Planet Ladder

Translator – Gabi Blumberg
Retouch and Lettering – Eric Pineda
Cover Designer – Akemi Imafuku
Graphic Designer – Anna Kernbaum
English Adaptation – Kristen Bailey Murphy
Senior Editor – Julie Taylor

Production Managers – Mario Rodriguez and Jennifer Wagner
Art Director – Matt Alford
VP Production – Ron Klamert
Publisher – Stuart Levy

Email: editor@TOKYOPOP.com
Come visit us online at www.TOKYOPOP.com

A 🐟**TOKYOPOP**® manga

TOKYOPOP® is an imprint of Mixx Entertainment, Inc.

5900 Wilshire Blvd. Ste 2000, Los Angeles, CA 90036

ISBN: 1-931514-64-X

First TOKYOPOP® printing: October 2002

10 9 8 7 6 5 4 3 2

Manufactured in the USA

Planet Ladder

Volume 3

Written and Illustrated by
Yuri Narushima

Los Angeles . Tokyo

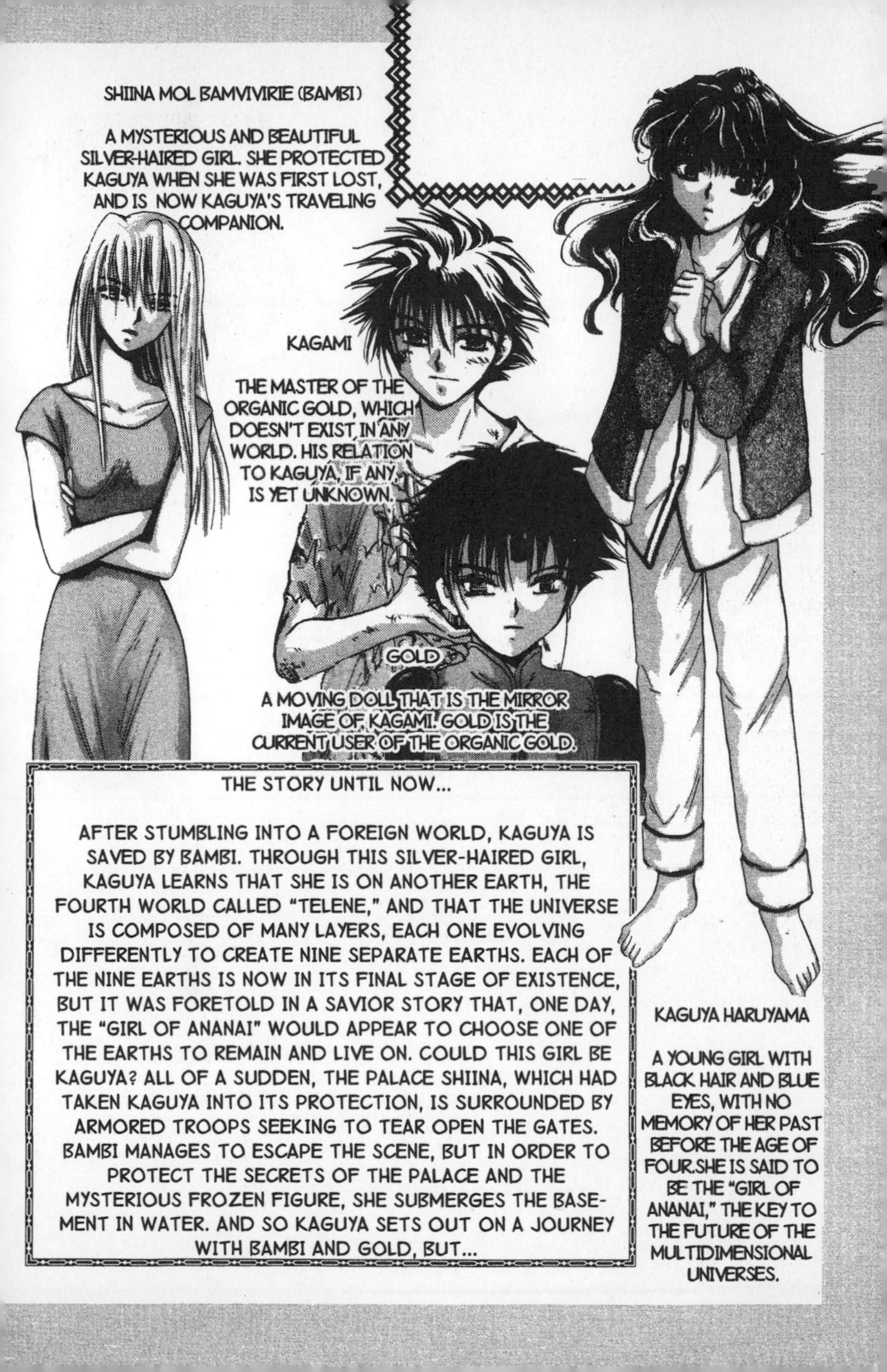

SHIINA MOL BAMVIVIRIE (BAMBI)

A MYSTERIOUS AND BEAUTIFUL SILVER-HAIRED GIRL. SHE PROTECTED KAGUYA WHEN SHE WAS FIRST LOST, AND IS NOW KAGUYA'S TRAVELING COMPANION.

KAGAMI

THE MASTER OF THE ORGANIC GOLD, WHICH DOESN'T EXIST IN ANY WORLD. HIS RELATION TO KAGUYA, IF ANY, IS YET UNKNOWN.

GOLD

A MOVING DOLL THAT IS THE MIRROR IMAGE OF KAGAMI. GOLD IS THE CURRENT USER OF THE ORGANIC GOLD.

THE STORY UNTIL NOW...

AFTER STUMBLING INTO A FOREIGN WORLD, KAGUYA IS SAVED BY BAMBI. THROUGH THIS SILVER-HAIRED GIRL, KAGUYA LEARNS THAT SHE IS ON ANOTHER EARTH, THE FOURTH WORLD CALLED "TELENE," AND THAT THE UNIVERSE IS COMPOSED OF MANY LAYERS, EACH ONE EVOLVING DIFFERENTLY TO CREATE NINE SEPARATE EARTHS. EACH OF THE NINE EARTHS IS NOW IN ITS FINAL STAGE OF EXISTENCE, BUT IT WAS FORETOLD IN A SAVIOR STORY THAT, ONE DAY, THE "GIRL OF ANANAI" WOULD APPEAR TO CHOOSE ONE OF THE EARTHS TO REMAIN AND LIVE ON. COULD THIS GIRL BE KAGUYA? ALL OF A SUDDEN, THE PALACE SHIINA, WHICH HAD TAKEN KAGUYA INTO ITS PROTECTION, IS SURROUNDED BY ARMORED TROOPS SEEKING TO TEAR OPEN THE GATES. BAMBI MANAGES TO ESCAPE THE SCENE, BUT IN ORDER TO PROTECT THE SECRETS OF THE PALACE AND THE MYSTERIOUS FROZEN FIGURE, SHE SUBMERGES THE BASEMENT IN WATER. AND SO KAGUYA SETS OUT ON A JOURNEY WITH BAMBI AND GOLD, BUT...

KAGUYA HARUYAMA

A YOUNG GIRL WITH BLACK HAIR AND BLUE EYES, WITH NO MEMORY OF HER PAST BEFORE THE AGE OF FOUR. SHE IS SAID TO BE THE "GIRL OF ANANAI," THE KEY TO THE FUTURE OF THE MULTIDIMENSIONAL UNIVERSES.

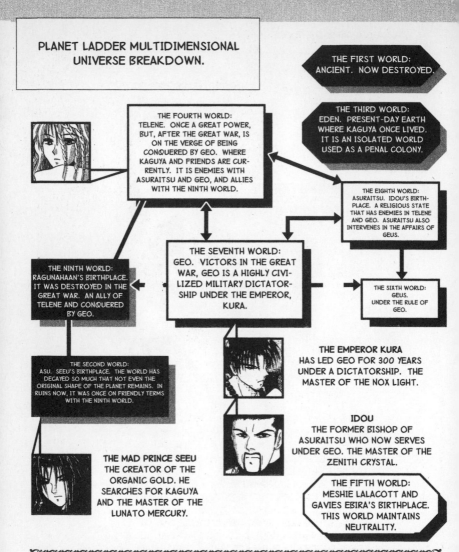

PLANET LADDER MULTIDIMENSIONAL UNIVERSE BREAKDOWN.

THE FIRST WORLD:
ANCIENT. NOW DESTROYED.

THE FOURTH WORLD:
TELENE. ONCE A GREAT POWER, BUT, AFTER THE GREAT WAR, IS ON THE VERGE OF BEING CONQUERED BY GEO. WHERE KAGUYA AND FRIENDS ARE CURRENTLY. IT IS ENEMIES WITH ASURAITSU AND GEO, AND ALLIES WITH THE NINTH WORLD.

THE THIRD WORLD:
EDEN. PRESENT-DAY EARTH WHERE KAGUYA ONCE LIVED. IT IS AN ISOLATED WORLD USED AS A PENAL COLONY.

THE EIGHTH WORLD:
ASURAITSU. IDOU'S BIRTHPLACE. A RELIGIOUS STATE THAT HAS ENEMIES IN TELENE AND GEO. ASURAITSU ALSO INTERVENES IN THE AFFAIRS OF GEUS.

THE SEVENTH WORLD:
GEO. VICTORS IN THE GREAT WAR, GEO IS A HIGHLY CIVILIZED MILITARY DICTATORSHIP UNDER THE EMPEROR, KURA.

THE NINTH WORLD:
RAGUNAHAAN'S BIRTHPLACE. IT WAS DESTROYED IN THE GREAT WAR. AN ALLY OF TELENE AND CONQUERED BY GEO.

THE SIXTH WORLD:
GEUS. UNDER THE RULE OF GEO.

THE SECOND WORLD:
ASU. SEEU'S BIRTHPLACE. THE WORLD HAS DECAYED SO MUCH THAT NOT EVEN THE ORIGINAL SHAPE OF THE PLANET REMAINS. IN RUINS NOW, IT WAS ONCE ON FRIENDLY TERMS WITH THE NINTH WORLD.

THE EMPEROR KURA
HAS LED GEO FOR 300 YEARS UNDER A DICTATORSHIP. THE MASTER OF THE NOX LIGHT.

IDOU
THE FORMER BISHOP OF ASURAITSU WHO NOW SERVES UNDER GEO. THE MASTER OF THE ZENITH CRYSTAL.

THE MAD PRINCE SEEU
THE CREATOR OF THE ORGANIC GOLD. HE SEARCHES FOR KAGUYA AND THE MASTER OF THE LUNATO MERCURY.

THE FIFTH WORLD:
MESHIE LALACOTT AND GAVIES EBIRA'S BIRTHPLACE. THIS WORLD MAINTAINS NEUTRALITY.

WHAT IS THE FINAL STAGE OF A MULTIDIMENSIONAL UNIVERSE? A MULTIDIMENSIONAL/PARALLEL UNIVERSE IS A UNIVERSE WITH LAYERS LOCATED IN MULTIPLE DIMENSIONS, AND EACH LAYER IS CALLED "A WORLD." THESE PARALLEL WORLDS ARE SUPPOSED TO BE ABLE TO EXIST SIDE BY SIDE. HOWEVER, DUE TO A TEAR IN THE FABRIC OF THE UNIVERSE, THE AXIS WHICH SUPPORTS THESE WORLDS SHAKES. THIS SHAKING WILL ULTIMATELY LEAD TO THE COLLISION, AND THUS DEMISE, OF ALL THE WORLDS WITHIN A MULTIDIMENSIONAL UNIVERSE.

WHAT IS THE SAVIOR STORY? A PROPHECY OF THE FIRST WORLD, ANCIENT. IN THE TIME OF THE END OF THE WORLDS, A YOUNG GIRL, "THE GIRL OF ANANAI," WILL APPEAR AND CHOOSE ONLY ONE WORLD TO SURVIVE.

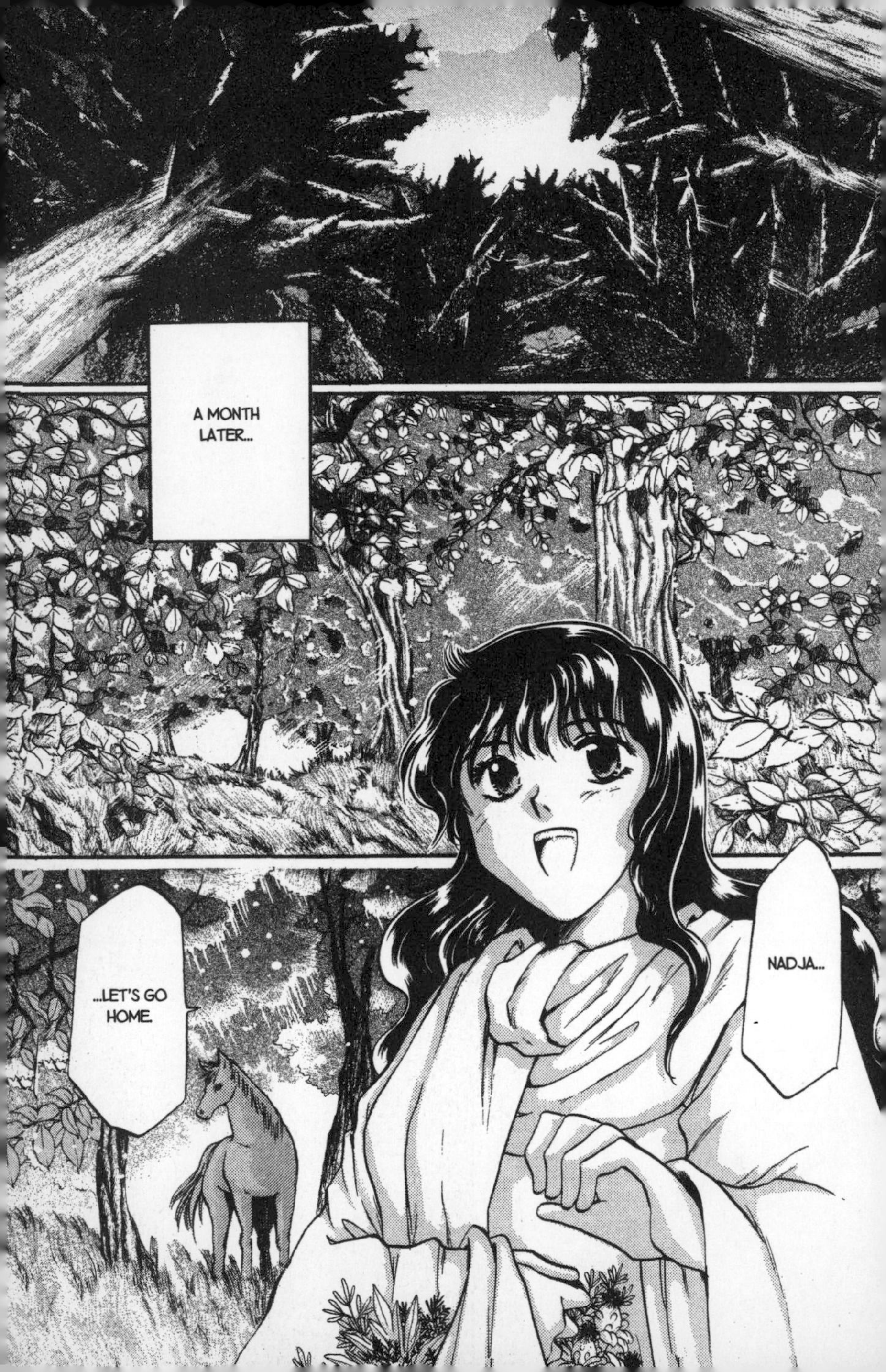
A MONTH LATER...
NADJA...
...LET'S GO HOME.

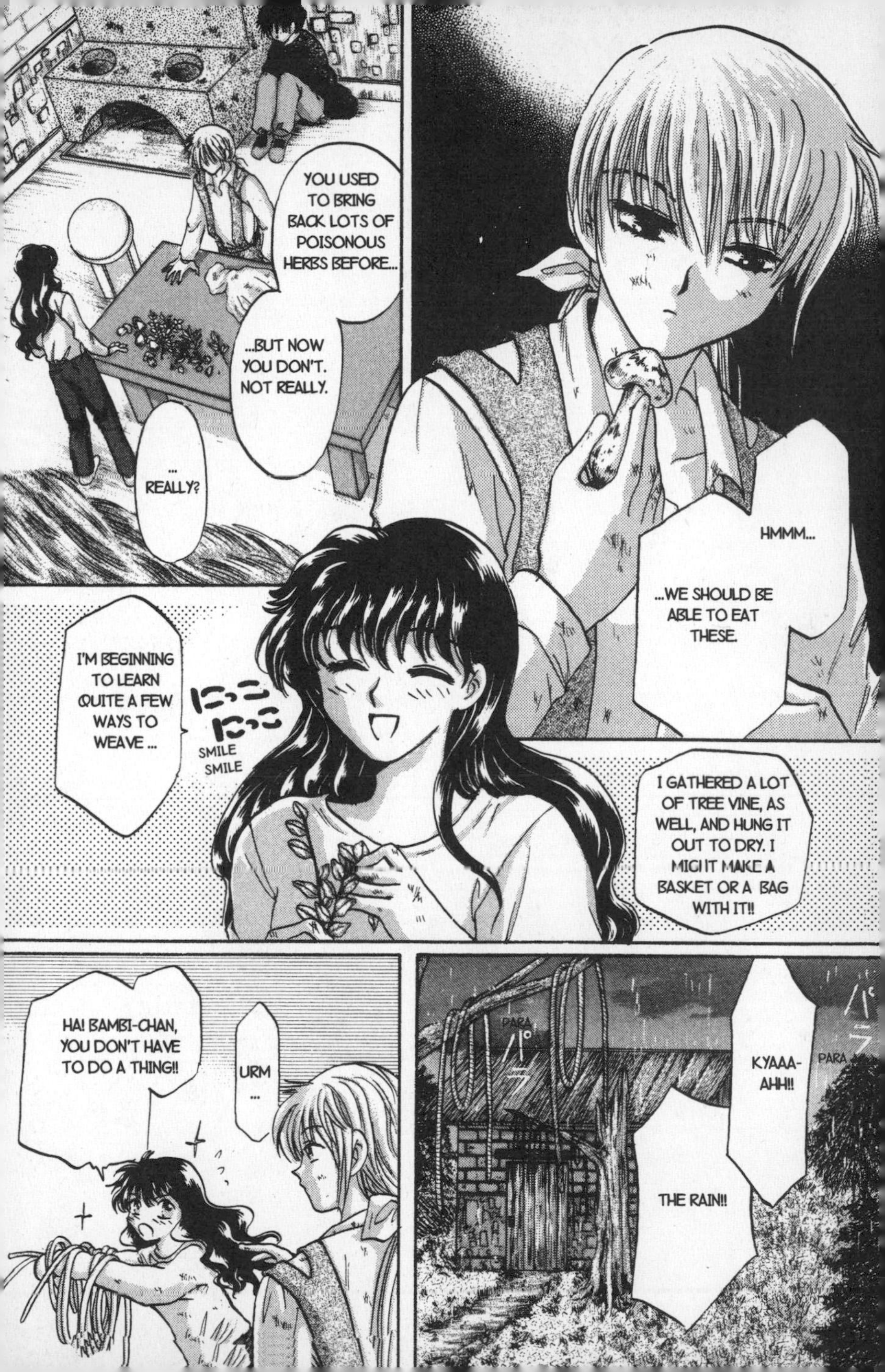
HMMM...
...WE SHOULD BE ABLE TO EAT THESE.
YOU USED TO BRING BACK LOTS OF POISONOUS HERBS BEFORE...
...BUT NOW YOU DON'T. NOT REALLY.
... REALLY?
I GATHERED A LOT OF TREE VINE, AS WELL, AND HUNG IT OUT TO DRY. I MIGHT MAKE A BASKET OR A BAG WITH IT!!
にっこにっこ
SMILE SMILE
I'M BEGINNING TO LEARN QUITE A FEW WAYS TO WEAVE ...
パ
ラ
PARA
KYAAA-AHH!!
パ
ラ
PARA
THE RAIN!!
URM ...
HA! BAMBI-CHAN, YOU DON'T HAVE TO DO A THING!!

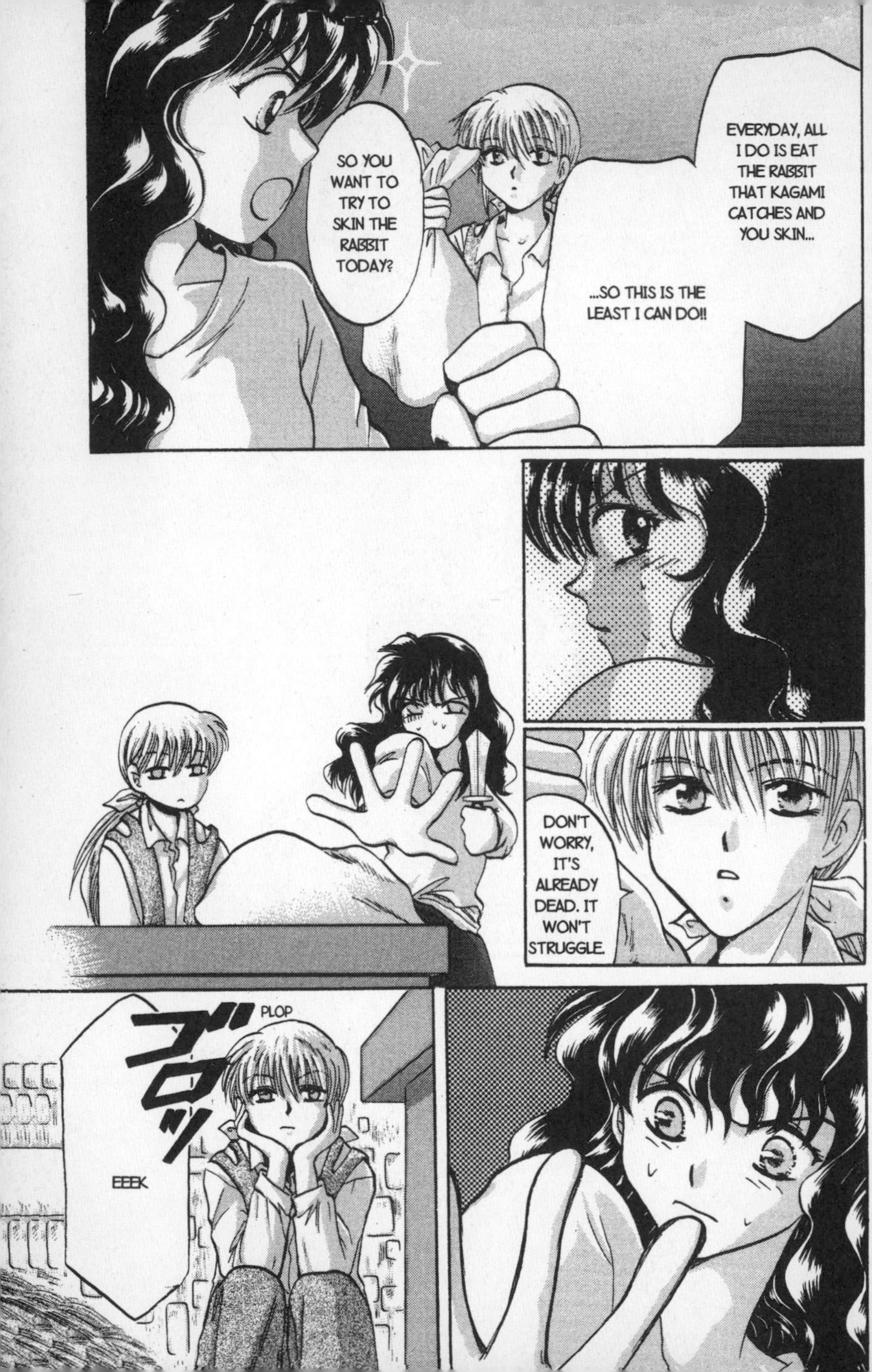
EVERYDAY, ALL I DO IS EAT THE RABBIT THAT KAGAMI CATCHES AND YOU SKIN...
...SO THIS IS THE LEAST I CAN DO!!
SO YOU WANT TO TRY TO SKIN THE RABBIT TODAY?
DON'T WORRY, IT'S ALREADY DEAD. IT WON'T STRUGGLE.
ゴロッ
PLOP
EEEK

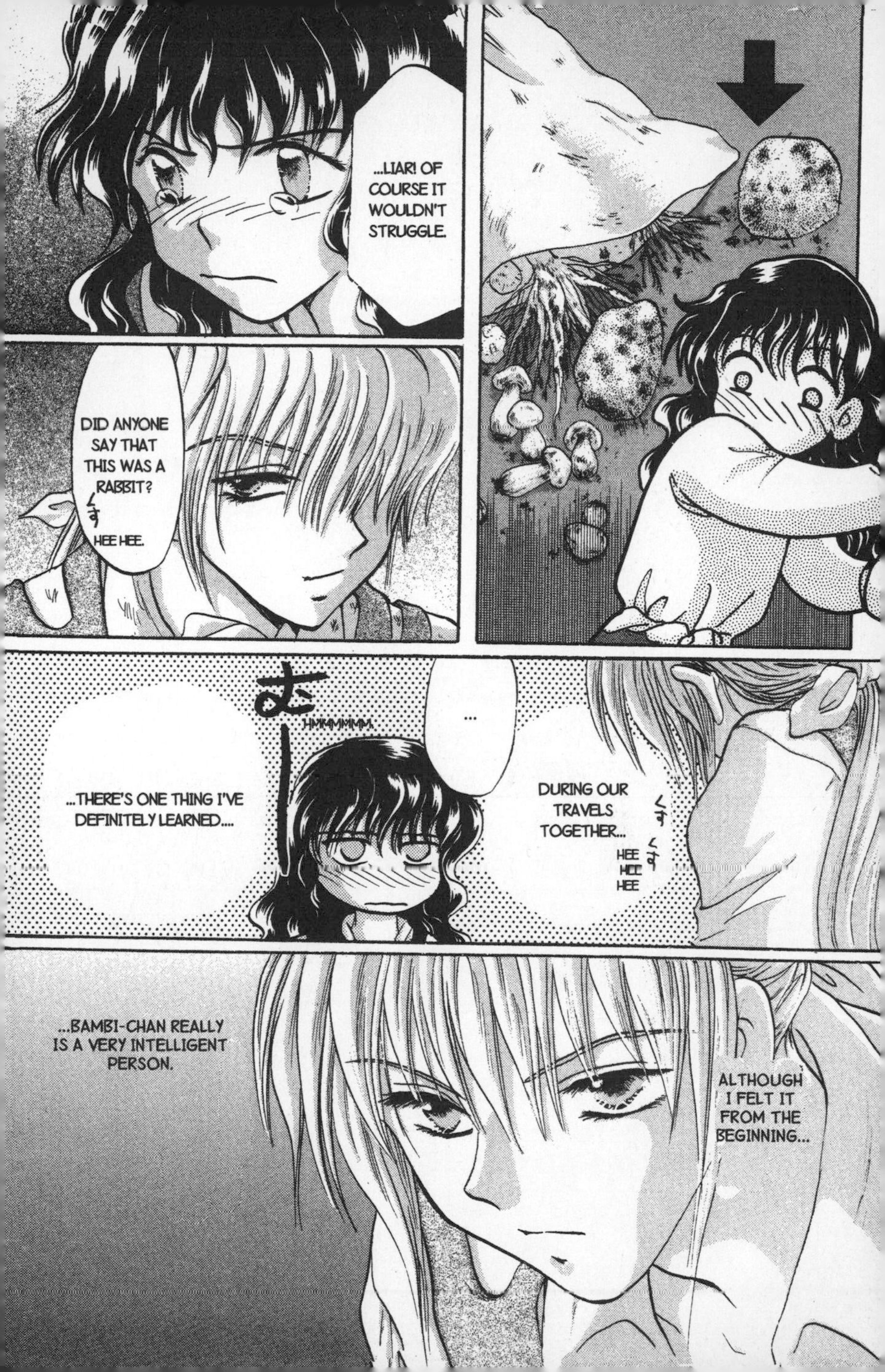
...LIAR! OF COURSE IT WOULDN'T STRUGGLE.
DID ANYONE SAY THAT THIS WAS A RABBIT?
くす
HEE HEE.
DURING OUR TRAVELS TOGETHER...
くす くす
HEE HEE HEE
...
むー
HMMMMMM.
...THERE'S ONE THING I'VE DEFINITELY LEARNED....
ALTHOUGH I FELT IT FROM THE BEGINNING...
...BAMBI-CHAN REALLY IS A VERY INTELLIGENT PERSON.

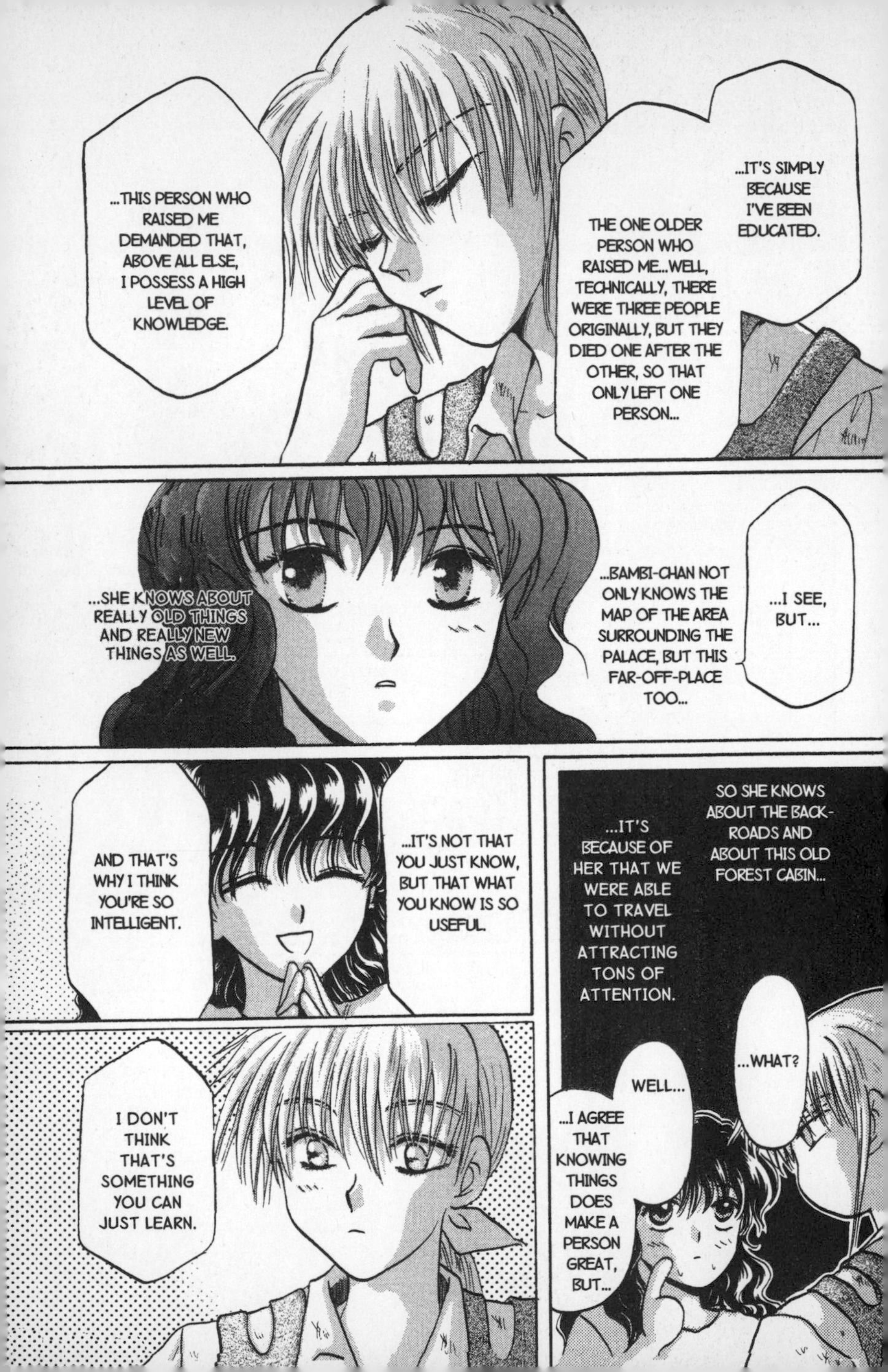
...IT'S SIMPLY BECAUSE I'VE BEEN EDUCATED.
THE ONE OLDER PERSON WHO RAISED ME...WELL, TECHNICALLY, THERE WERE THREE PEOPLE ORIGINALLY, BUT THEY DIED ONE AFTER THE OTHER, SO THAT ONLY LEFT ONE PERSON...
...THIS PERSON WHO RAISED ME DEMANDED THAT, ABOVE ALL ELSE, I POSSESS A HIGH LEVEL OF KNOWLEDGE.
...I SEE, BUT...
...BAMBI-CHAN NOT ONLY KNOWS THE MAP OF THE AREA SURROUNDING THE PALACE, BUT THIS FAR-OFF-PLACE TOO...
...SHE KNOWS ABOUT REALLY OLD THINGS AND REALLY NEW THINGS AS WELL.
SO SHE KNOWS ABOUT THE BACK-ROADS AND ABOUT THIS OLD FOREST CABIN...
...IT'S BECAUSE OF HER THAT WE WERE ABLE TO TRAVEL WITHOUT ATTRACTING TONS OF ATTENTION.
...WHAT?
WELL...
...I AGREE THAT KNOWING THINGS DOES MAKE A PERSON GREAT, BUT...
...IT'S NOT THAT YOU JUST KNOW, BUT THAT WHAT YOU KNOW IS SO USEFUL.
AND THAT'S WHY I THINK YOU'RE SO INTELLIGENT.
I DON'T THINK THAT'S SOMETHING YOU CAN JUST LEARN.

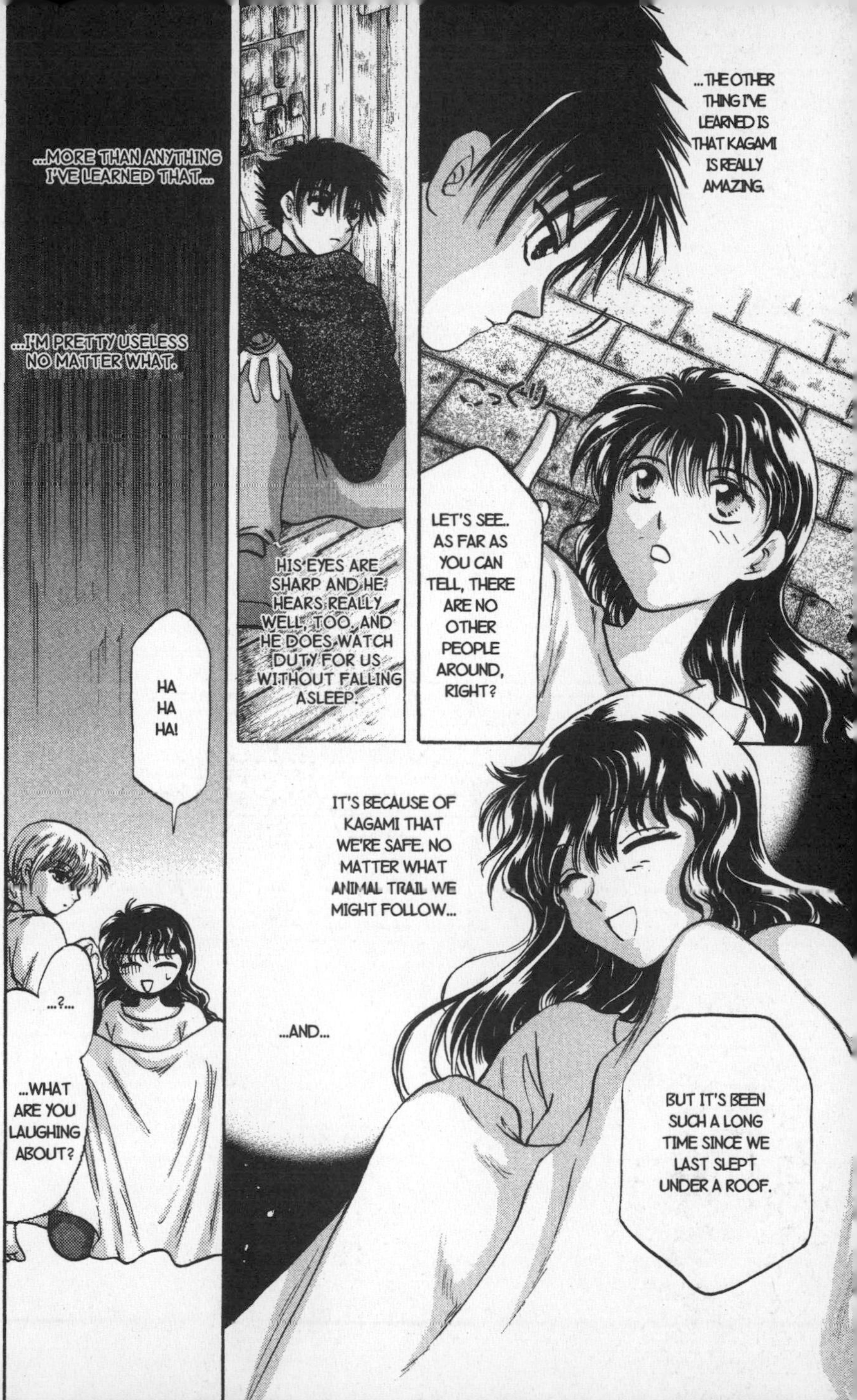

...THE OTHER THING I'VE LEARNED IS THAT KAGAMI IS REALLY AMAZING.
LET'S SEE.. AS FAR AS YOU CAN TELL, THERE ARE NO OTHER PEOPLE AROUND, RIGHT?
HIS EYES ARE SHARP AND HE HEARS REALLY WELL, TOO. AND HE DOES WATCH DUTY FOR US WITHOUT FALLING ASLEEP.
IT'S BECAUSE OF KAGAMI THAT WE'RE SAFE. NO MATTER WHAT ANIMAL TRAIL WE MIGHT FOLLOW...
...AND...
BUT IT'S BEEN SUCH A LONG TIME SINCE WE LAST SLEPT UNDER A ROOF.
...MORE THAN ANYTHING I'VE LEARNED THAT...
...I'M PRETTY USELESS NO MATTER WHAT.
HA HA HA!
...?...
...WHAT ARE YOU LAUGHING ABOUT?

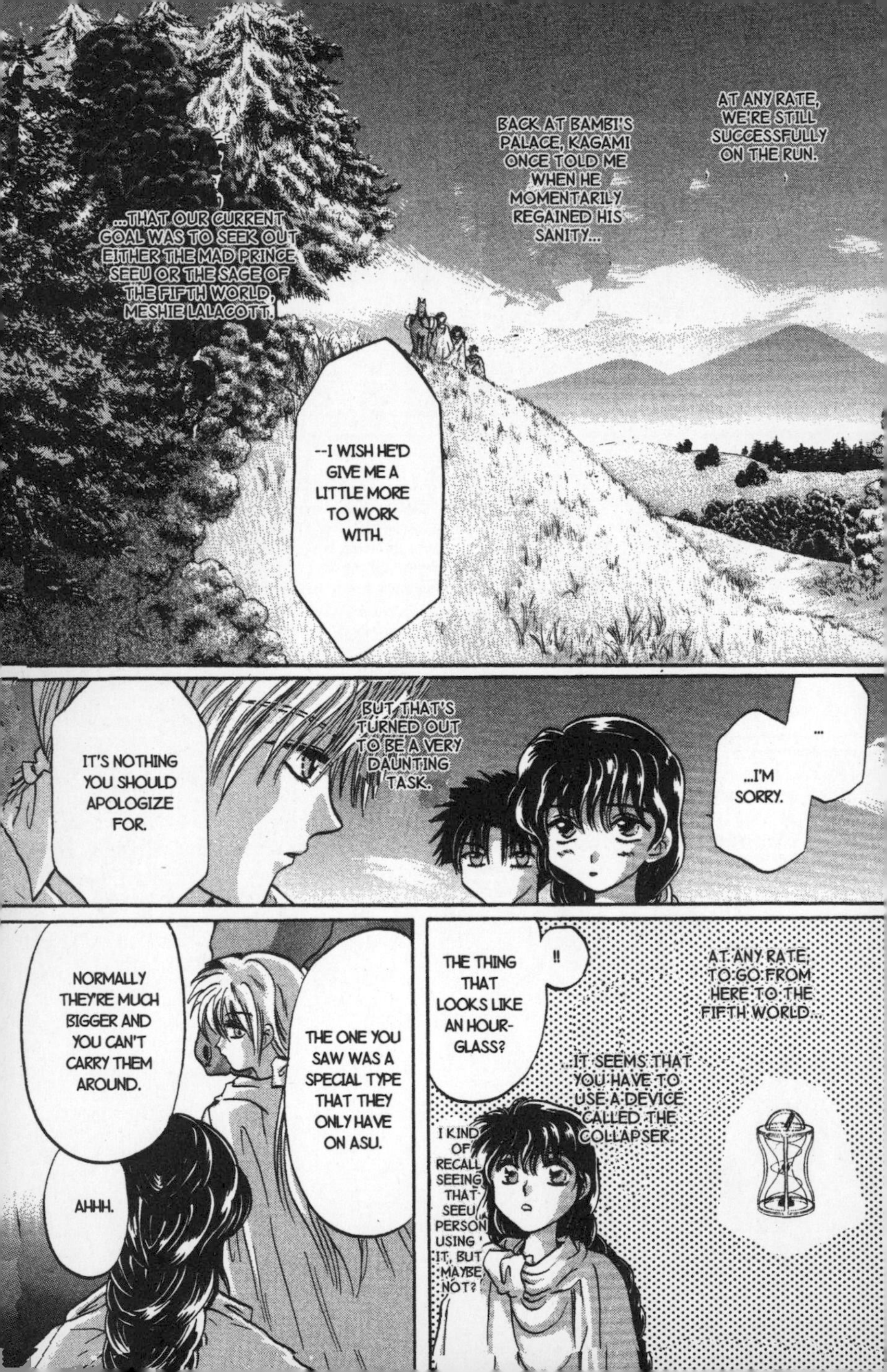
AT ANY RATE, WE'RE STILL SUCCESSFULLY ON THE RUN.
BACK AT BAMBI'S PALACE, KAGAMI ONCE TOLD ME WHEN HE MOMENTARILY REGAINED HIS SANITY...
...THAT OUR CURRENT GOAL WAS TO SEEK OUT EITHER THE MAD PRINCE SEEU OR THE SAGE OF THE FIFTH WORLD, MESHIE LALACOTT.
--I WISH HE'D GIVE ME A LITTLE MORE TO WORK WITH.
...
...I'M SORRY.
BUT THAT'S TURNED OUT TO BE A VERY DAUNTING TASK.
IT'S NOTHING YOU SHOULD APOLOGIZE FOR.
AT ANY RATE, TO GO FROM HERE TO THE FIFTH WORLD...
...IT SEEMS THAT YOU HAVE TO USE A DEVICE CALLED THE COLLAPSER.
!!
THE THING THAT LOOKS LIKE AN HOUR-GLASS?
I KIND OF RECALL SEEING THAT SEEU PERSON USING IT, BUT MAYBE NOT?
THE ONE YOU SAW WAS A SPECIAL TYPE THAT THEY ONLY HAVE ON ASU.
NORMALLY THEY'RE MUCH BIGGER AND YOU CAN'T CARRY THEM AROUND.
AHHH.

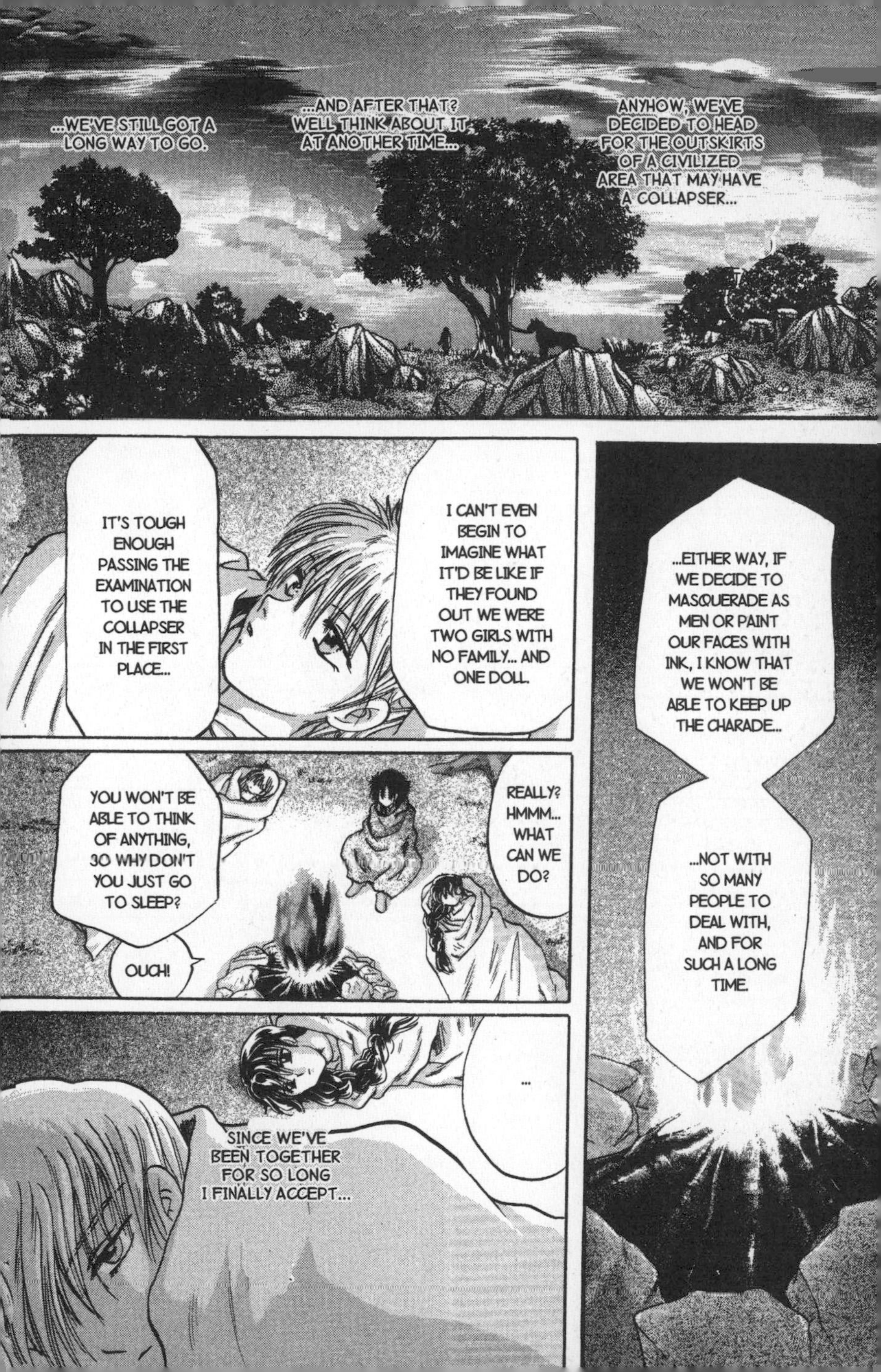
ANYHOW, WE'VE DECIDED TO HEAD FOR THE OUTSKIRTS OF A CIVILIZED AREA THAT MAY HAVE A COLLAPSER...
...AND AFTER THAT? WELL THINK ABOUT IT AT ANOTHER TIME...
...WE'VE STILL GOT A LONG WAY TO GO.
...EITHER WAY, IF WE DECIDE TO MASQUERADE AS MEN OR PAINT OUR FACES WITH INK, I KNOW THAT WE WON'T BE ABLE TO KEEP UP THE CHARADE...
...NOT WITH SO MANY PEOPLE TO DEAL WITH, AND FOR SUCH A LONG TIME.
I CAN'T EVEN BEGIN TO IMAGINE WHAT IT'D BE LIKE IF THEY FOUND OUT WE WERE TWO GIRLS WITH NO FAMILY... AND ONE DOLL.
IT'S TOUGH ENOUGH PASSING THE EXAMINATION TO USE THE COLLAPSER IN THE FIRST PLACE...
REALLY? HMMM... WHAT CAN WE DO?
YOU WON'T BE ABLE TO THINK OF ANYTHING, SO WHY DON'T YOU JUST GO TO SLEEP?
OUCH!
...
SINCE WE'VE BEEN TOGETHER FOR SO LONG I FINALLY ACCEPT...

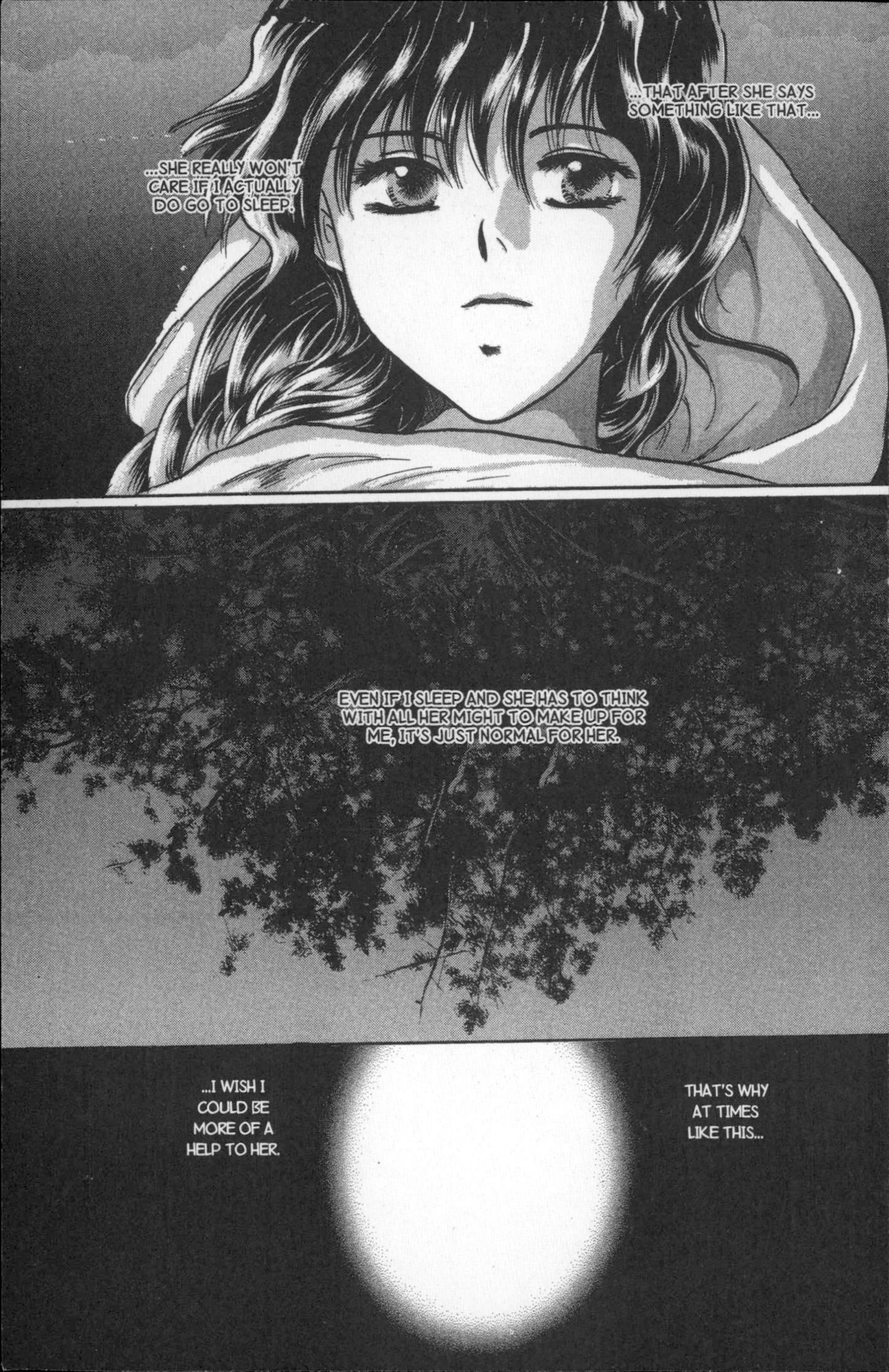
...THAT AFTER SHE SAYS SOMETHING LIKE THAT...
...SHE REALLY WON'T CARE IF I ACTUALLY DO GO TO SLEEP.
EVEN IF I SLEEP AND SHE HAS TO THINK WITH ALL HER MIGHT TO MAKE UP FOR ME, IT'S JUST NORMAL FOR HER.
THAT'S WHY AT TIMES LIKE THIS...
...I WISH I COULD BE MORE OF A HELP TO HER.

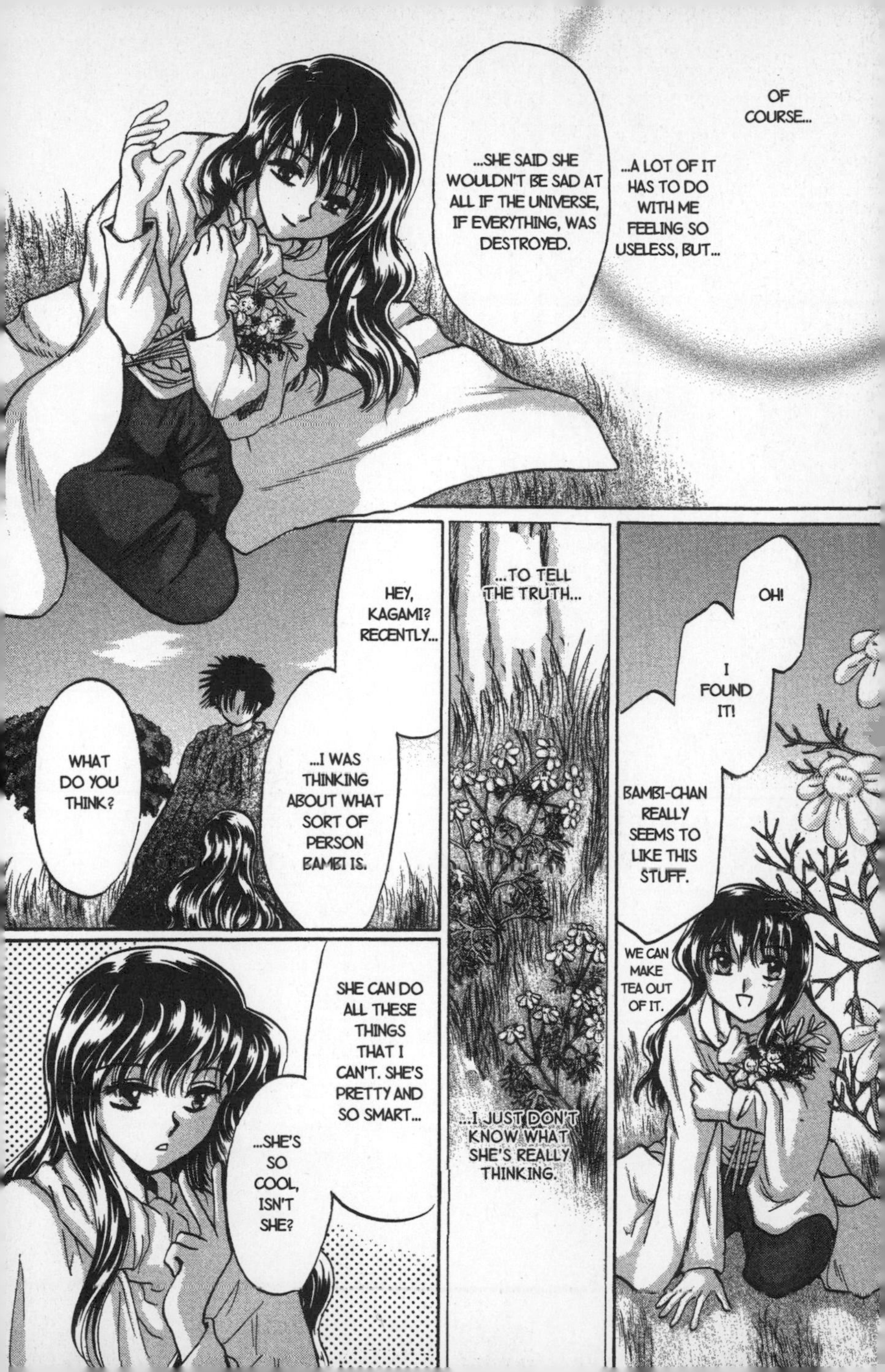
OF COURSE...
...A LOT OF IT HAS TO DO WITH ME FEELING SO USELESS, BUT...
...SHE SAID SHE WOULDN'T BE SAD AT ALL IF THE UNIVERSE, IF EVERYTHING, WAS DESTROYED.
OH!
I FOUND IT!
BAMBI-CHAN REALLY SEEMS TO LIKE THIS STUFF.
WE CAN MAKE TEA OUT OF IT.
...TO TELL THE TRUTH...
...I JUST DON'T KNOW WHAT SHE'S REALLY THINKING.
HEY, KAGAMI? RECENTLY...
...I WAS THINKING ABOUT WHAT SORT OF PERSON BAMBI IS.
WHAT DO YOU THINK?
SHE CAN DO ALL THESE THINGS THAT I CAN'T. SHE'S PRETTY AND SO SMART...
...SHE'S SO COOL, ISN'T SHE?

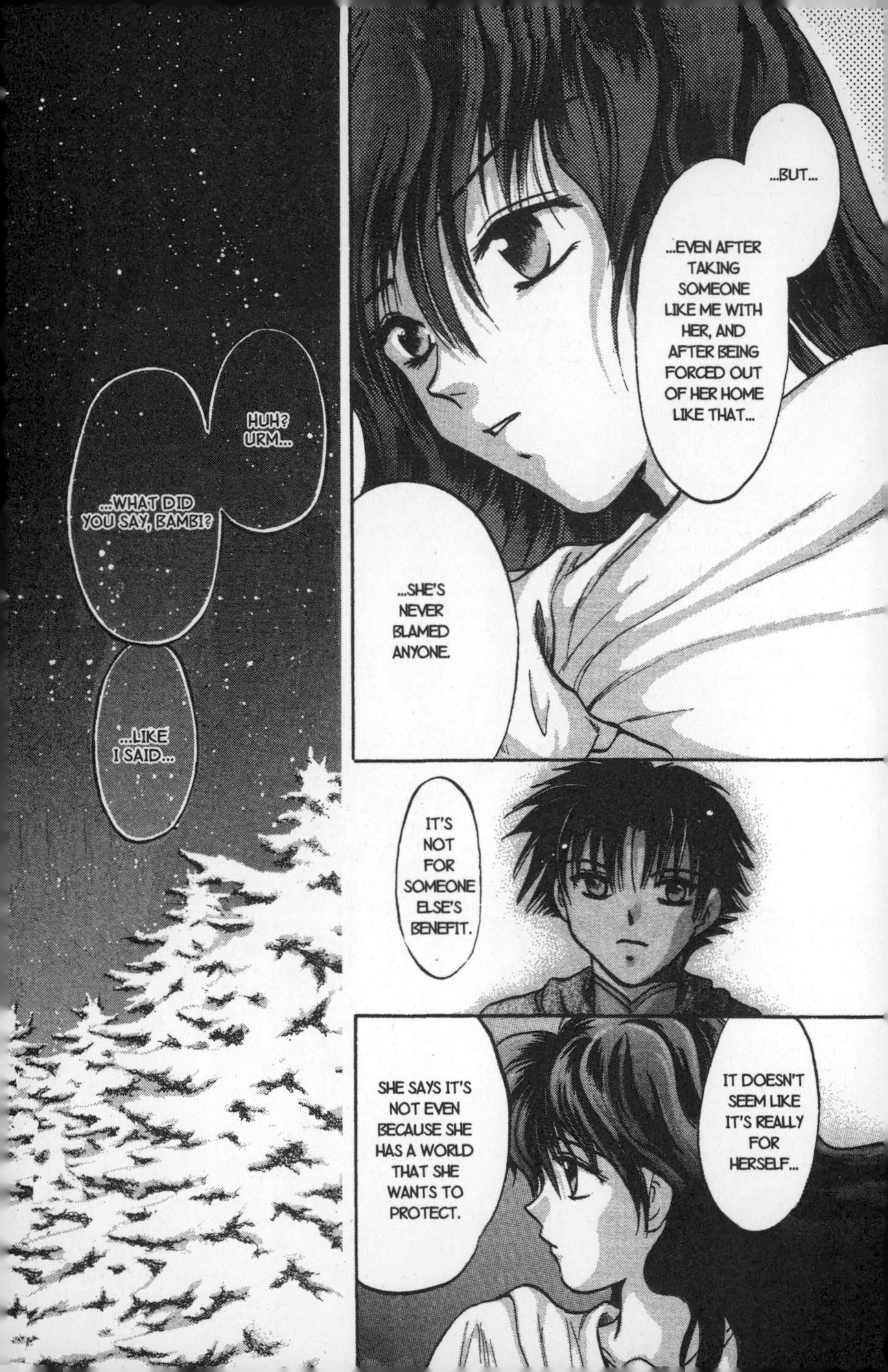
...BUT...
...EVEN AFTER TAKING SOMEONE LIKE ME WITH HER, AND AFTER BEING FORCED OUT OF HER HOME LIKE THAT...
...SHE'S NEVER BLAMED ANYONE.
IT'S NOT FOR SOMEONE ELSE'S BENEFIT.
IT DOESN'T SEEM LIKE IT'S REALLY FOR HERSELF...
SHE SAYS IT'S NOT EVEN BECAUSE SHE HAS A WORLD THAT SHE WANTS TO PROTECT.
HUH? URM...
...WHAT DID YOU SAY, BAMBI?
...LIKE I SAID...

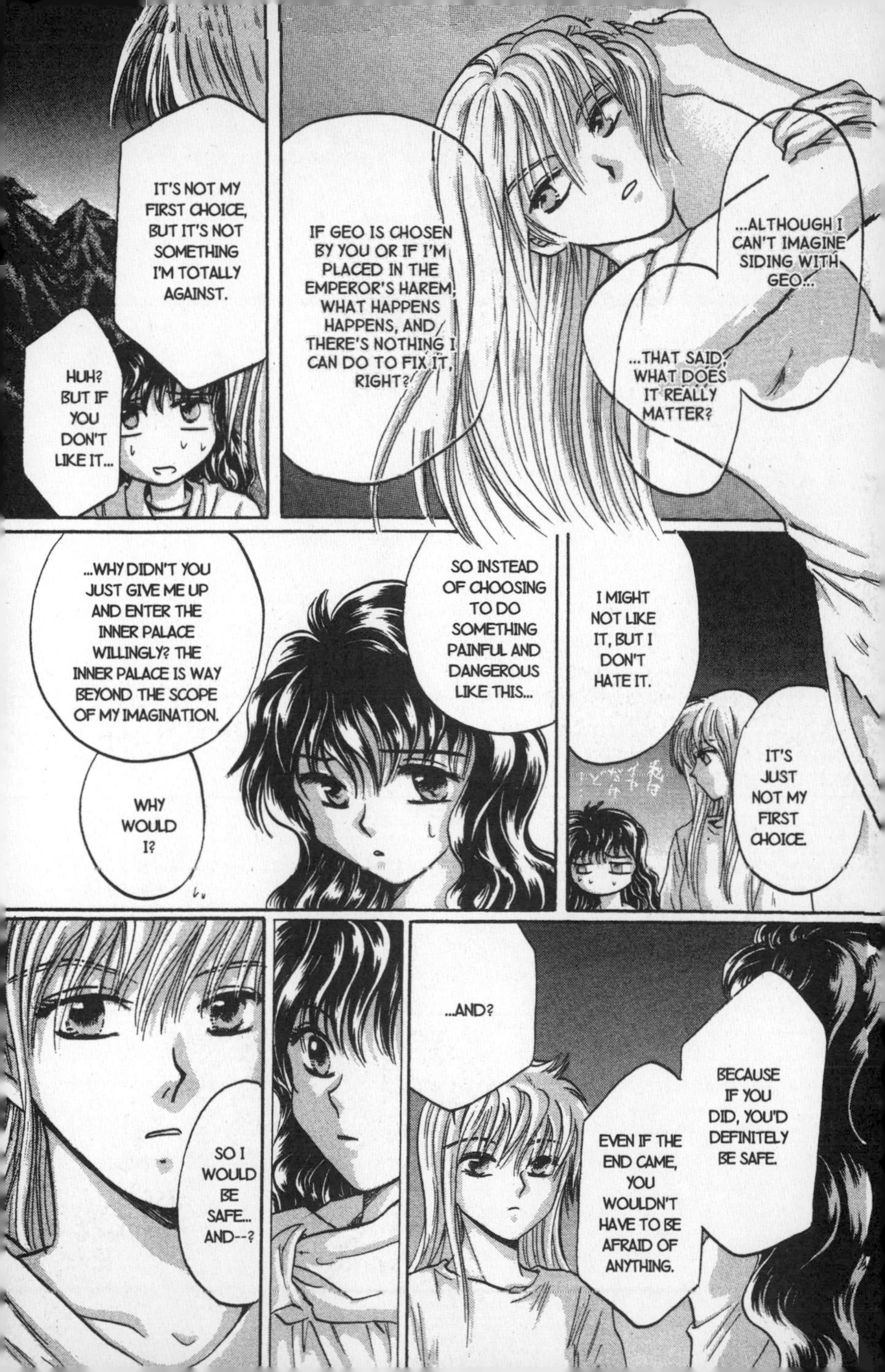
...ALTHOUGH I CAN'T IMAGINE SIDING WITH GEO...
...THAT SAID, WHAT DOES IT REALLY MATTER?
IF GEO IS CHOSEN BY YOU OR IF I'M PLACED IN THE EMPEROR'S HAREM, WHAT HAPPENS HAPPENS, AND THERE'S NOTHING I CAN DO TO FIX IT, RIGHT?
IT'S NOT MY FIRST CHOICE, BUT IT'S NOT SOMETHING I'M TOTALLY AGAINST.
HUH? BUT IF YOU DON'T LIKE IT...
I MIGHT NOT LIKE IT, BUT I DON'T HATE IT.
IT'S JUST NOT MY FIRST CHOICE.
SO INSTEAD OF CHOOSING TO DO SOMETHING PAINFUL AND DANGEROUS LIKE THIS...
...WHY DIDN'T YOU JUST GIVE ME UP AND ENTER THE INNER PALACE WILLINGLY? THE INNER PALACE IS WAY BEYOND THE SCOPE OF MY IMAGINATION.
WHY WOULD I?
...AND?
BECAUSE IF YOU DID, YOU'D DEFINITELY BE SAFE.
EVEN IF THE END CAME, YOU WOULDN'T HAVE TO BE AFRAID OF ANYTHING.
SO I WOULD BE SAFE... AND--?

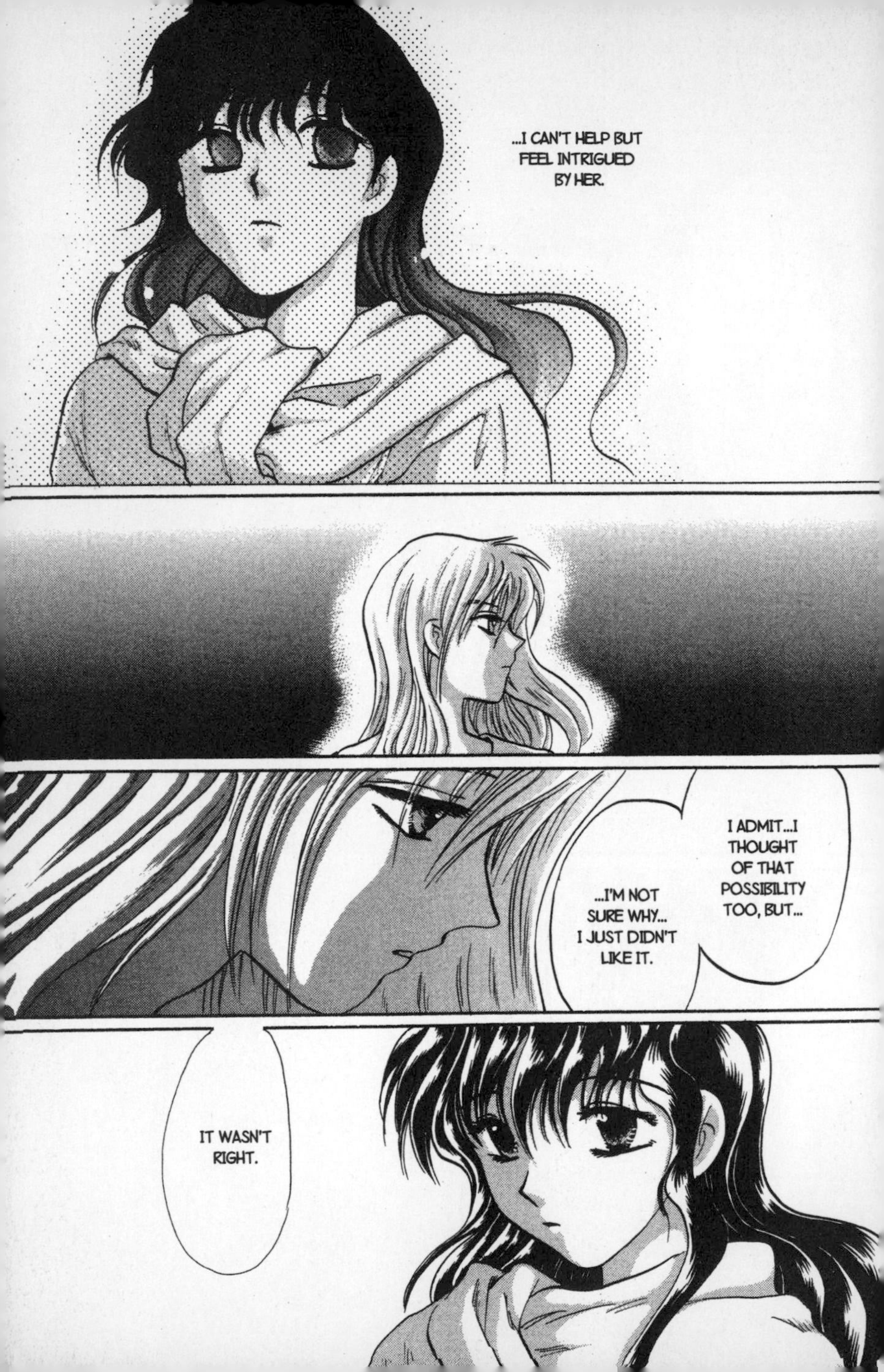
...I CAN'T HELP BUT FEEL INTRIGUED BY HER.
I ADMIT...I THOUGHT OF THAT POSSIBILITY TOO, BUT...
...I'M NOT SURE WHY... I JUST DIDN'T LIKE IT.
IT WASN'T RIGHT.

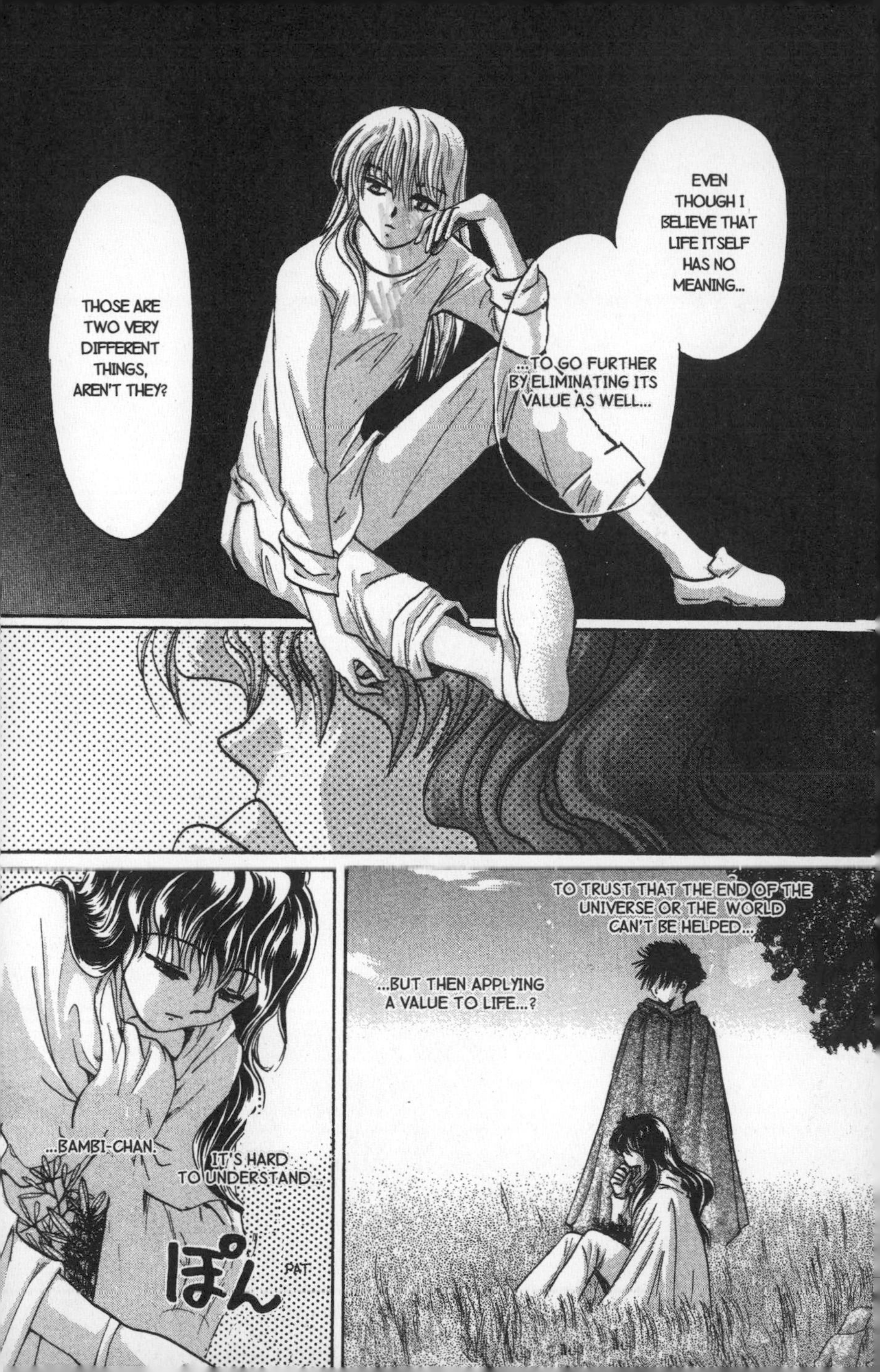
EVEN THOUGH I BELIEVE THAT LIFE ITSELF HAS NO MEANING...
...TO GO FURTHER BY ELIMINATING ITS VALUE AS WELL...
THOSE ARE TWO VERY DIFFERENT THINGS, AREN'T THEY?
TO TRUST THAT THE END OF THE UNIVERSE OR THE WORLD CAN'T BE HELPED...
...BUT THEN APPLYING A VALUE TO LIFE...?
IT'S HARD TO UNDERSTAND...
...BAMBI-CHAN.
ぽん
PAT

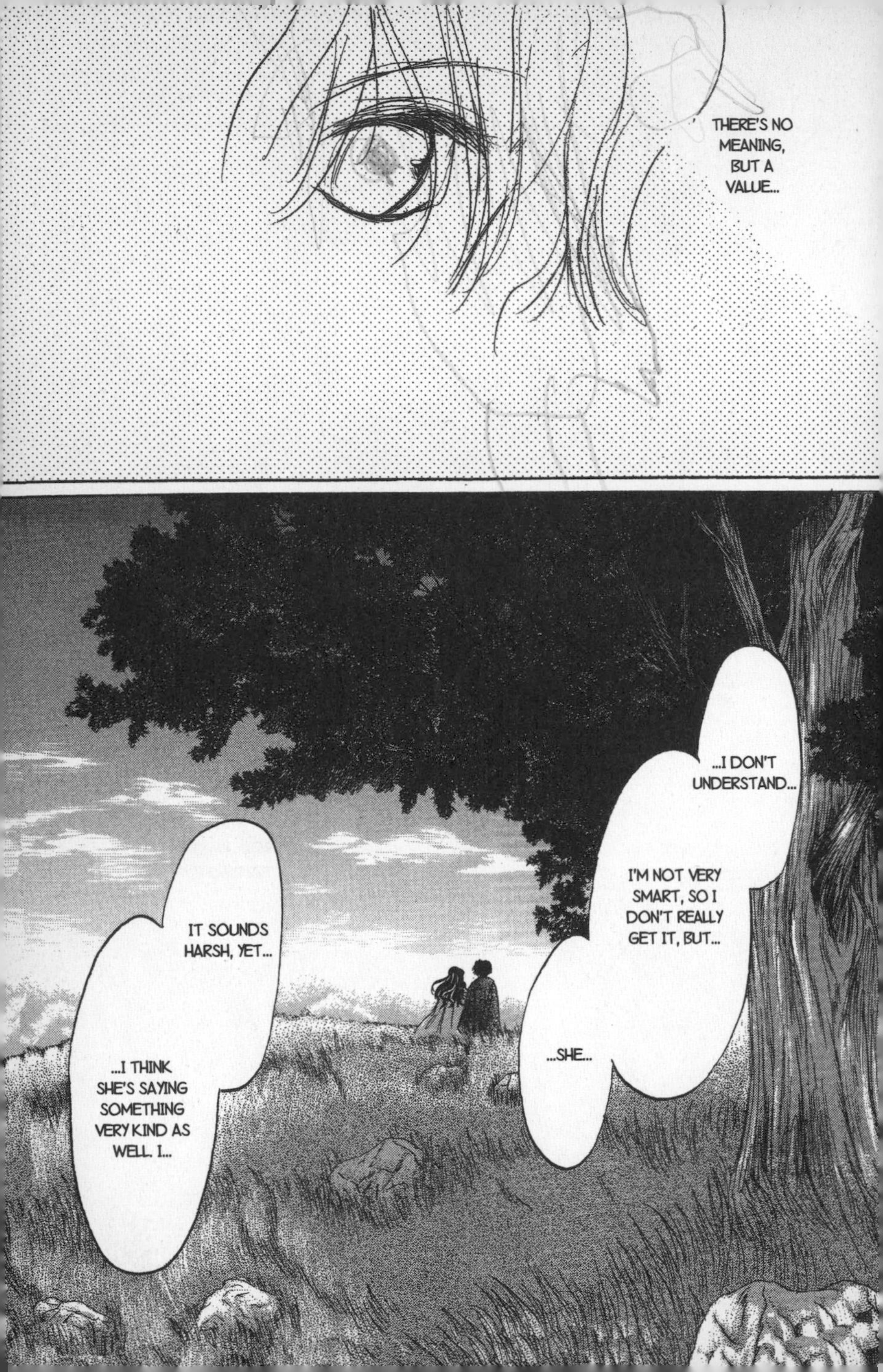
THERE'S NO MEANING, BUT A VALUE...
...I DON'T UNDERSTAND...
I'M NOT VERY SMART, SO I DON'T REALLY GET IT, BUT...
...SHE...
IT SOUNDS HARSH, YET...
...I THINK SHE'S SAYING SOMETHING VERY KIND AS WELL. I...

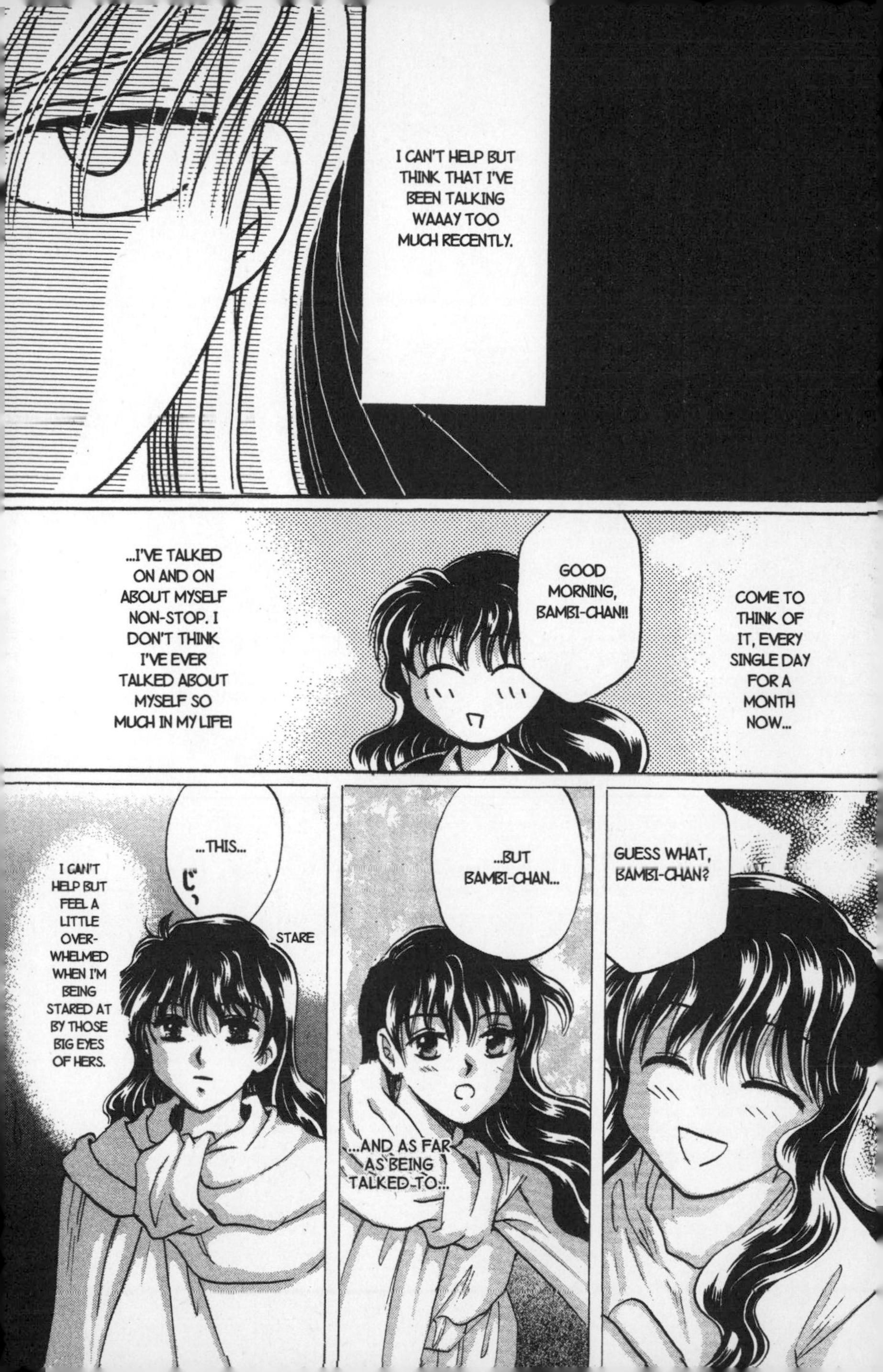
I CAN'T HELP BUT THINK THAT I'VE BEEN TALKING WAAAY TOO MUCH RECENTLY.
COME TO THINK OF IT, EVERY SINGLE DAY FOR A MONTH NOW...
GOOD MORNING, BAMBI-CHAN!!
...I'VE TALKED ON AND ON ABOUT MYSELF NON-STOP. I DON'T THINK I'VE EVER TALKED ABOUT MYSELF SO MUCH IN MY LIFE!
GUESS WHAT, BAMBI-CHAN?
...BUT BAMBI-CHAN...
...AND AS FAR AS BEING TALKED TO...
...THIS...
STARE
I CAN'T HELP BUT FEEL A LITTLE OVER-WHELMED WHEN I'M BEING STARED AT BY THOSE BIG EYES OF HERS.

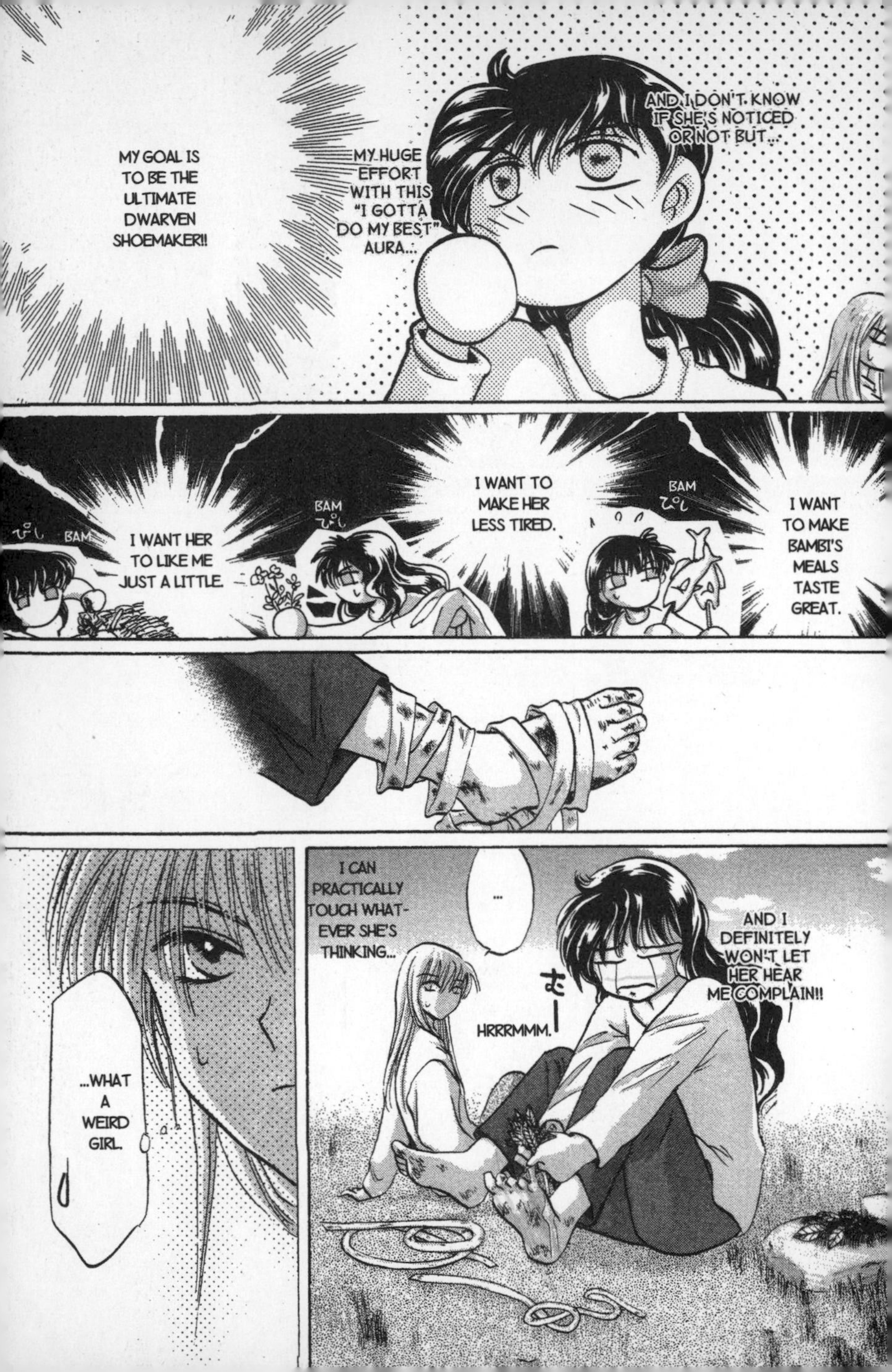
AND I DON'T KNOW IF SHE'S NOTICED OR NOT BUT...
MY HUGE EFFORT WITH THIS "I GOTTA DO MY BEST" AURA...
MY GOAL IS TO BE THE ULTIMATE DWARVEN SHOEMAKER!!
I WANT TO MAKE BAMBI'S MEALS TASTE GREAT.
BAM ぴし
I WANT TO MAKE HER LESS TIRED.
BAM ぴし
I WANT HER TO LIKE ME JUST A LITTLE.
ぴし BAM
AND I DEFINITELY WON'T LET HER HEAR ME COMPLAIN!!
むー
HRRRMMM.
...
I CAN PRACTICALLY TOUCH WHAT-EVER SHE'S THINKING...
...WHAT A WEIRD GIRL.

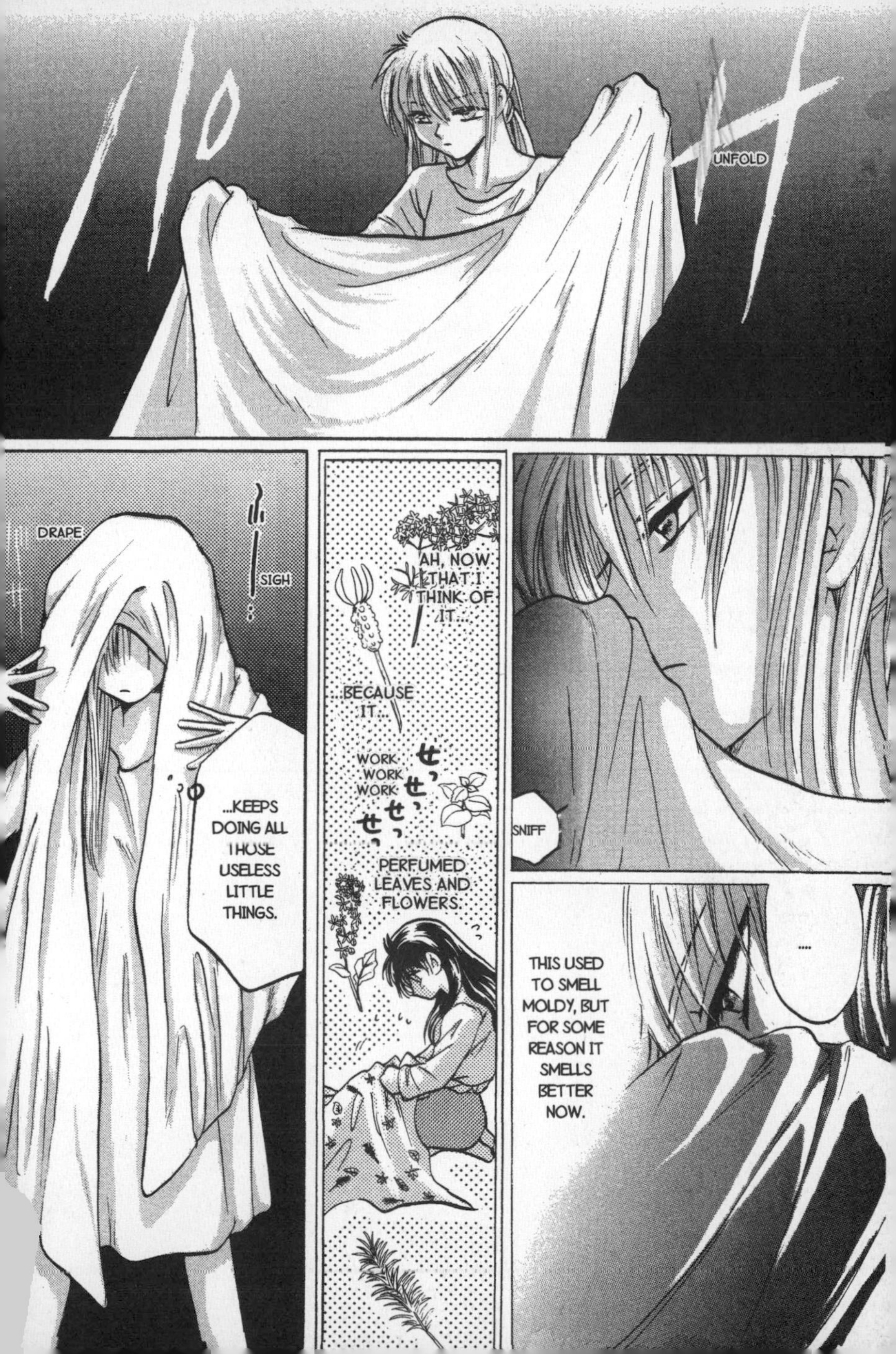

UNFOLD
SNIFF
...
THIS USED TO SMELL MOLDY, BUT FOR SOME REASON IT SMELLS BETTER NOW.
AH, NOW THAT I THINK OF IT...
...BECAUSE IT...
せっ せっ せっ せっ
WORK WORK WORK
PERFUMED LEAVES AND FLOWERS.
DRAPE
ふー…
SIGH
...KEEPS DOING ALL THOSE USELESS LITTLE THINGS.

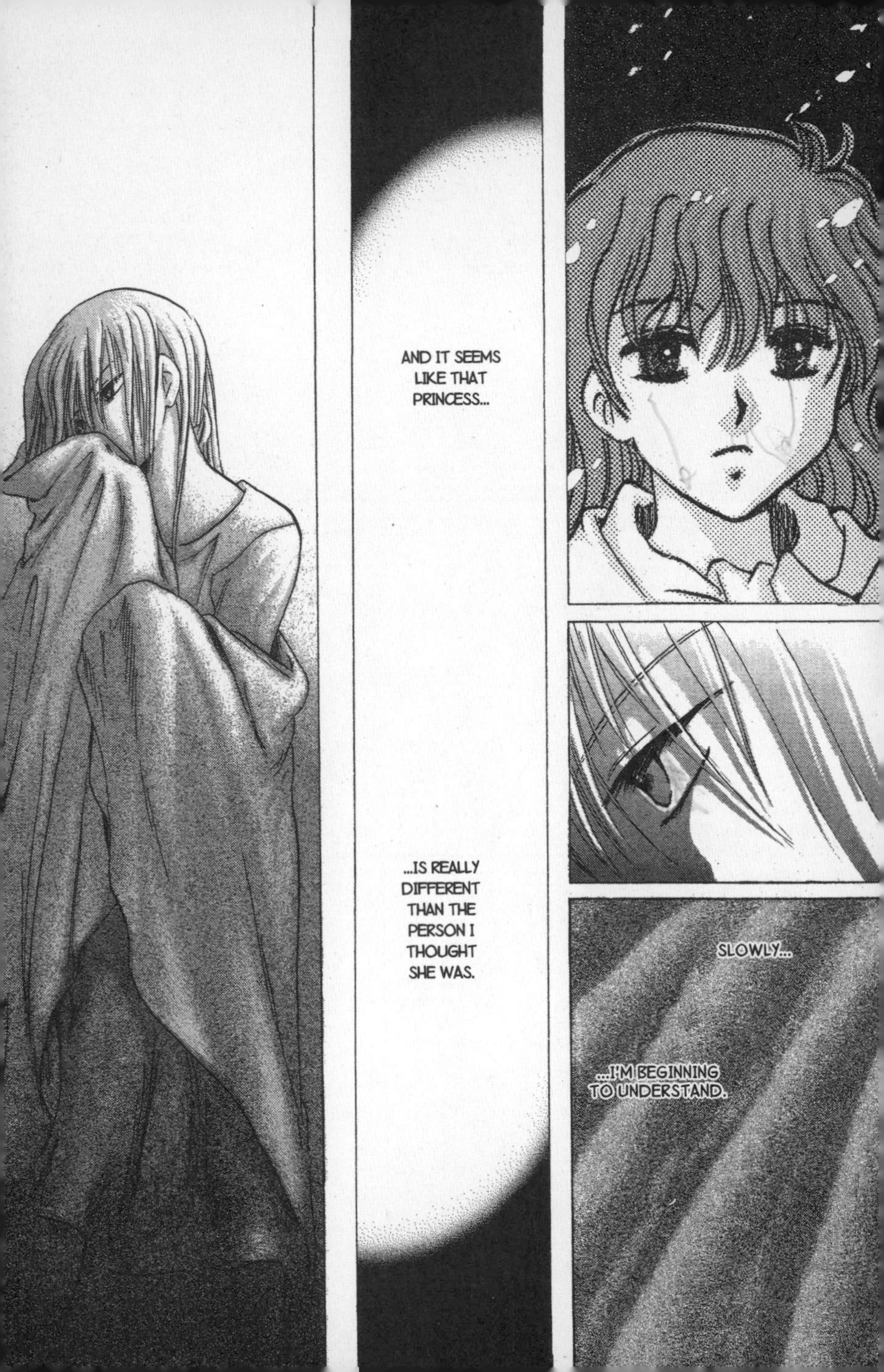
SLOWLY...
...I'M BEGINNING TO UNDERSTAND.
AND IT SEEMS LIKE THAT PRINCESS...
...IS REALLY DIFFERENT THAN THE PERSON I THOUGHT SHE WAS.

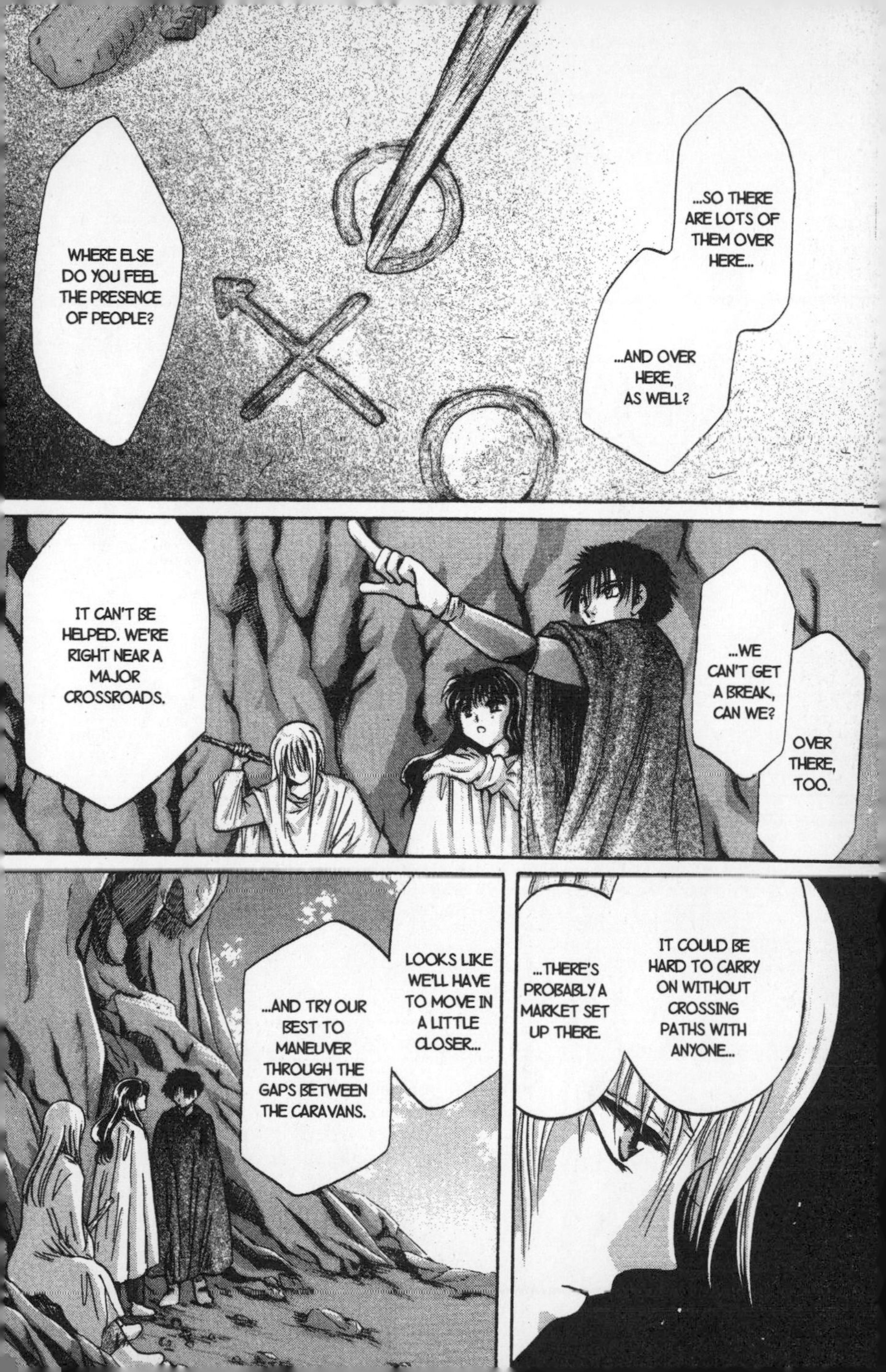
...SO THERE ARE LOTS OF THEM OVER HERE...
...AND OVER HERE, AS WELL?
WHERE ELSE DO YOU FEEL THE PRESENCE OF PEOPLE?
OVER THERE, TOO.
...WE CAN'T GET A BREAK, CAN WE?
IT CAN'T BE HELPED. WE'RE RIGHT NEAR A MAJOR CROSSROADS.
IT COULD BE HARD TO CARRY ON WITHOUT CROSSING PATHS WITH ANYONE...
...THERE'S PROBABLY A MARKET SET UP THERE.
LOOKS LIKE WE'LL HAVE TO MOVE IN A LITTLE CLOSER...
...AND TRY OUR BEST TO MANEUVER THROUGH THE GAPS BETWEEN THE CARAVANS.

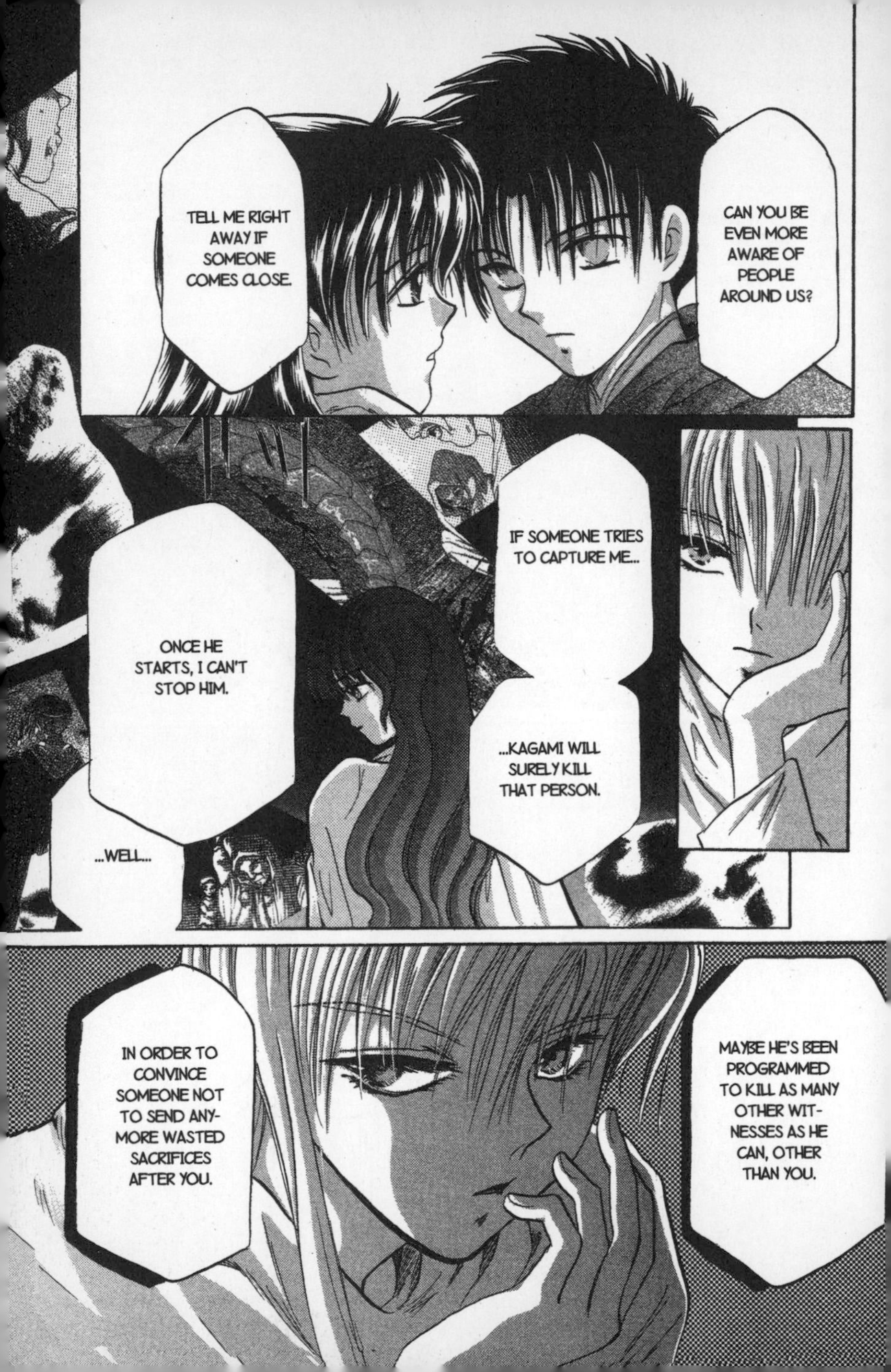

CAN YOU BE EVEN MORE AWARE OF PEOPLE AROUND US?
TELL ME RIGHT AWAY IF SOMEONE COMES CLOSE.
IF SOMEONE TRIES TO CAPTURE ME...
...KAGAMI WILL SURELY KILL THAT PERSON.
ONCE HE STARTS, I CAN'T STOP HIM.
...WELL...
MAYBE HE'S BEEN PROGRAMMED TO KILL AS MANY OTHER WIT-NESSES AS HE CAN, OTHER THAN YOU.
IN ORDER TO CONVINCE SOMEONE NOT TO SEND ANY-MORE WASTED SACRIFICES AFTER YOU.

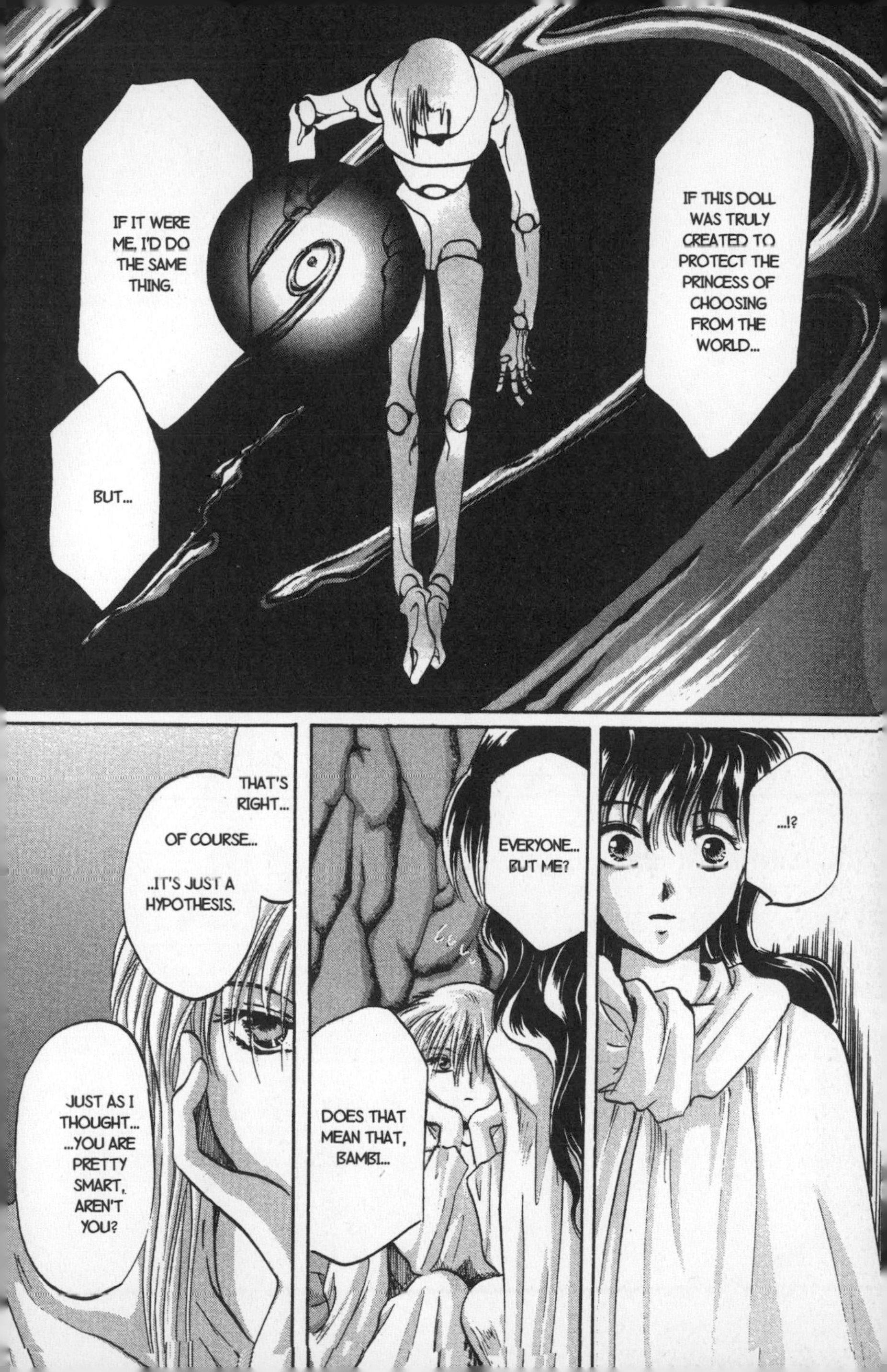
IF THIS DOLL WAS TRULY CREATED TO PROTECT THE PRINCESS OF CHOOSING FROM THE WORLD...
IF IT WERE ME, I'D DO THE SAME THING.
BUT...
...!?
EVERYONE... BUT ME?
DOES THAT MEAN THAT, BAMBI...
THAT'S RIGHT...
OF COURSE...
..IT'S JUST A HYPOTHESIS.
JUST AS I THOUGHT... ...YOU ARE PRETTY SMART, AREN'T YOU?

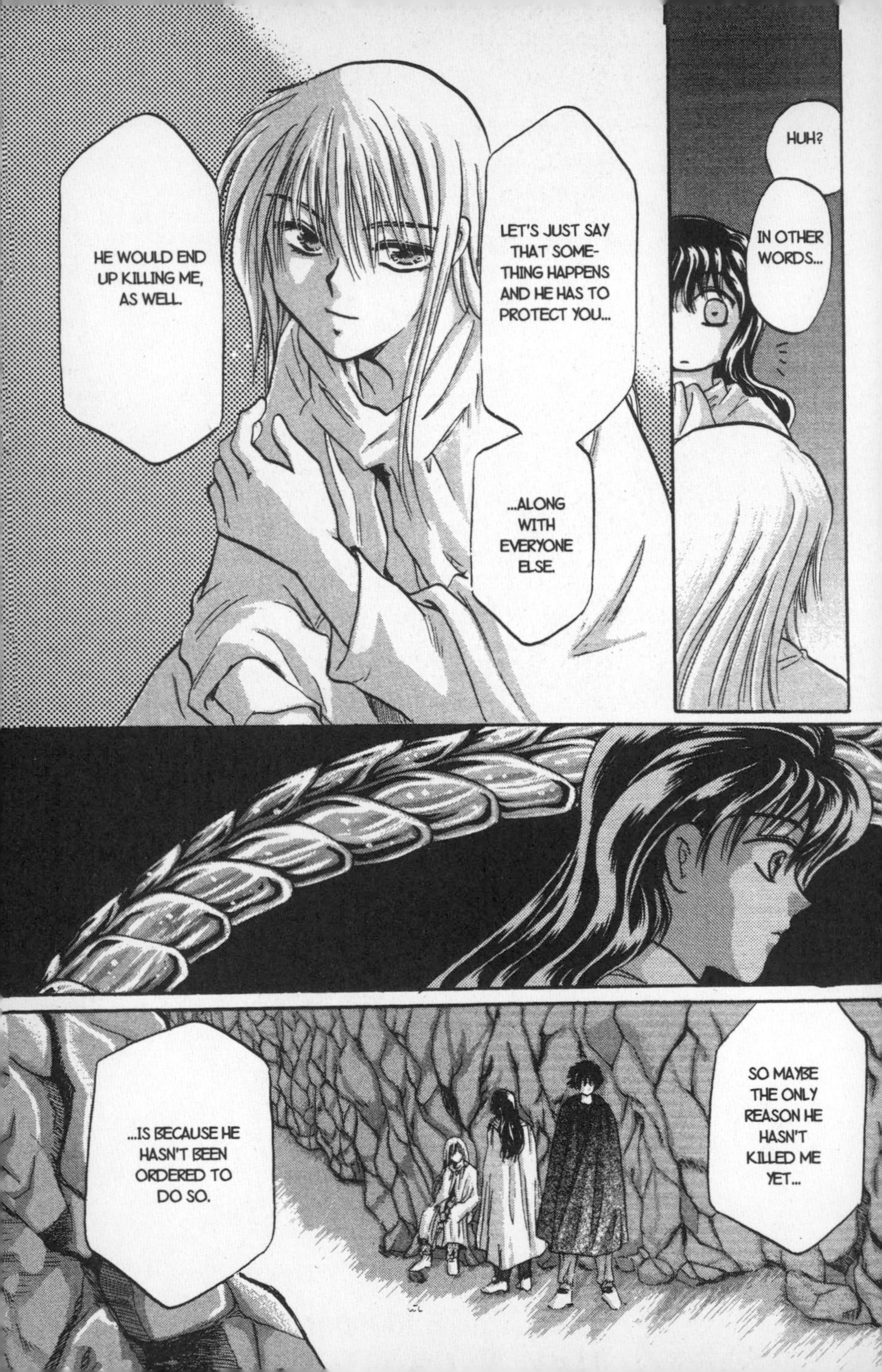
HUH?
IN OTHER WORDS...
LET'S JUST SAY THAT SOME-THING HAPPENS AND HE HAS TO PROTECT YOU...
HE WOULD END UP KILLING ME, AS WELL.
...ALONG WITH EVERYONE ELSE.
SO MAYBE THE ONLY REASON HE HASN'T KILLED ME YET...
...IS BECAUSE HE HASN'T BEEN ORDERED TO DO SO.

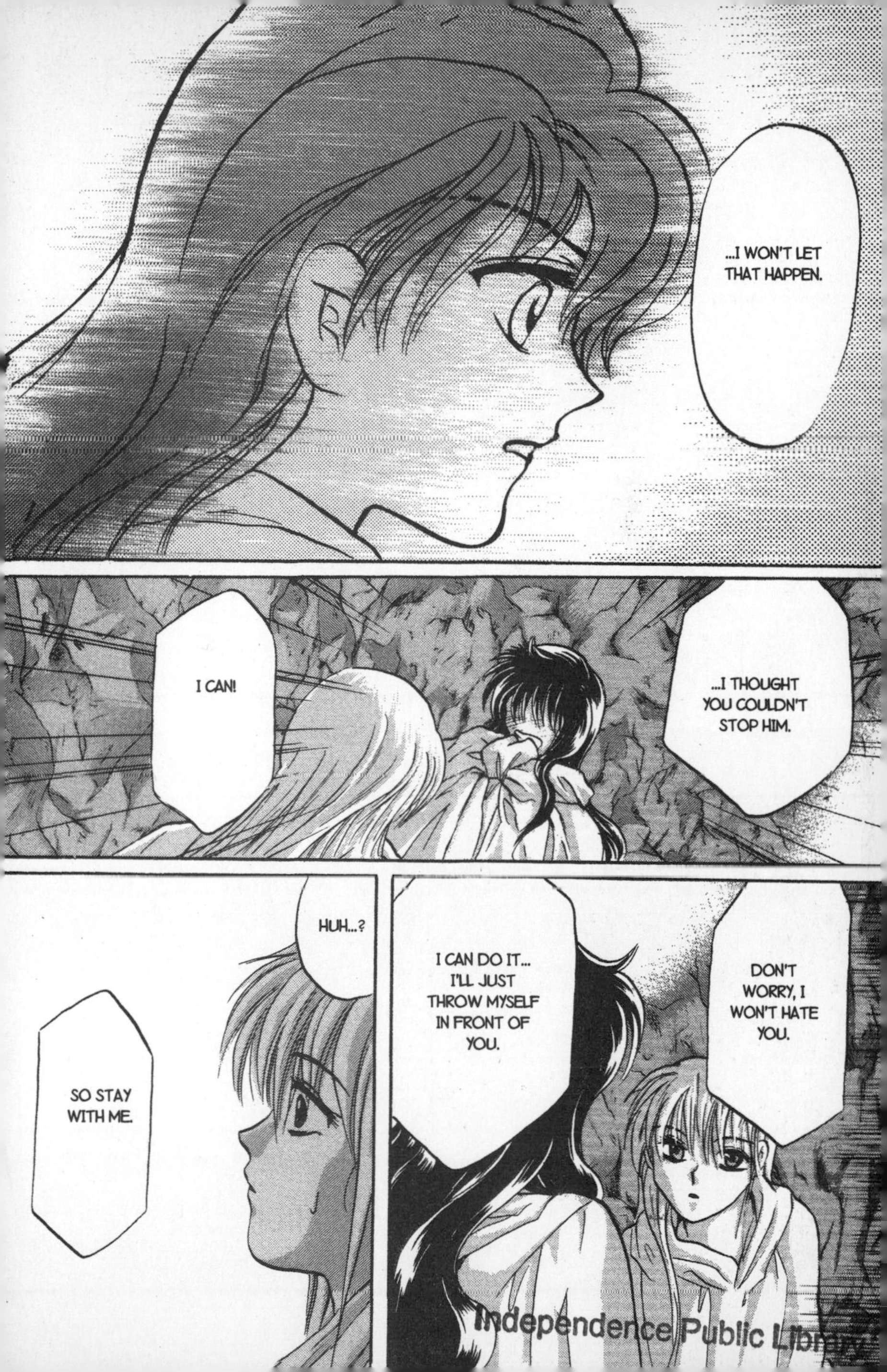
...I WON'T LET THAT HAPPEN.
...I THOUGHT YOU COULDN'T STOP HIM.
I CAN!
DON'T WORRY, I WON'T HATE YOU.
I CAN DO IT... I'LL JUST THROW MYSELF IN FRONT OF YOU.
HUH...?
SO STAY WITH ME.

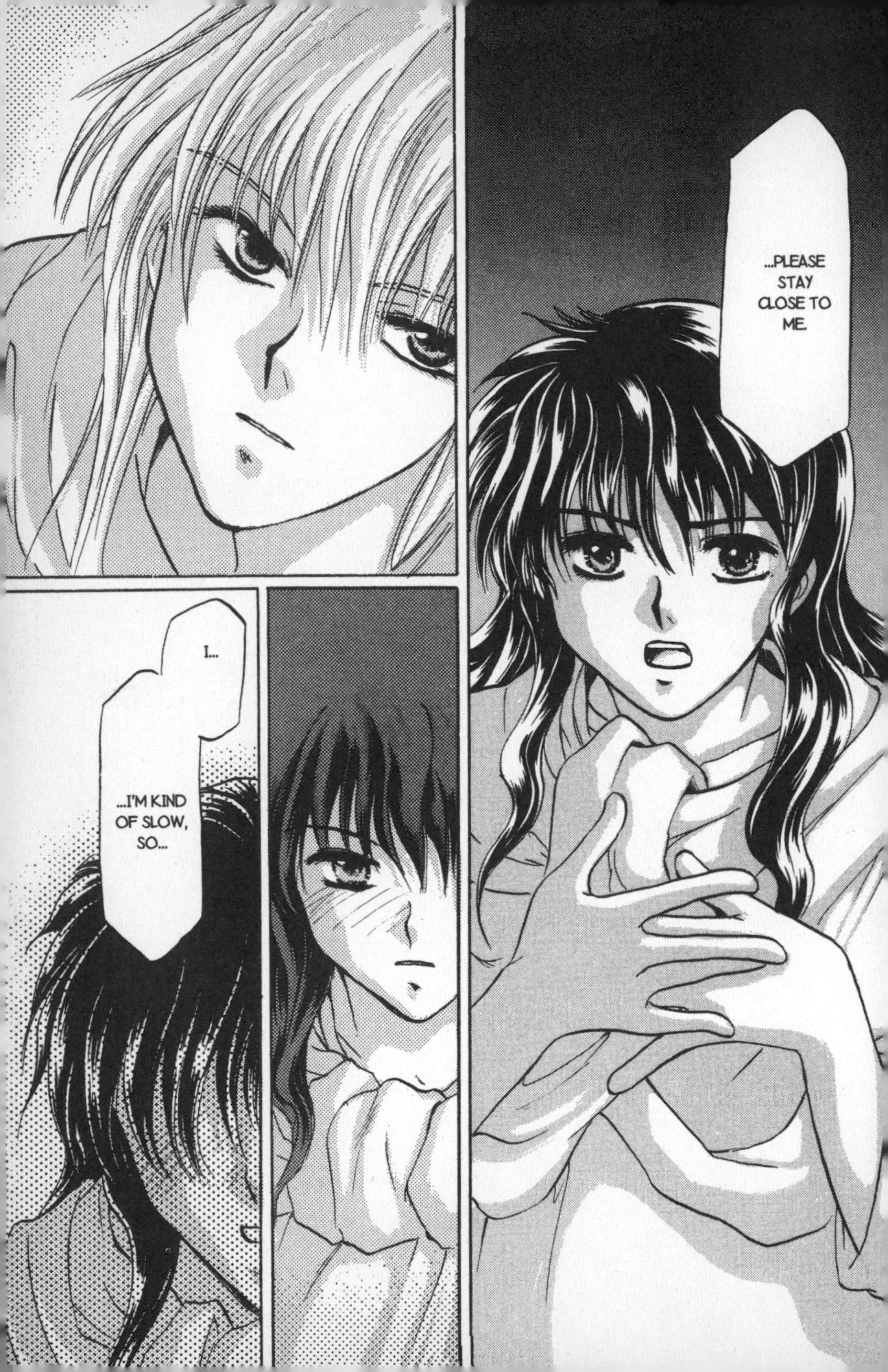
I...
...I'M KIND OF SLOW, SO...
...PLEASE STAY CLOSE TO ME.

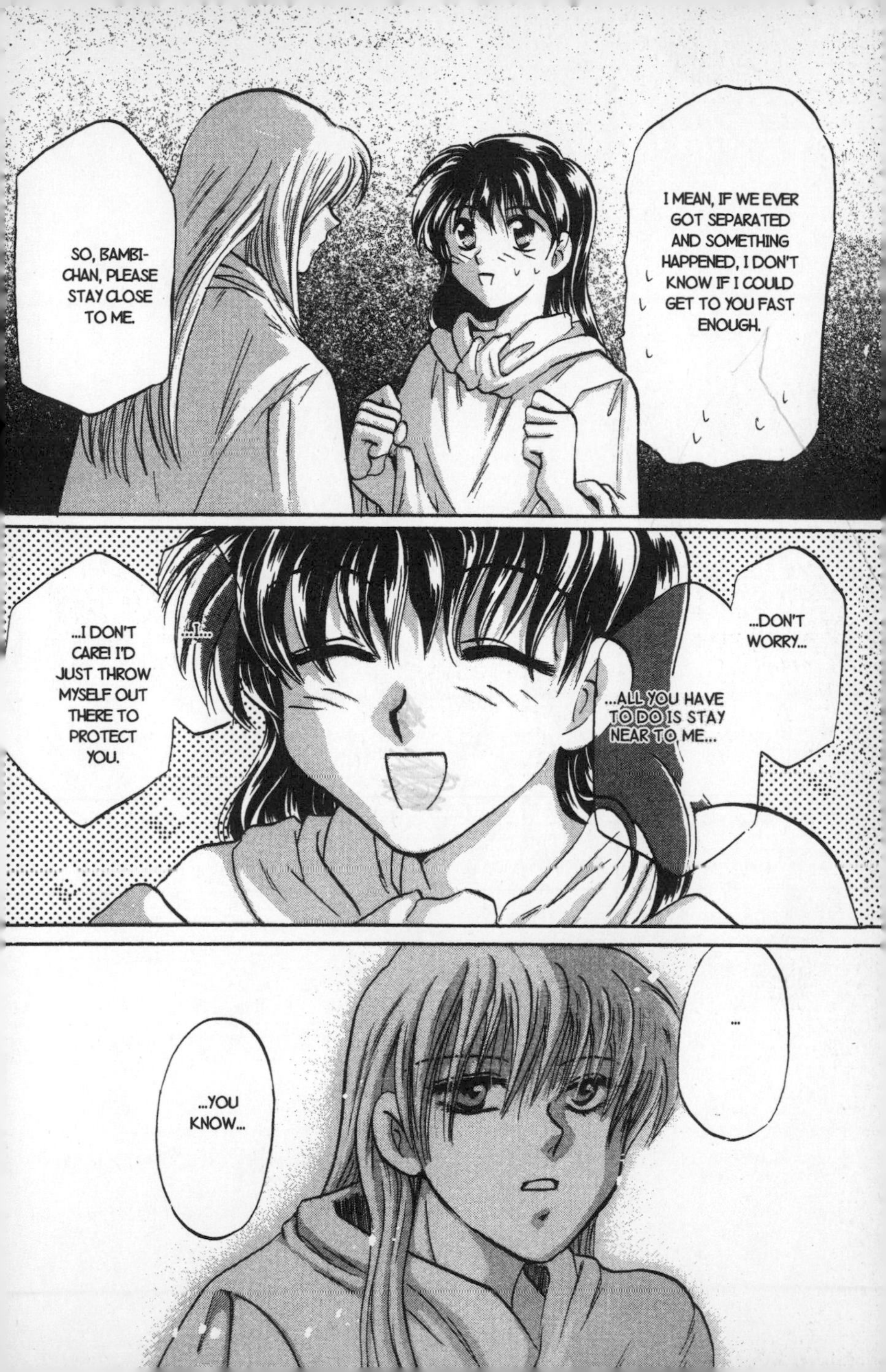
I MEAN, IF WE EVER GOT SEPARATED AND SOMETHING HAPPENED, I DON'T KNOW IF I COULD GET TO YOU FAST ENOUGH.
SO, BAMBI-CHAN, PLEASE STAY CLOSE TO ME.
...DON'T WORRY...
...ALL YOU HAVE TO DO IS STAY NEAR TO ME...
...I DON'T CARE! I'D JUST THROW MYSELF OUT THERE TO PROTECT YOU.
...
...YOU KNOW...

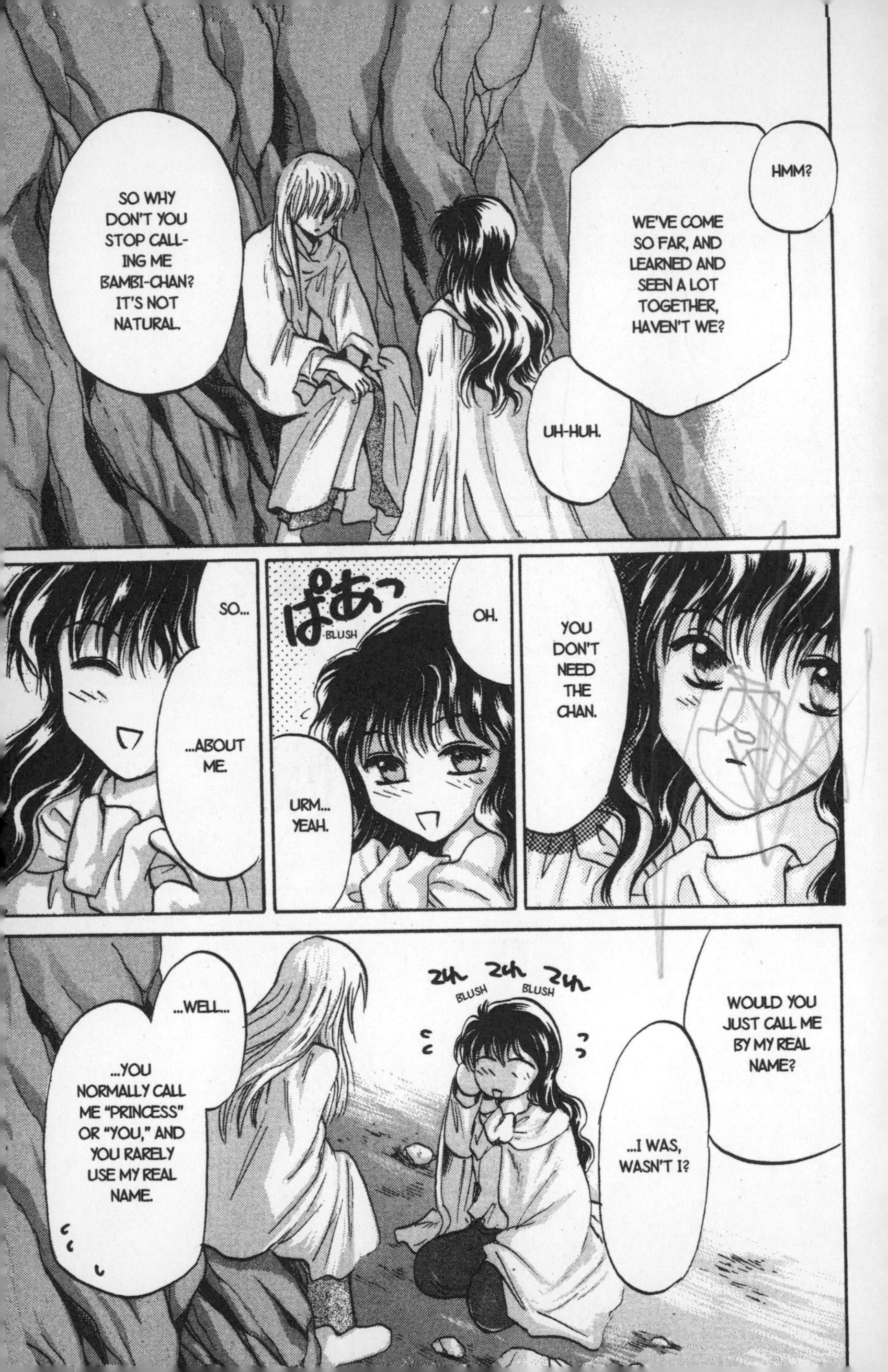
HMM?
WE'VE COME SO FAR, AND LEARNED AND SEEN A LOT TOGETHER, HAVEN'T WE?
UH-HUH.
SO WHY DON'T YOU STOP CALLING-ING ME BAMBI-CHAN? IT'S NOT NATURAL.
YOU DON'T NEED THE CHAN.
OH.
ぱあっ
BLUSH
URM... YEAH.
SO...
...ABOUT ME.
WOULD YOU JUST CALL ME BY MY REAL NAME?
...I WAS, WASN'T I?
てれ てれ てれ
BLUSH BLUSH
...WELL...
...YOU NORMALLY CALL ME "PRINCESS" OR "YOU," AND YOU RARELY USE MY REAL NAME.

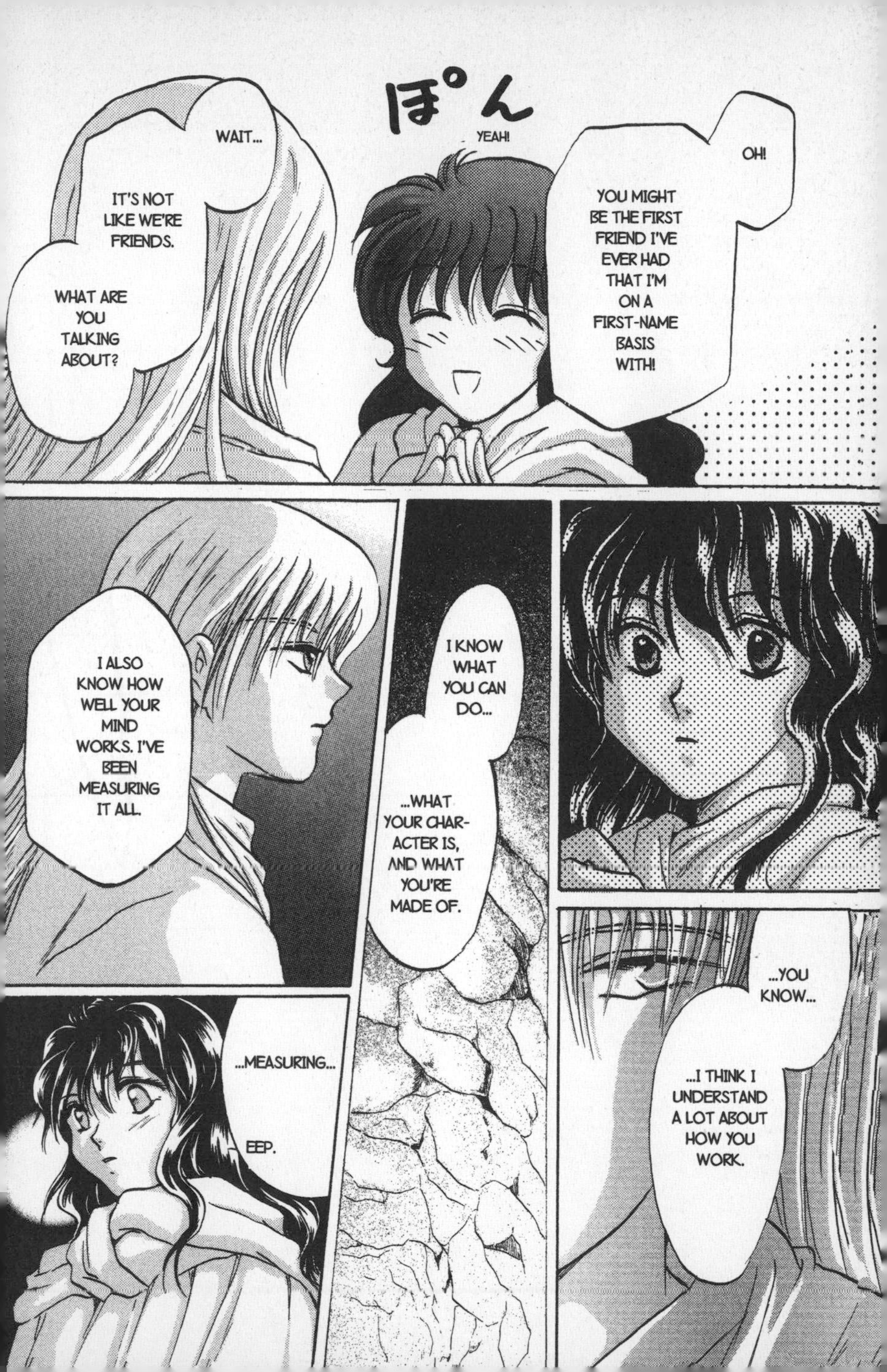
OH!
YOU MIGHT BE THE FIRST FRIEND I'VE EVER HAD THAT I'M ON A FIRST-NAME BASIS WITH!
ぽん
YEAH!
WAIT...
IT'S NOT LIKE WE'RE FRIENDS.
WHAT ARE YOU TALKING ABOUT?
...YOU KNOW...
...I THINK I UNDERSTAND A LOT ABOUT HOW YOU WORK.
I KNOW WHAT YOU CAN DO...
...WHAT YOUR CHAR-ACTER IS, AND WHAT YOU'RE MADE OF.
I ALSO KNOW HOW WELL YOUR MIND WORKS. I'VE BEEN MEASURING IT ALL.
...MEASURING...
EEP.

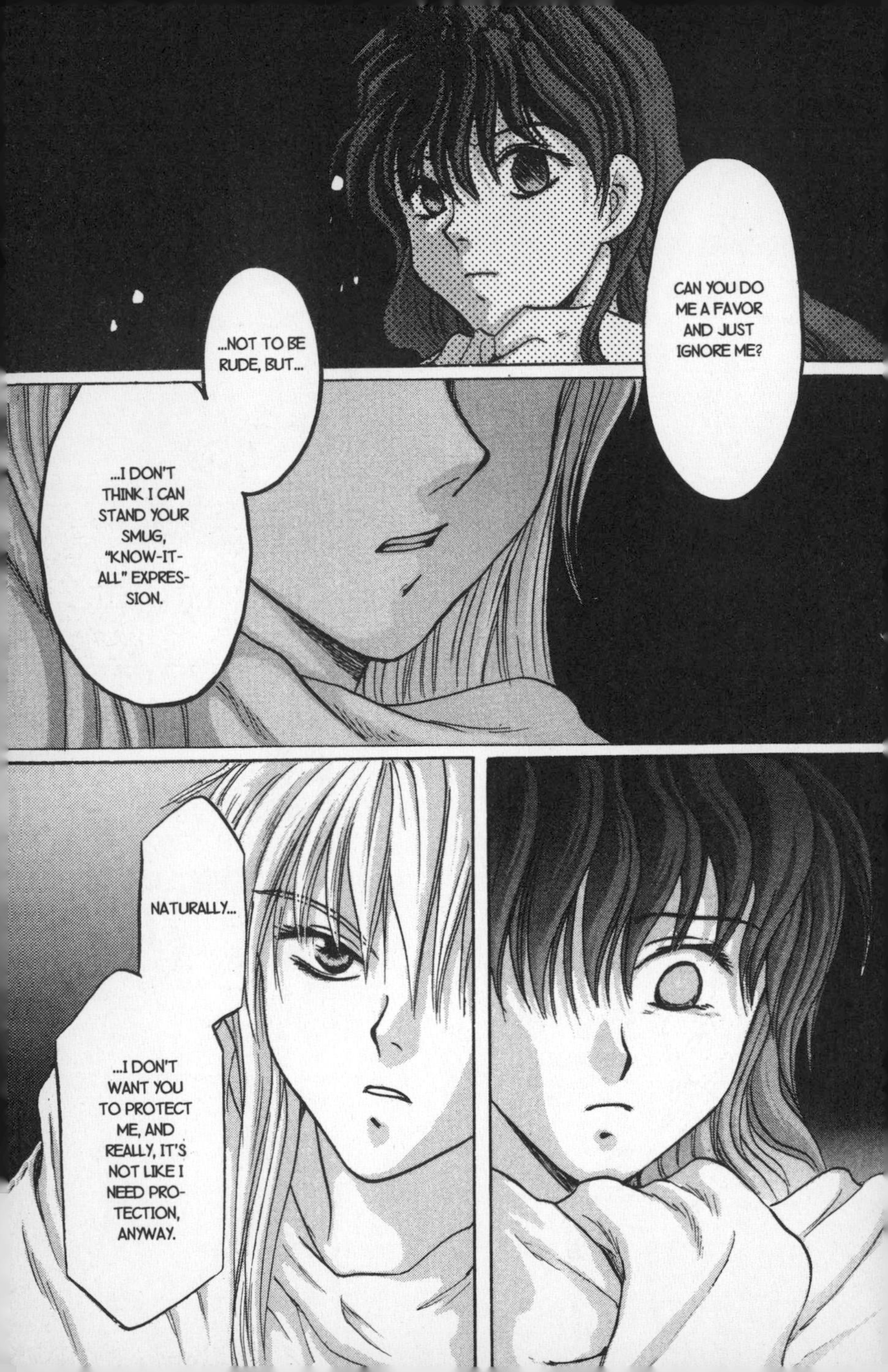
CAN YOU DO ME A FAVOR AND JUST IGNORE ME?
...NOT TO BE RUDE, BUT...
...I DON'T THINK I CAN STAND YOUR SMUG, "KNOW-IT-ALL" EXPRES-SION.
NATURALLY...
...I DON'T WANT YOU TO PROTECT ME, AND REALLY, IT'S NOT LIKE I NEED PRO-TECTION, ANYWAY.

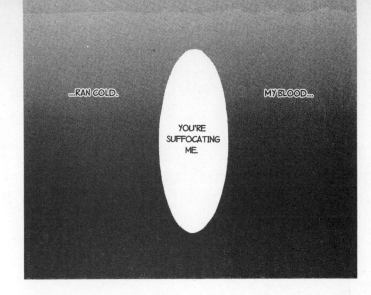

MY BLOOD...
YOU'RE SUFFOCATING ME.
...RAN COLD.
...I...
...I BETTER...GO LOOK FOR SOME MORE BERRIES...OR SOMETHING.
...ALRIGHT.
BUT I REALLY WANT TO GET STARTED WITH SETTING UP CAMP FOR TONIGHT.
I'LL BE BACK!!
I PROMISE I'LL BE RIGHT BACK...SO...

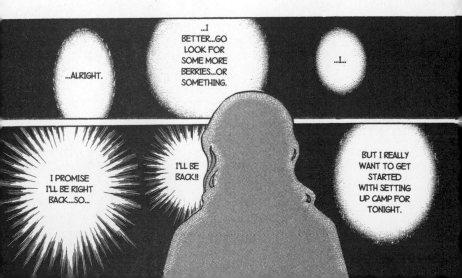

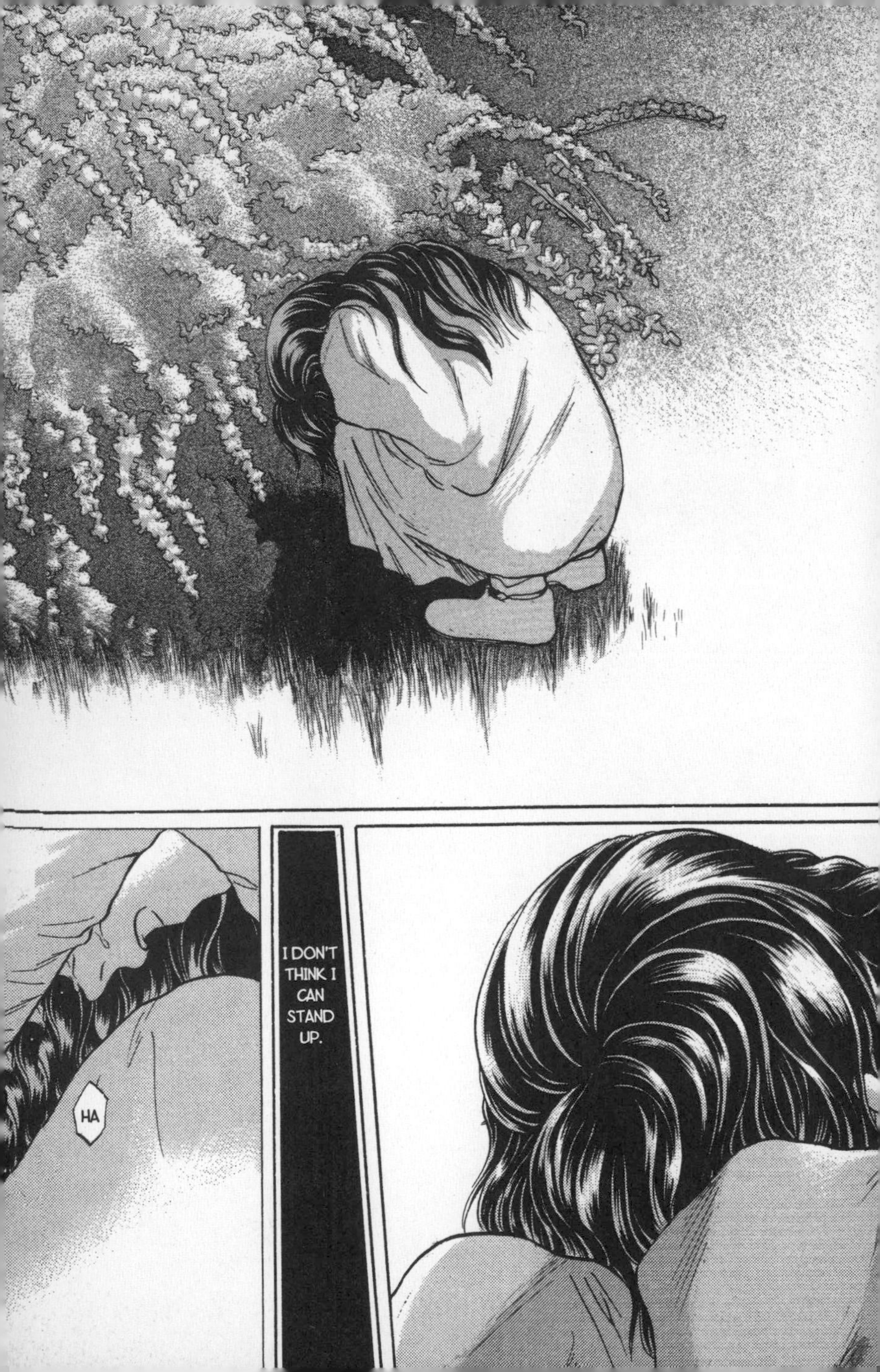
I DON'T THINK I CAN STAND UP.
HA

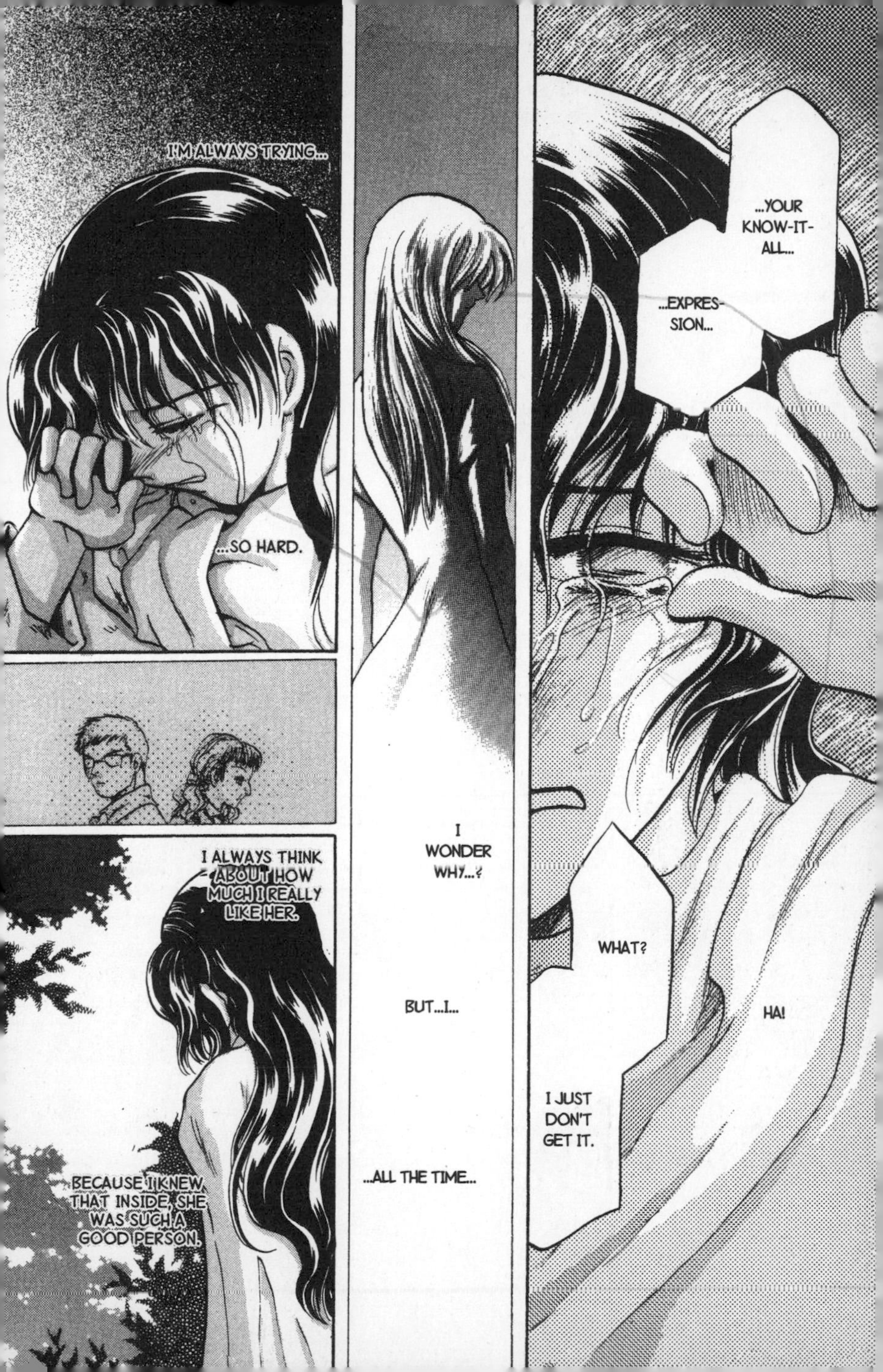
...YOUR KNOW-IT-ALL...
...EXPRES-SION...
HA!
WHAT?
I JUST DON'T GET IT.
I WONDER WHY...?
BUT...I...
...ALL THE TIME...
I'M ALWAYS TRYING...
...SO HARD.
I ALWAYS THINK ABOUT HOW MUCH I REALLY LIKE HER.
BECAUSE I KNEW THAT INSIDE, SHE WAS SUCH A GOOD PERSON.

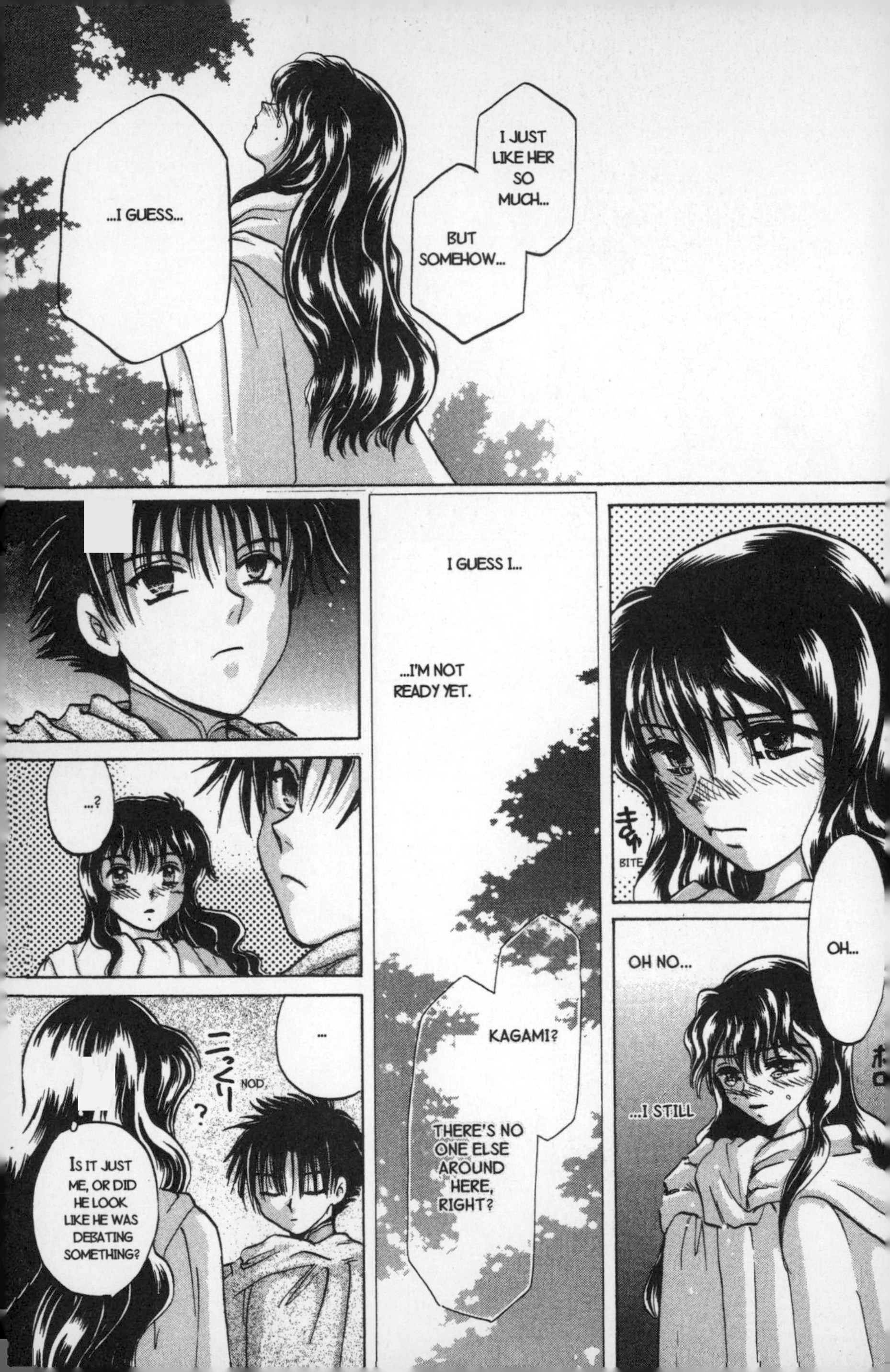
I JUST LIKE HER SO MUCH...
BUT SOMEHOW...
...I GUESS...
BITE
OH...
OH NO...
...I STILL
I GUESS I...
...I'M NOT READY YET.
KAGAMI?
THERE'S NO ONE ELSE AROUND HERE, RIGHT?
...?
...
NOD
?
IS IT JUST ME, OR DID HE LOOK LIKE HE WAS DEBATING SOMETHING?

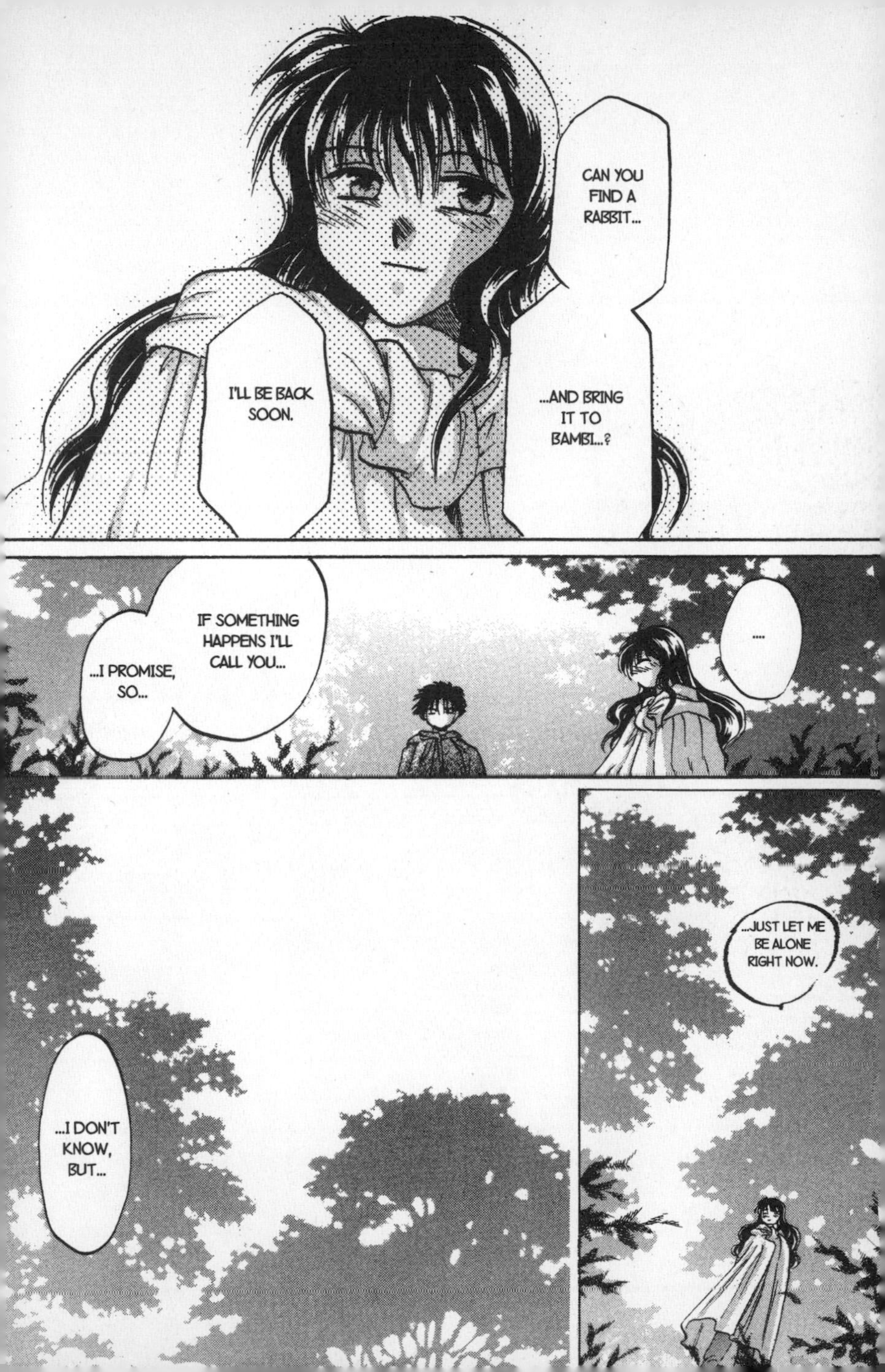
CAN YOU FIND A RABBIT...
...AND BRING IT TO BAMBI...?
I'LL BE BACK SOON.
....
IF SOMETHING HAPPENS I'LL CALL YOU...
...I PROMISE, SO...
...JUST LET ME BE ALONE RIGHT NOW.
...I DON'T KNOW, BUT...

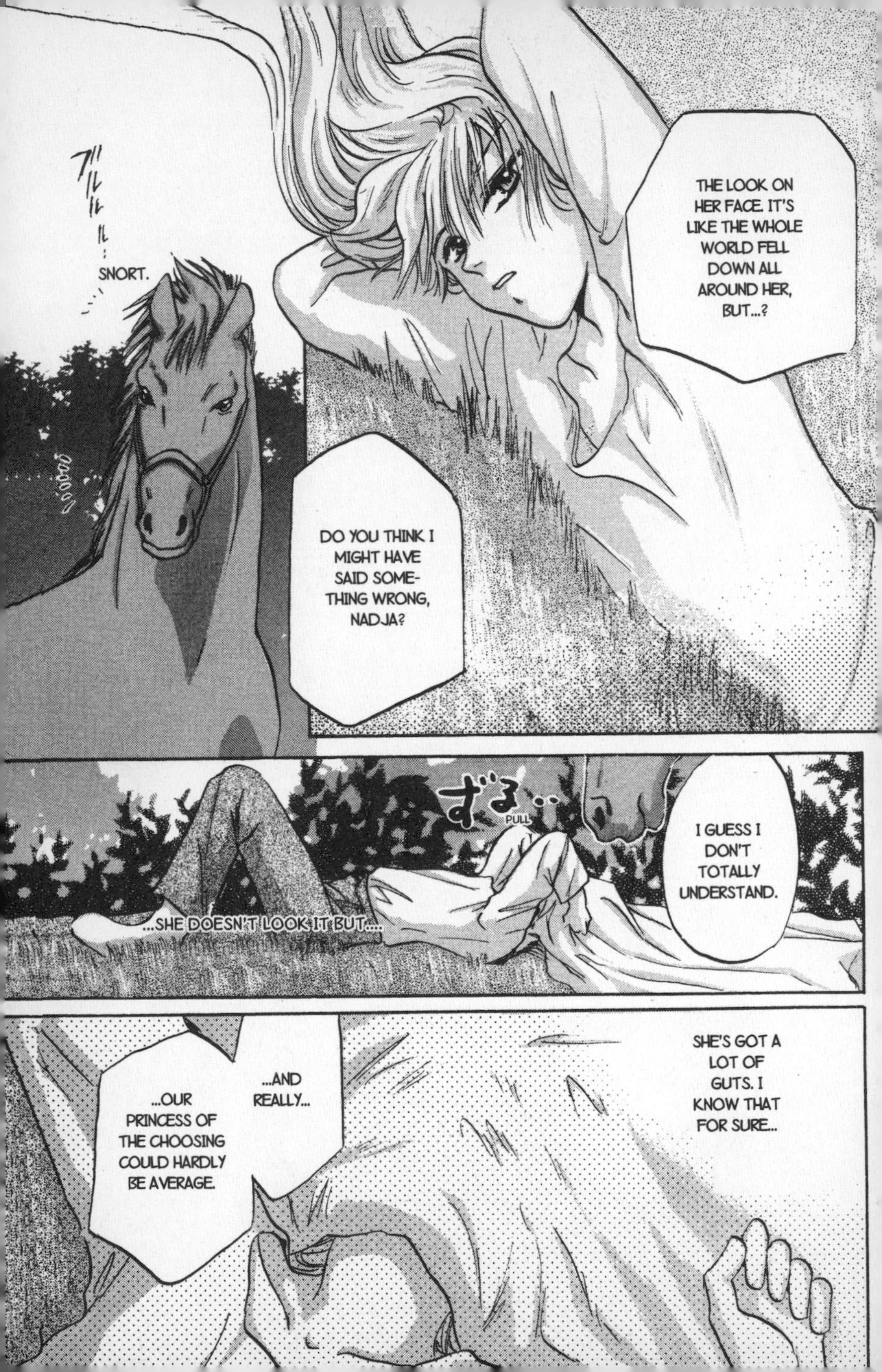
THE LOOK ON HER FACE. IT'S LIKE THE WHOLE WORLD FELL DOWN ALL AROUND HER, BUT...?
ブルルル…
SNORT.
DO YOU THINK I MIGHT HAVE SAID SOME-THING WRONG, NADJA?
I GUESS I DON'T TOTALLY UNDERSTAND.
ずる…
PULL
...SHE DOESN'T LOOK IT BUT....
SHE'S GOT A LOT OF GUTS. I KNOW THAT FOR SURE...
...AND REALLY...
...OUR PRINCESS OF THE CHOOSING COULD HARDLY BE AVERAGE.

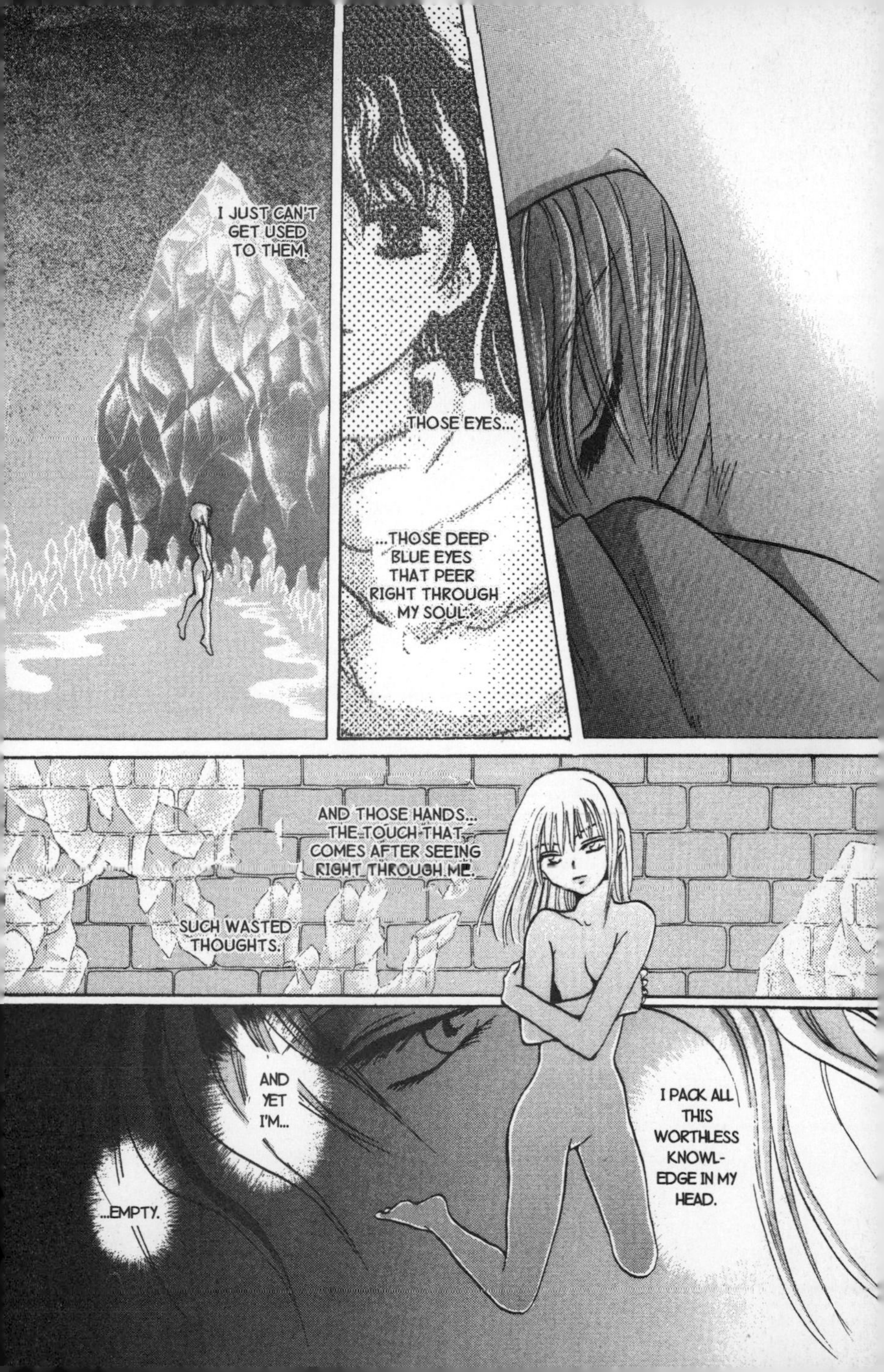
THOSE EYES...
...THOSE DEEP BLUE EYES THAT PEER RIGHT THROUGH MY SOUL.
I JUST CAN'T GET USED TO THEM.
AND THOSE HANDS... THE TOUCH THAT COMES AFTER SEEING RIGHT THROUGH ME.
SUCH WASTED THOUGHTS.
I PACK ALL THIS WORTHLESS KNOWL-EDGE IN MY HEAD.
AND YET I'M...
...EMPTY.

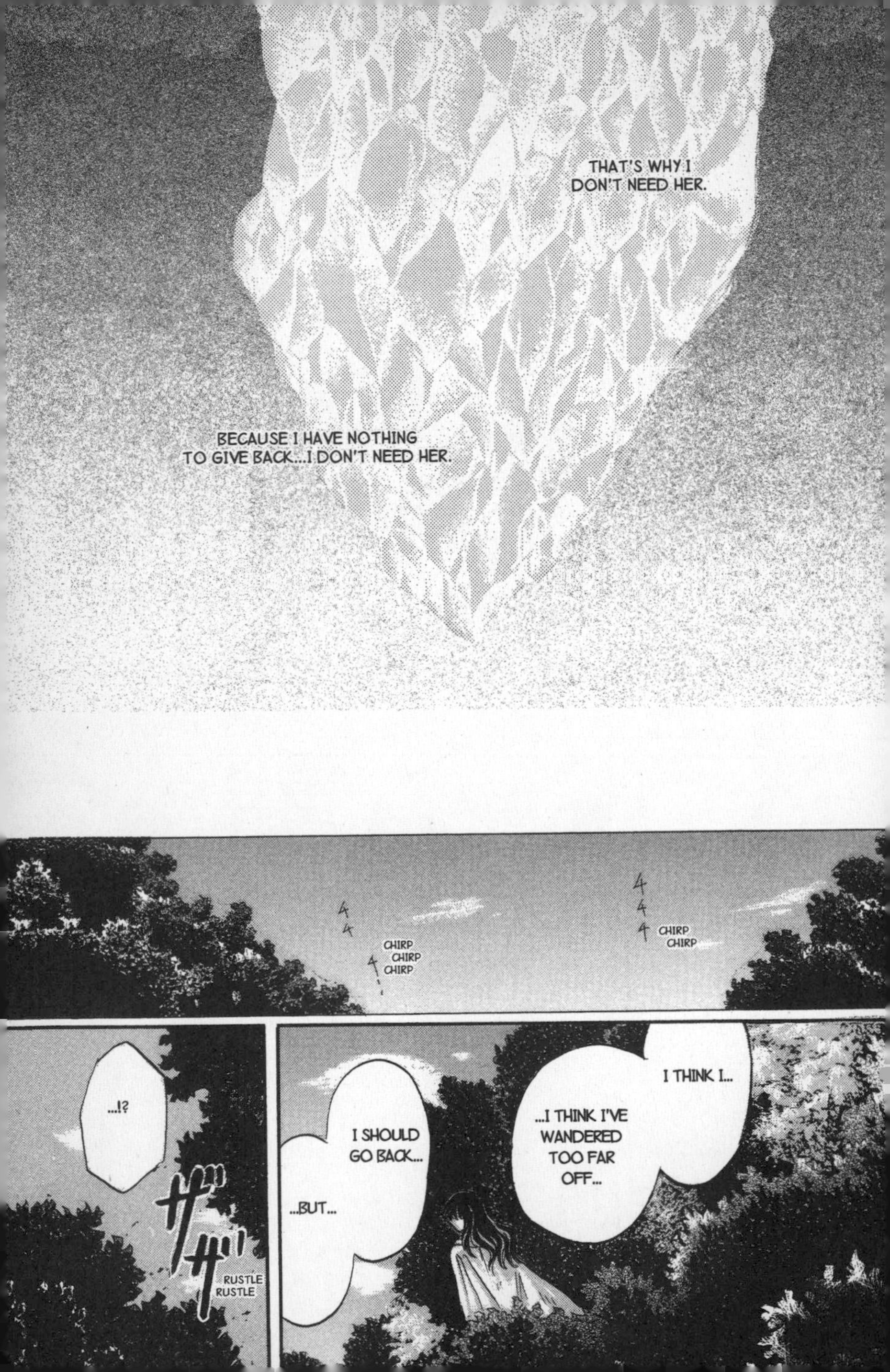
THAT'S WHY I DON'T NEED HER.
BECAUSE I HAVE NOTHING TO GIVE BACK...I DON'T NEED HER.
CHIRP CHIRP
CHIRP CHIRP CHIRP
I THINK I...
...I THINK I'VE WANDERED TOO FAR OFF...
I SHOULD GO BACK...
...BUT...
...!?
RUSTLE RUSTLE

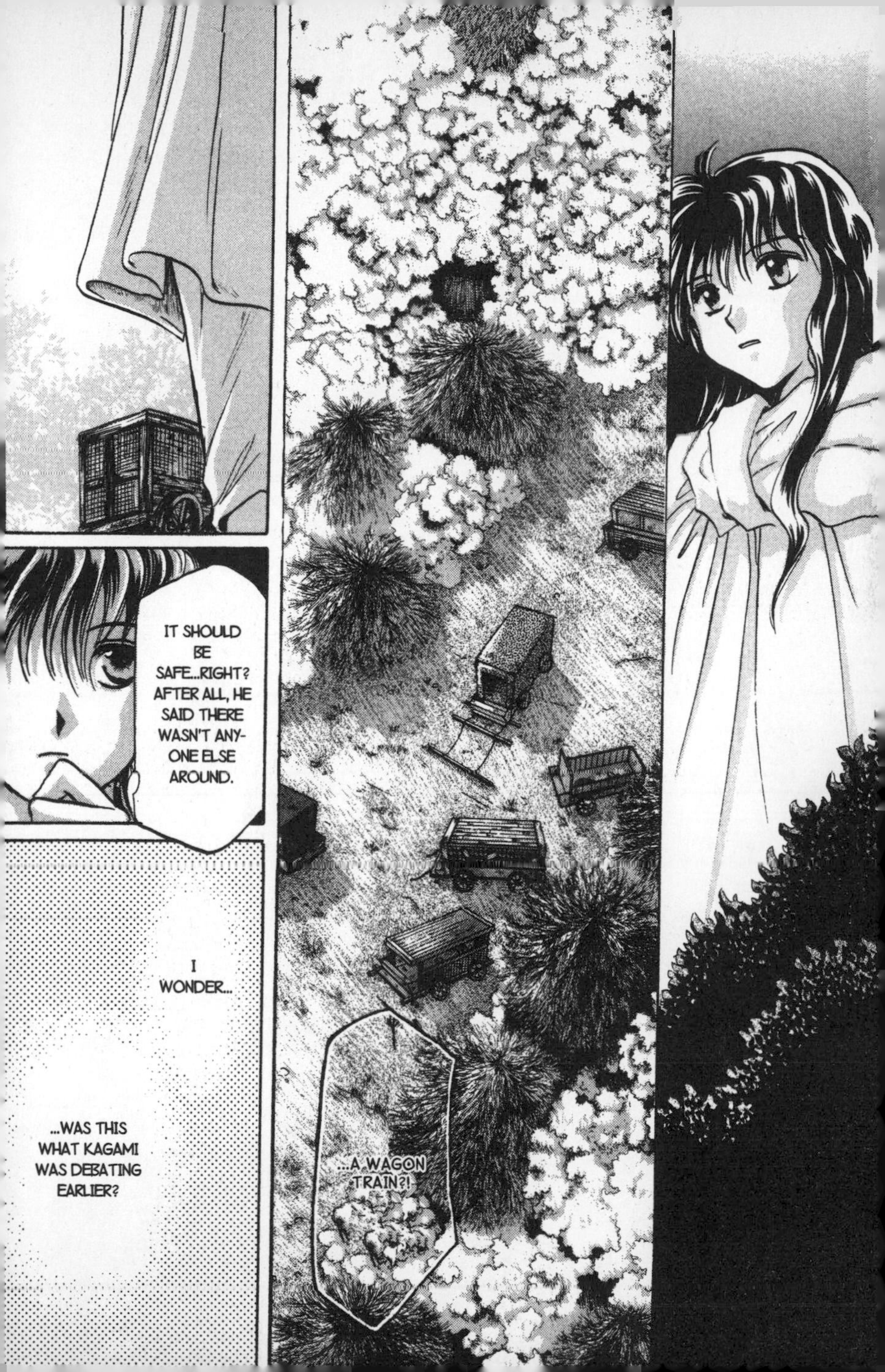
...A WAGON TRAIN?!
IT SHOULD BE SAFE...RIGHT? AFTER ALL, HE SAID THERE WASN'T ANY-ONE ELSE AROUND.
I WONDER...
...WAS THIS WHAT KAGAMI WAS DEBATING EARLIER?

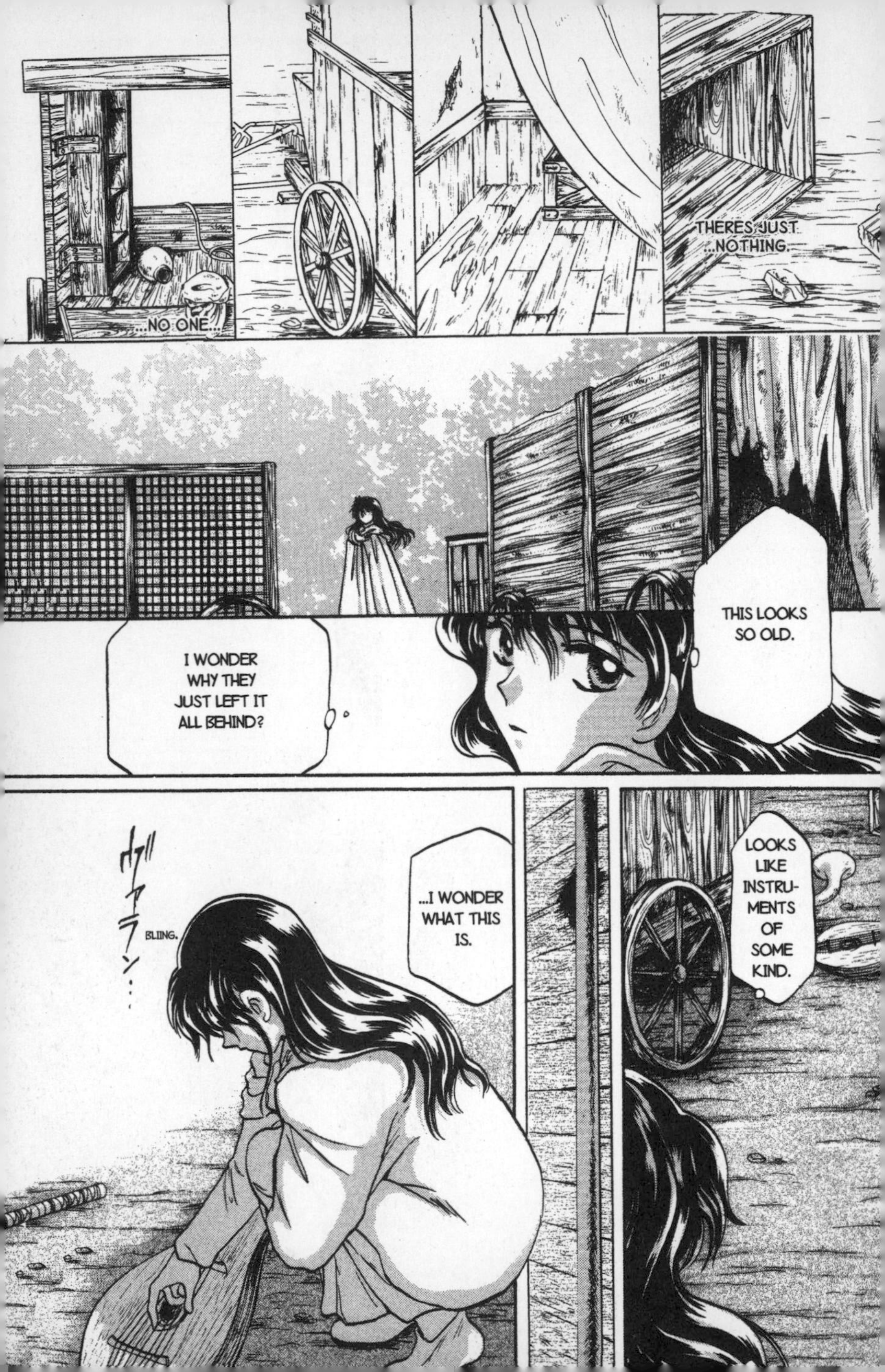
THERES JUST ...NOTHING.
...NO ONE...
THIS LOOKS SO OLD.
I WONDER WHY THEY JUST LEFT IT ALL BEHIND?
LOOKS LIKE INSTRUMENTS OF SOME KIND.
...I WONDER WHAT THIS IS.
BLIING.

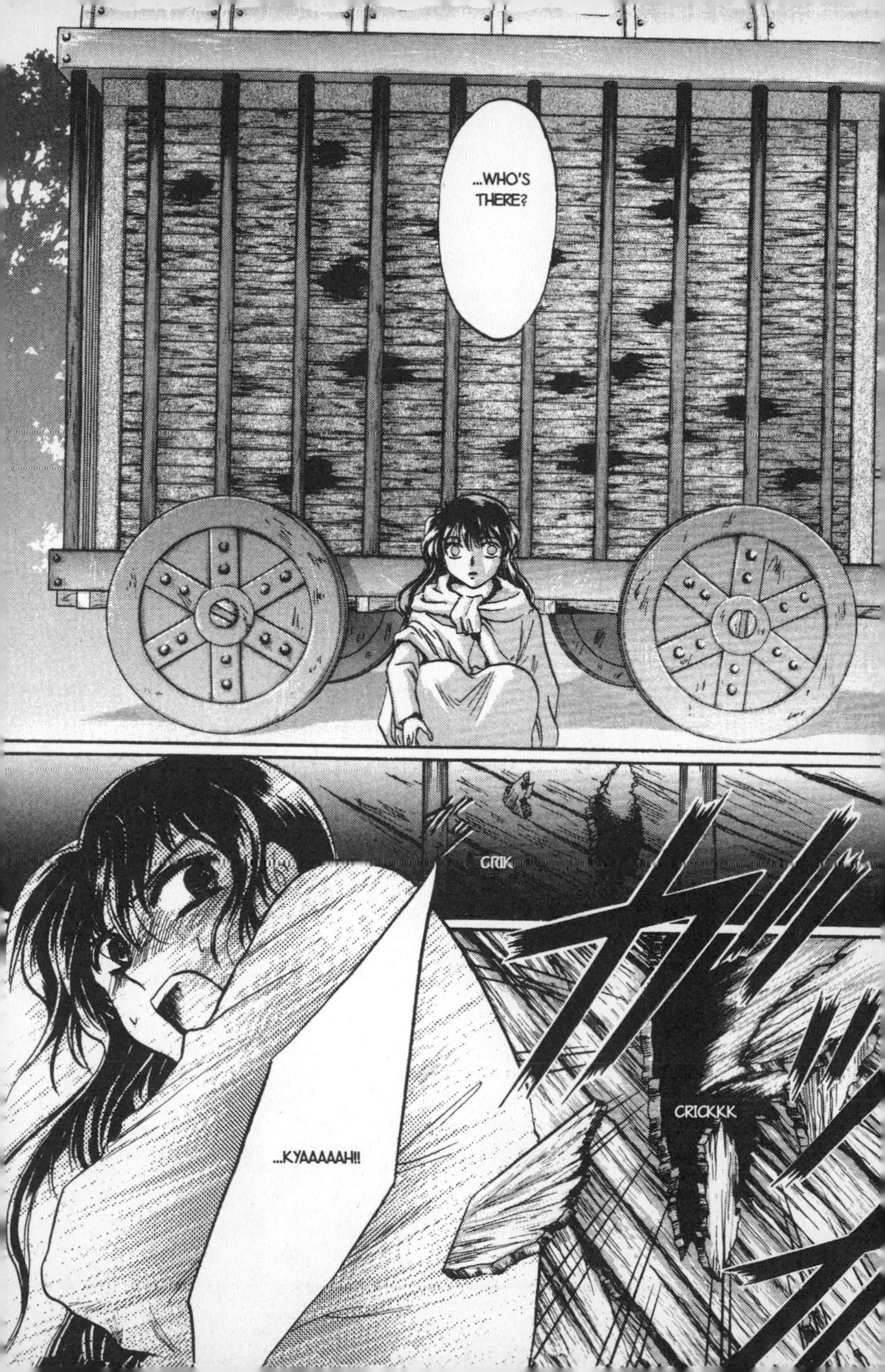
...WHO'S THERE?
GRIK
CRICKKK
...KYAAAAAH!!

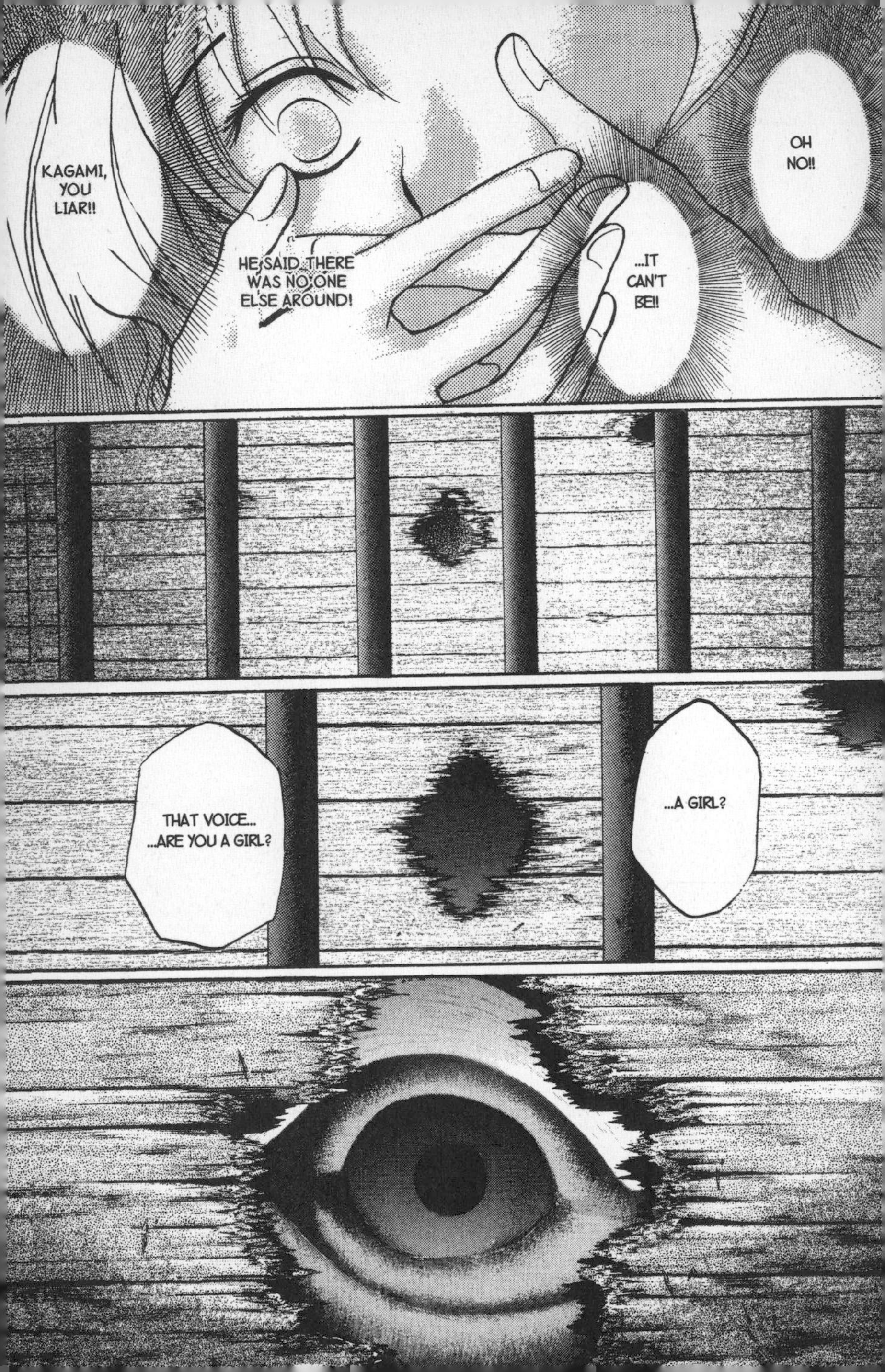
OH NO!!
...IT CAN'T BE!!
HE SAID THERE WAS NO ONE ELSE AROUND!
KAGAMI, YOU LIAR!!
...A GIRL?
THAT VOICE... ...ARE YOU A GIRL?

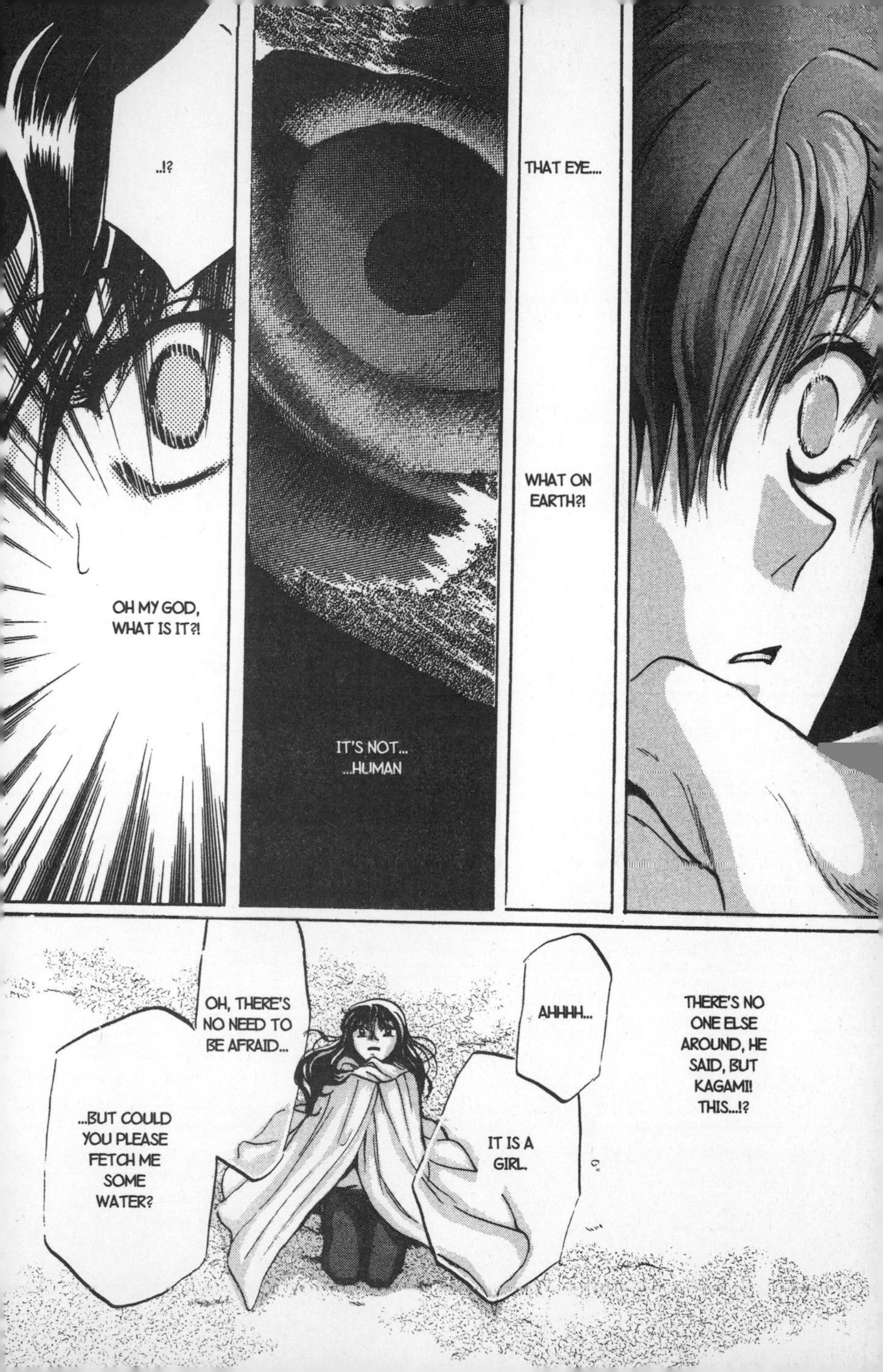
THAT EYE...
WHAT ON EARTH?!
IT'S NOT... ...HUMAN
..!?
OH MY GOD, WHAT IS IT?!
THERE'S NO ONE ELSE AROUND, HE SAID, BUT KAGAMI! THIS...!?
AHHHH...
IT IS A GIRL.
OH, THERE'S NO NEED TO BE AFRAID...
...BUT COULD YOU PLEASE FETCH ME SOME WATER?

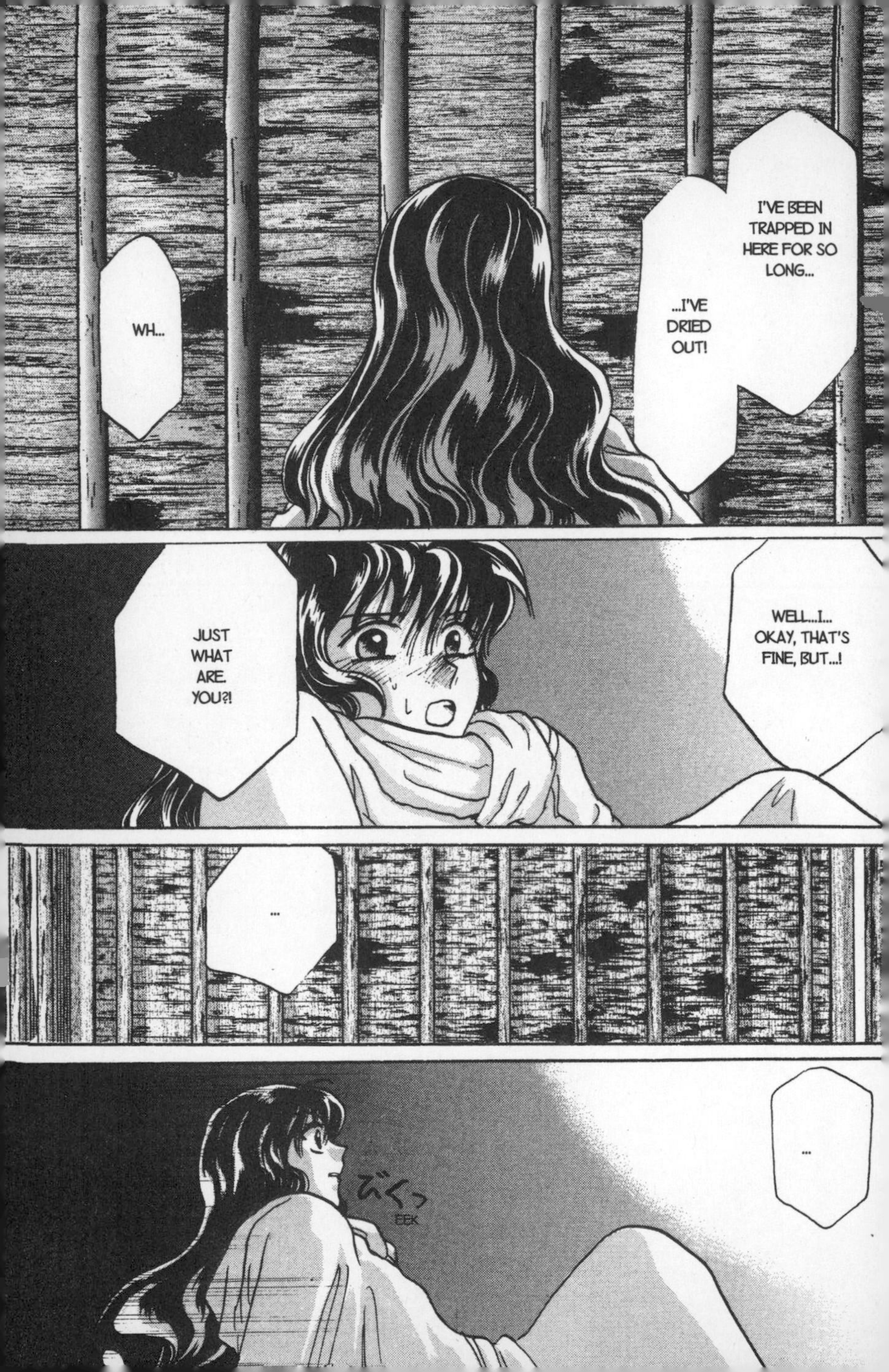
I'VE BEEN TRAPPED IN HERE FOR SO LONG...
...I'VE DRIED OUT!
WH...
WELL...I... OKAY, THAT'S FINE, BUT...!
JUST WHAT ARE. YOU?!
...
...
びくっ
EEK

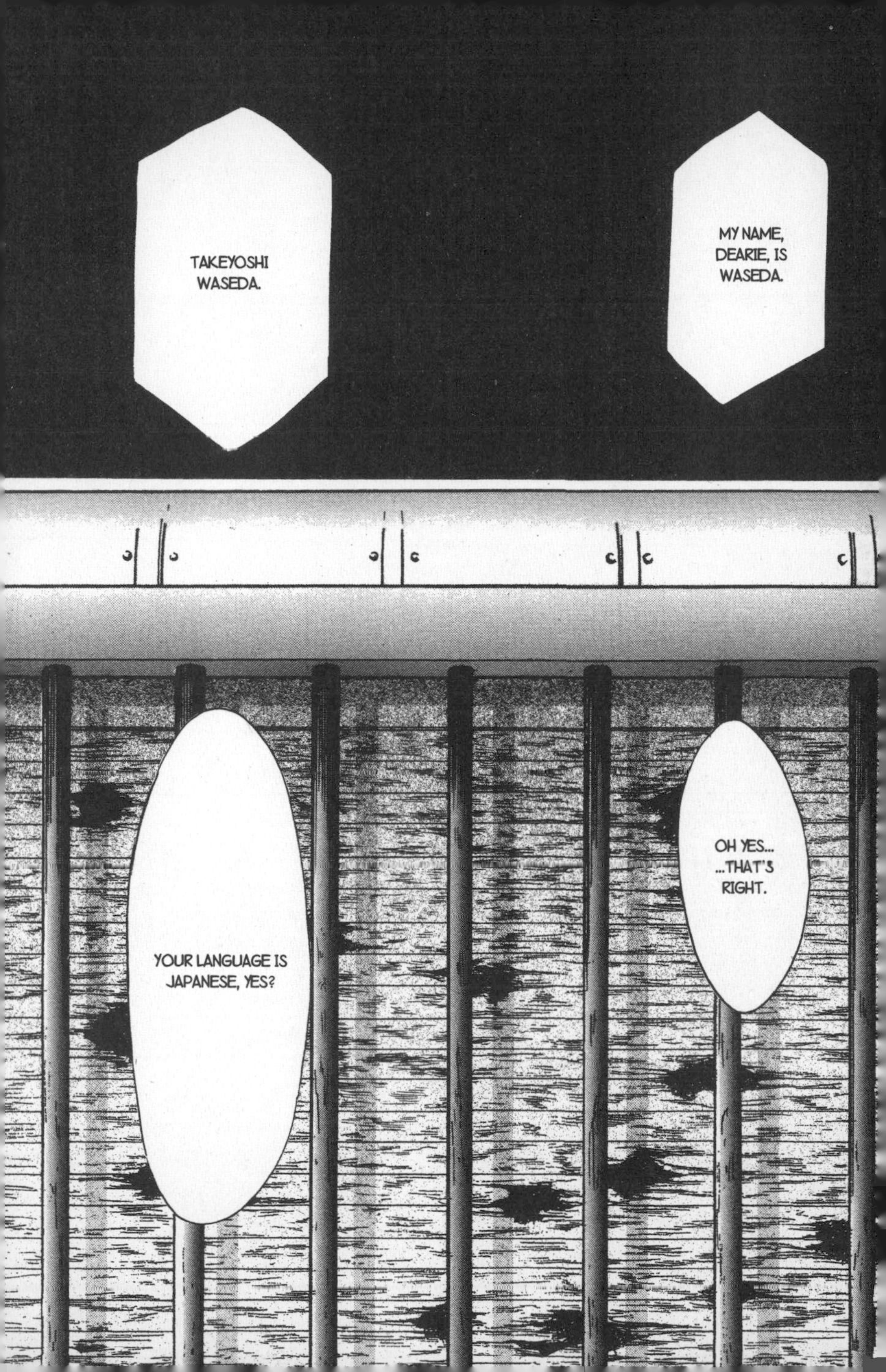
MY NAME, DEARIE, IS WASEDA.
TAKEYOSHI WASEDA.
OH YES... ...THAT'S RIGHT.
YOUR LANGUAGE IS JAPANESE, YES?

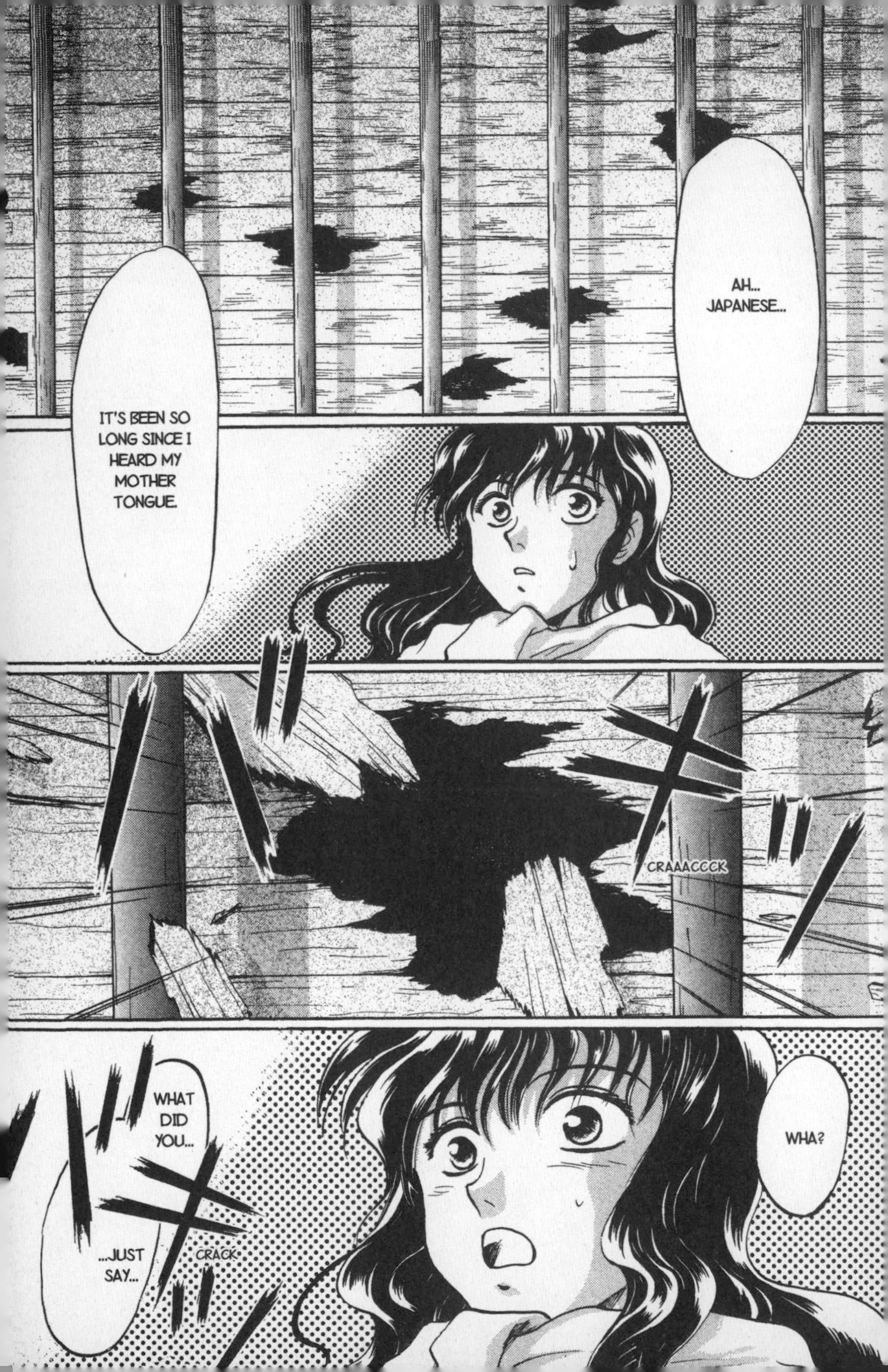
AH... JAPANESE...
IT'S BEEN SO LONG SINCE I HEARD MY MOTHER TONGUE.
CRAAACCCK
WHA?
WHAT DID YOU...
...JUST SAY...
CRACK

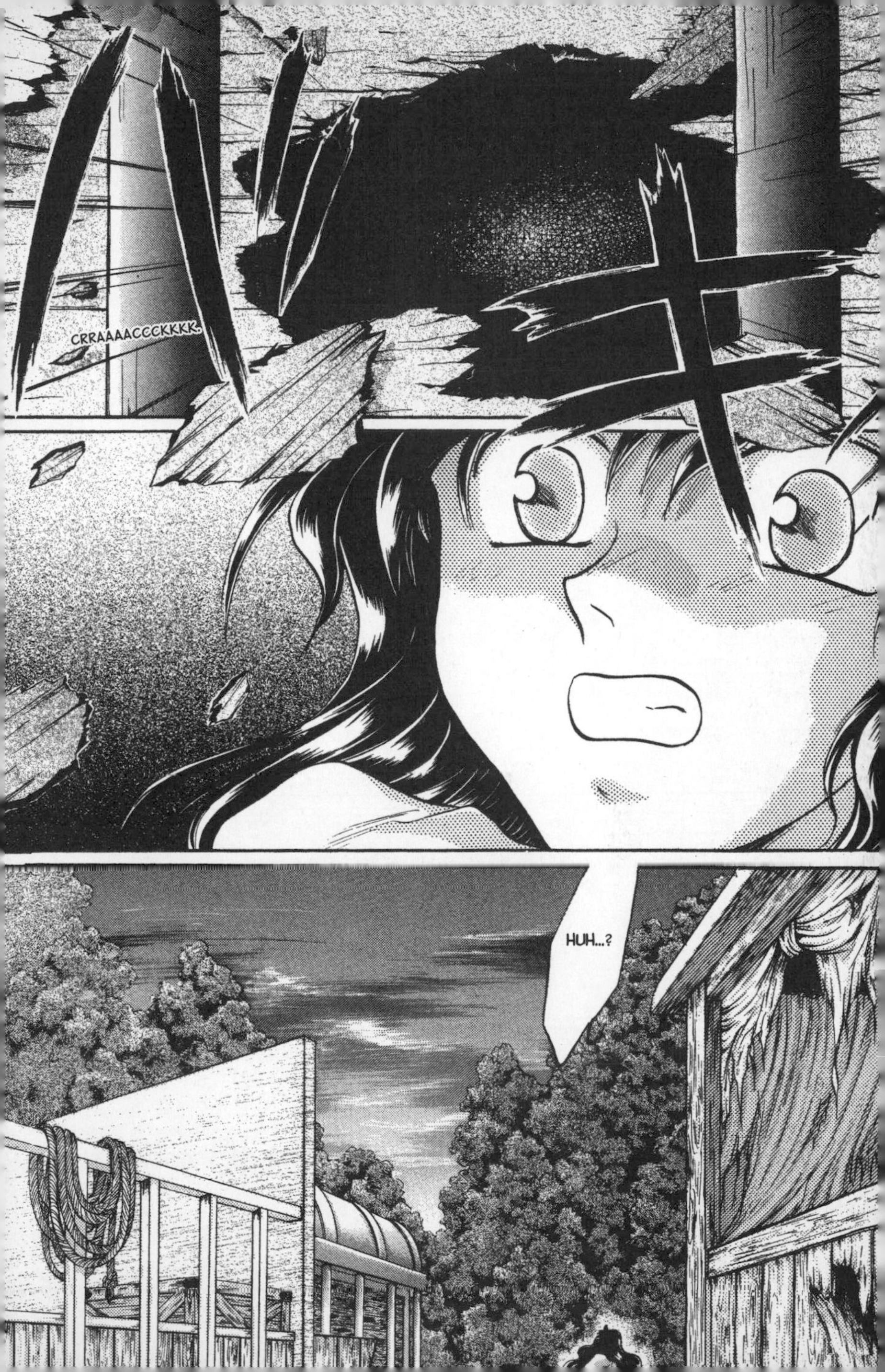
CRRAAAACCCKKKK.
HUH...?

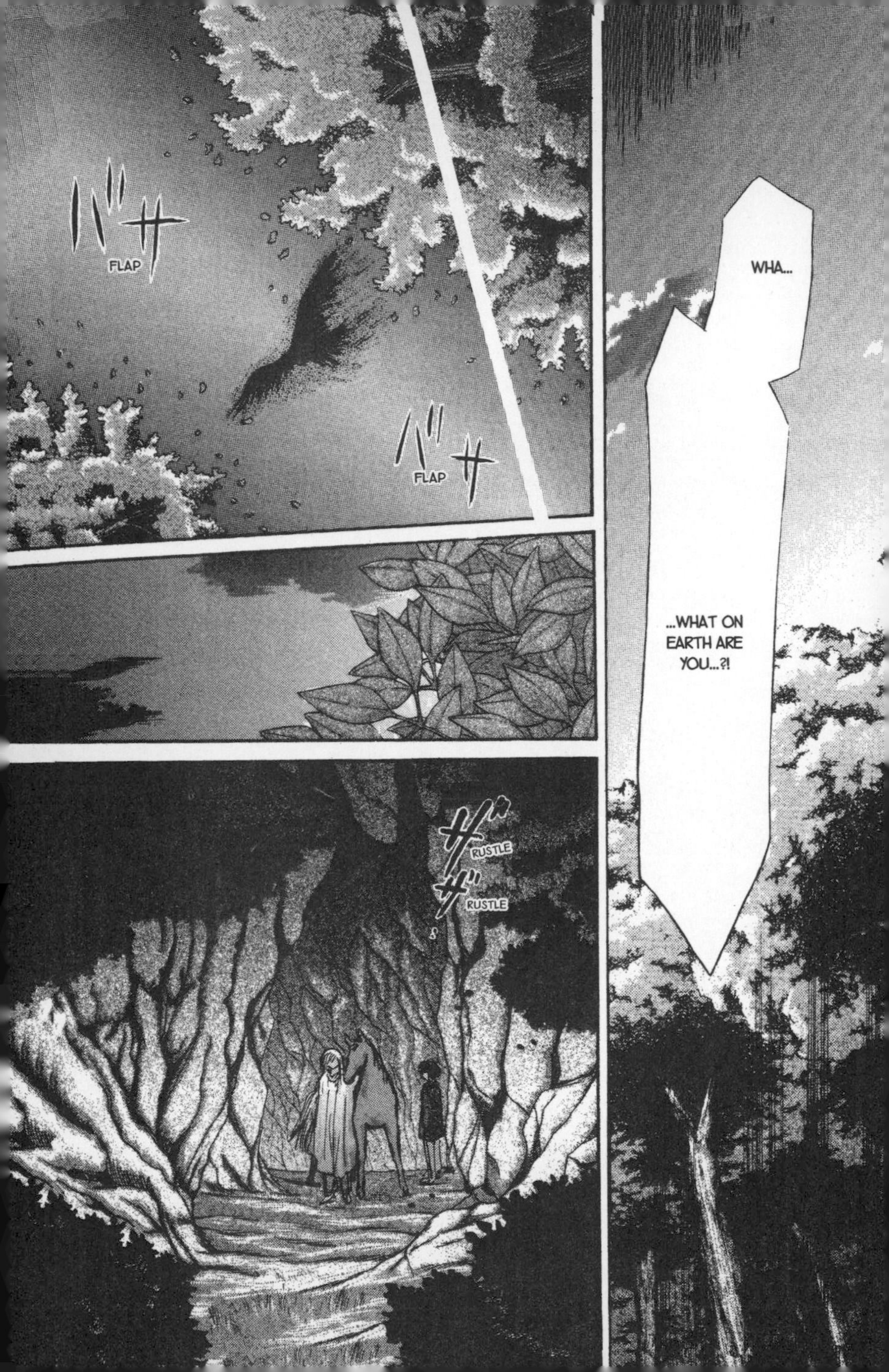
WHA...
...WHAT ON EARTH ARE YOU...?!
FLAP
FLAP
RUSTLE
RUSTLE

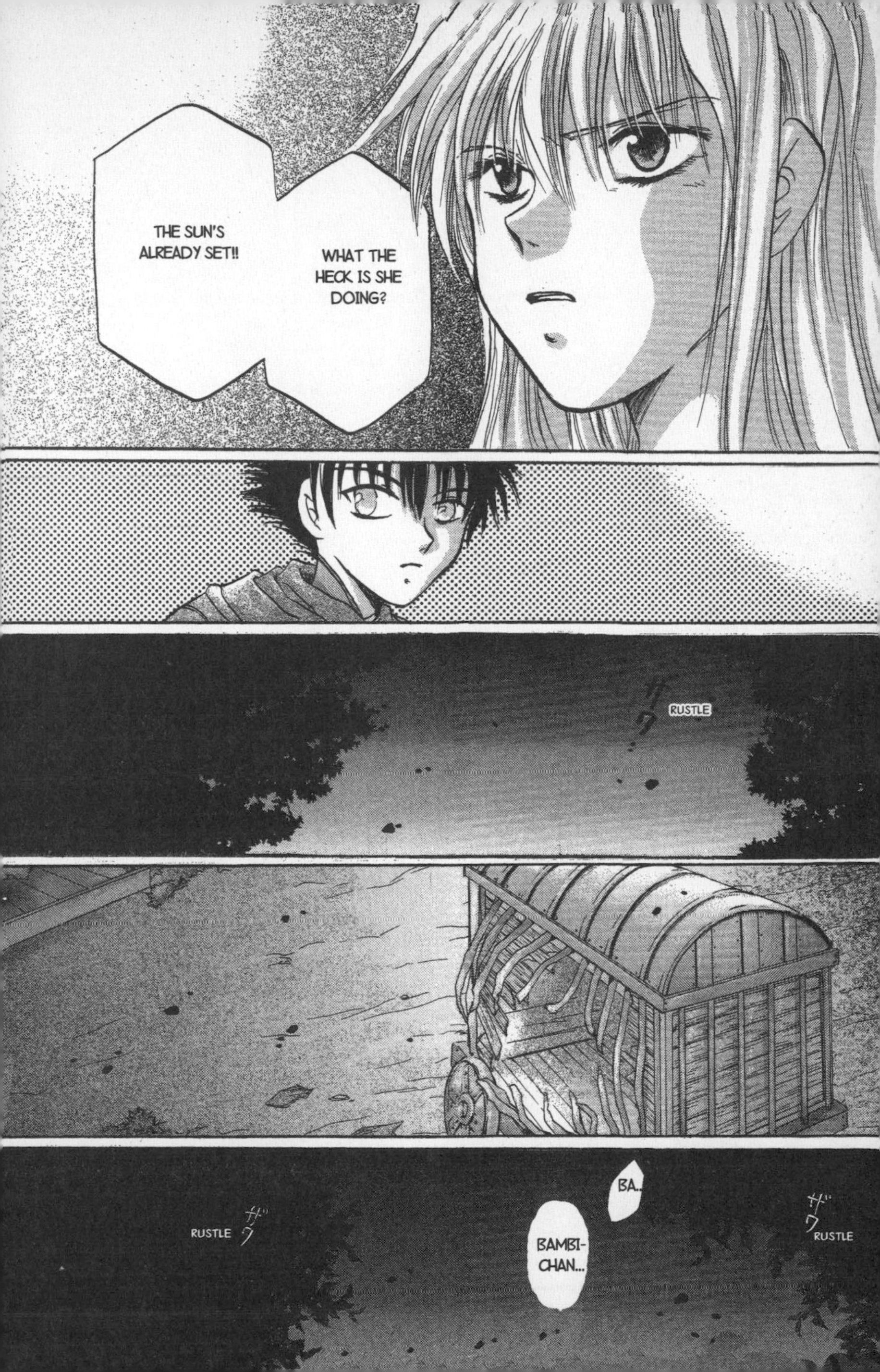
WHAT THE HECK IS SHE DOING?
THE SUN'S ALREADY SET!!
ザワ
RUSTLE
ザワ
RUSTLE
BA...
BAMBI-CHAN...
ザワ
RUSTLE

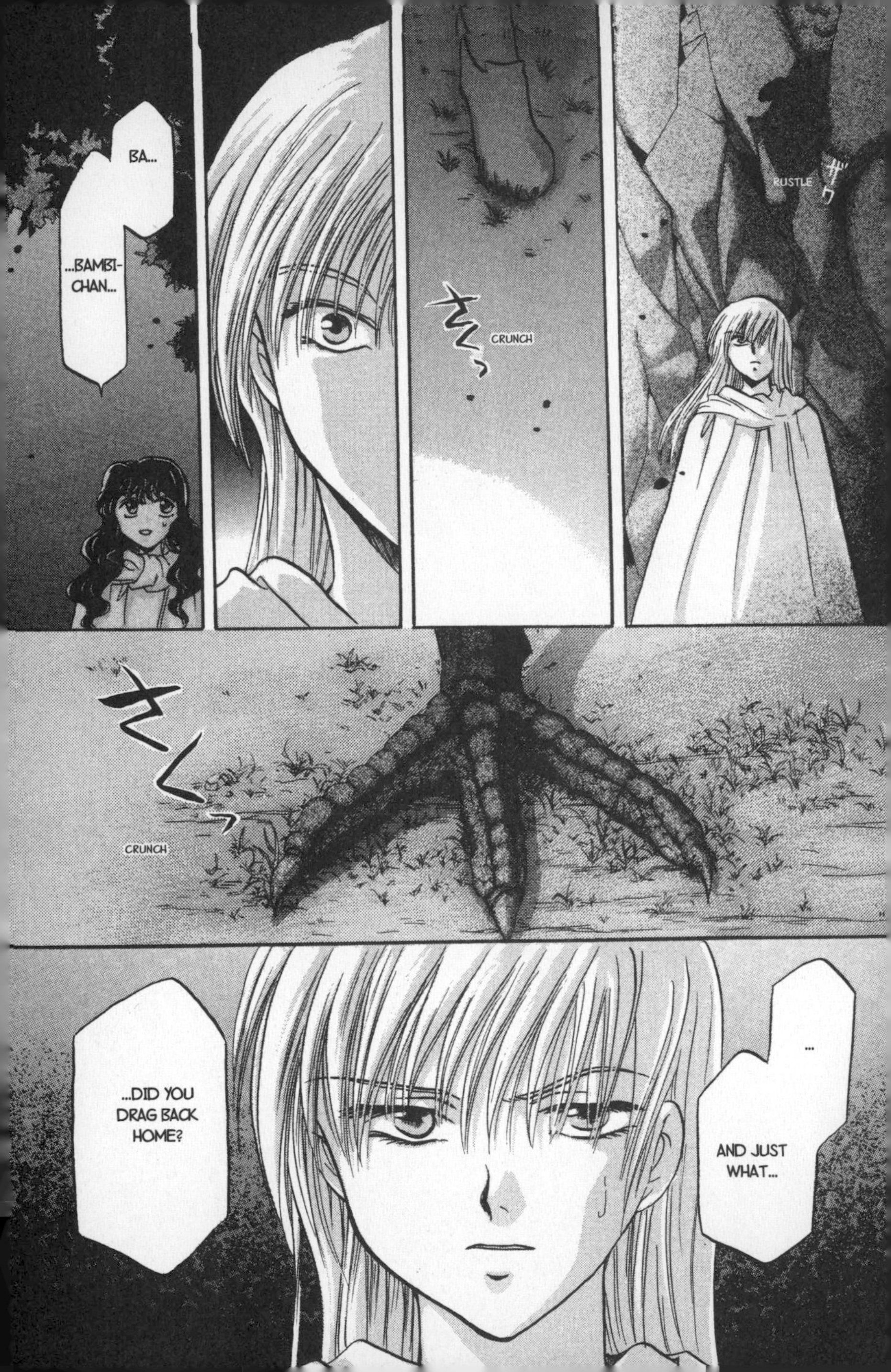
ザク
RUSTLE
さくっ
CRUNCH
BA...
...BAMBI-CHAN...
さくっ
CRUNCH
...
AND JUST WHAT...
...DID YOU DRAG BACK HOME?

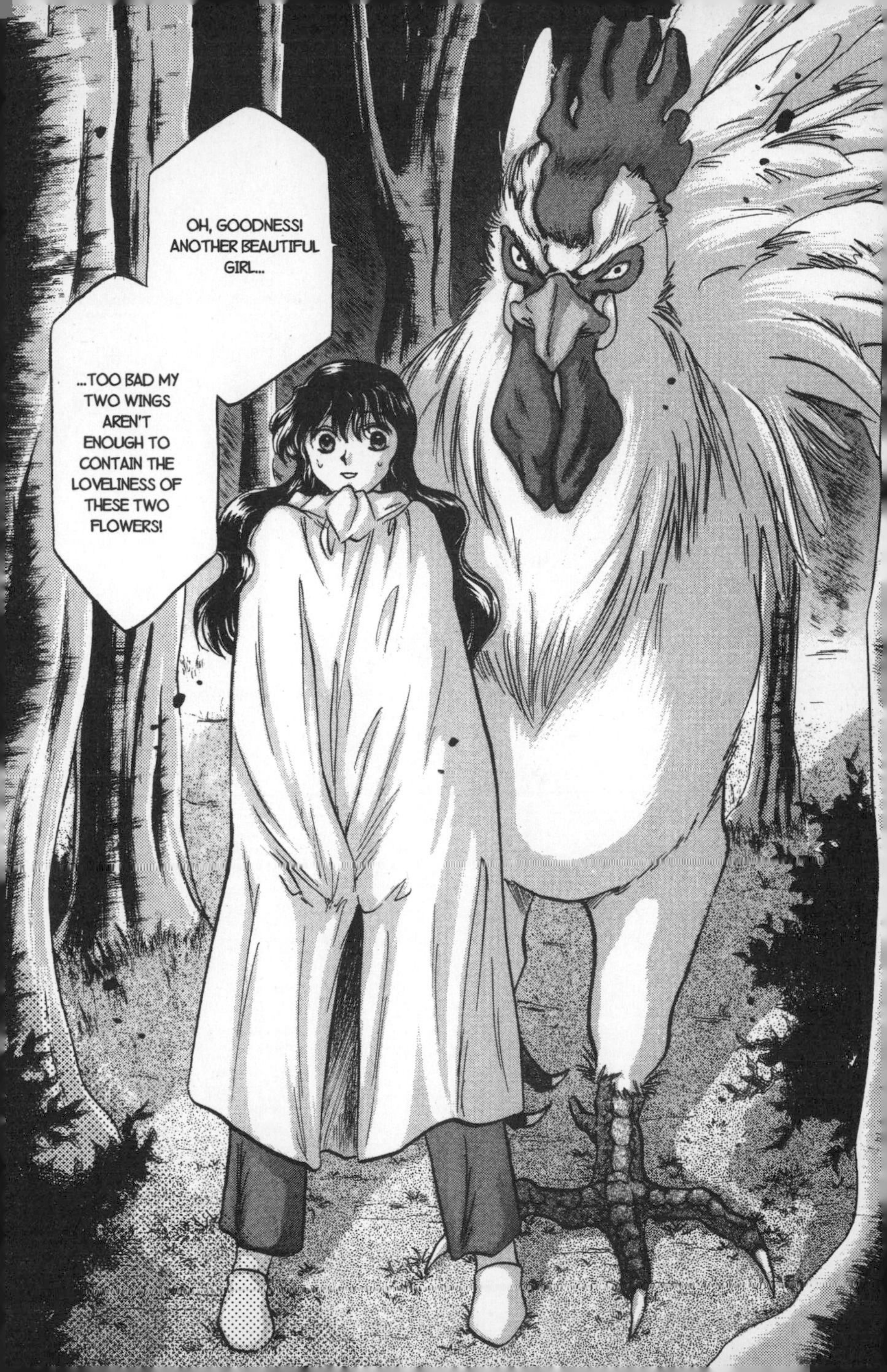
OH, GOODNESS! ANOTHER BEAUTIFUL GIRL...
...TOO BAD MY TWO WINGS AREN'T ENOUGH TO CONTAIN THE LOVELINESS OF THESE TWO FLOWERS!

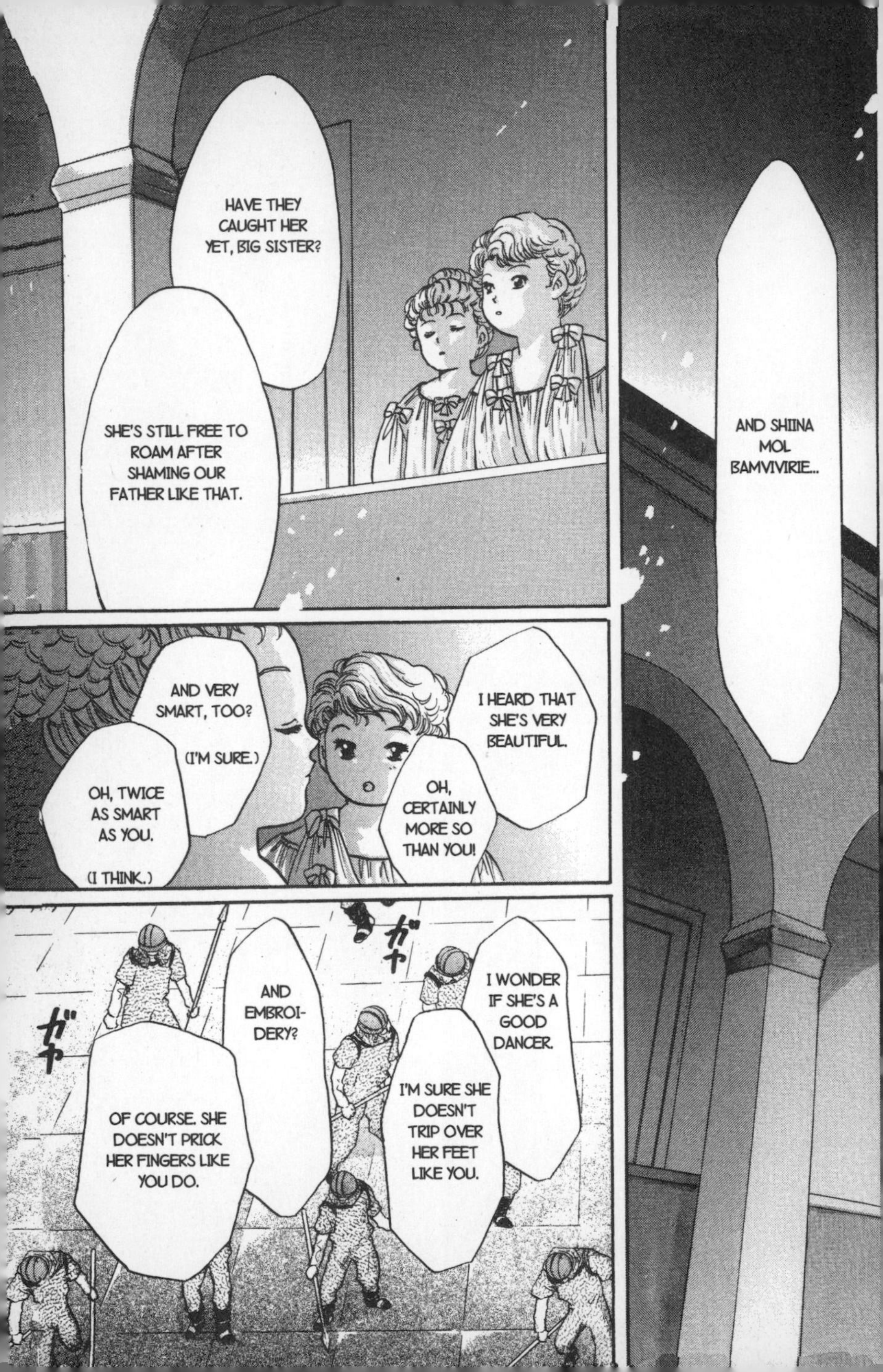
AND SHIINA MOL BAMVIVIRIE...
HAVE THEY CAUGHT HER YET, BIG SISTER?
SHE'S STILL FREE TO ROAM AFTER SHAMING OUR FATHER LIKE THAT.
I HEARD THAT SHE'S VERY BEAUTIFUL.
OH, CERTAINLY MORE SO THAN YOU!
AND VERY SMART, TOO? (I'M SURE.)
OH, TWICE AS SMART AS YOU. (I THINK.)
ガヤ
I WONDER IF SHE'S A GOOD DANCER.
I'M SURE SHE DOESN'T TRIP OVER HER FEET LIKE YOU.
AND EMBROIDERY?
OF COURSE. SHE DOESN'T PRICK HER FINGERS LIKE YOU DO.
ガヤ

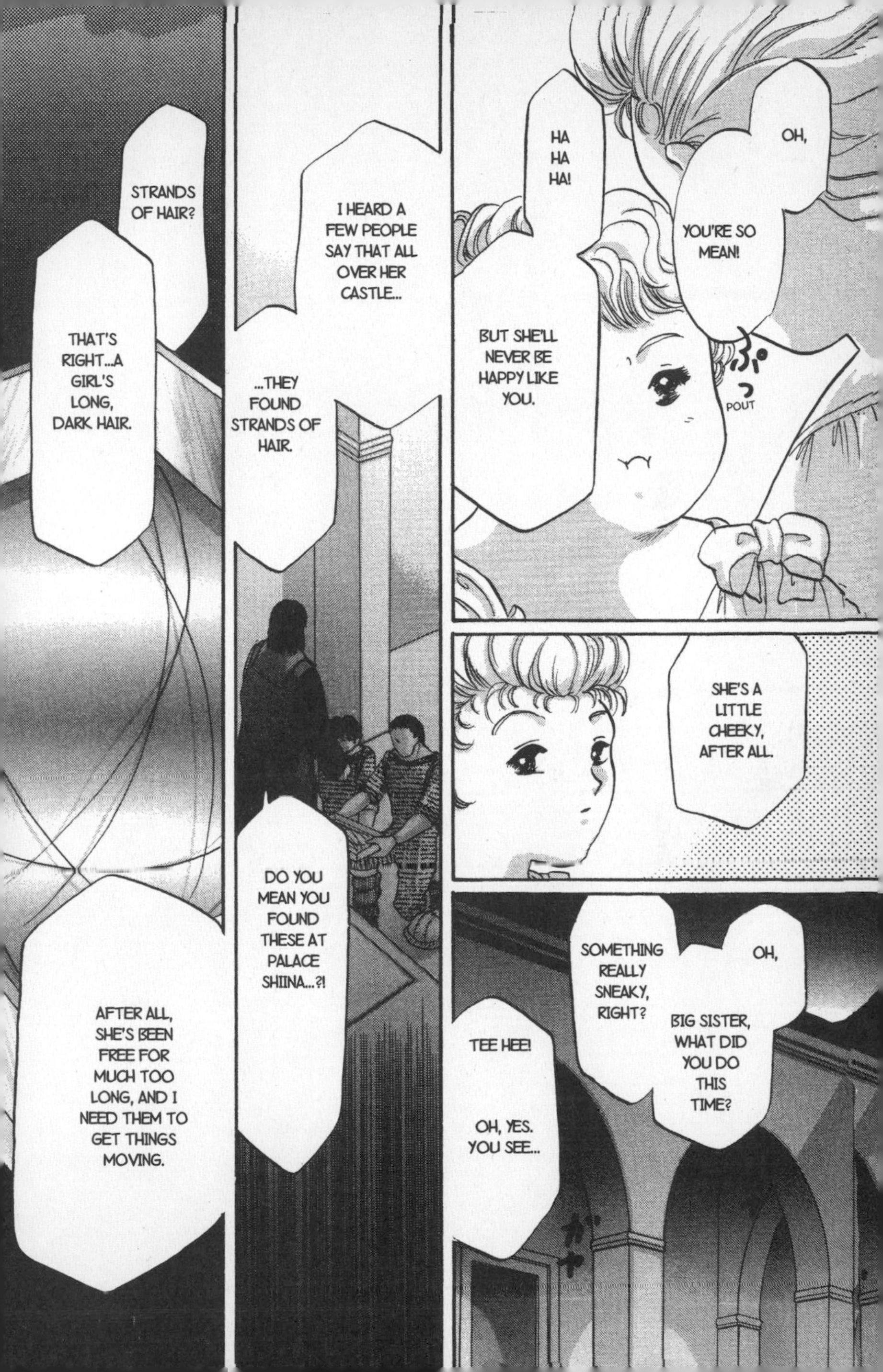
OH,
YOU'RE SO MEAN!
POUT
HA HA HA!
BUT SHE'LL NEVER BE HAPPY LIKE YOU.
SHE'S A LITTLE CHEEKY, AFTER ALL.
OH,
BIG SISTER, WHAT DID YOU DO THIS TIME?
SOMETHING REALLY SNEAKY, RIGHT?
TEE HEE!
OH, YES. YOU SEE...
I HEARD A FEW PEOPLE SAY THAT ALL OVER HER CASTLE...
...THEY FOUND STRANDS OF HAIR.
DO YOU MEAN YOU FOUND THESE AT PALACE SHIINA...?!
STRANDS OF HAIR?
THAT'S RIGHT...A GIRL'S LONG, DARK HAIR.
AFTER ALL, SHE'S BEEN FREE FOR MUCH TOO LONG, AND I NEED THEM TO GET THINGS MOVING.

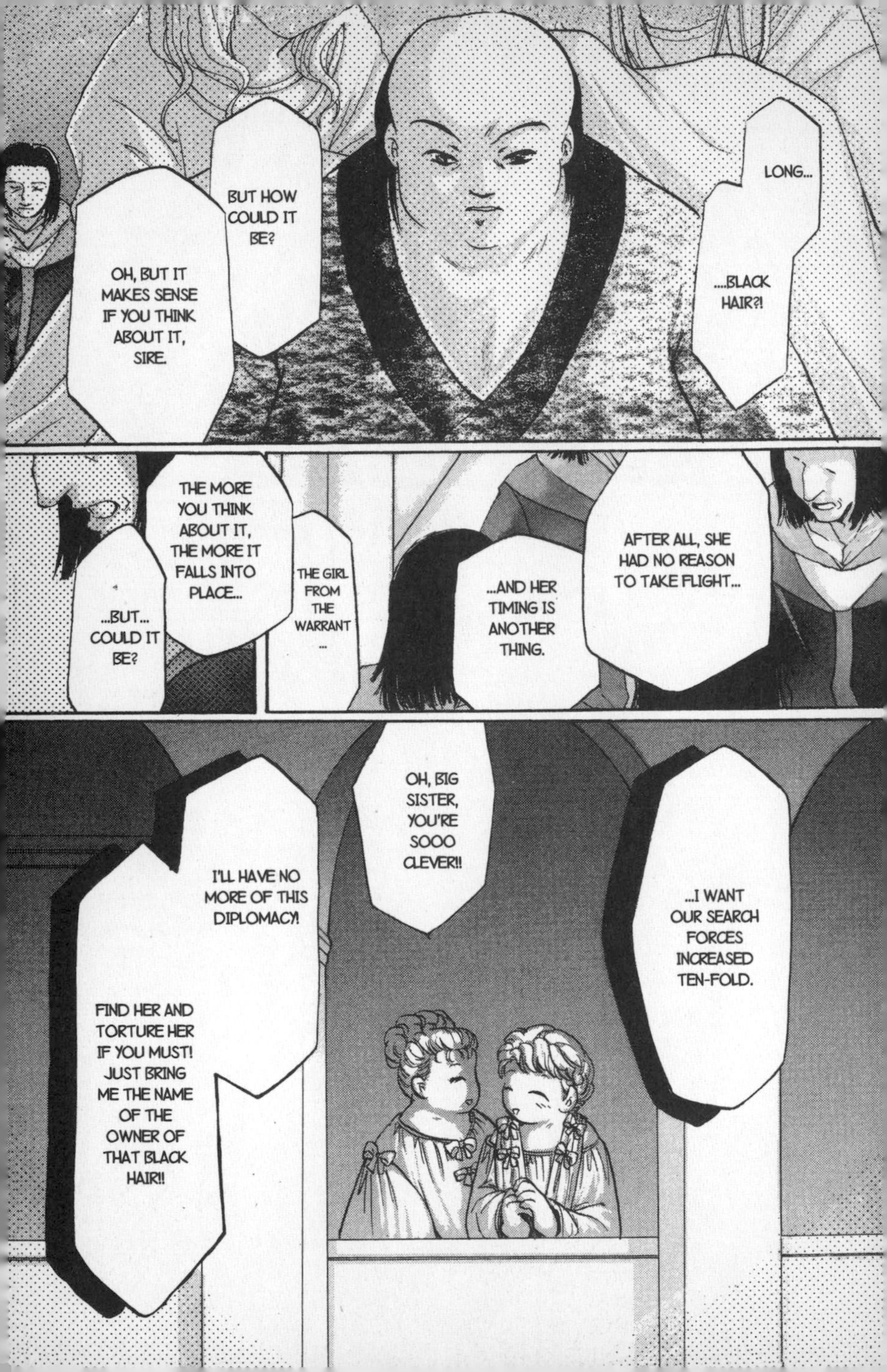
LONG...
...BLACK HAIR?!
BUT HOW COULD IT BE?
OH, BUT IT MAKES SENSE IF YOU THINK ABOUT IT, SIRE.
AFTER ALL, SHE HAD NO REASON TO TAKE FLIGHT...
...AND HER TIMING IS ANOTHER THING.
THE GIRL FROM THE WARRANT ...
THE MORE YOU THINK ABOUT IT, THE MORE IT FALLS INTO PLACE...
...BUT... COULD IT BE?
...I WANT OUR SEARCH FORCES INCREASED TEN-FOLD.
OH, BIG SISTER, YOU'RE SOOO CLEVER!!
I'LL HAVE NO MORE OF THIS DIPLOMACY!
FIND HER AND TORTURE HER IF YOU MUST! JUST BRING ME THE NAME OF THE OWNER OF THAT BLACK HAIR!!

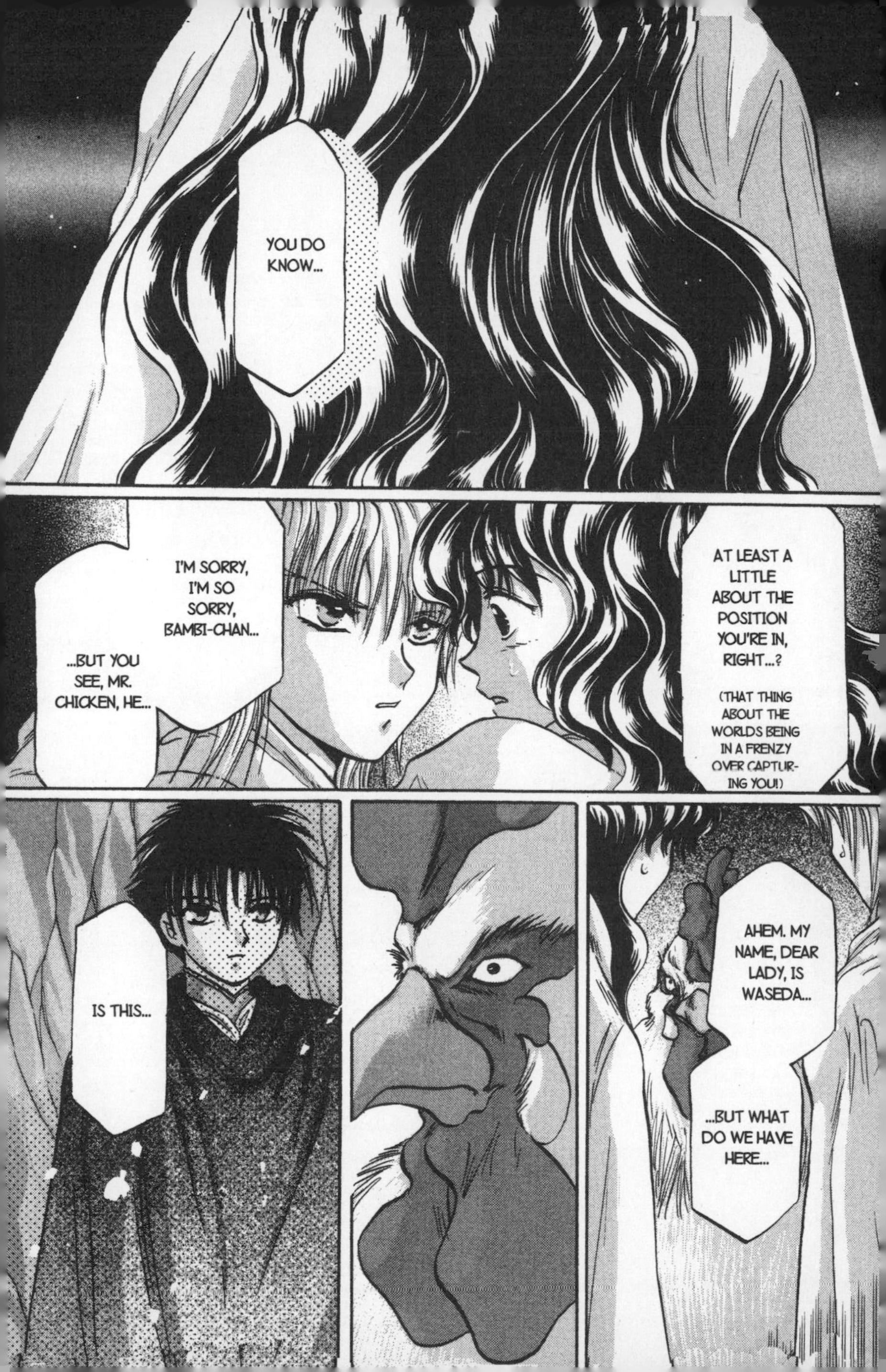
YOU DO KNOW...
AT LEAST A LITTLE ABOUT THE POSITION YOU'RE IN, RIGHT...?
(THAT THING ABOUT THE WORLDS BEING IN A FRENZY OVER CAPTURING YOU!)
I'M SORRY, I'M SO SORRY, BAMBI-CHAN...
...BUT YOU SEE, MR. CHICKEN, HE...
AHEM. MY NAME, DEAR LADY, IS WASEDA...
...BUT WHAT DO WE HAVE HERE...
IS THIS...

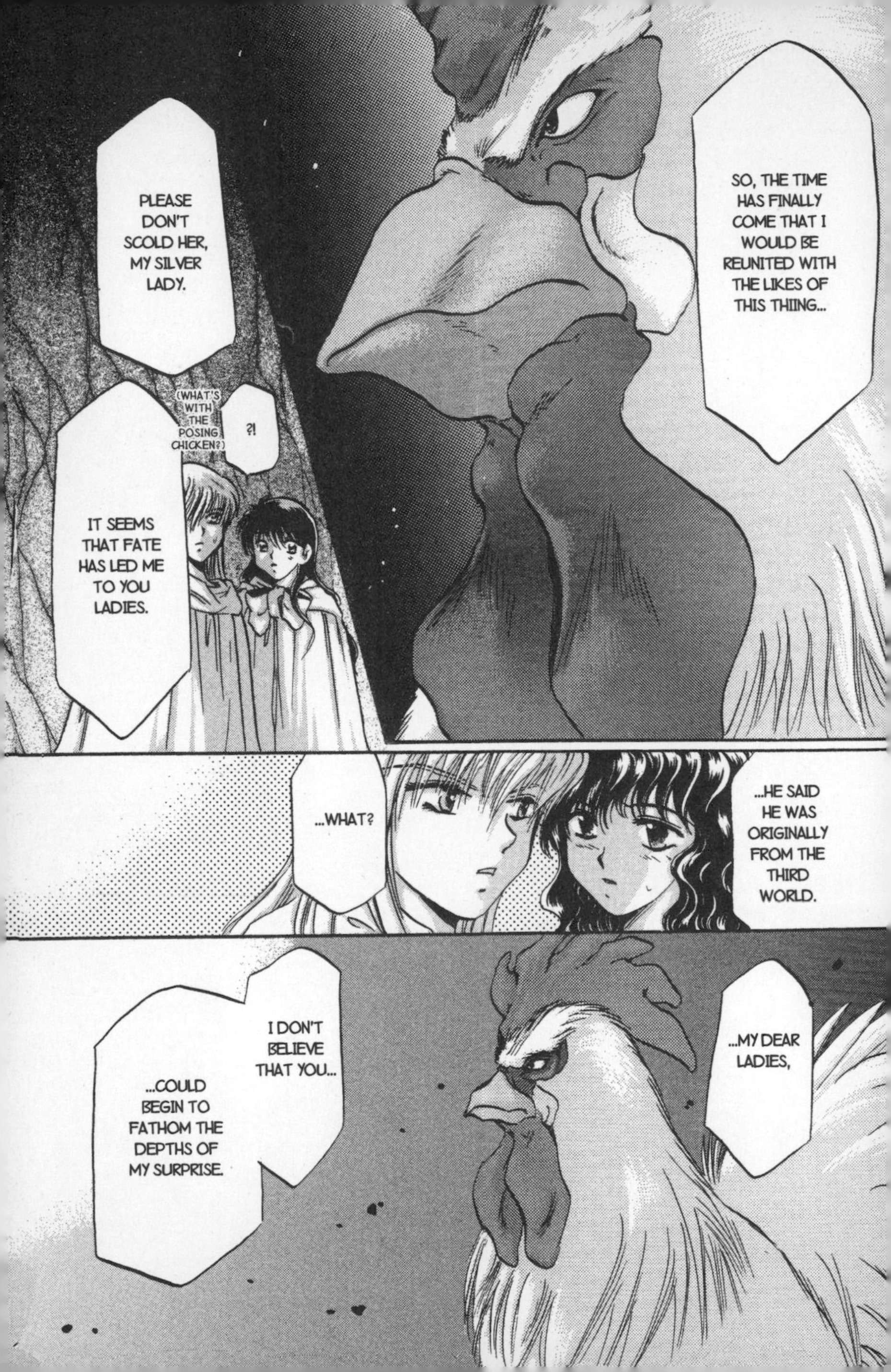
SO, THE TIME HAS FINALLY COME THAT I WOULD BE REUNITED WITH THE LIKES OF THIS THIING...
PLEASE DON'T SCOLD HER, MY SILVER LADY.
?!
(WHAT'S WITH THE POSING CHICKEN?)
IT SEEMS THAT FATE HAS LED ME TO YOU LADIES.
...HE SAID HE WAS ORIGINALLY FROM THE THIRD WORLD.
...WHAT?
...MY DEAR LADIES,
I DON'T BELIEVE THAT YOU...
...COULD BEGIN TO FATHOM THE DEPTHS OF MY SURPRISE.

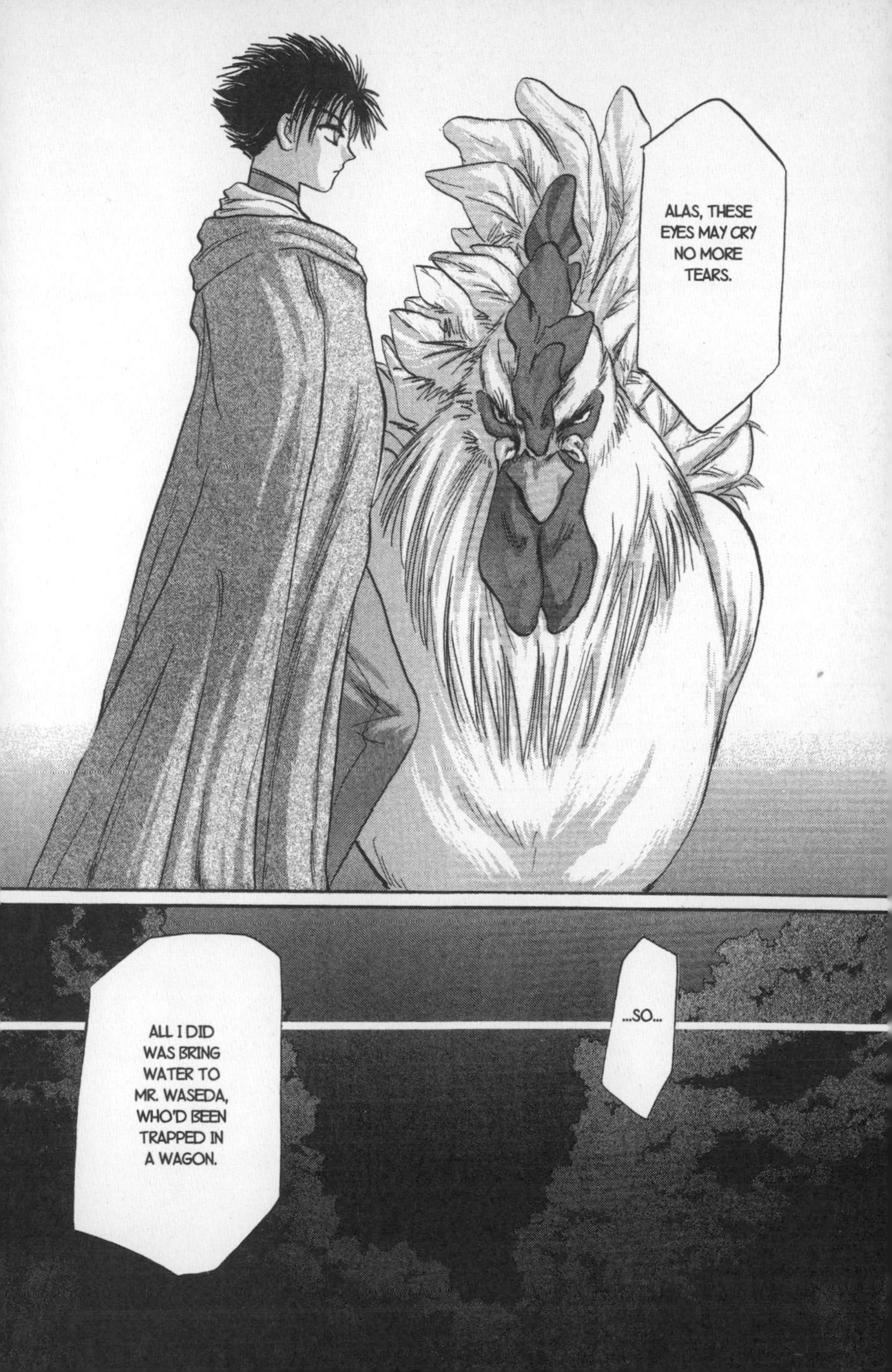
ALAS, THESE EYES MAY CRY NO MORE TEARS.
...SO...
ALL I DID WAS BRING WATER TO MR. WASEDA, WHO'D BEEN TRAPPED IN A WAGON.

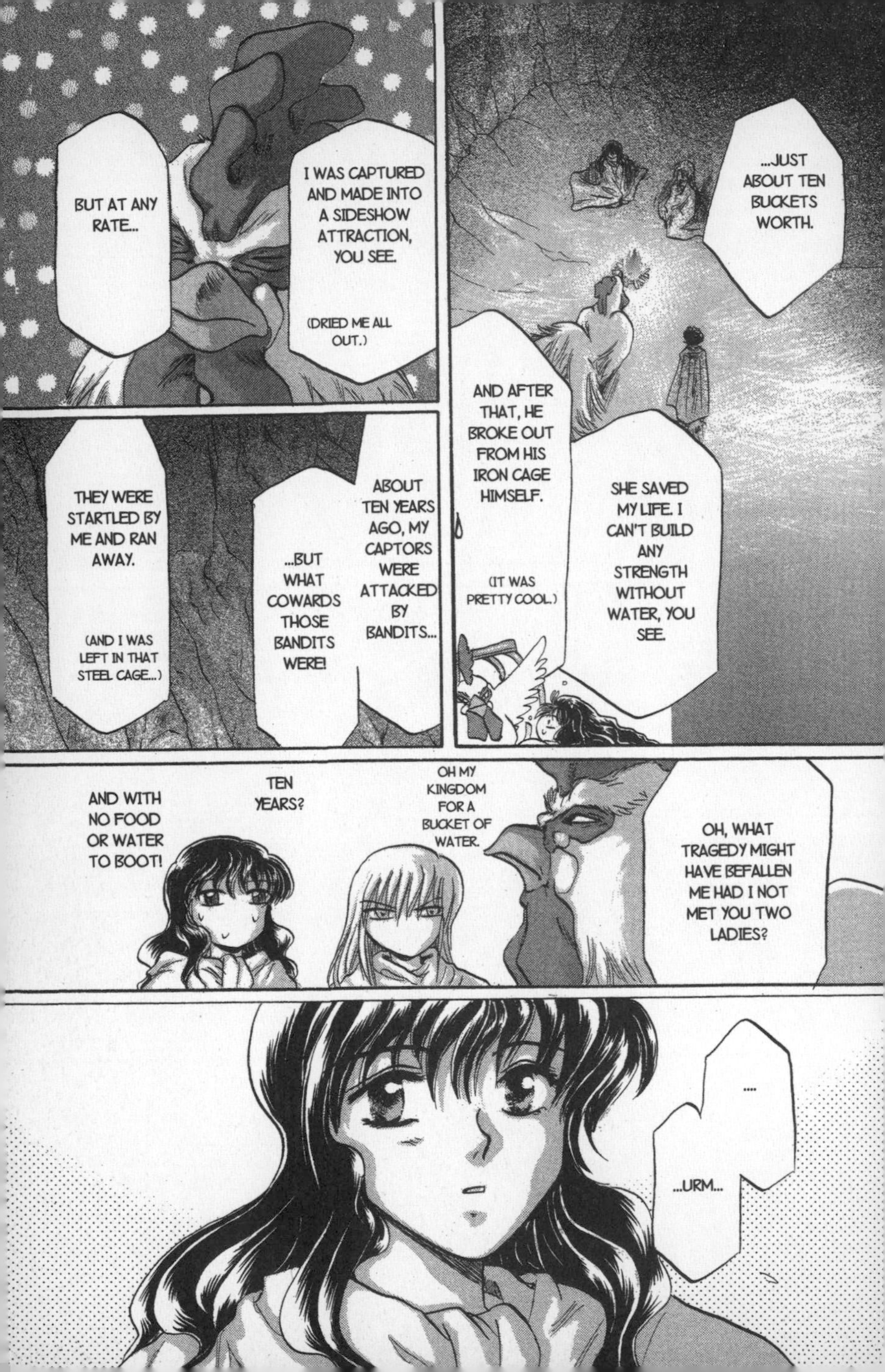

...JUST ABOUT TEN BUCKETS WORTH.
AND AFTER THAT, HE BROKE OUT FROM HIS IRON CAGE HIMSELF.
SHE SAVED MY LIFE. I CAN'T BUILD ANY STRENGTH WITHOUT WATER, YOU SEE.
(IT WAS PRETTY COOL.)
I WAS CAPTURED AND MADE INTO A SIDESHOW ATTRACTION, YOU SEE.
(DRIED ME ALL OUT.)
BUT AT ANY RATE...
ABOUT TEN YEARS AGO, MY CAPTORS WERE ATTACKED BY BANDITS...
...BUT WHAT COWARDS THOSE BANDITS WERE!
THEY WERE STARTLED BY ME AND RAN AWAY.
(AND I WAS LEFT IN THAT STEEL CAGE...)
OH, WHAT TRAGEDY MIGHT HAVE BEFALLEN ME HAD I NOT MET YOU TWO LADIES?
OH MY KINGDOM FOR A BUCKET OF WATER.
TEN YEARS?
AND WITH NO FOOD OR WATER TO BOOT!
....
...URM...

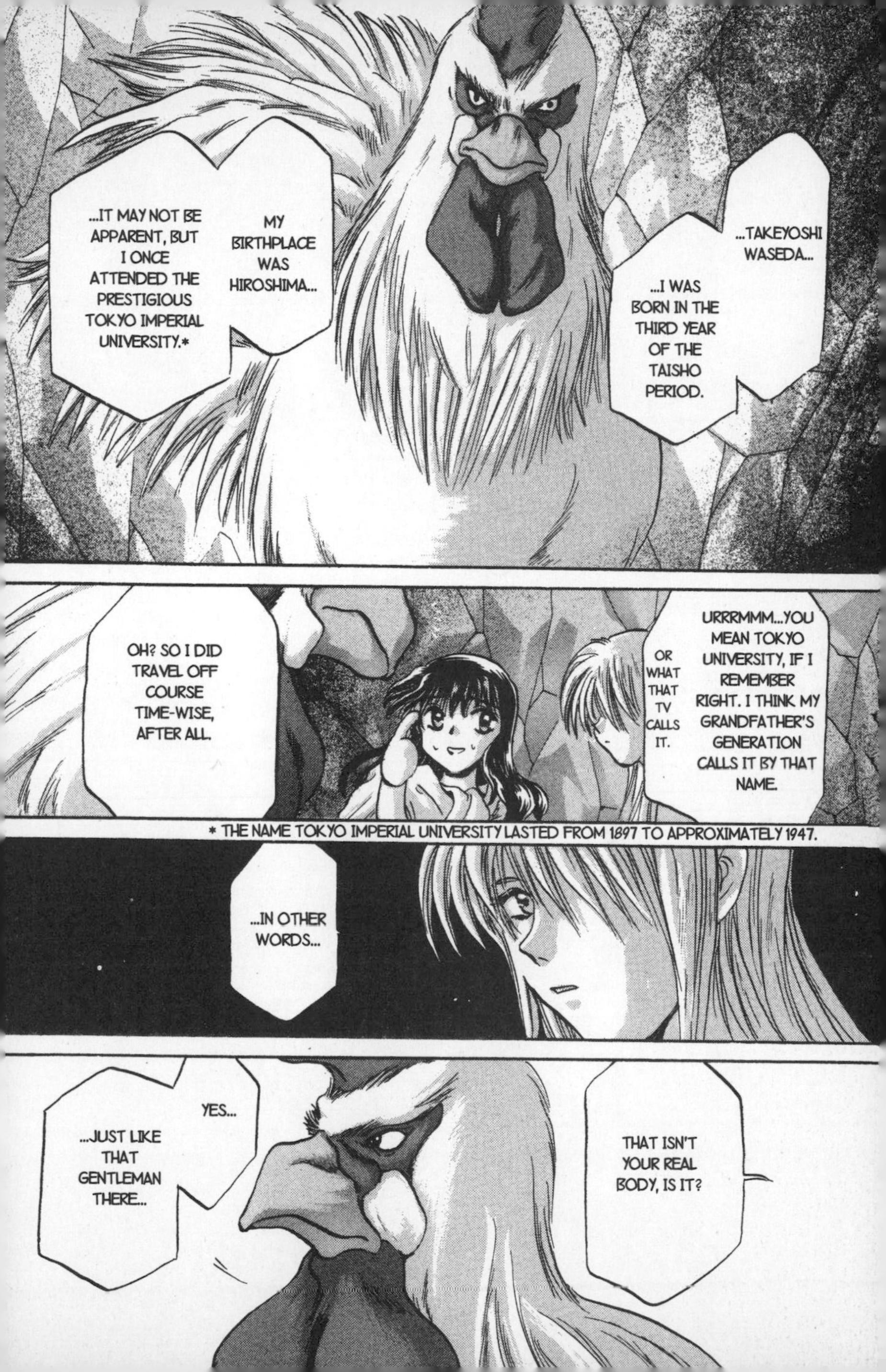
...TAKEYOSHI WASEDA...
...I WAS BORN IN THE THIRD YEAR OF THE TAISHO PERIOD.
MY BIRTHPLACE WAS HIROSHIMA...
...IT MAY NOT BE APPARENT, BUT I ONCE ATTENDED THE PRESTIGIOUS TOKYO IMPERIAL UNIVERSITY.*
URRRMMM...YOU MEAN TOKYO UNIVERSITY, IF I REMEMBER RIGHT. I THINK MY GRANDFATHER'S GENERATION CALLS IT BY THAT NAME.
OR WHAT THAT TV CALLS IT.
OH? SO I DID TRAVEL OFF COURSE TIME-WISE, AFTER ALL.
...IN OTHER WORDS...
THAT ISN'T YOUR REAL BODY, IS IT?
YES...
...JUST LIKE THAT GENTLEMAN THERE...

* THE NAME TOKYO IMPERIAL UNIVERSITY LASTED FROM 1897 TO APPROXIMATELY 1947.

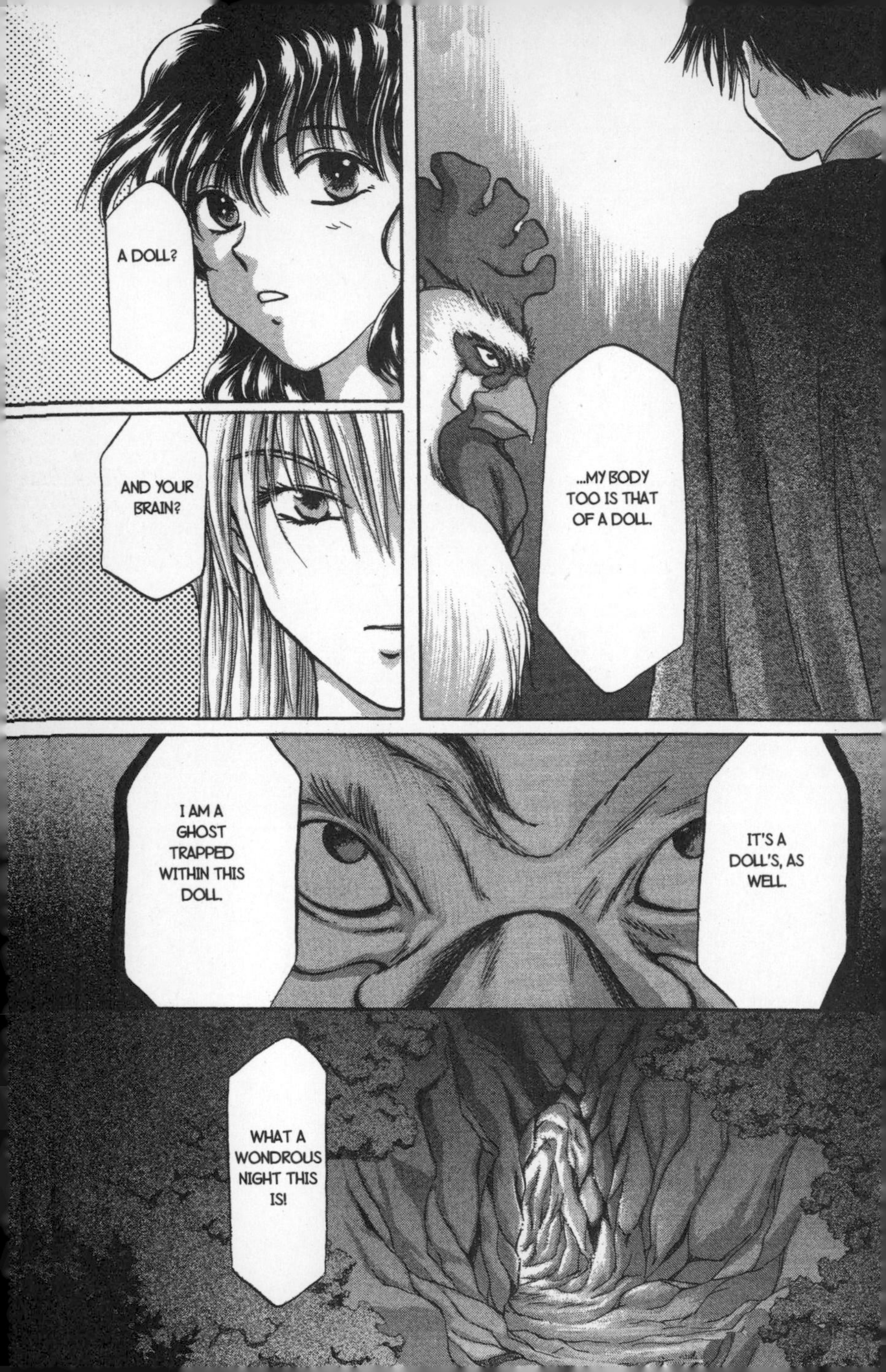
...MY BODY TOO IS THAT OF A DOLL.
A DOLL?
AND YOUR BRAIN?
IT'S A DOLL'S, AS WELL.
I AM A GHOST TRAPPED WITHIN THIS DOLL.
WHAT A WONDROUS NIGHT THIS IS!

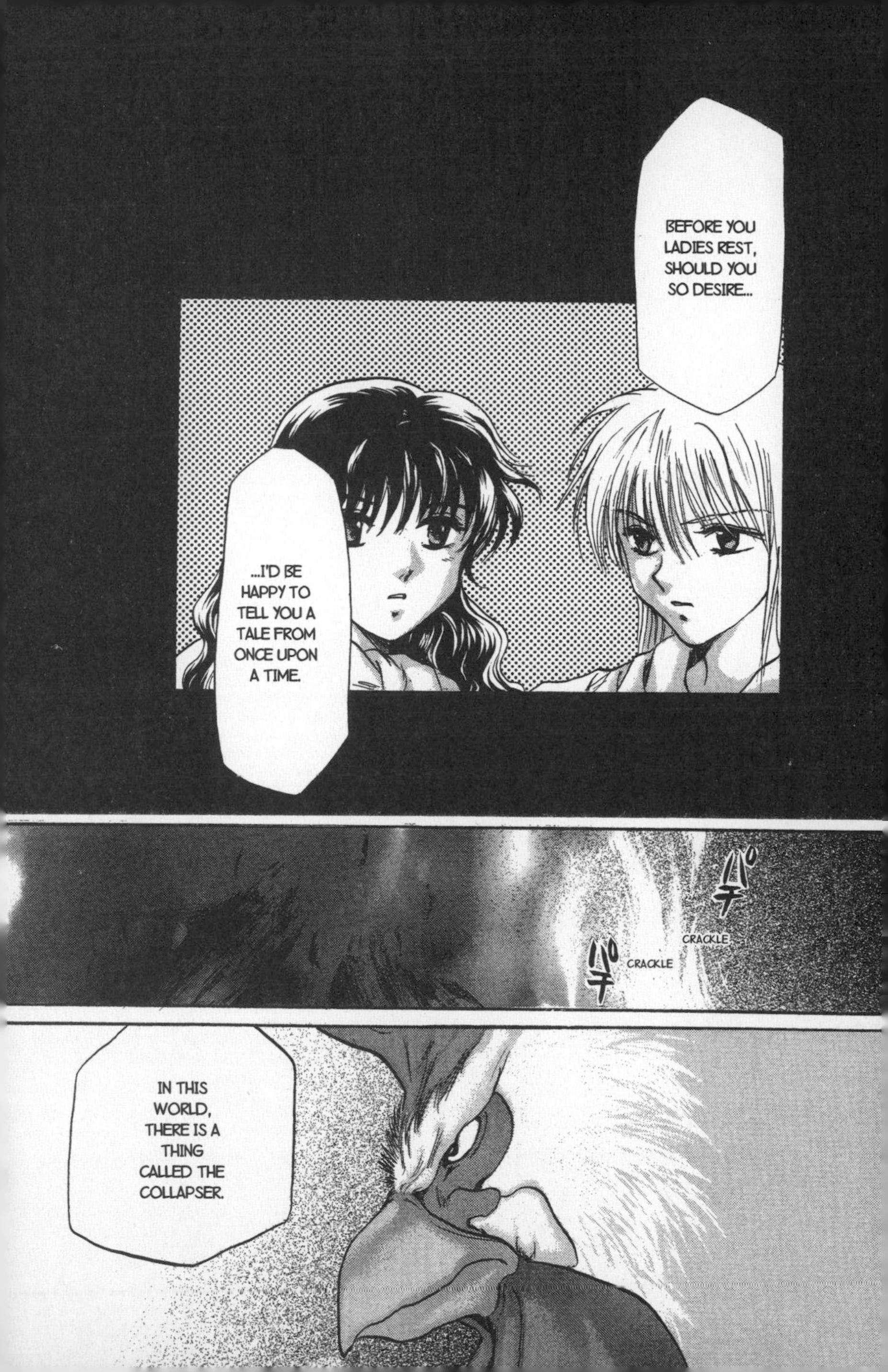
BEFORE YOU LADIES REST, SHOULD YOU SO DESIRE...
...I'D BE HAPPY TO TELL YOU A TALE FROM ONCE UPON A TIME.
パチ
CRACKLE
パチ
CRACKLE
IN THIS WORLD, THERE IS A THING CALLED THE COLLAPSER.

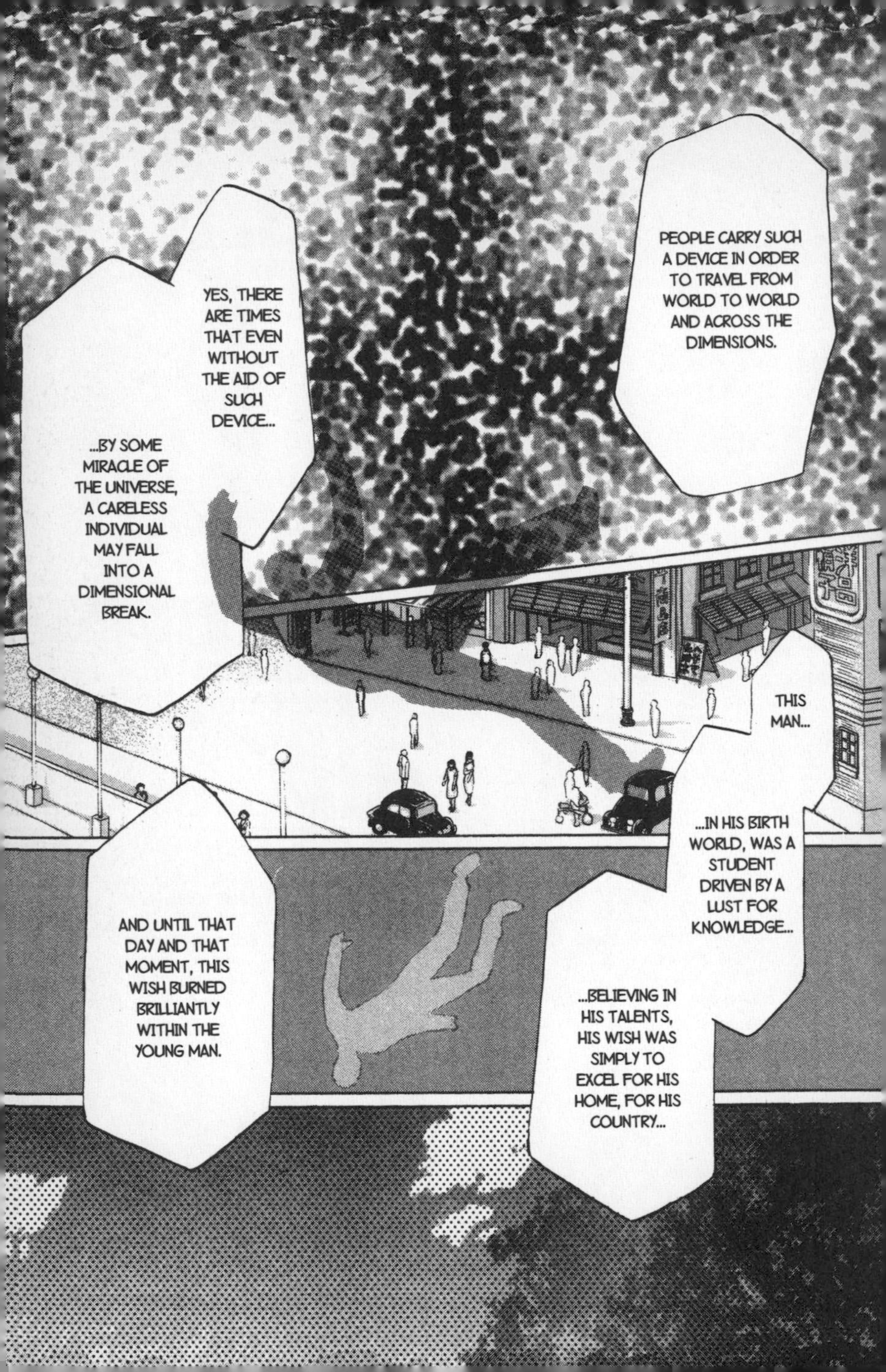
PEOPLE CARRY SUCH A DEVICE IN ORDER TO TRAVEL FROM WORLD TO WORLD AND ACROSS THE DIMENSIONS.
YES, THERE ARE TIMES THAT EVEN WITHOUT THE AID OF SUCH DEVICE...
...BY SOME MIRACLE OF THE UNIVERSE, A CARELESS INDIVIDUAL MAY FALL INTO A DIMENSIONAL BREAK.
THIS MAN...
...IN HIS BIRTH WORLD, WAS A STUDENT DRIVEN BY A LUST FOR KNOWLEDGE...
...BELIEVING IN HIS TALENTS, HIS WISH WAS SIMPLY TO EXCEL FOR HIS HOME, FOR HIS COUNTRY...
AND UNTIL THAT DAY AND THAT MOMENT, THIS WISH BURNED BRILLIANTLY WITHIN THE YOUNG MAN.

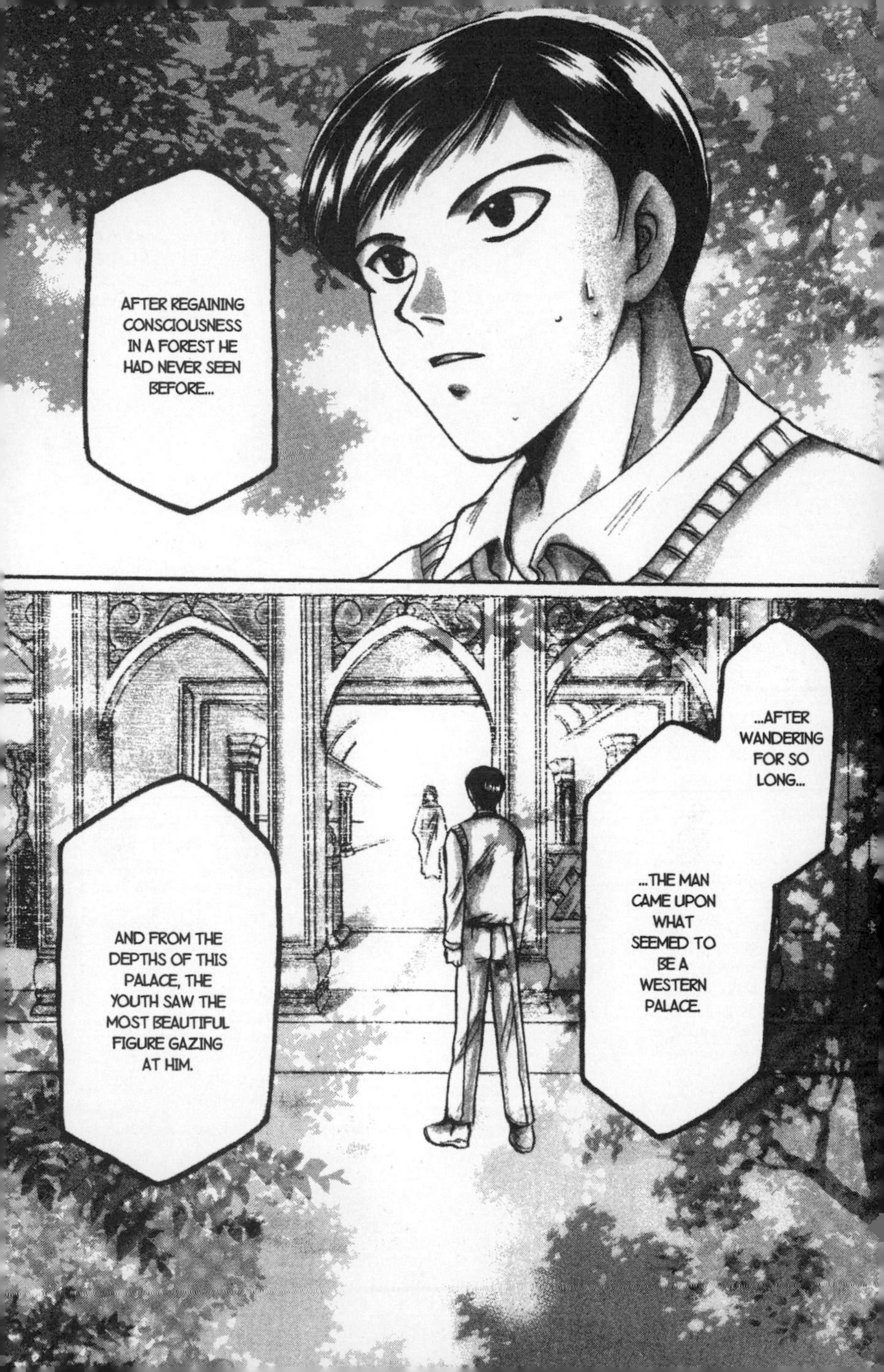
AFTER REGAINING CONSCIOUSNESS IN A FOREST HE HAD NEVER SEEN BEFORE...
...AFTER WANDERING FOR SO LONG...
...THE MAN CAME UPON WHAT SEEMED TO BE A WESTERN PALACE.
AND FROM THE DEPTHS OF THIS PALACE, THE YOUTH SAW THE MOST BEAUTIFUL FIGURE GAZING AT HIM.

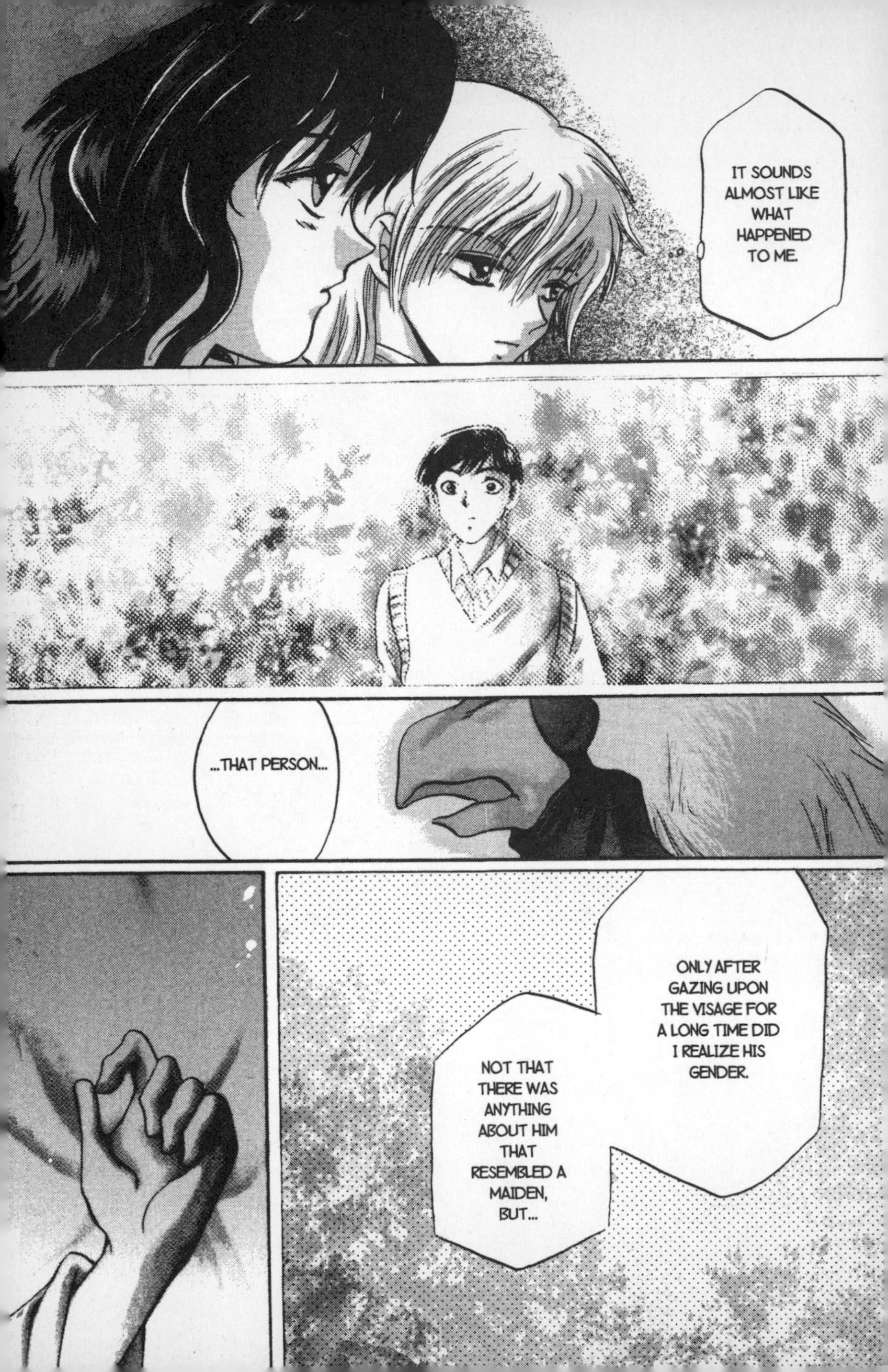
IT SOUNDS ALMOST LIKE WHAT HAPPENED TO ME.
...THAT PERSON...
ONLY AFTER GAZING UPON THE VISAGE FOR A LONG TIME DID I REALIZE HIS GENDER.
NOT THAT THERE WAS ANYTHING ABOUT HIM THAT RESEMBLED A MAIDEN, BUT...

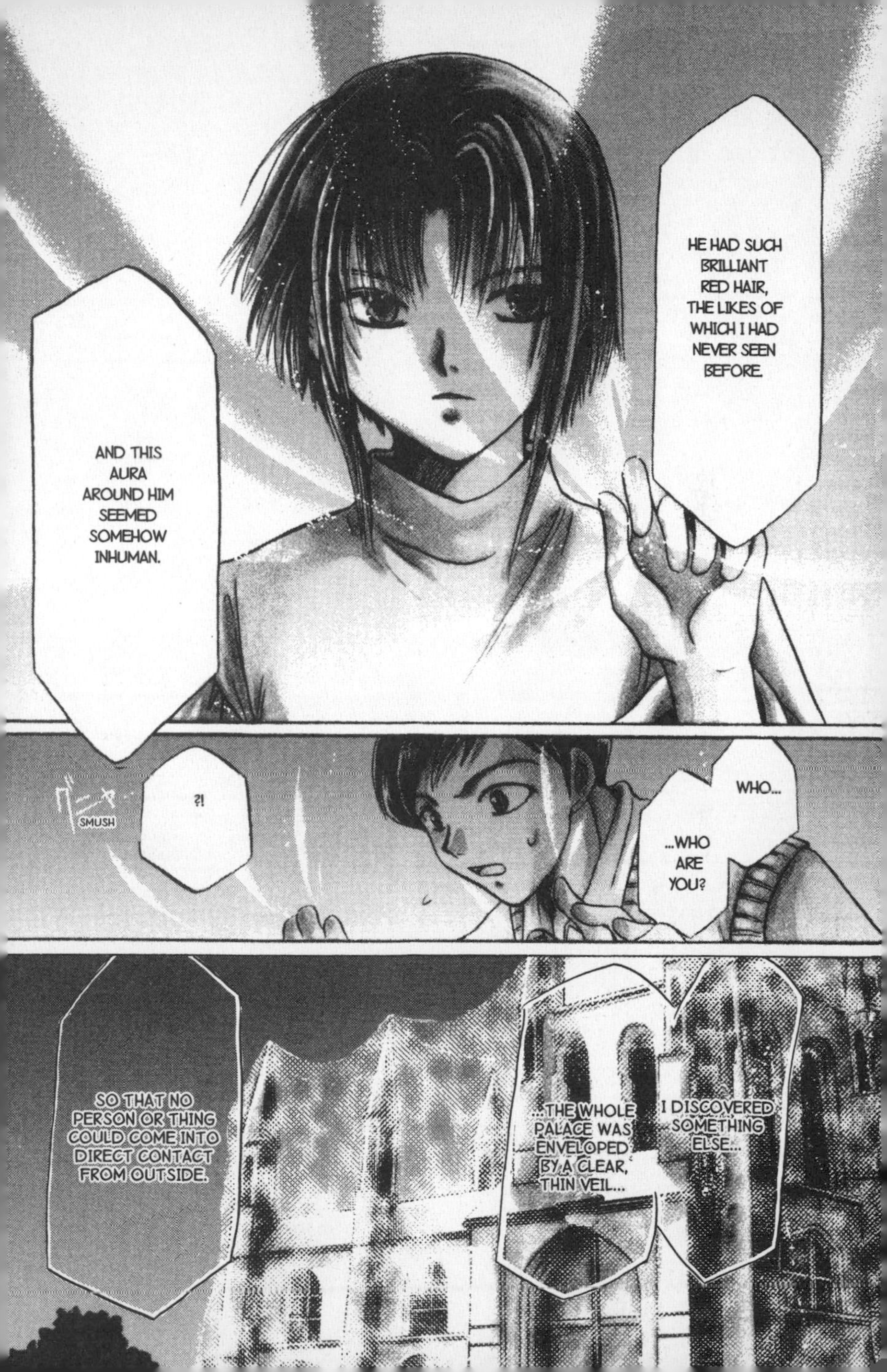
HE HAD SUCH BRILLIANT RED HAIR, THE LIKES OF WHICH I HAD NEVER SEEN BEFORE.
AND THIS AURA AROUND HIM SEEMED SOMEHOW INHUMAN.
WHO...
...WHO ARE YOU?
?!
SMUSH
I DISCOVERED SOMETHING ELSE...
...THE WHOLE PALACE WAS ENVELOPED BY A CLEAR, THIN VEIL...
SO THAT NO PERSON OR THING COULD COME INTO DIRECT CONTACT FROM OUTSIDE.

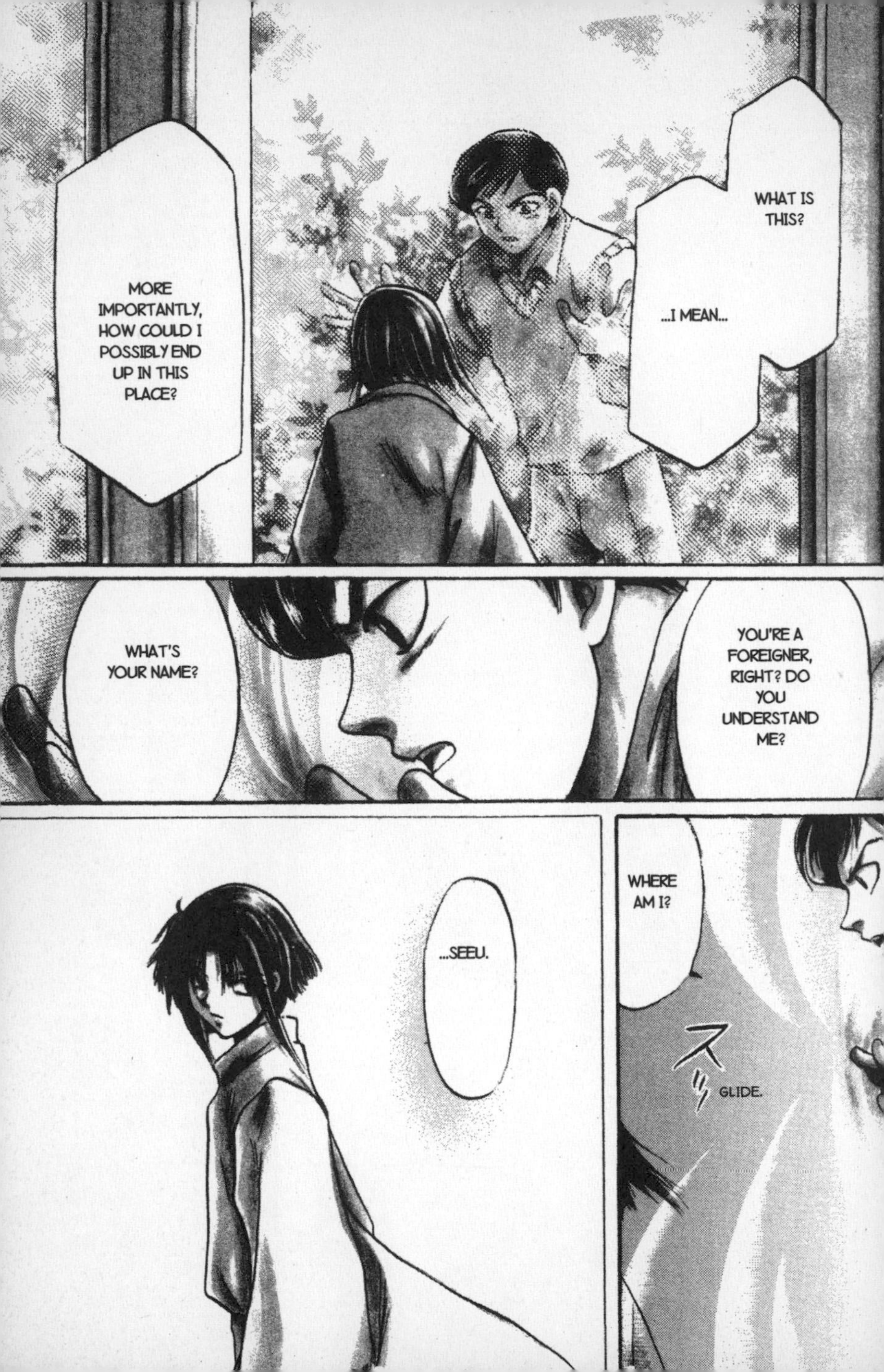
WHAT IS THIS?
...I MEAN...
MORE IMPORTANTLY, HOW COULD I POSSIBLY END UP IN THIS PLACE?
YOU'RE A FOREIGNER, RIGHT? DO YOU UNDERSTAND ME?
WHAT'S YOUR NAME?
WHERE AM I?
スッ
GLIDE.
...SEEU.

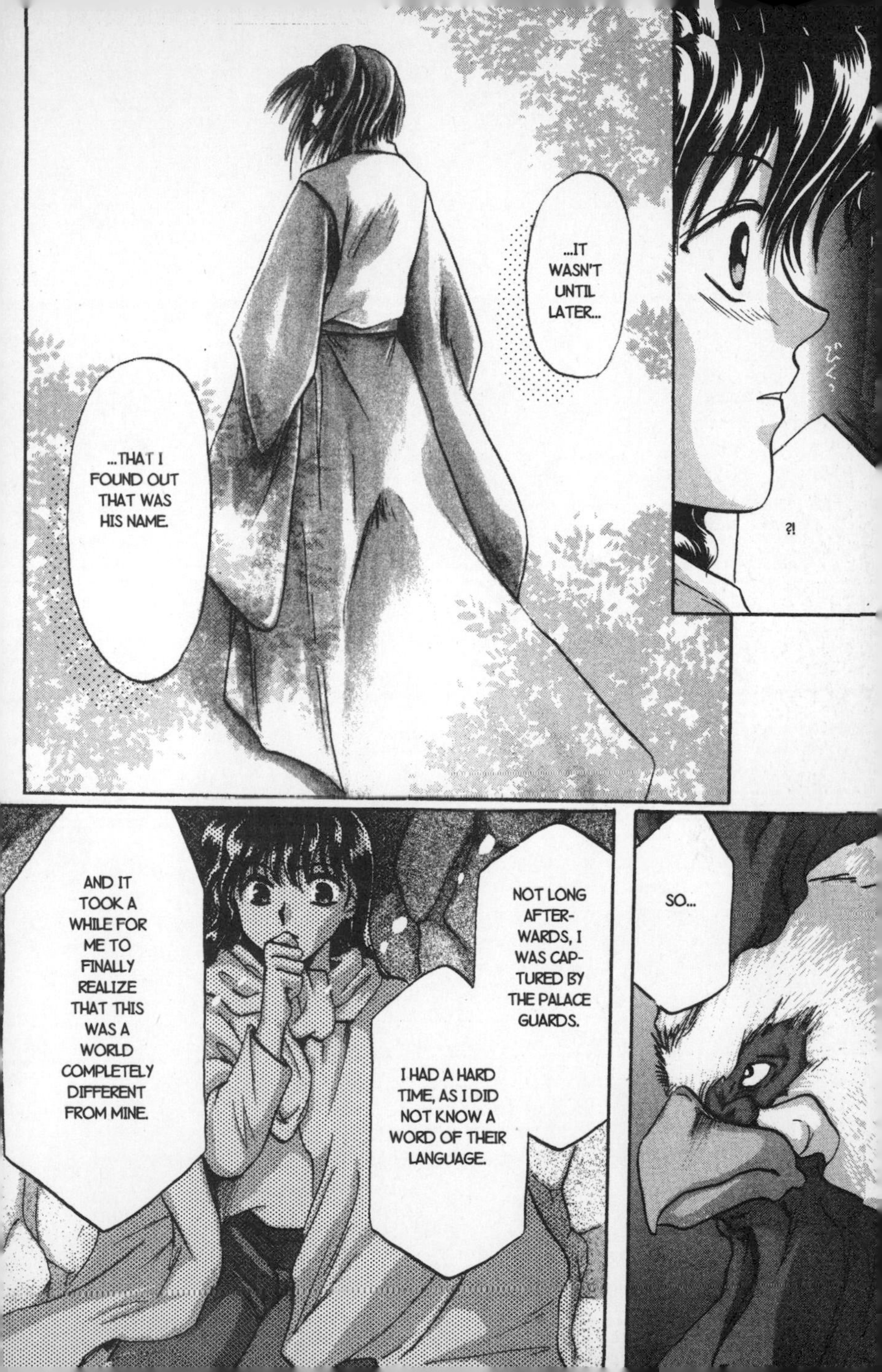
?!
...IT WASN'T UNTIL LATER...
...THAT I FOUND OUT THAT WAS HIS NAME.
SO...
NOT LONG AFTER-WARDS, I WAS CAP-TURED BY THE PALACE GUARDS.
I HAD A HARD TIME, AS I DID NOT KNOW A WORD OF THEIR LANGUAGE.
AND IT TOOK A WHILE FOR ME TO FINALLY REALIZE THAT THIS WAS A WORLD COMPLETELY DIFFERENT FROM MINE.

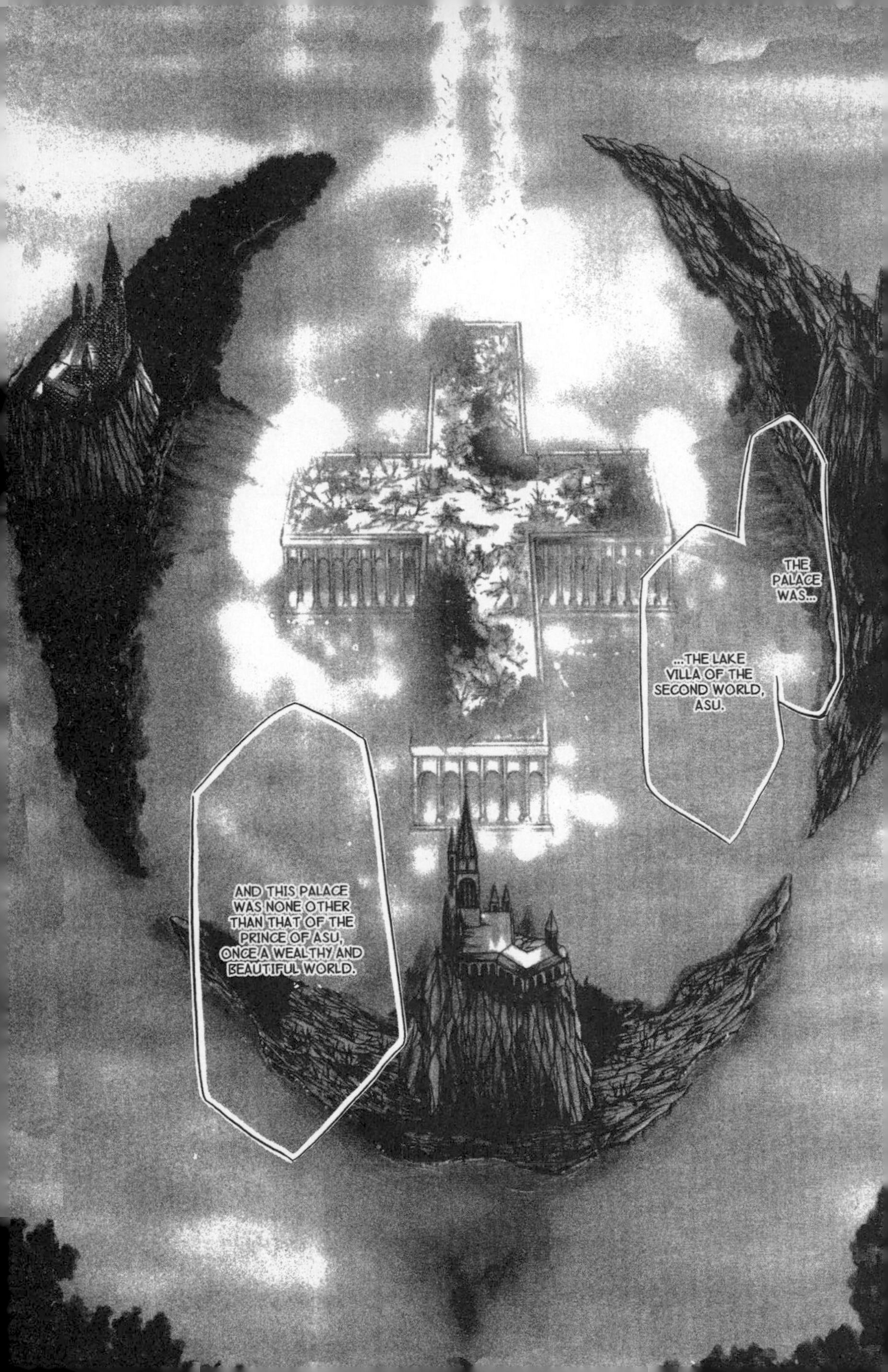
THE PALACE WAS...
...THE LAKE VILLA OF THE SECOND WORLD, ASU.
AND THIS PALACE WAS NONE OTHER THAN THAT OF THE PRINCE OF ASU, ONCE A WEALTHY AND BEAUTIFUL WORLD.

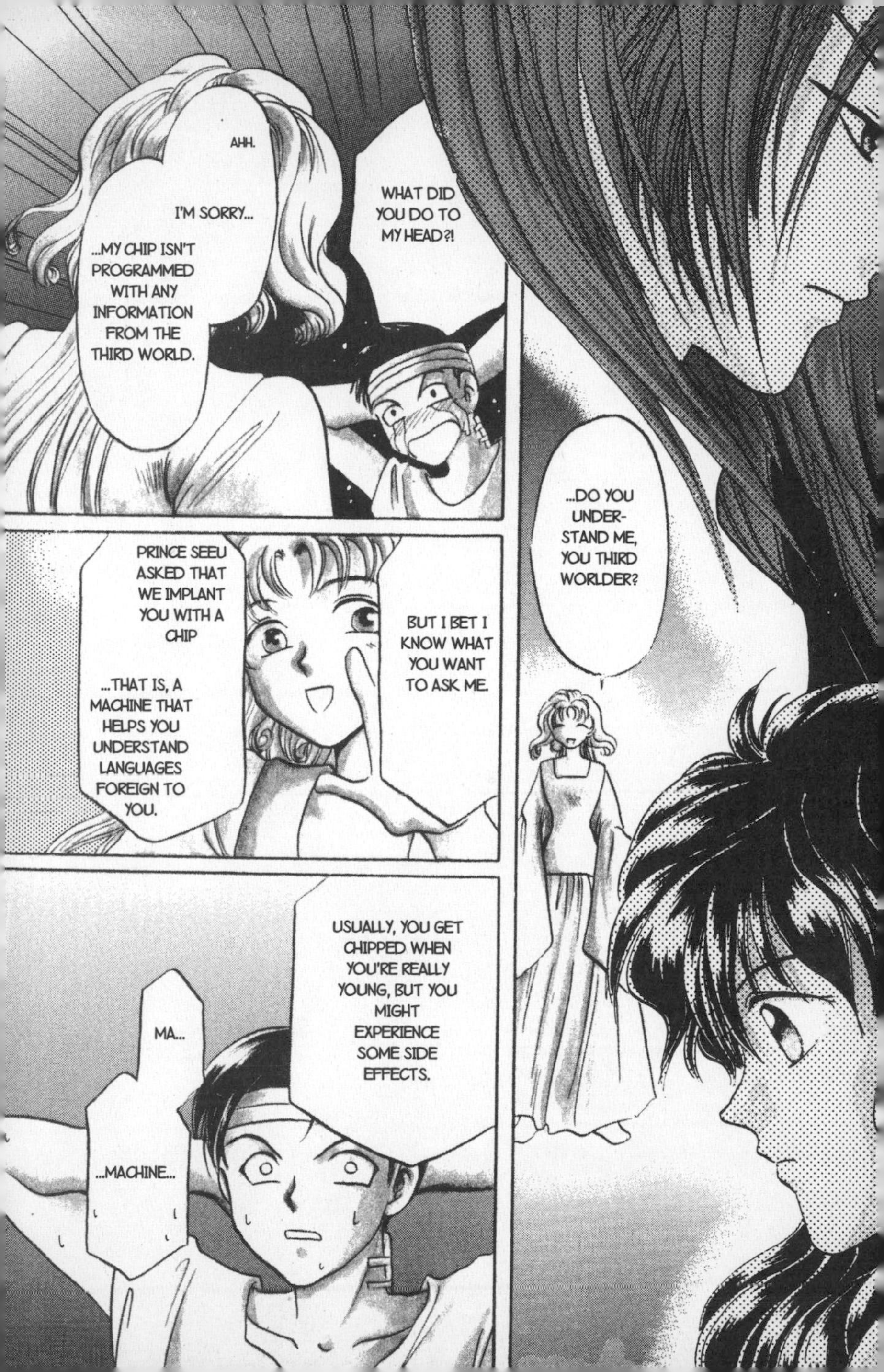
...DO YOU UNDERSTAND ME, YOU THIRD WORLDER?
WHAT DID YOU DO TO MY HEAD?!
AHH.
I'M SORRY...
...MY CHIP ISN'T PROGRAMMED WITH ANY INFORMATION FROM THE THIRD WORLD.
BUT I BET I KNOW WHAT YOU WANT TO ASK ME.
PRINCE SEEU ASKED THAT WE IMPLANT YOU WITH A CHIP
...THAT IS, A MACHINE THAT HELPS YOU UNDERSTAND LANGUAGES FOREIGN TO YOU.
USUALLY, YOU GET CHIPPED WHEN YOU'RE REALLY YOUNG, BUT YOU MIGHT EXPERIENCE SOME SIDE EFFECTS.
MA...
...MACHINE...

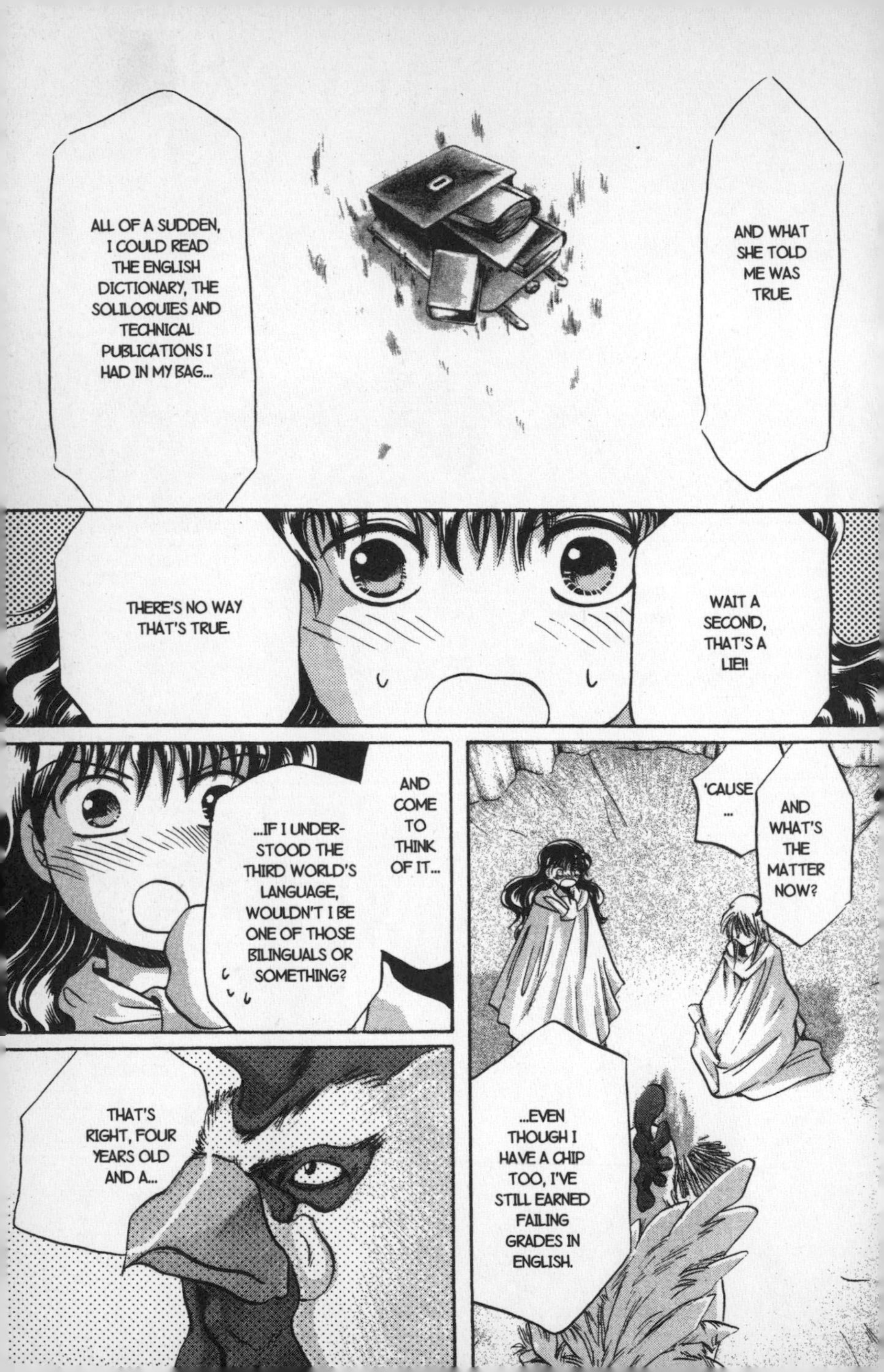
AND WHAT SHE TOLD ME WAS TRUE.
ALL OF A SUDDEN, I COULD READ THE ENGLISH DICTIONARY, THE SOLILOQUIES AND TECHNICAL PUBLICATIONS I HAD IN MY BAG...
WAIT A SECOND, THAT'S A LIE!!
THERE'S NO WAY THAT'S TRUE.
AND WHAT'S THE MATTER NOW?
'CAUSE ...
...EVEN THOUGH I HAVE A CHIP TOO, I'VE STILL EARNED FAILING GRADES IN ENGLISH.
AND COME TO THINK OF IT...
...IF I UNDER-STOOD THE THIRD WORLD'S LANGUAGE, WOULDN'T I BE ONE OF THOSE BILINGUALS OR SOMETHING?
THAT'S RIGHT, FOUR YEARS OLD AND A...

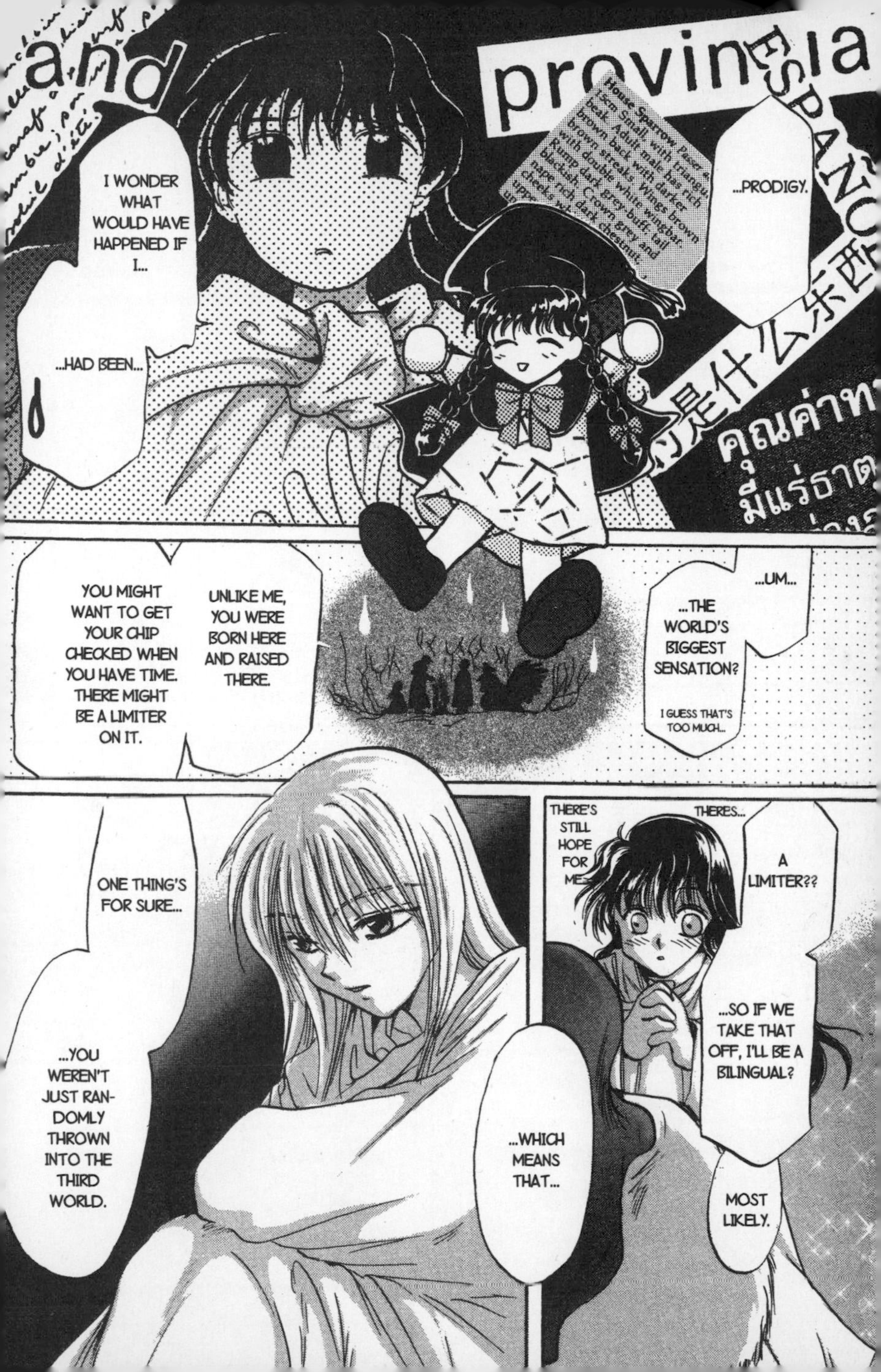
and
provincia
ESPAÑO
I WONDER WHAT WOULD HAVE HAPPENED IF I...
...HAD BEEN...
...PRODIGY.
是什么东西
คุณค่าท
มีแร่ธาต
...UM...
...THE WORLD'S BIGGEST SENSATION?
I GUESS THAT'S TOO MUCH...
UNLIKE ME, YOU WERE BORN HERE AND RAISED THERE.
YOU MIGHT WANT TO GET YOUR CHIP CHECKED WHEN YOU HAVE TIME. THERE MIGHT BE A LIMITER ON IT.
THERES...
A LIMITER??
THERE'S STILL HOPE FOR ME
...SO IF WE TAKE THAT OFF, I'LL BE A BILINGUAL?
MOST LIKELY.
ONE THING'S FOR SURE...
...WHICH MEANS THAT...
...YOU WEREN'T JUST RAN-DOMLY THROWN INTO THE THIRD WORLD.

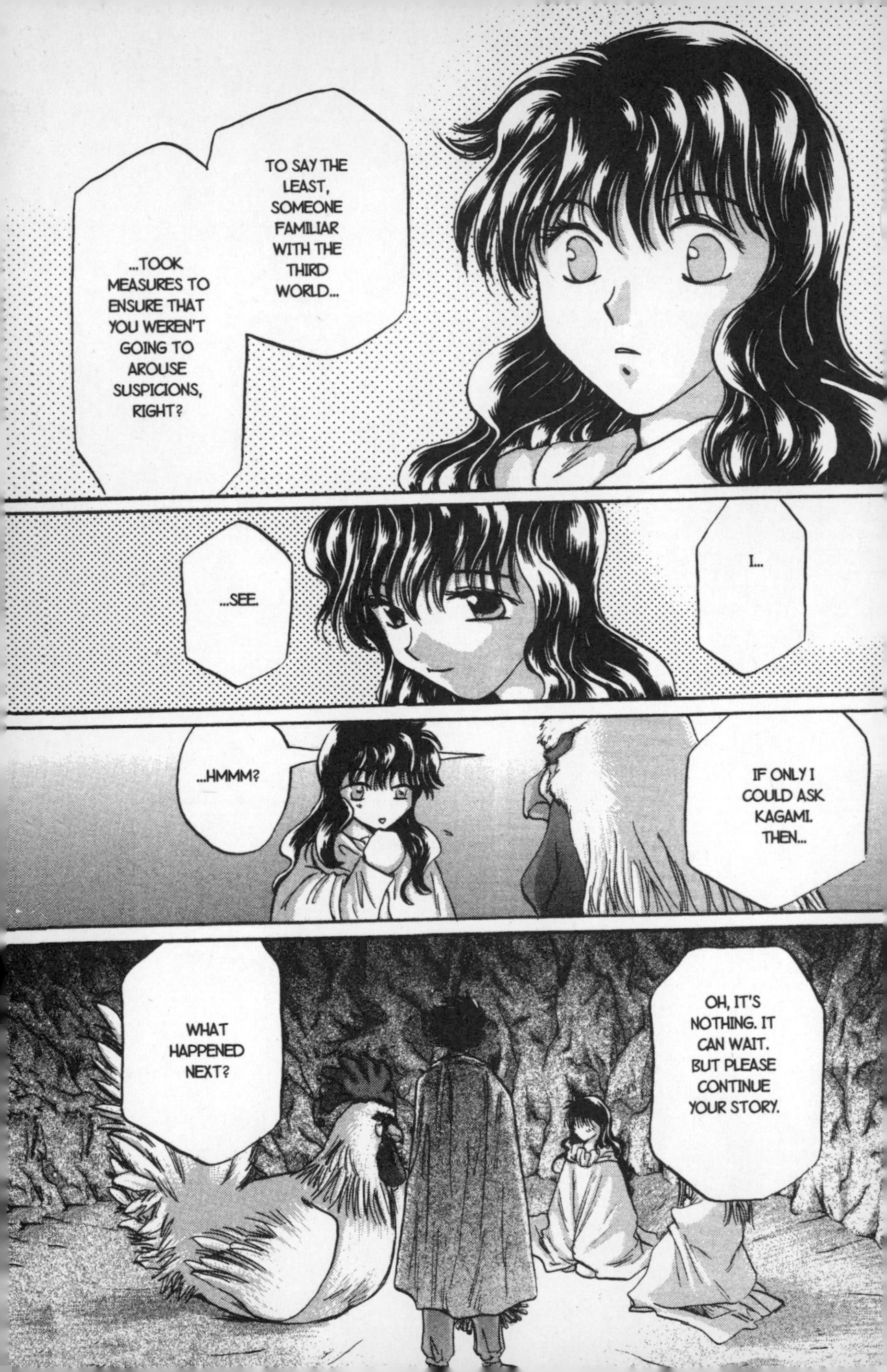
TO SAY THE LEAST, SOMEONE FAMILIAR WITH THE THIRD WORLD...
...TOOK MEASURES TO ENSURE THAT YOU WEREN'T GOING TO AROUSE SUSPICIONS, RIGHT?
I...
...SEE.
IF ONLY I COULD ASK KAGAMI. THEN...
...HMMM?
OH, IT'S NOTHING. IT CAN WAIT. BUT PLEASE CONTINUE YOUR STORY.
WHAT HAPPENED NEXT?

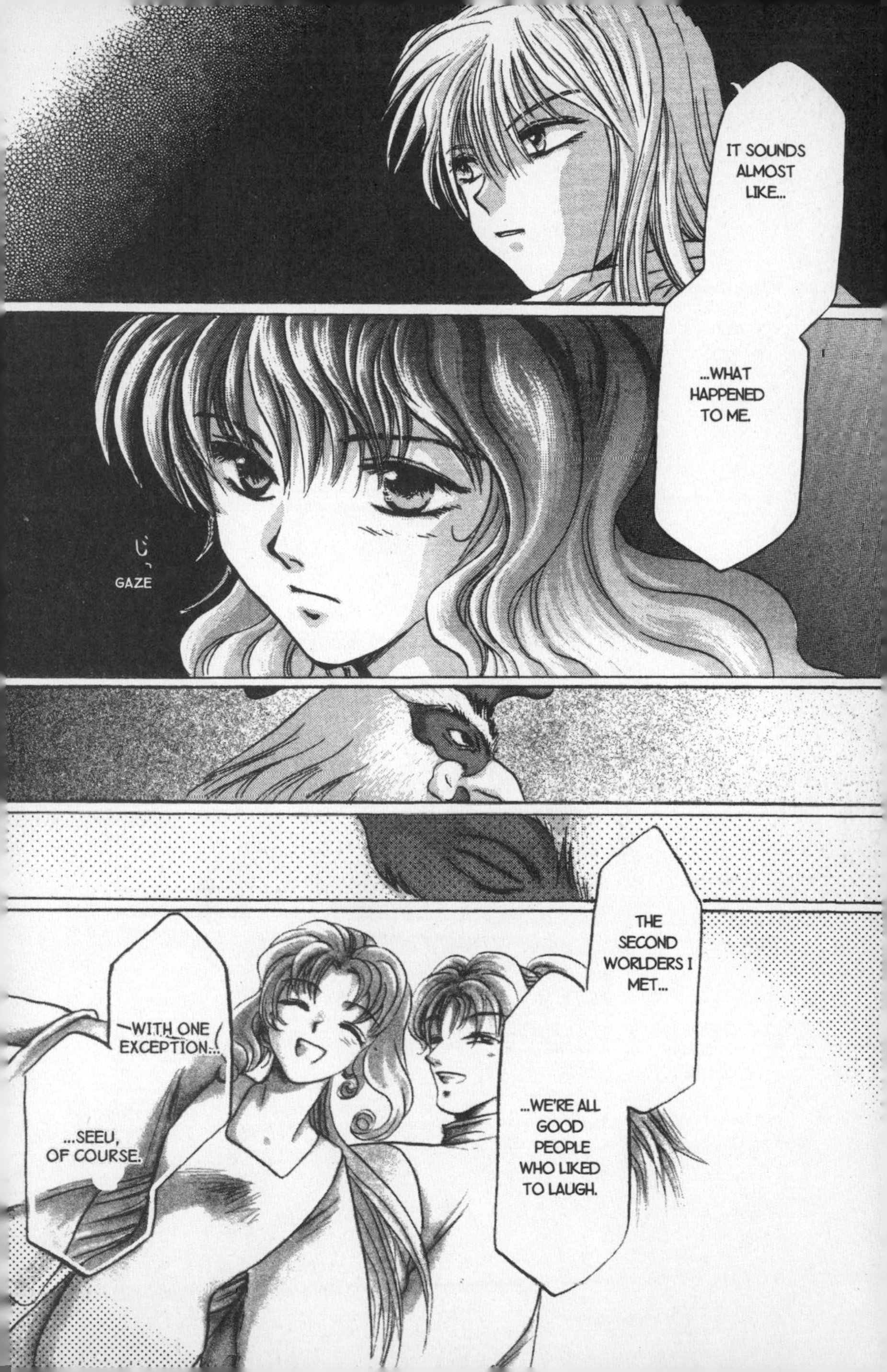
IT SOUNDS ALMOST LIKE...
...WHAT HAPPENED TO ME.
じっ
GAZE
THE SECOND WORLDERS I MET...
...WE'RE ALL GOOD PEOPLE WHO LIKED TO LAUGH.
—WITH ONE EXCEPTION...
...SEEU, OF COURSE.

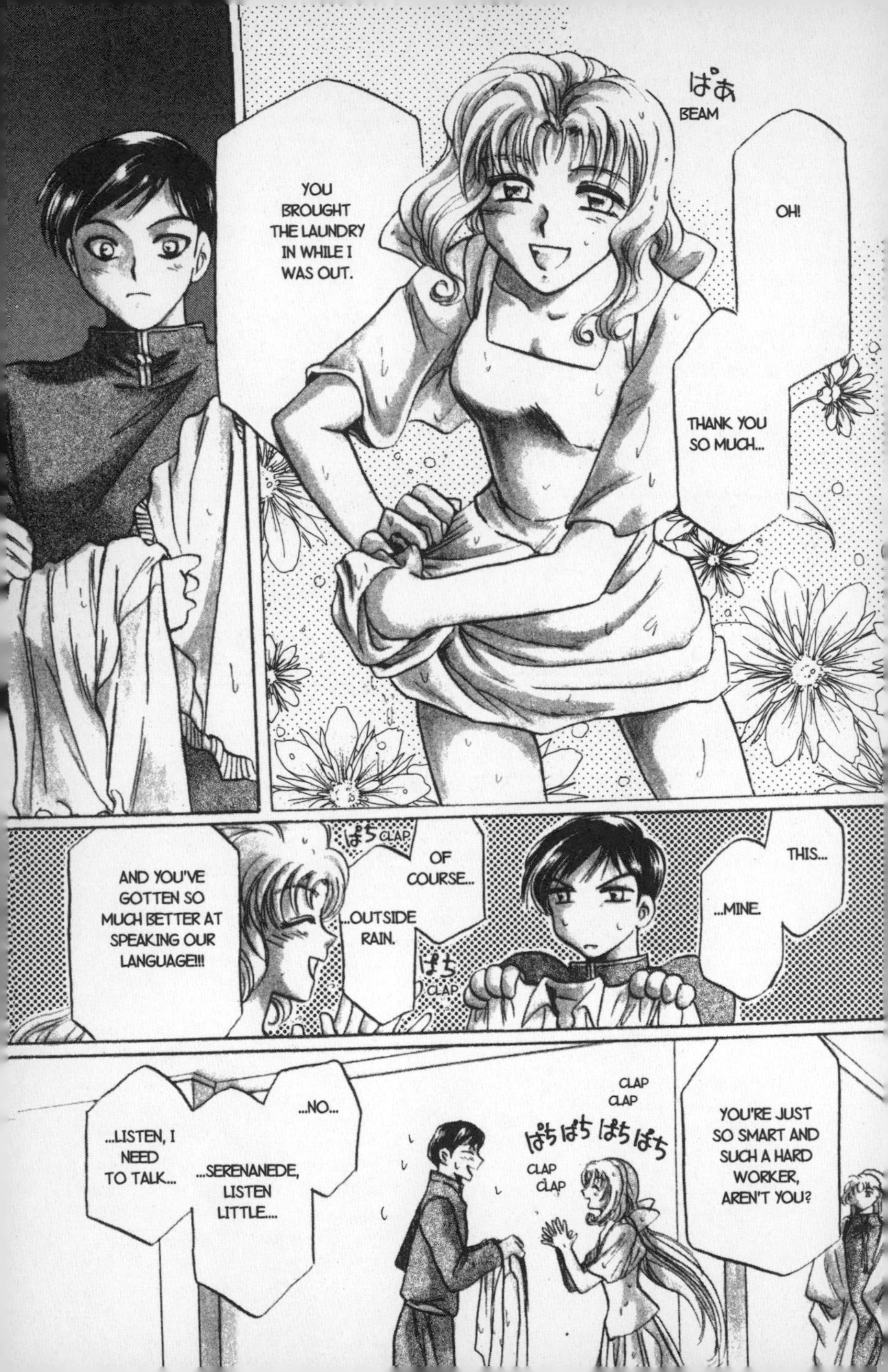
ぱぁ
BEAM
OH!
YOU BROUGHT THE LAUNDRY IN WHILE I WAS OUT.
THANK YOU SO MUCH...
THIS...
...MINE.
OF COURSE...
...OUTSIDE RAIN.
ぱち
CLAP
AND YOU'VE GOTTEN SO MUCH BETTER AT SPEAKING OUR LANGUAGE!!!
ぱち
CLAP
YOU'RE JUST SO SMART AND SUCH A HARD WORKER, AREN'T YOU?
CLAP CLAP
ぱちぱち ぱちぱち
CLAP CLAP
...NO...
...SERENANEDE, LISTEN LITTLE...
...LISTEN, I NEED TO TALK...

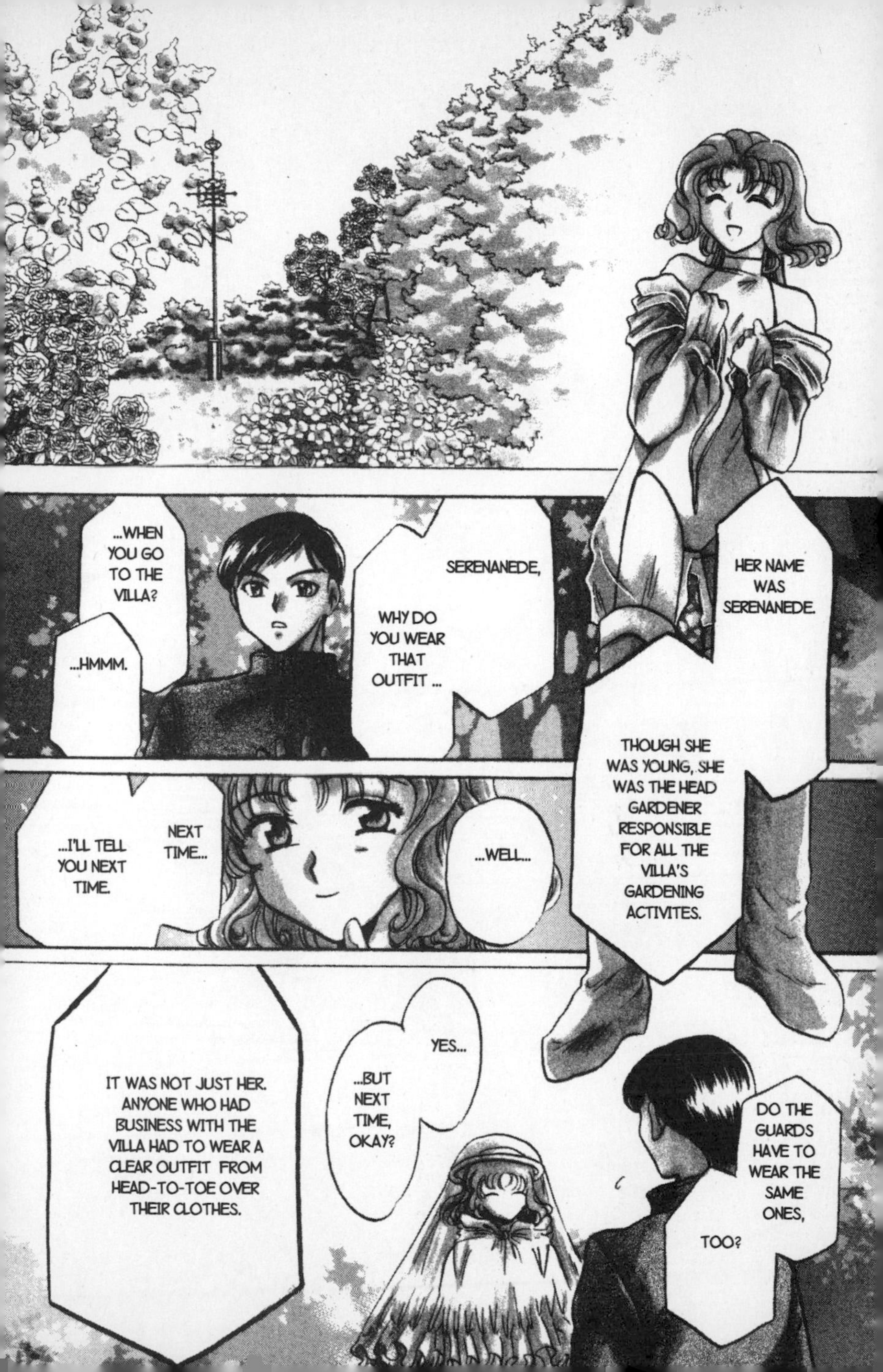
HER NAME WAS SERENANEDE.
THOUGH SHE WAS YOUNG, SHE WAS THE HEAD GARDENER RESPONSIBLE FOR ALL THE VILLA'S GARDENING ACTIVITES.
SERENANEDE,
WHY DO YOU WEAR THAT OUTFIT ...
...WHEN YOU GO TO THE VILLA?
...HMMM.
...WELL...
NEXT TIME...
...I'LL TELL YOU NEXT TIME.
DO THE GUARDS HAVE TO WEAR THE SAME ONES,
TOO?
YES...
...BUT NEXT TIME, OKAY?
IT WAS NOT JUST HER. ANYONE WHO HAD BUSINESS WITH THE VILLA HAD TO WEAR A CLEAR OUTFIT FROM HEAD-TO-TOE OVER THEIR CLOTHES.

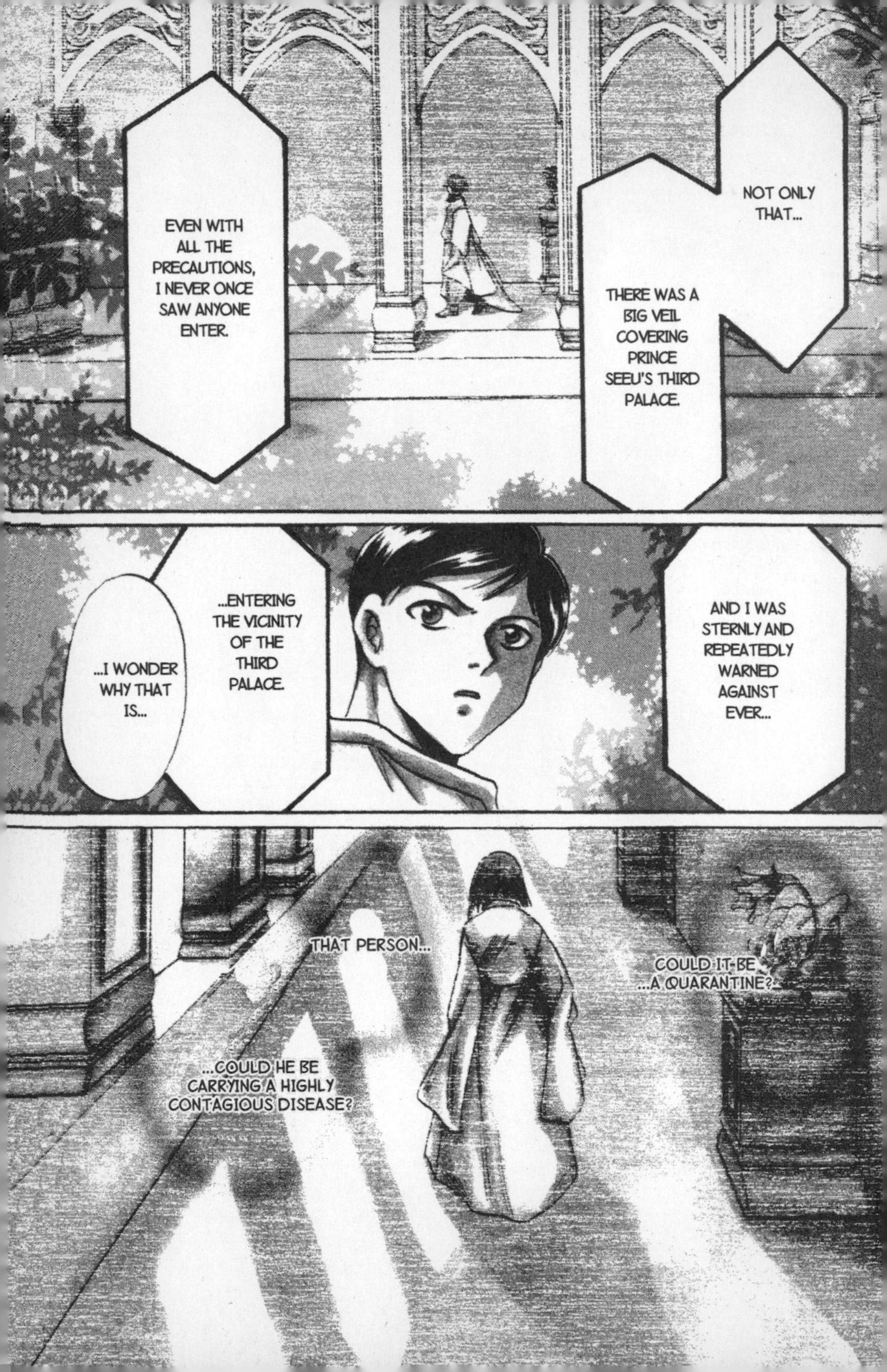
NOT ONLY THAT...
THERE WAS A BIG VEIL COVERING PRINCE SEEU'S THIRD PALACE.
EVEN WITH ALL THE PRECAUTIONS, I NEVER ONCE SAW ANYONE ENTER.
AND I WAS STERNLY AND REPEATEDLY WARNED AGAINST EVER...
...ENTERING THE VICINITY OF THE THIRD PALACE.
...I WONDER WHY THAT IS...
THAT PERSON...
COULD IT BE ...A QUARANTINE?
...COULD HE BE CARRYING A HIGHLY CONTAGIOUS DISEASE?

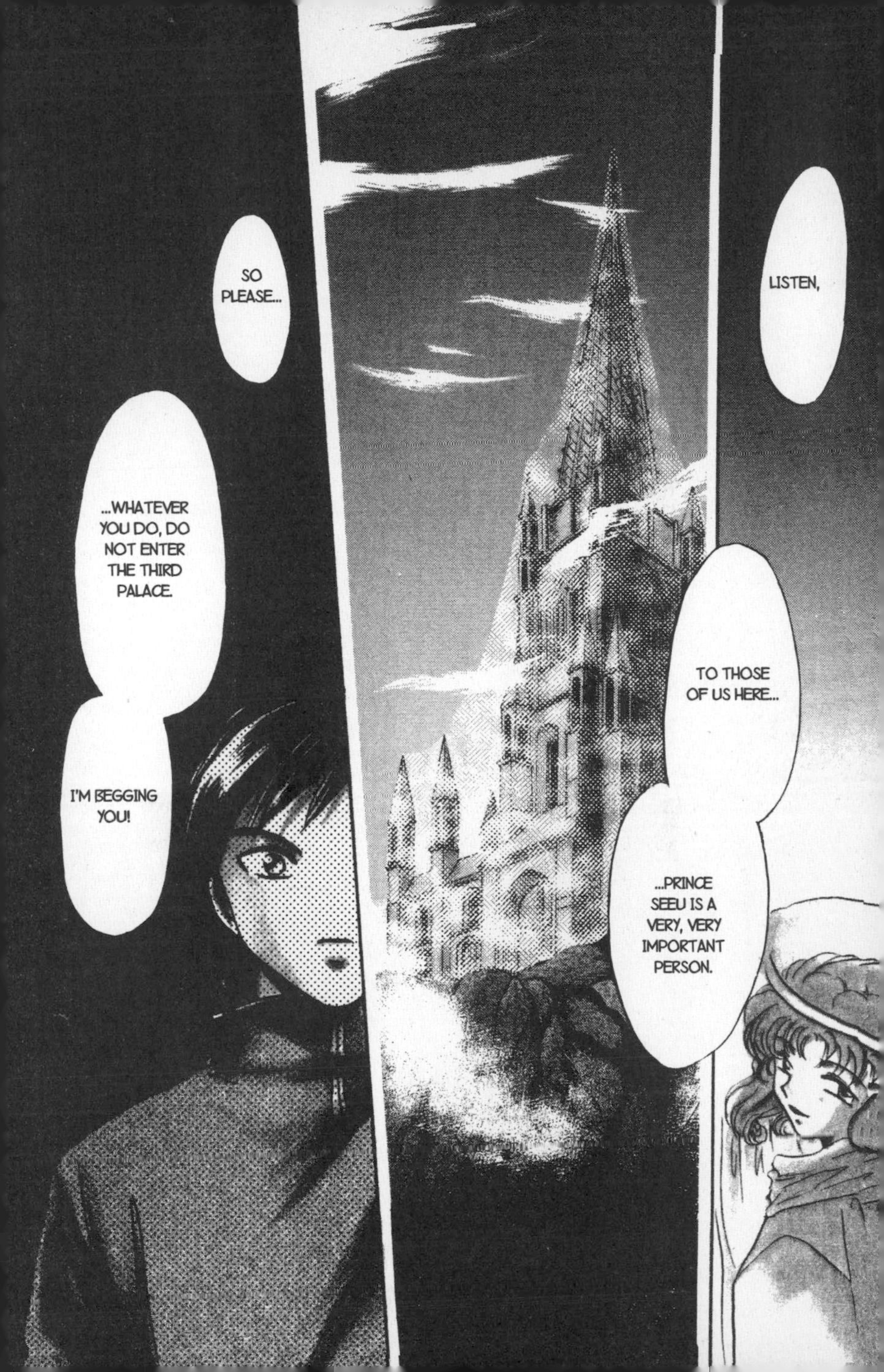
LISTEN,
TO THOSE OF US HERE...
...PRINCE SEEU IS A VERY, VERY IMPORTANT PERSON.
SO PLEASE...
...WHATEVER YOU DO, DO NOT ENTER THE THIRD PALACE.
I'M BEGGING YOU!

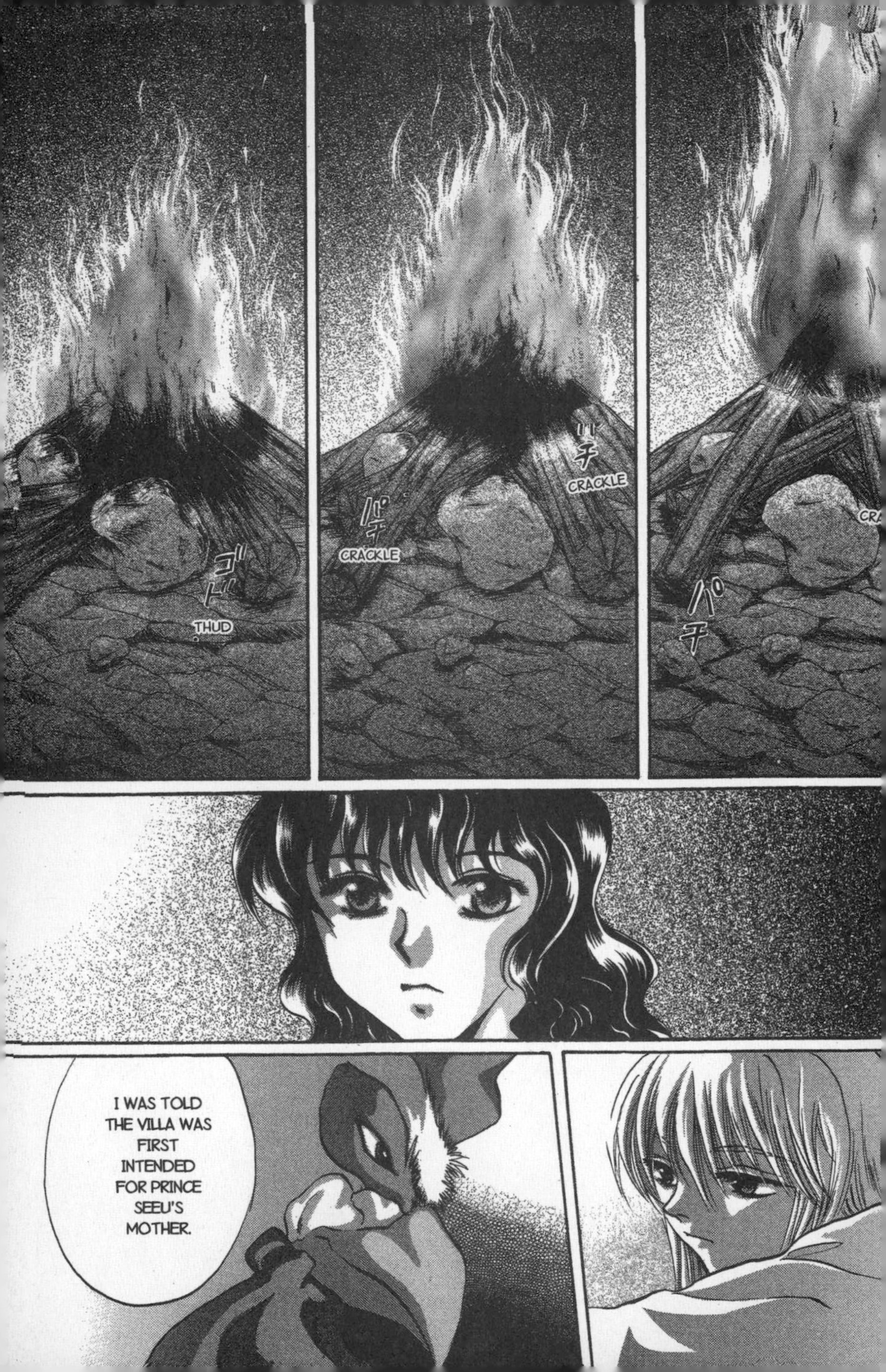

パチ
パチ
CRACKLE
パチ
CRACKLE
ゴド
THUD
I WAS TOLD THE VILLA WAS FIRST INTENDED FOR PRINCE SEEU'S MOTHER.

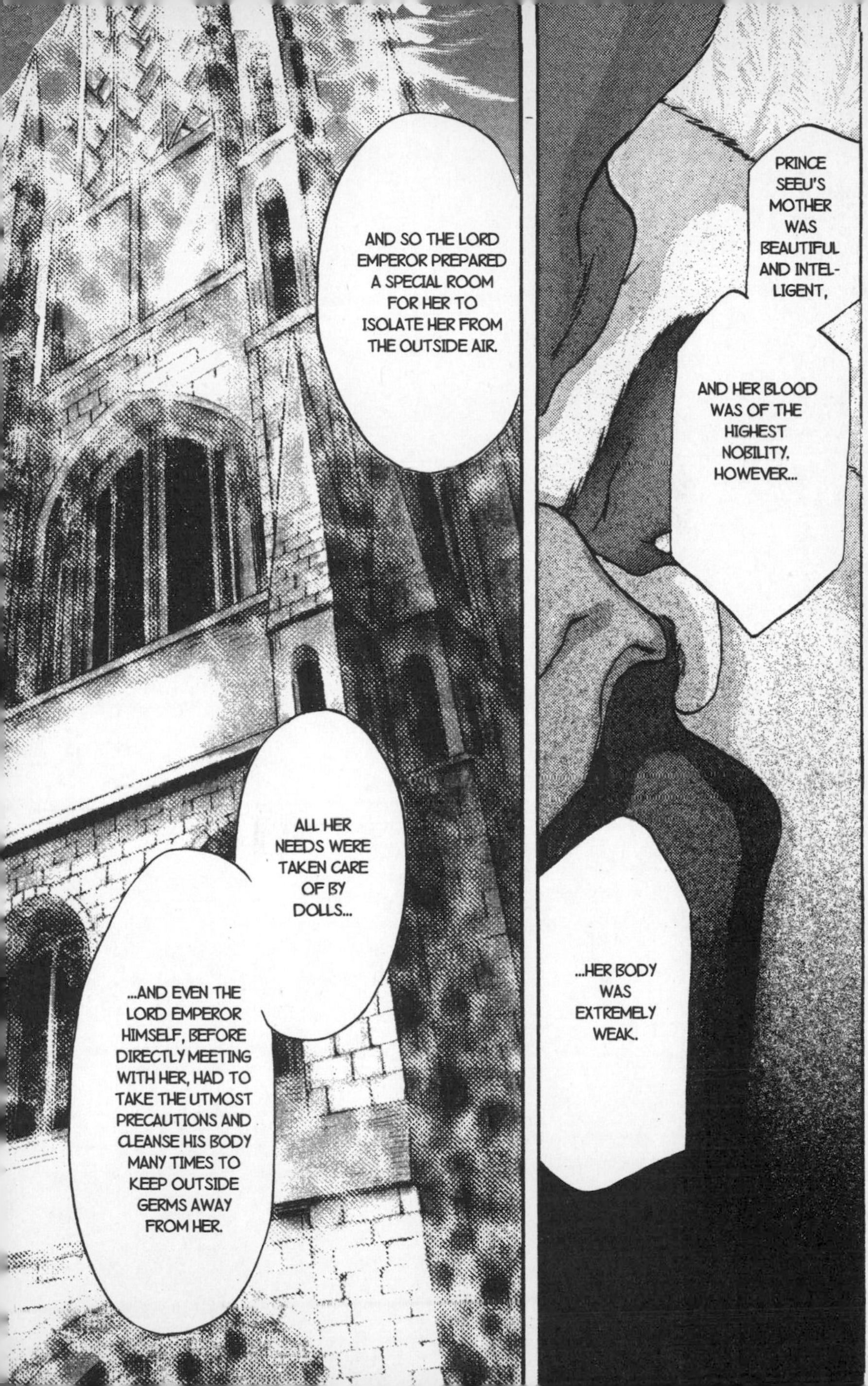
PRINCE SEEU'S MOTHER WAS BEAUTIFUL AND INTEL-LIGENT,
AND HER BLOOD WAS OF THE HIGHEST NOBILITY. HOWEVER...
...HER BODY WAS EXTREMELY WEAK.
AND SO THE LORD EMPEROR PREPARED A SPECIAL ROOM FOR HER TO ISOLATE HER FROM THE OUTSIDE AIR.
ALL HER NEEDS WERE TAKEN CARE OF BY DOLLS...
...AND EVEN THE LORD EMPEROR HIMSELF, BEFORE DIRECTLY MEETING WITH HER, HAD TO TAKE THE UTMOST PRECAUTIONS AND CLEANSE HIS BODY MANY TIMES TO KEEP OUTSIDE GERMS AWAY FROM HER.

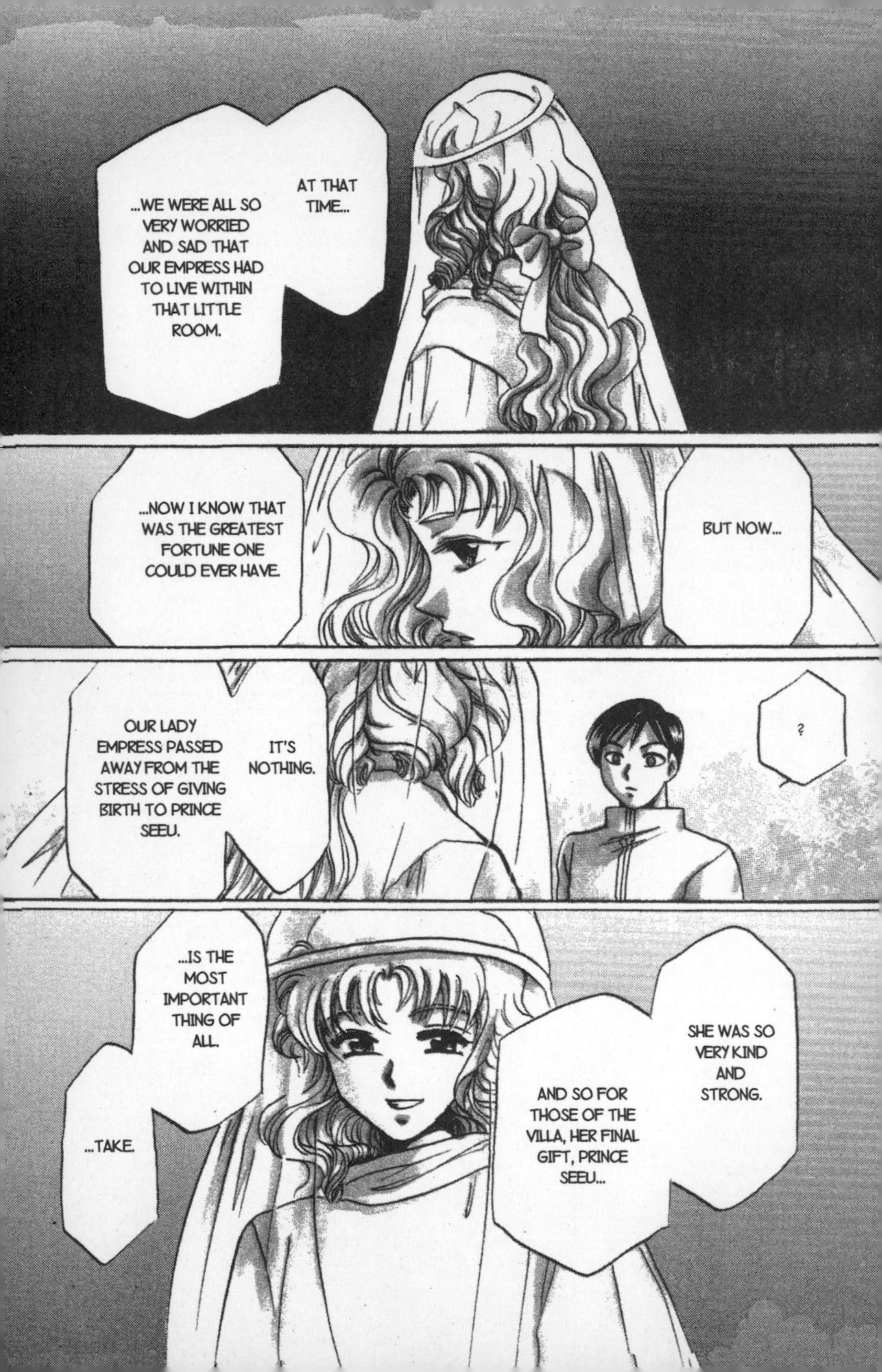
AT THAT TIME...
...WE WERE ALL SO VERY WORRIED AND SAD THAT OUR EMPRESS HAD TO LIVE WITHIN THAT LITTLE ROOM.
BUT NOW...
...NOW I KNOW THAT WAS THE GREATEST FORTUNE ONE COULD EVER HAVE.
?
IT'S NOTHING.
OUR LADY EMPRESS PASSED AWAY FROM THE STRESS OF GIVING BIRTH TO PRINCE SEEU.
SHE WAS SO VERY KIND AND STRONG.
AND SO FOR THOSE OF THE VILLA, HER FINAL GIFT, PRINCE SEEU...
...IS THE MOST IMPORTANT THING OF ALL.
...TAKE.

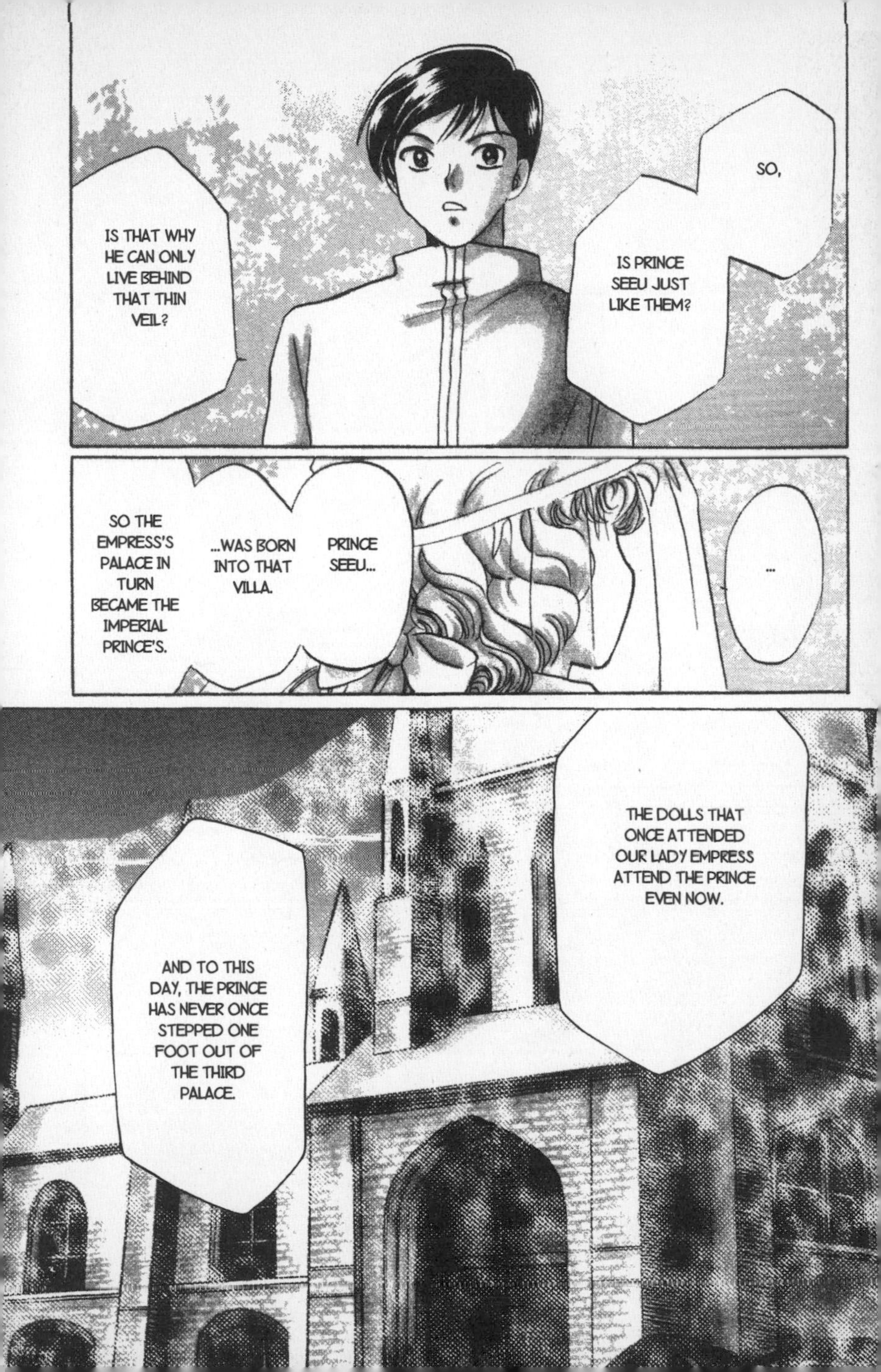
SO,
IS PRINCE SEEU JUST LIKE THEM?
IS THAT WHY HE CAN ONLY LIVE BEHIND THAT THIN VEIL?
...
PRINCE SEEU...
...WAS BORN INTO THAT VILLA.
SO THE EMPRESS'S PALACE IN TURN BECAME THE IMPERIAL PRINCE'S.
THE DOLLS THAT ONCE ATTENDED OUR LADY EMPRESS ATTEND THE PRINCE EVEN NOW.
AND TO THIS DAY, THE PRINCE HAS NEVER ONCE STEPPED ONE FOOT OUT OF THE THIRD PALACE.

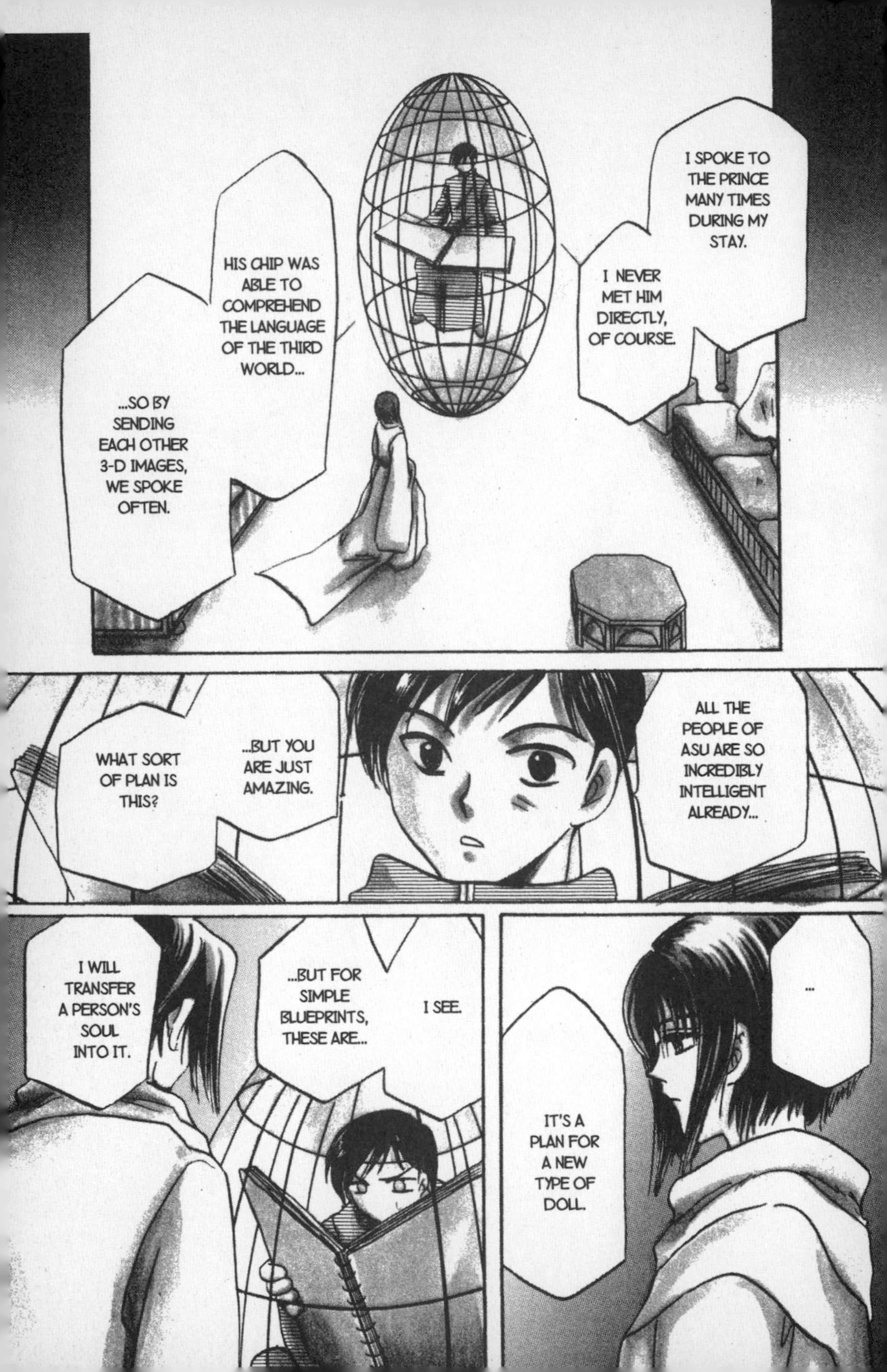
I SPOKE TO THE PRINCE MANY TIMES DURING MY STAY.
I NEVER MET HIM DIRECTLY, OF COURSE.
HIS CHIP WAS ABLE TO COMPREHEND THE LANGUAGE OF THE THIRD WORLD...
...SO BY SENDING EACH OTHER 3-D IMAGES, WE SPOKE OFTEN.
ALL THE PEOPLE OF ASU ARE SO INCREDIBLY INTELLIGENT ALREADY...
...BUT YOU ARE JUST AMAZING.
WHAT SORT OF PLAN IS THIS?
...
IT'S A PLAN FOR A NEW TYPE OF DOLL.
I SEE.
...BUT FOR SIMPLE BLUEPRINTS, THESE ARE...
I WILL TRANSFER A PERSON'S SOUL INTO IT.

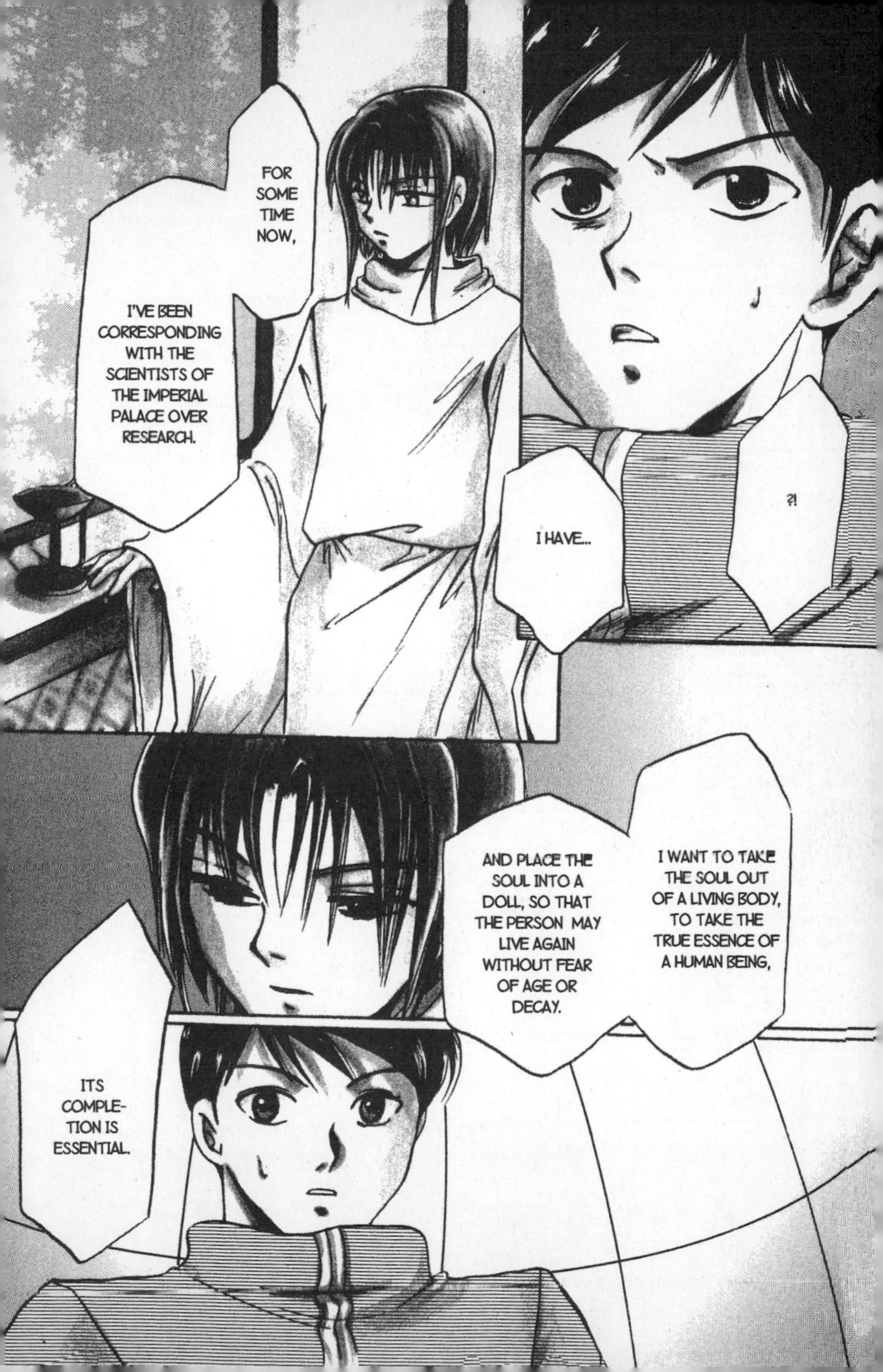
?!
I HAVE...
FOR SOME TIME NOW,
I'VE BEEN CORRESPONDING WITH THE SCIENTISTS OF THE IMPERIAL PALACE OVER RESEARCH.
I WANT TO TAKE THE SOUL OUT OF A LIVING BODY, TO TAKE THE TRUE ESSENCE OF A HUMAN BEING,
AND PLACE THE SOUL INTO A DOLL, SO THAT THE PERSON MAY LIVE AGAIN WITHOUT FEAR OF AGE OR DECAY.
ITS COMPLETION IS ESSENTIAL.

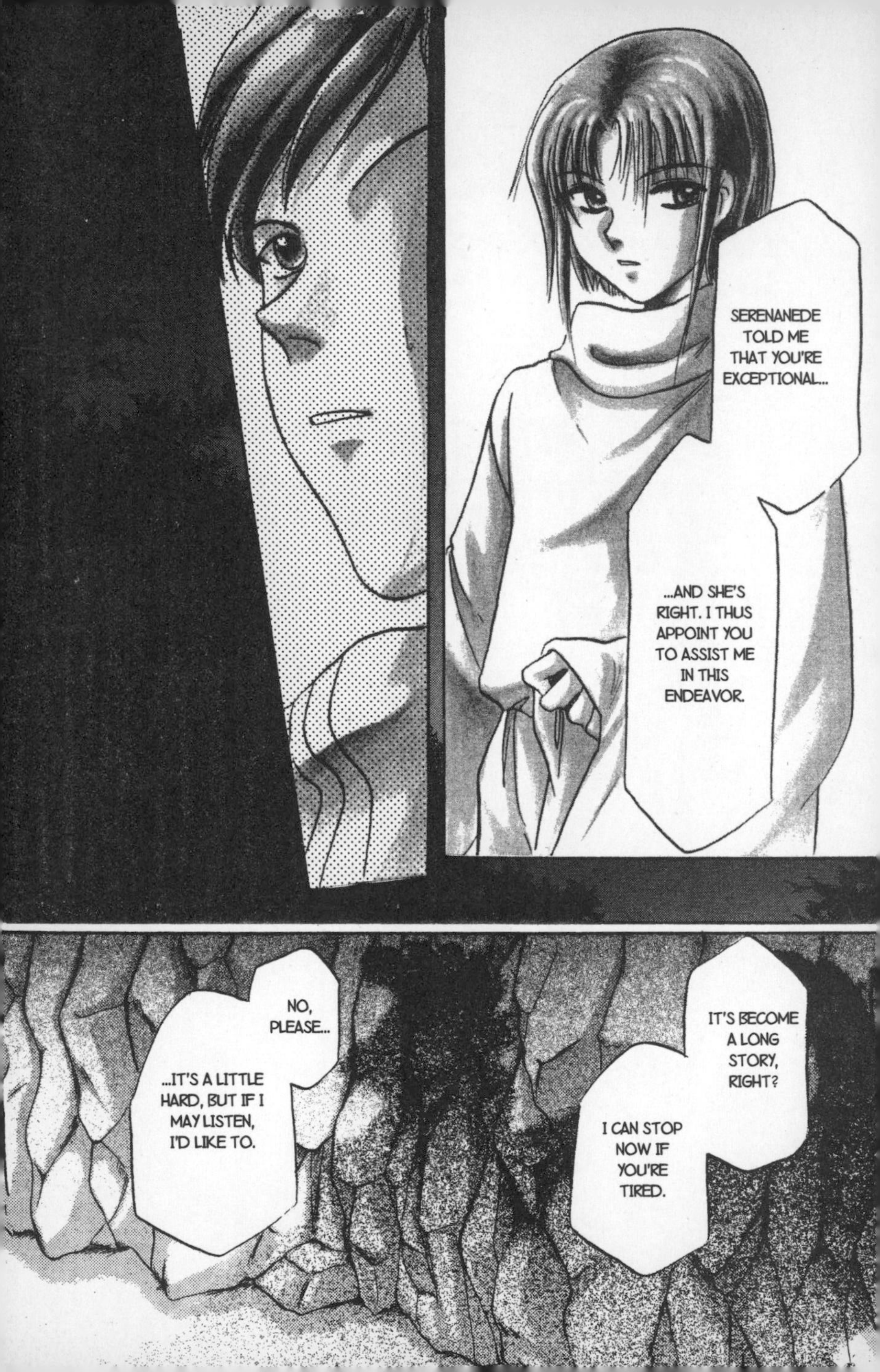
SERENANEDE TOLD ME THAT YOU'RE EXCEPTIONAL...
...AND SHE'S RIGHT. I THUS APPOINT YOU TO ASSIST ME IN THIS ENDEAVOR.
IT'S BECOME A LONG STORY, RIGHT?
I CAN STOP NOW IF YOU'RE TIRED.
NO, PLEASE...
...IT'S A LITTLE HARD, BUT IF I MAY LISTEN, I'D LIKE TO.

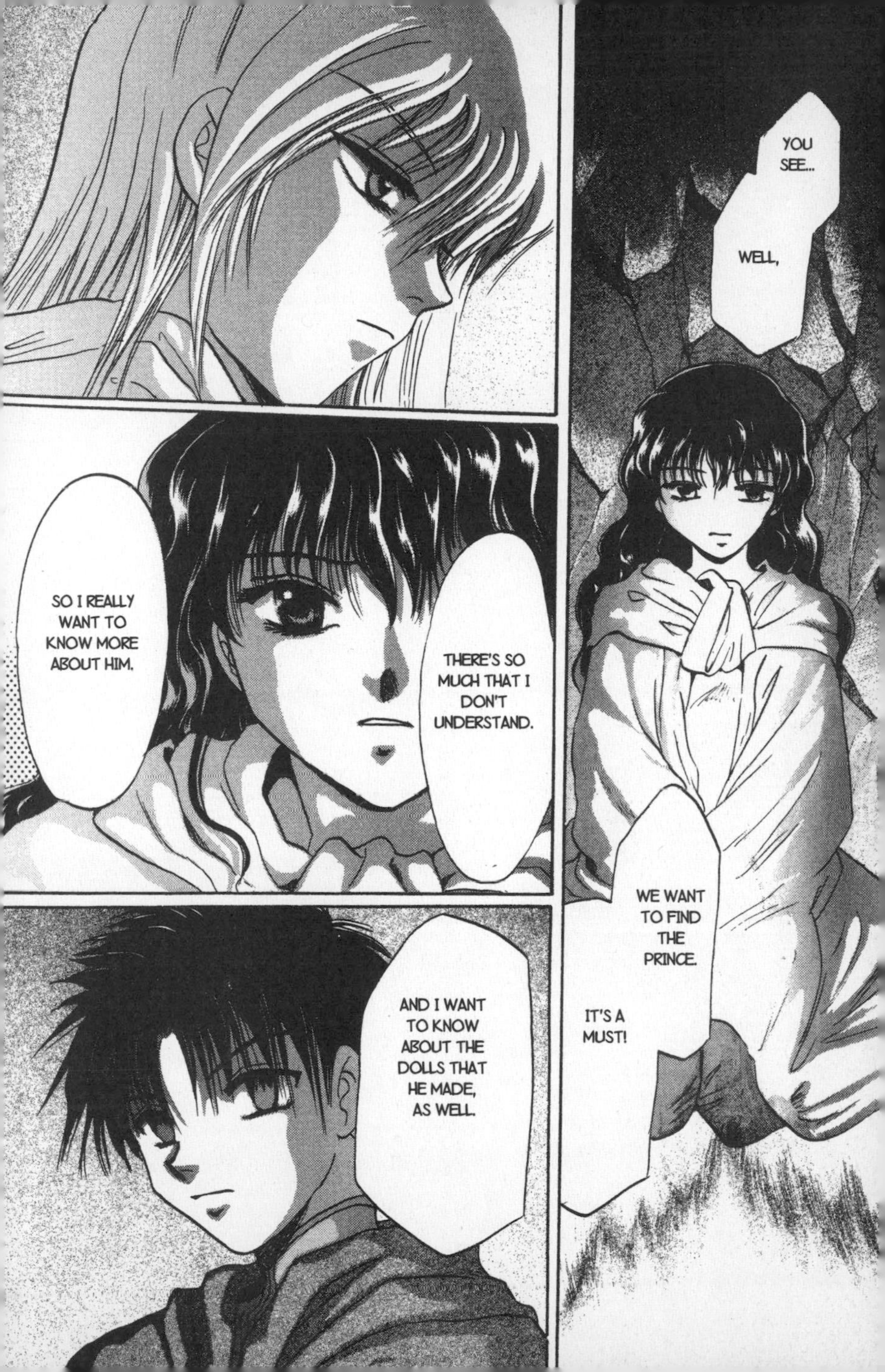
YOU SEE...
WELL,
WE WANT TO FIND THE PRINCE.
IT'S A MUST!
THERE'S SO MUCH THAT I DON'T UNDERSTAND.
SO I REALLY WANT TO KNOW MORE ABOUT HIM.
AND I WANT TO KNOW ABOUT THE DOLLS THAT HE MADE, AS WELL.

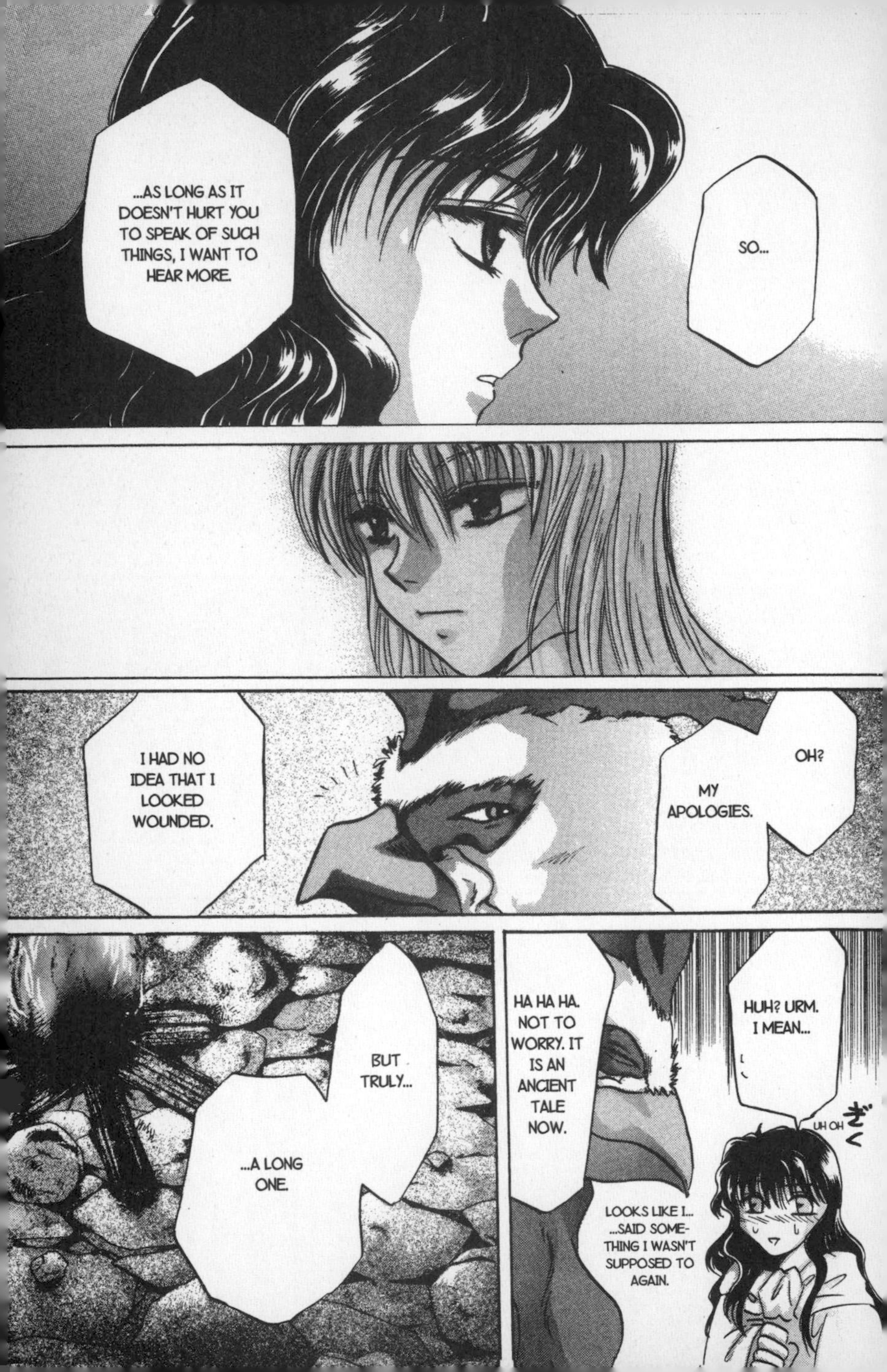
SO...
...AS LONG AS IT DOESN'T HURT YOU TO SPEAK OF SUCH THINGS, I WANT TO HEAR MORE.
OH? MY APOLOGIES.
I HAD NO IDEA THAT I LOOKED WOUNDED.
HUH? URM. I MEAN...
HA HA HA. NOT TO WORRY. IT IS AN ANCIENT TALE NOW.
ぎく
UH OH
LOOKS LIKE I... ...SAID SOME-THING I WASN'T SUPPOSED TO AGAIN.
BUT TRULY...
...A LONG ONE.

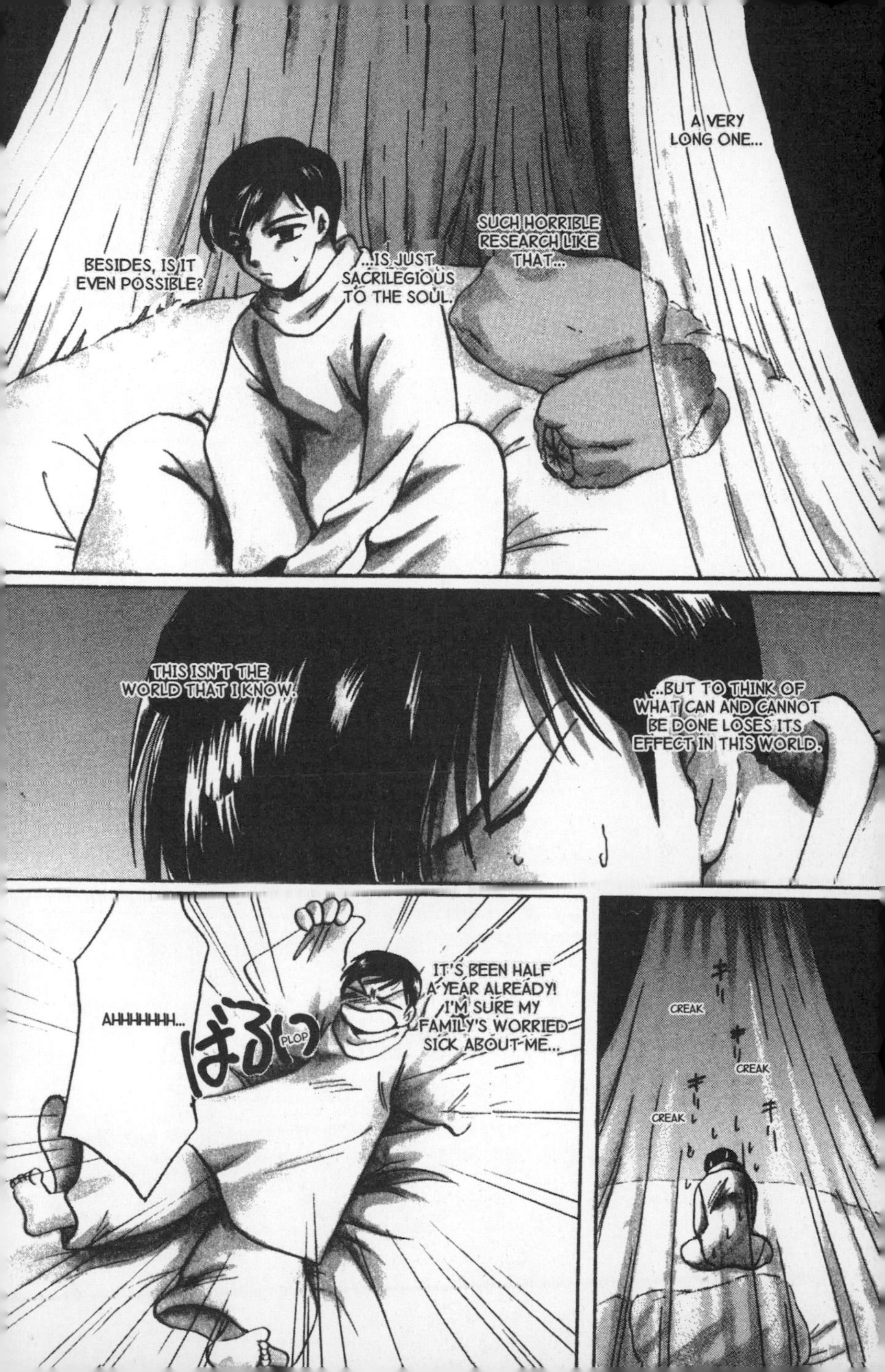
A VERY LONG ONE...
SUCH HORRIBLE RESEARCH LIKE THAT...
...IS JUST SACRILEGIOUS TO THE SOUL.
BESIDES, IS IT EVEN POSSIBLE?
...BUT TO THINK OF WHAT CAN AND CANNOT BE DONE LOSES ITS EFFECT IN THIS WORLD.
THIS ISN'T THE WORLD THAT I KNOW.
CREAK
CREAK
CREAK
IT'S BEEN HALF A YEAR ALREADY! I'M SURE MY FAMILY'S WORRIED SICK ABOUT ME...
PLOP
AHHHHHHH...

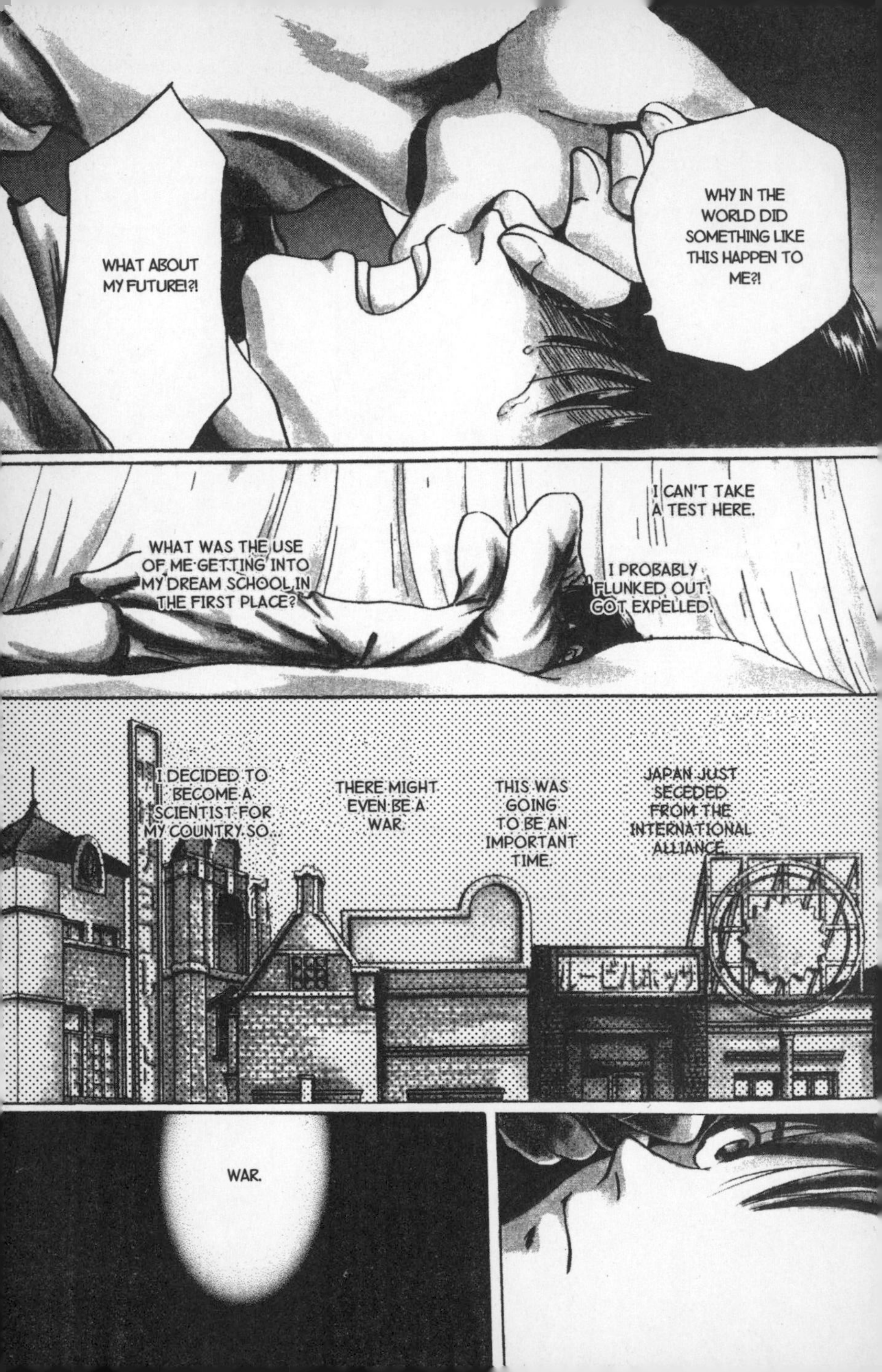
WHY IN THE WORLD DID SOMETHING LIKE THIS HAPPEN TO ME?!
WHAT ABOUT MY FUTURE!?!
I CAN'T TAKE A TEST HERE.
I PROBABLY FLUNKED OUT. GOT EXPELLED.
WHAT WAS THE USE OF ME GETTING INTO MY DREAM SCHOOL IN THE FIRST PLACE?
JAPAN JUST SECEDED FROM THE INTERNATIONAL ALLIANCE.
THIS WAS GOING TO BE AN IMPORTANT TIME.
THERE MIGHT EVEN BE A WAR.
I DECIDED TO BECOME A SCIENTIST FOR MY COUNTRY SO...
WAR.

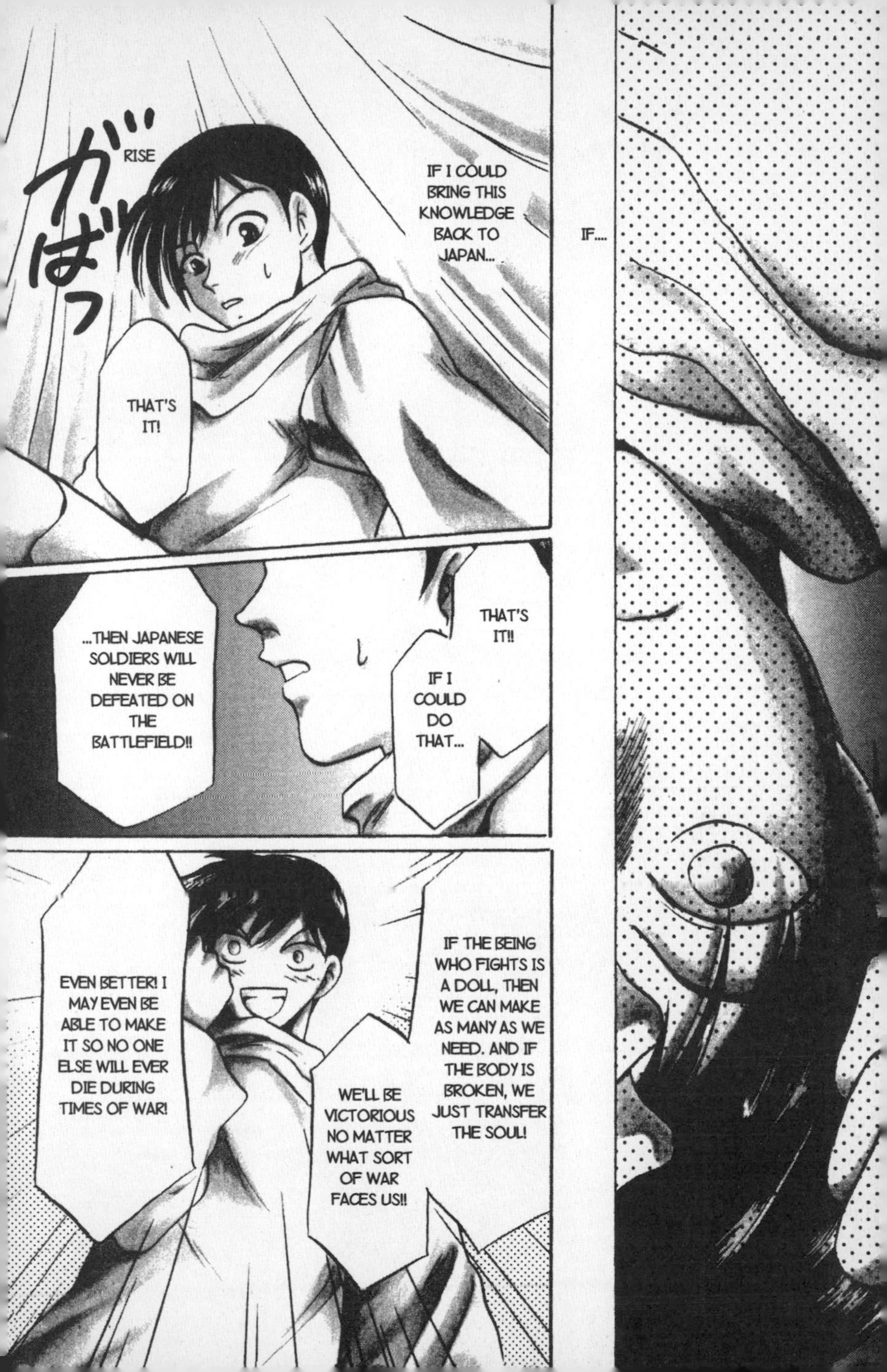
IF....
がばっ
RISE
IF I COULD BRING THIS KNOWLEDGE BACK TO JAPAN...
THAT'S IT!
THAT'S IT!!
IF I COULD DO THAT...
...THEN JAPANESE SOLDIERS WILL NEVER BE DEFEATED ON THE BATTLEFIELD!!
IF THE BEING WHO FIGHTS IS A DOLL, THEN WE CAN MAKE AS MANY AS WE NEED. AND IF THE BODY IS BROKEN, WE JUST TRANSFER THE SOUL!
WE'LL BE VICTORIOUS NO MATTER WHAT SORT OF WAR FACES US!!
EVEN BETTER! I MAY EVEN BE ABLE TO MAKE IT SO NO ONE ELSE WILL EVER DIE DURING TIMES OF WAR!

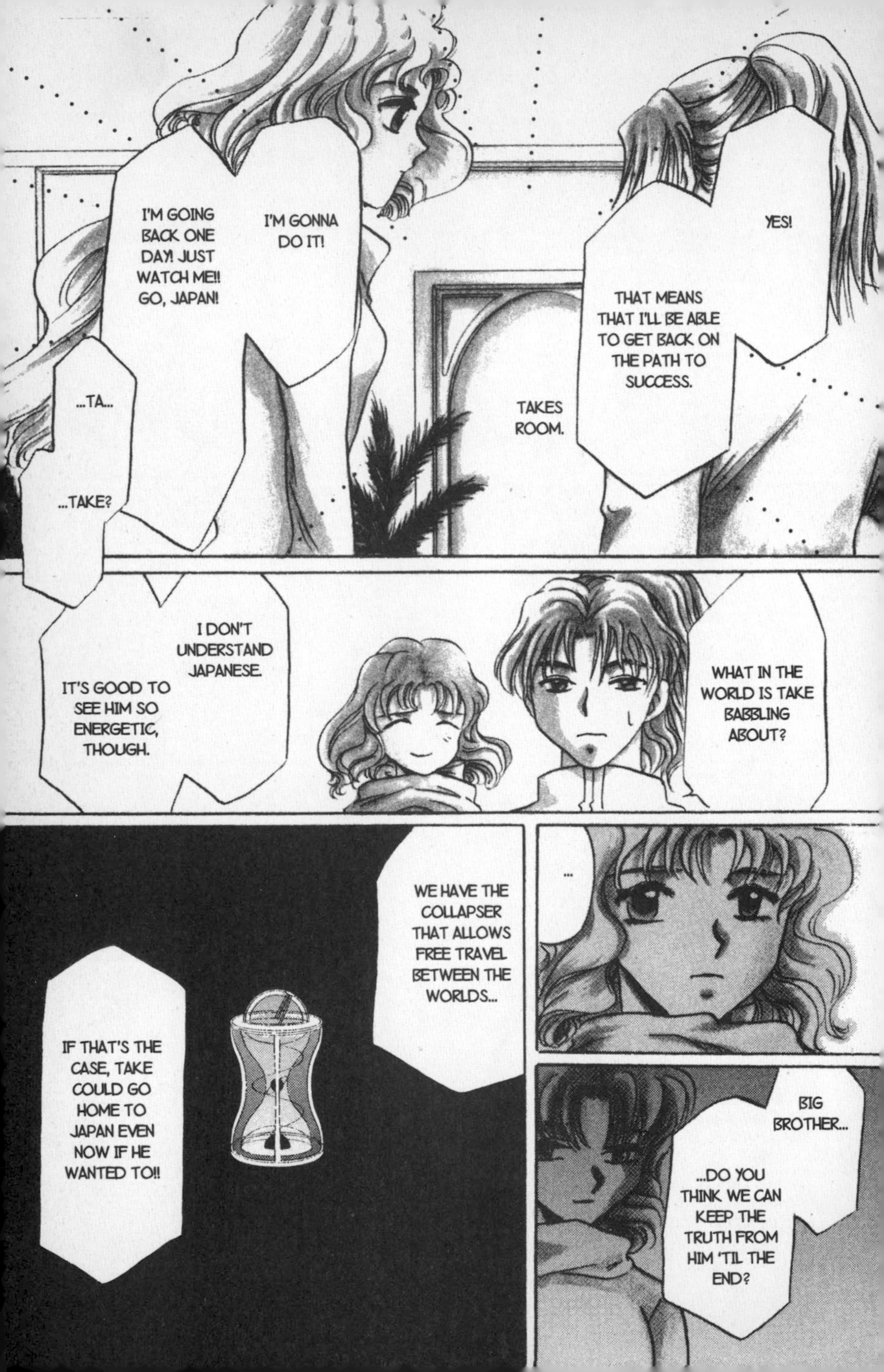
YES!
THAT MEANS THAT I'LL BE ABLE TO GET BACK ON THE PATH TO SUCCESS.
TAKES ROOM.
I'M GONNA DO IT!
I'M GOING BACK ONE DAY! JUST WATCH ME!! GO, JAPAN!
...TA...
...TAKE?
WHAT IN THE WORLD IS TAKE BABBLING ABOUT?
I DON'T UNDERSTAND JAPANESE.
IT'S GOOD TO SEE HIM SO ENERGETIC, THOUGH.
...
BIG BROTHER...
...DO YOU THINK WE CAN KEEP THE TRUTH FROM HIM 'TIL THE END?
WE HAVE THE COLLAPSER THAT ALLOWS FREE TRAVEL BETWEEN THE WORLDS...
IF THAT'S THE CASE, TAKE COULD GO HOME TO JAPAN EVEN NOW IF HE WANTED TO!!

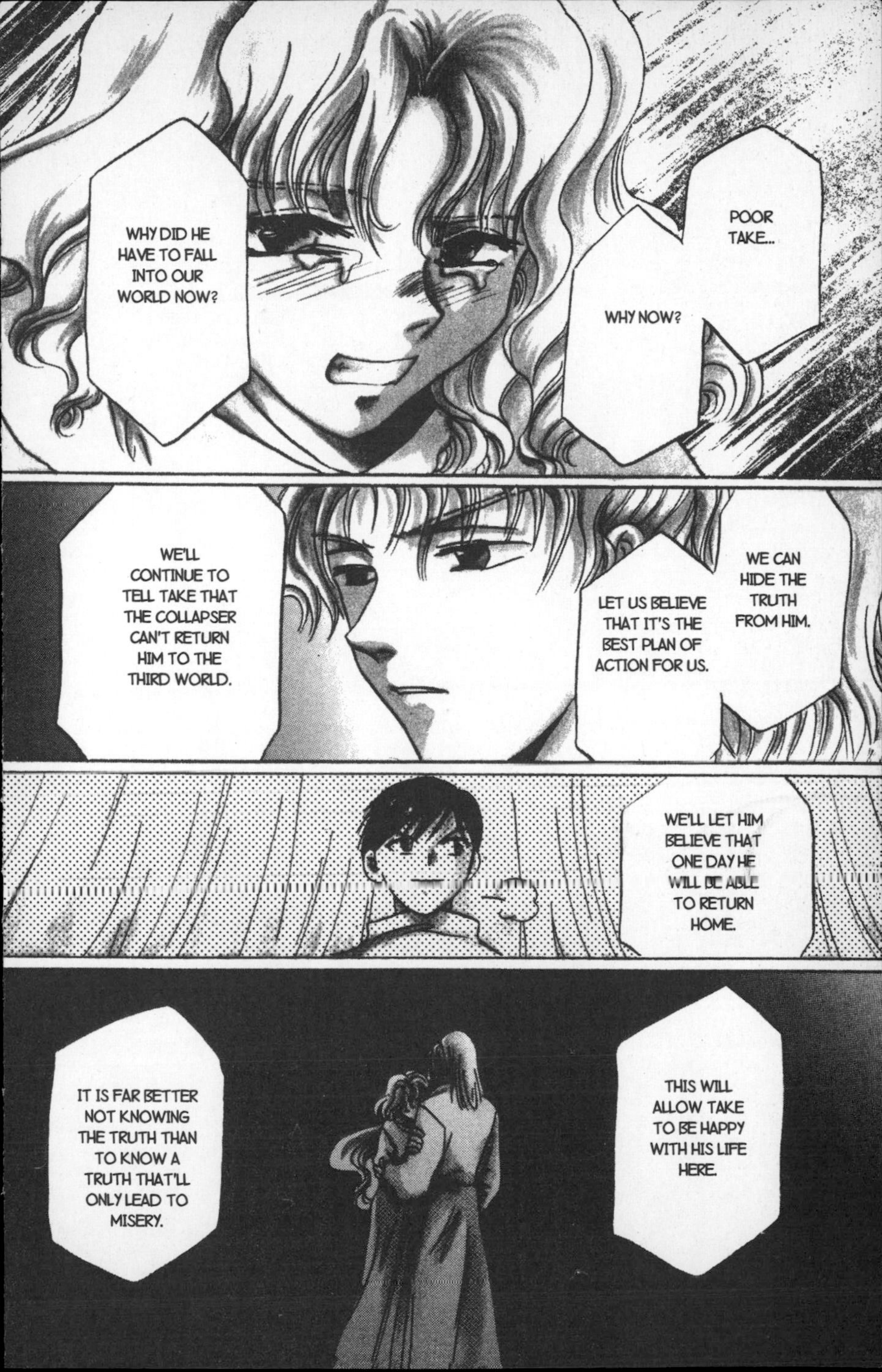
POOR TAKE...
WHY NOW?
WHY DID HE HAVE TO FALL INTO OUR WORLD NOW?
WE CAN HIDE THE TRUTH FROM HIM.
LET US BELIEVE THAT IT'S THE BEST PLAN OF ACTION FOR US.
WE'LL CONTINUE TO TELL TAKE THAT THE COLLAPSER CAN'T RETURN HIM TO THE THIRD WORLD.
WE'LL LET HIM BELIEVE THAT ONE DAY HE WILL BE ABLE TO RETURN HOME.
THIS WILL ALLOW TAKE TO BE HAPPY WITH HIS LIFE HERE.
IT IS FAR BETTER NOT KNOWING THE TRUTH THAN TO KNOW A TRUTH THAT'LL ONLY LEAD TO MISERY.

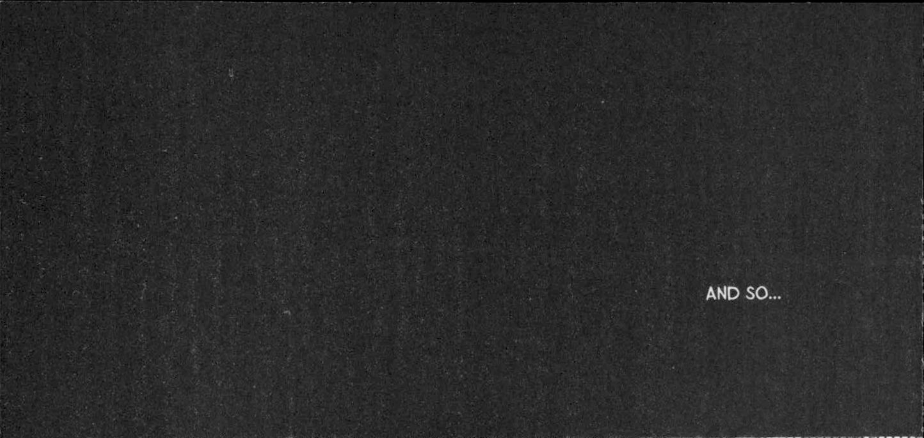
AND SO...

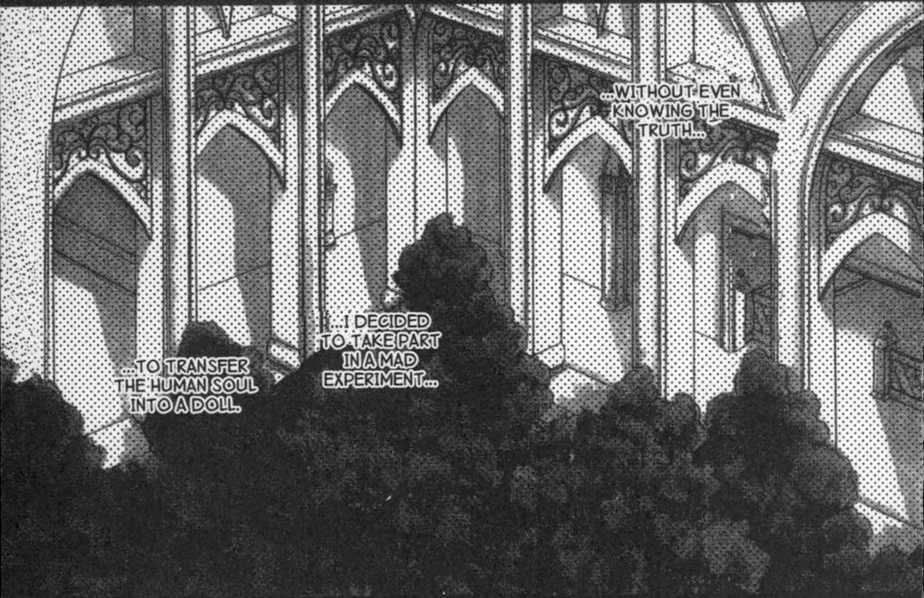
...WITHOUT EVEN KNOWING THE TRUTH...
...I DECIDED TO TAKE PART IN A MAD EXPERIMENT...
...TO TRANSFER THE HUMAN SOUL INTO A DOLL.

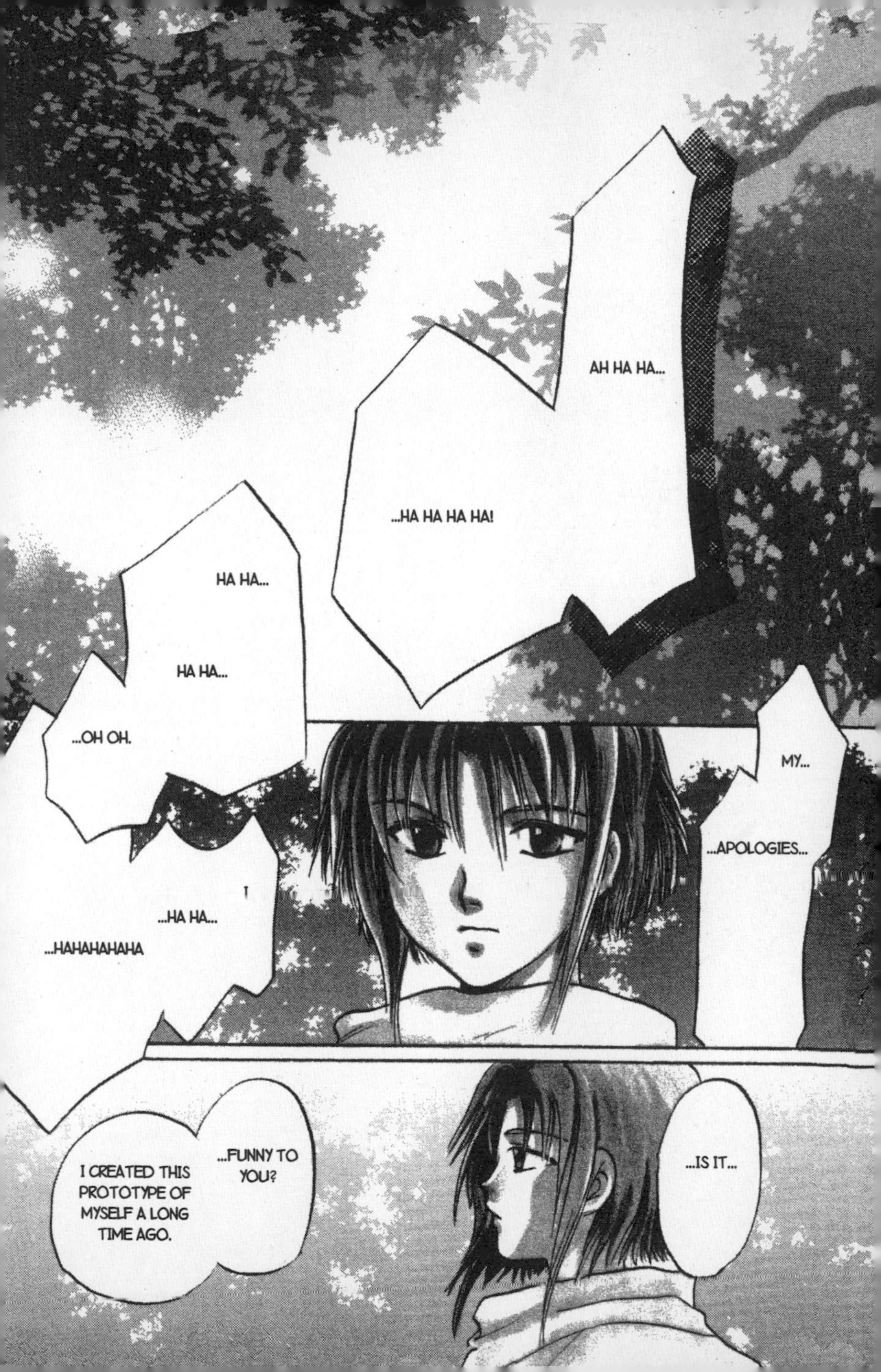
AH HA HA...
...HA HA HA HA!
HA HA...
HA HA...
...OH OH.
MY...
...APOLOGIES...
...HA HA...
...HAHAHAHAHA
...IS IT...
...FUNNY TO YOU?
I CREATED THIS PROTOTYPE OF MYSELF A LONG TIME AGO.

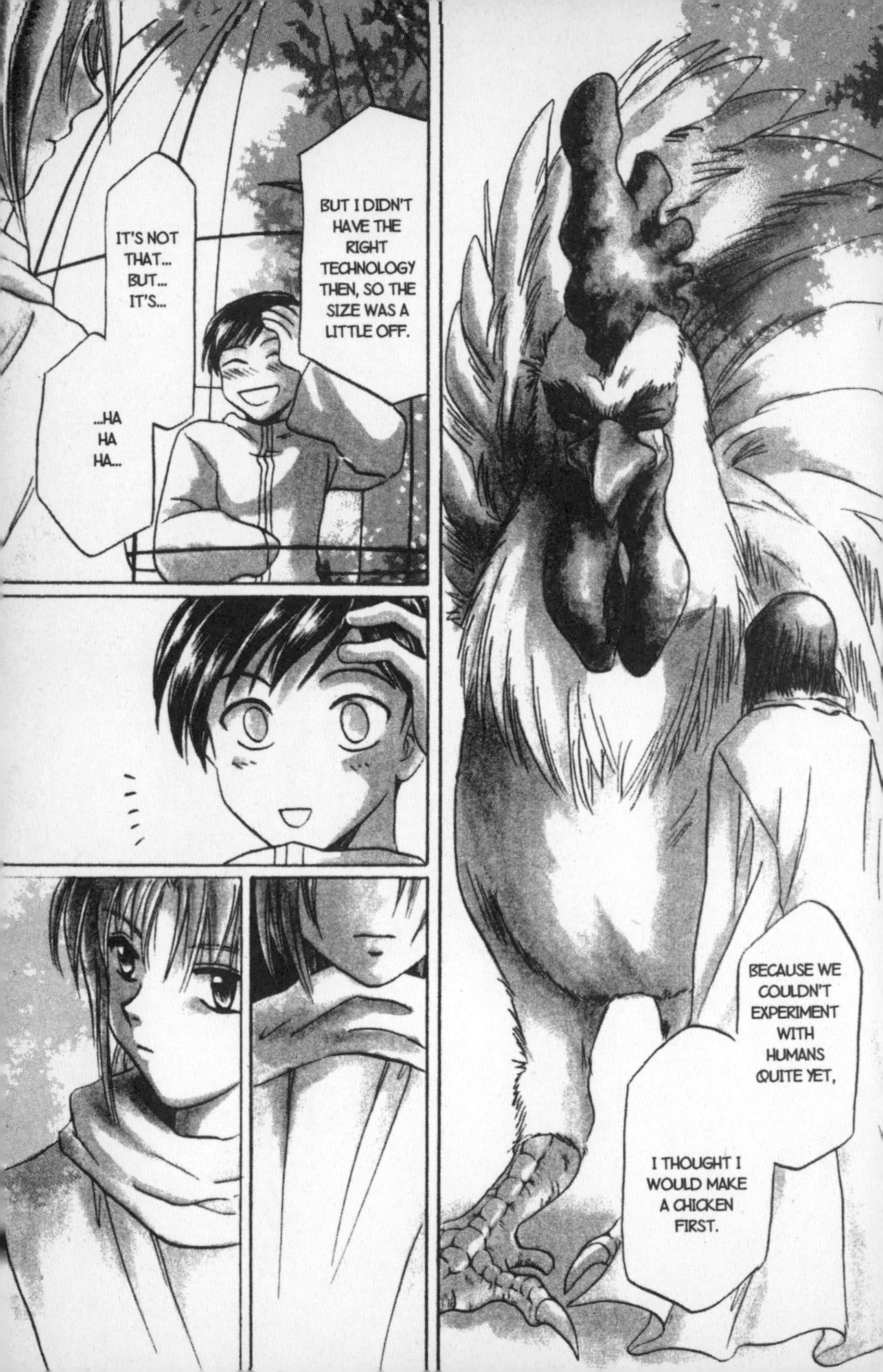
BECAUSE WE COULDN'T EXPERIMENT WITH HUMANS QUITE YET,
I THOUGHT I WOULD MAKE A CHICKEN FIRST.
BUT I DIDN'T HAVE THE RIGHT TECHNOLOGY THEN, SO THE SIZE WAS A LITTLE OFF.
IT'S NOT THAT... BUT... IT'S...
...HA HA HA...

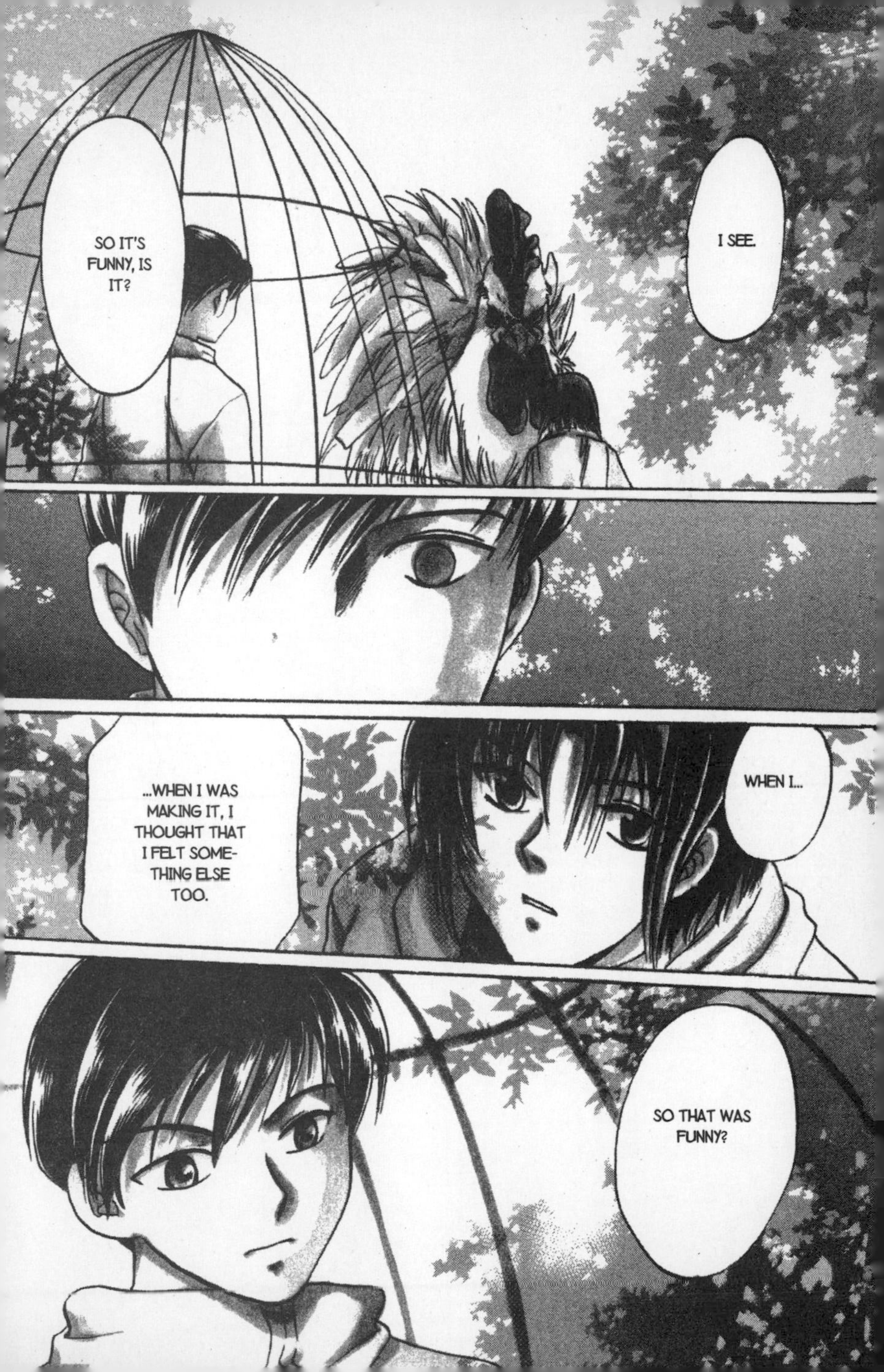
I SEE.
SO IT'S FUNNY, IS IT?
WHEN I...
...WHEN I WAS MAKING IT, I THOUGHT THAT I FELT SOME-THING ELSE TOO.
SO THAT WAS FUNNY?

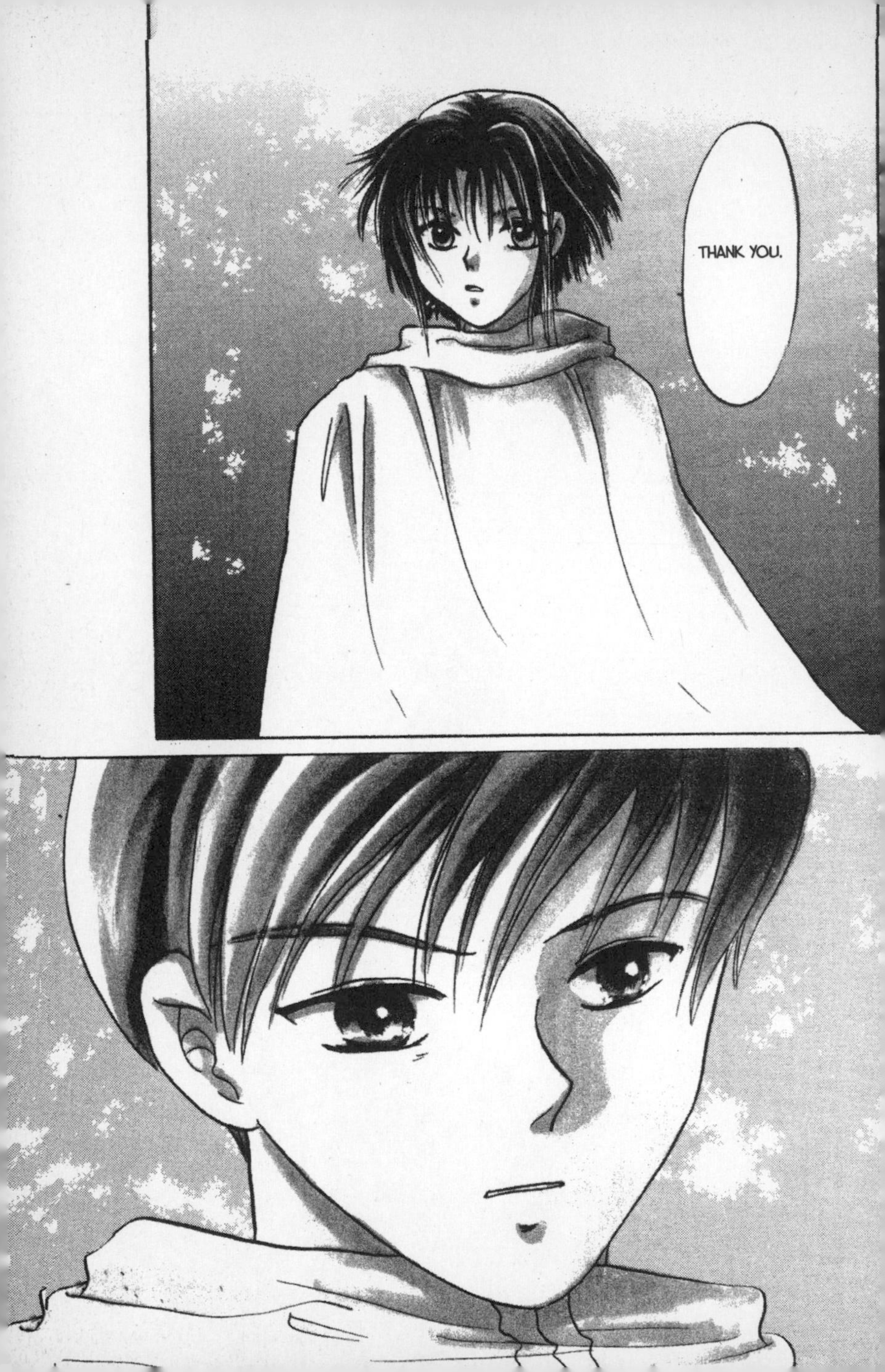
THANK YOU.

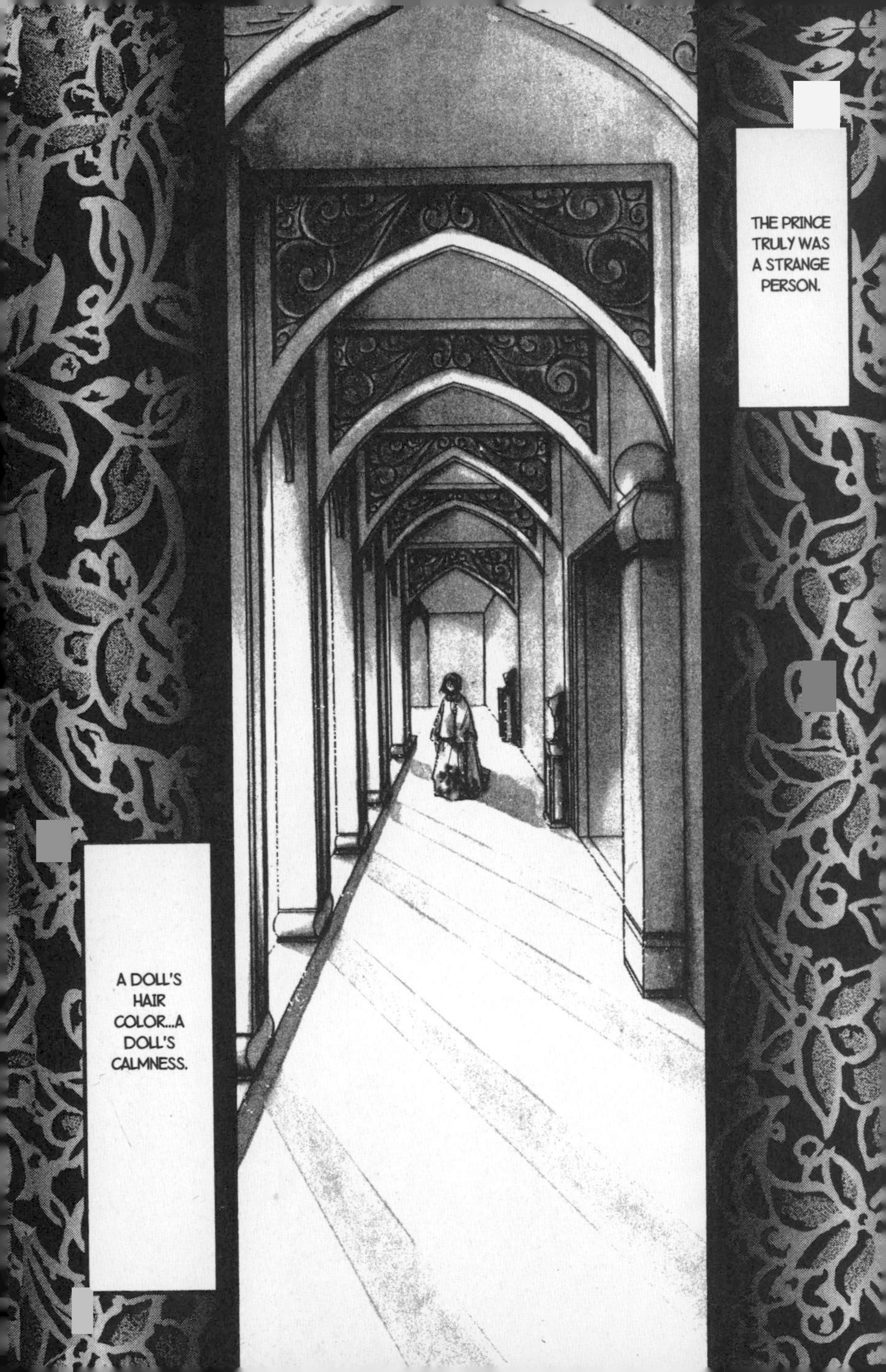
THE PRINCE TRULY WAS A STRANGE PERSON.
A DOLL'S HAIR COLOR...A DOLL'S CALMNESS.

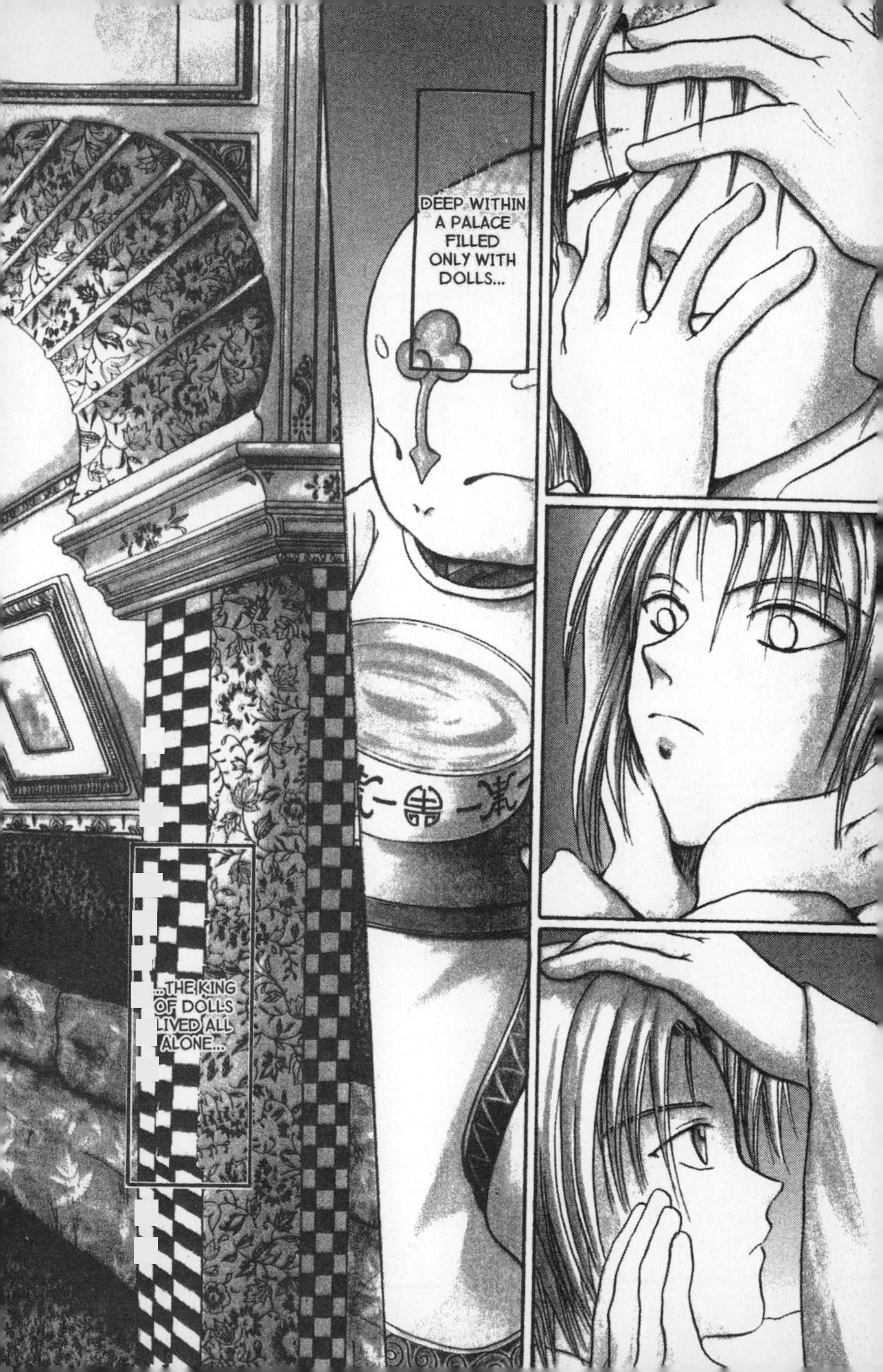
DEEP WITHIN A PALACE FILLED ONLY WITH DOLLS...
...THE KING OF DOLLS LIVED ALL ALONE...

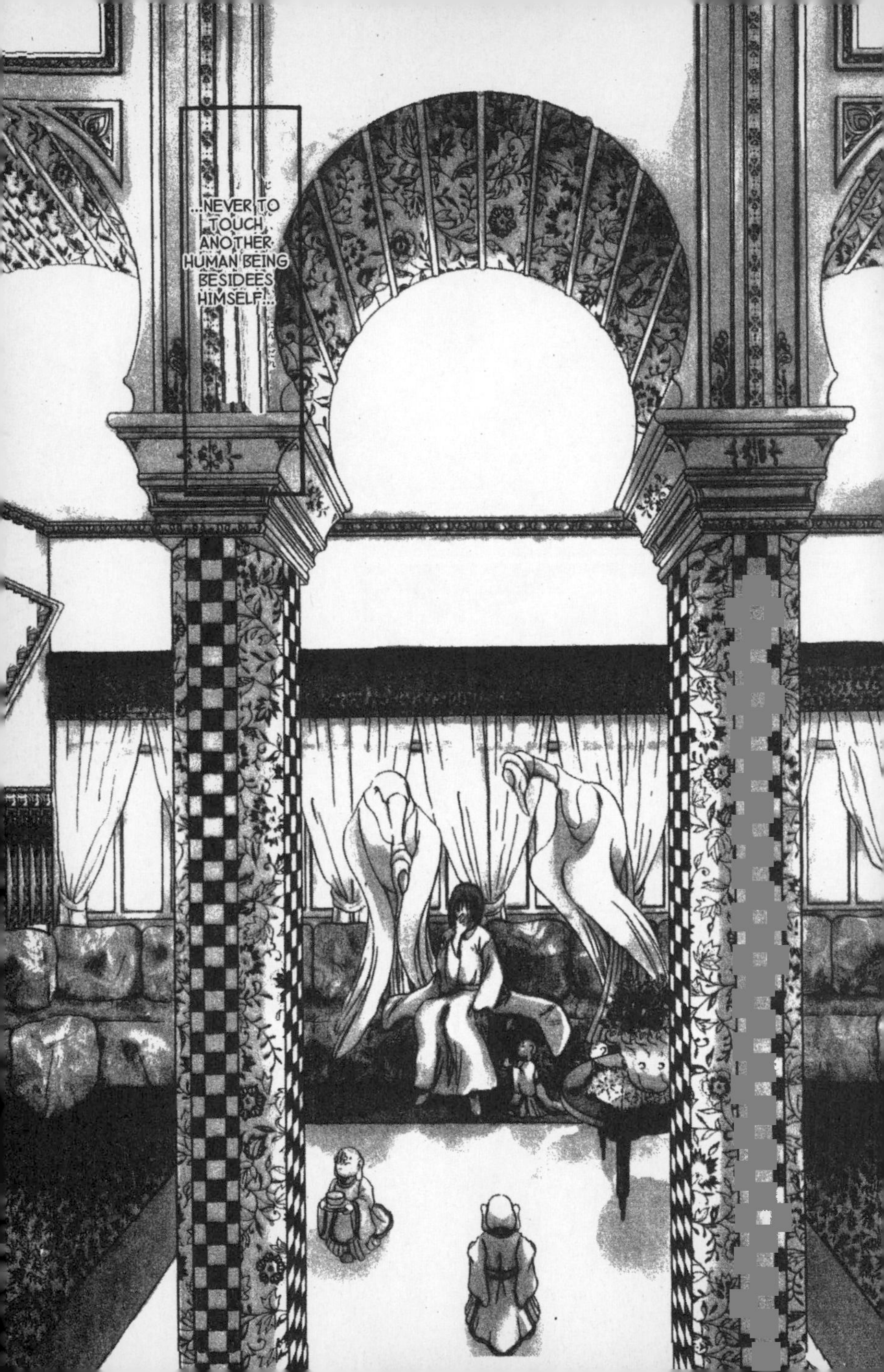
...NEVER TO TOUCH ANOTHER HUMAN BEING BESIDEES HIMSELF!...

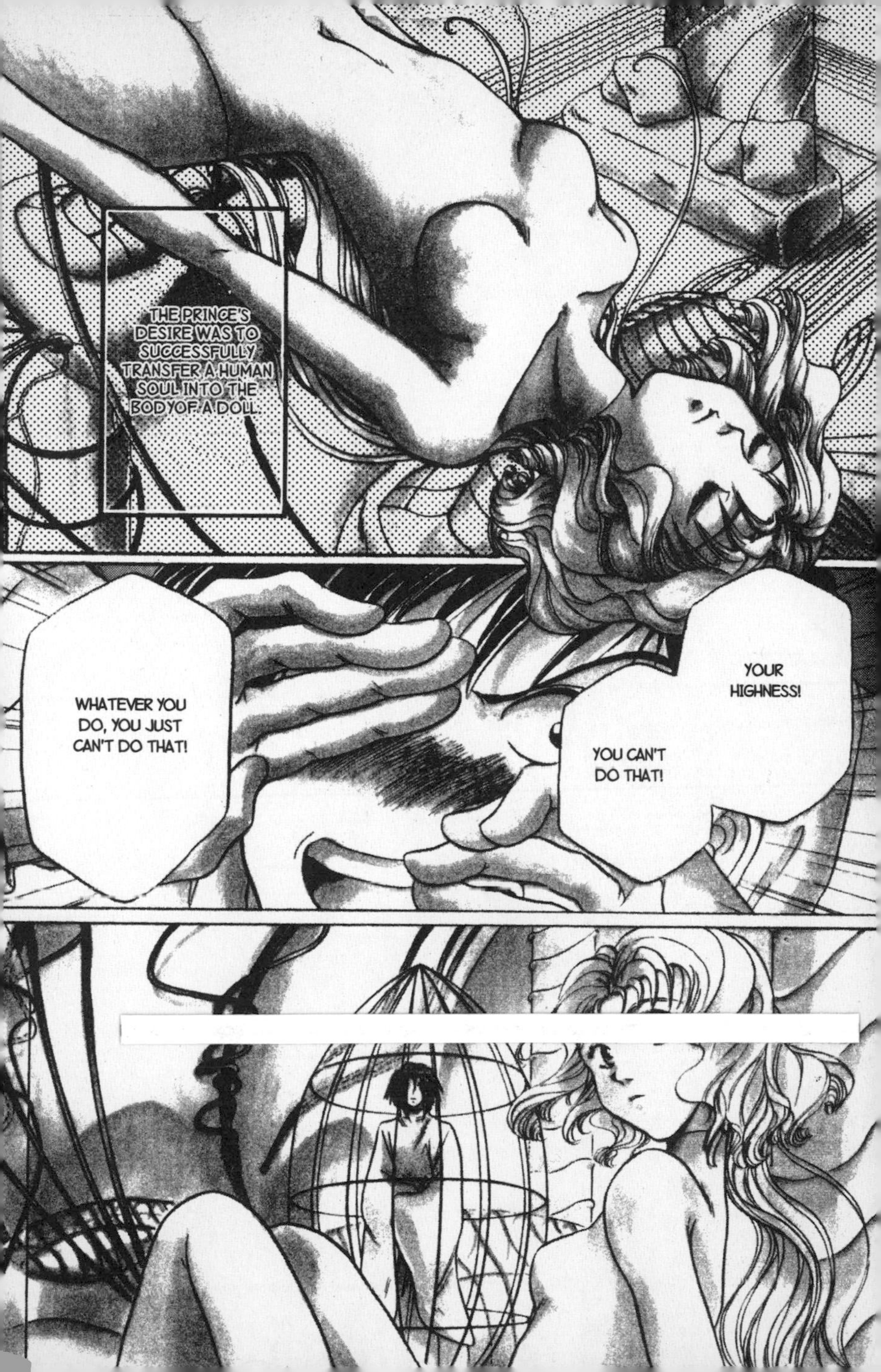
THE PRINCE'S DESIRE WAS TO SUCCESSFULLY TRANSFER A HUMAN SOUL INTO THE BODYOF A DOLL.
YOUR HIGHNESS!
YOU CAN'T DO THAT!
WHATEVER YOU DO, YOU JUST CAN'T DO THAT!

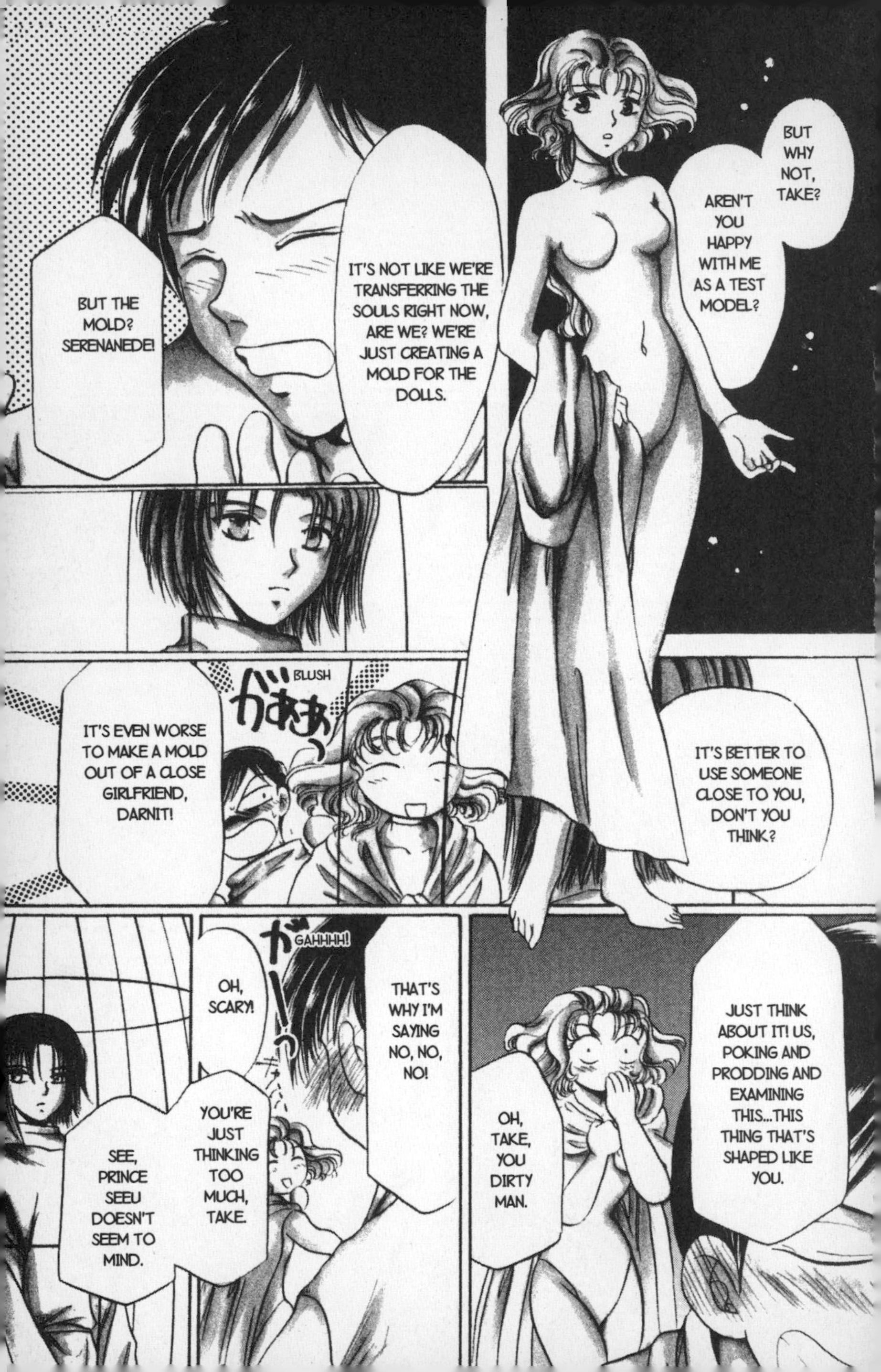

BUT WHY NOT, TAKE?
AREN'T YOU HAPPY WITH ME AS A TEST MODEL?
IT'S NOT LIKE WE'RE TRANSFERRING THE SOULS RIGHT NOW, ARE WE? WE'RE JUST CREATING A MOLD FOR THE DOLLS.
BUT THE MOLD? SERENANEDE!
IT'S BETTER TO USE SOMEONE CLOSE TO YOU, DON'T YOU THINK?
BLUSH
IT'S EVEN WORSE TO MAKE A MOLD OUT OF A CLOSE GIRLFRIEND, DARNIT!
JUST THINK ABOUT IT! US, POKING AND PRODDING AND EXAMINING THIS...THIS THING THAT'S SHAPED LIKE YOU.
OH, TAKE, YOU DIRTY MAN.
GAHHHH!
THAT'S WHY I'M SAYING NO, NO, NO!
OH, SCARY!
YOU'RE JUST THINKING TOO MUCH, TAKE.
SEE, PRINCE SEEU DOESN'T SEEM TO MIND.

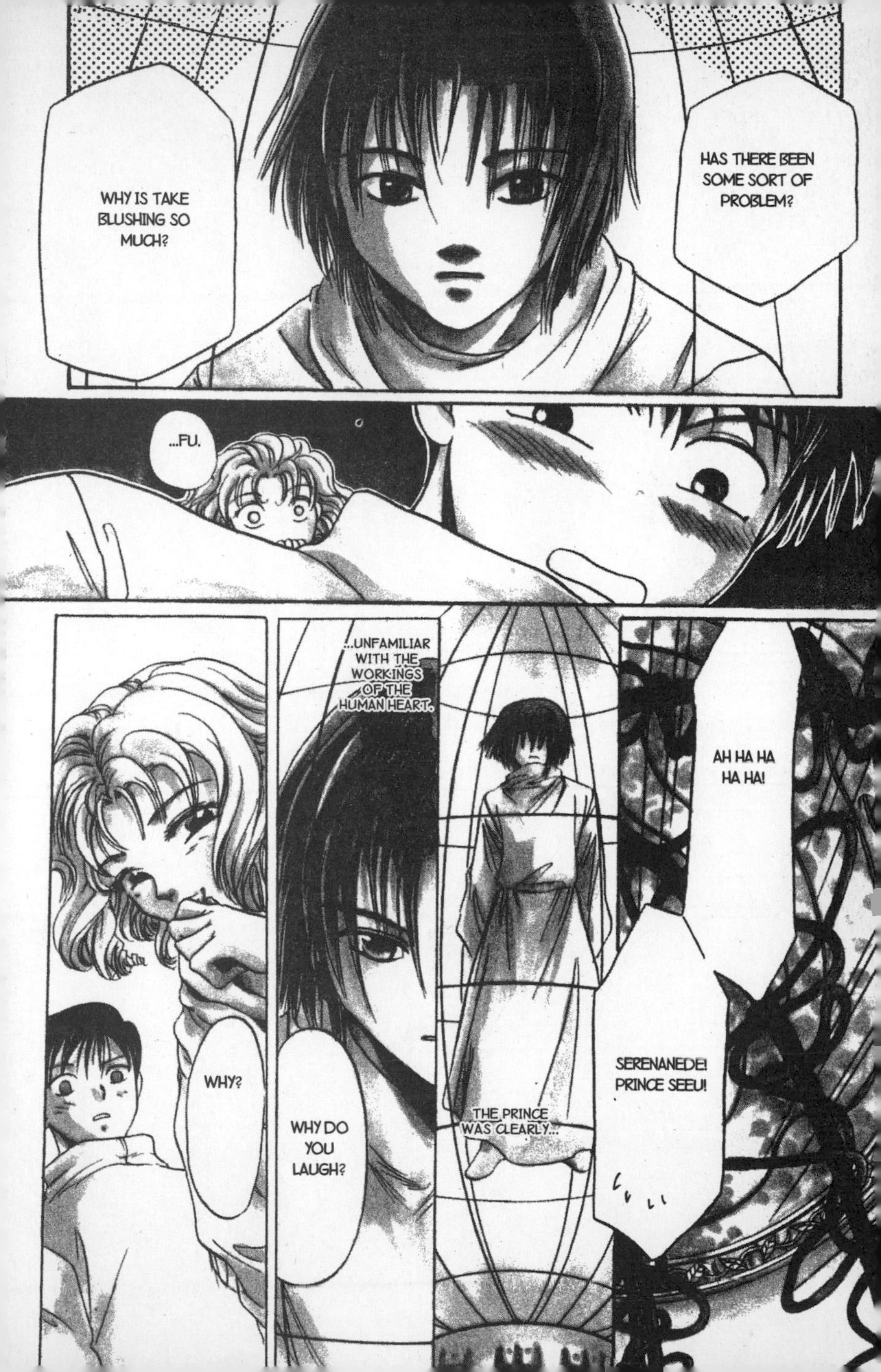
HAS THERE BEEN SOME SORT OF PROBLEM?
WHY IS TAKE BLUSHING SO MUCH?
...FU.
AH HA HA HA HA!
SERENANEDE! PRINCE SEEU!
THE PRINCE WAS CLEARLY...
...UNFAMILIAR WITH THE WORKINGS OF THE HUMAN HEART.
WHY DO YOU LAUGH?
WHY?

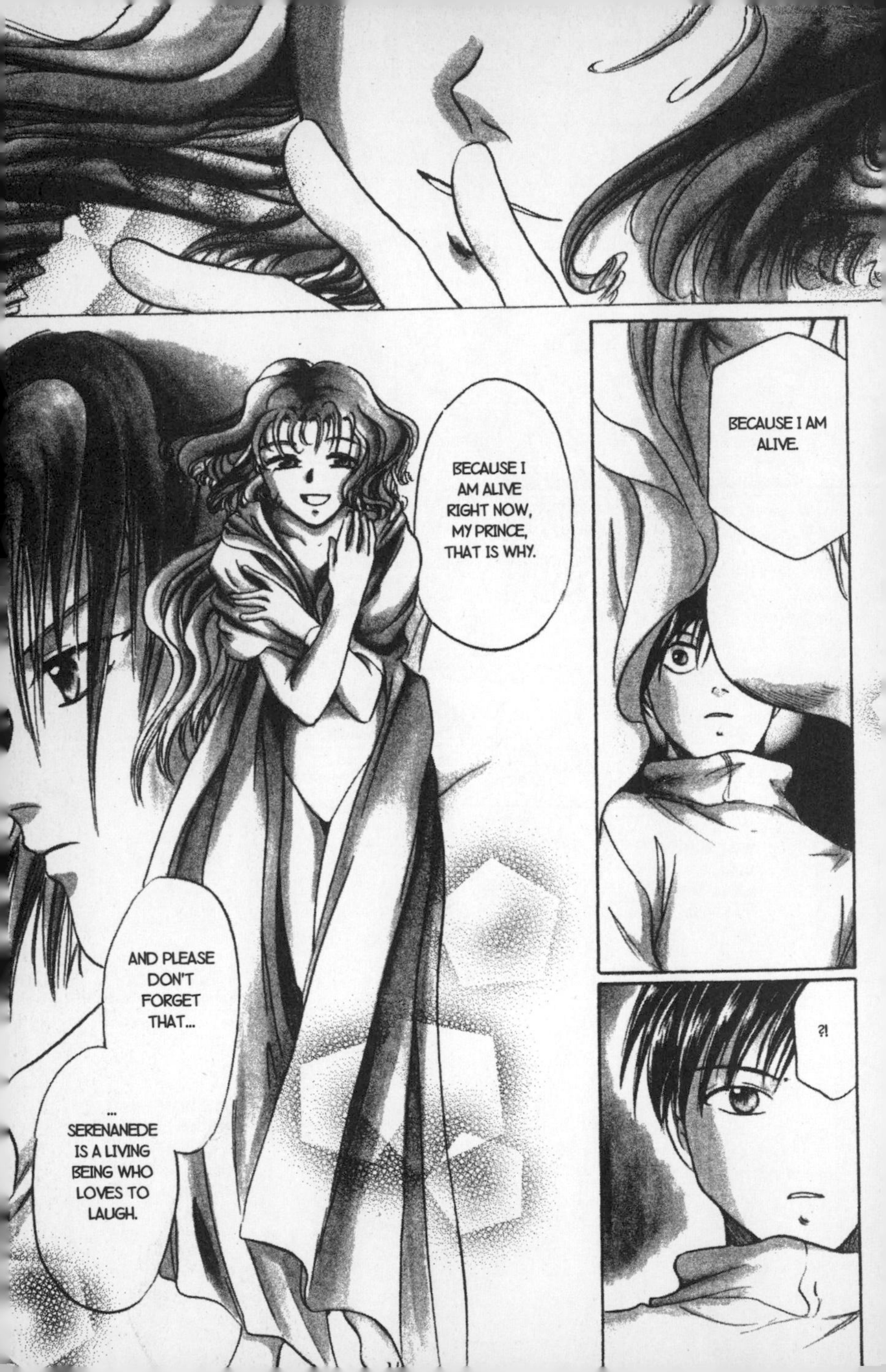
BECAUSE I AM ALIVE.
?!
BECAUSE I AM ALIVE RIGHT NOW, MY PRINCE, THAT IS WHY.
AND PLEASE DON'T FORGET THAT...
... SERENANEDE IS A LIVING BEING WHO LOVES TO LAUGH.

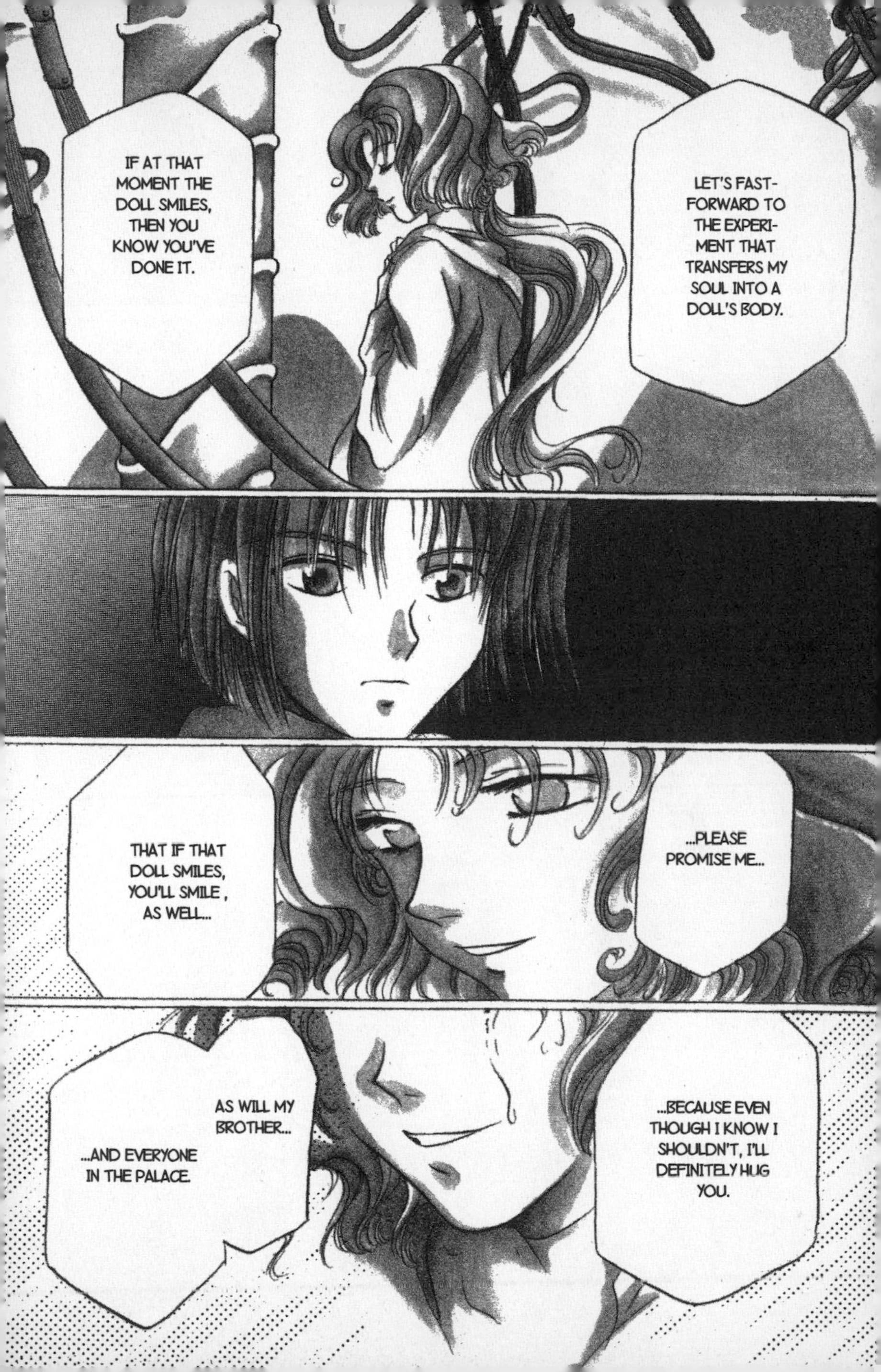
LET'S FAST-FORWARD TO THE EXPERIMENT THAT TRANSFERS MY SOUL INTO A DOLL'S BODY.
IF AT THAT MOMENT THE DOLL SMILES, THEN YOU KNOW YOU'VE DONE IT.
...PLEASE PROMISE ME...
THAT IF THAT DOLL SMILES, YOU'LL SMILE , AS WELL...
...BECAUSE EVEN THOUGH I KNOW I SHOULDN'T, I'LL DEFINITELY HUG YOU.
AS WILL MY BROTHER...
...AND EVERYONE IN THE PALACE.

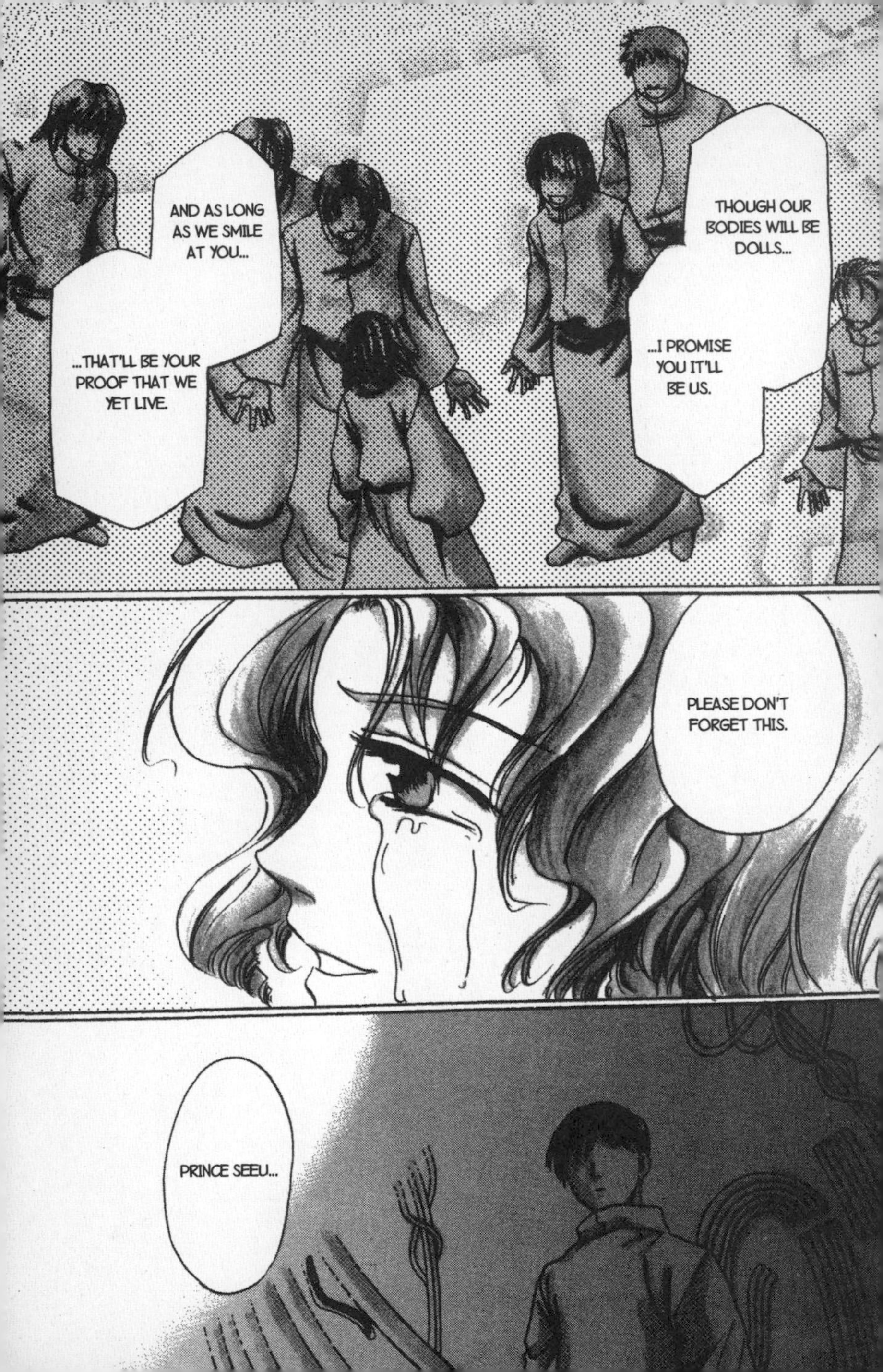
THOUGH OUR BODIES WILL BE DOLLS...
...I PROMISE YOU IT'LL BE US.
AND AS LONG AS WE SMILE AT YOU...
...THAT'LL BE YOUR PROOF THAT WE YET LIVE.
PLEASE DON'T FORGET THIS.
PRINCE SEEU...

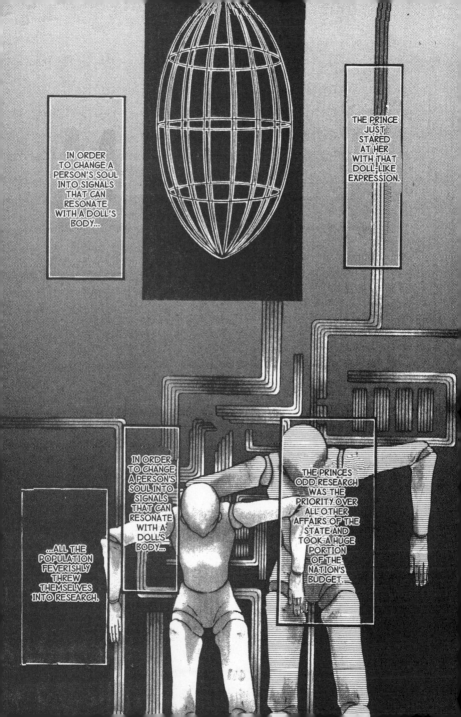

IN ORDER TO CHANGE A PERSON'S SOUL INTO SIGNALS THAT CAN RESONATE WITH A DOLL'S BODY...

THE PRINCE JUST STARED AT HER WITH THAT DOLL-LIKE EXPRESSION.

IN ORDER TO CHANGE A PERSON'S SOUL INTO SIGNALS THAT CAN RESONATE WITH A DOLL'S BODY...

THE PRINCE'S ODD RESEARCH WAS THE PRIORITY OVER ALL OTHER AFFAIRS OF THE STATE AND TOOK A HUGE PORTION OF THE NATION'S BUDGET.

...ALL THE POPULATION FEVERISHLY THREW THEMSELVES INTO RESEARCH.

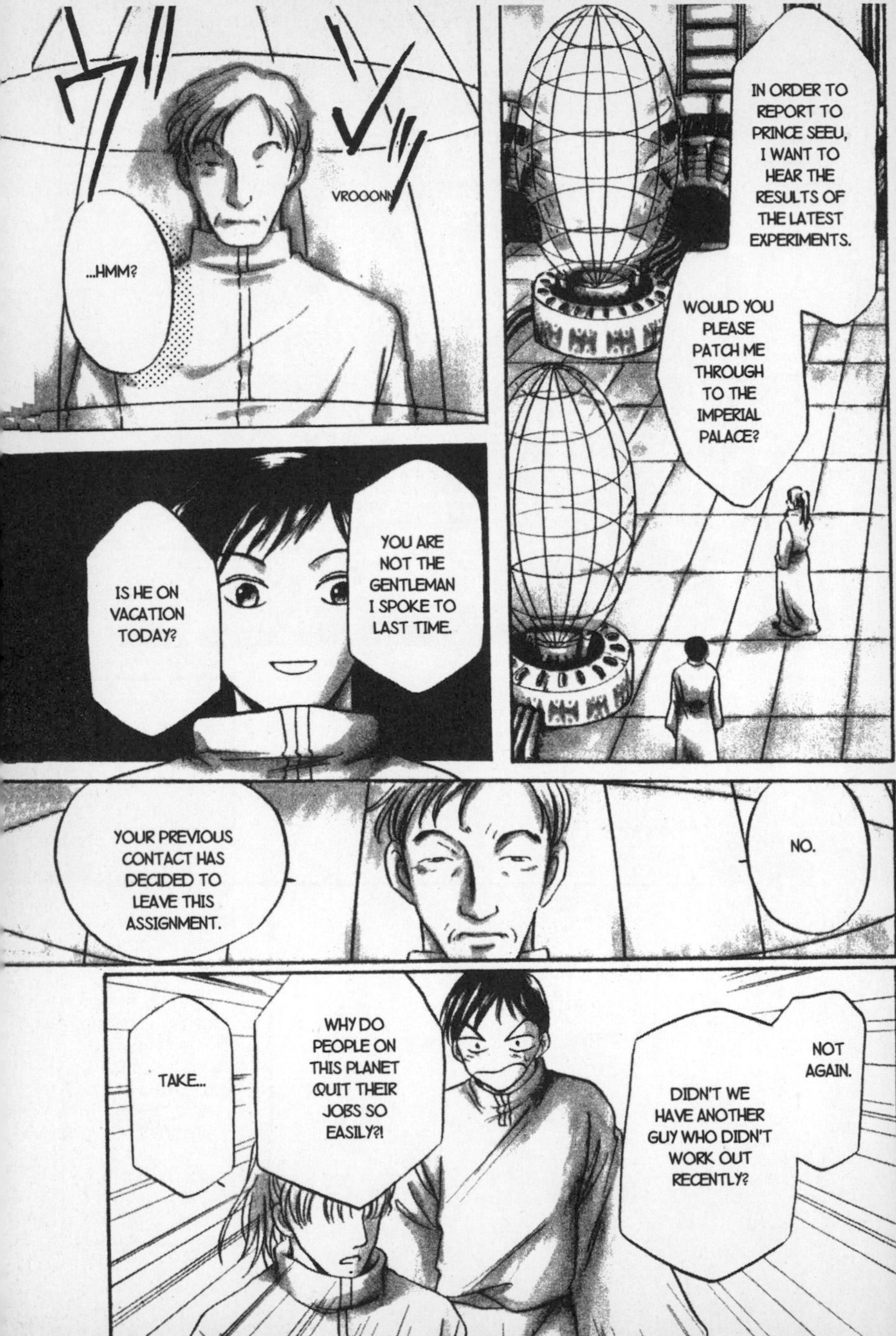
IN ORDER TO REPORT TO PRINCE SEEU, I WANT TO HEAR THE RESULTS OF THE LATEST EXPERIMENTS.
WOULD YOU PLEASE PATCH ME THROUGH TO THE IMPERIAL PALACE?
VROOONN
...HMM?
YOU ARE NOT THE GENTLEMAN I SPOKE TO LAST TIME.
IS HE ON VACATION TODAY?
NO.
YOUR PREVIOUS CONTACT HAS DECIDED TO LEAVE THIS ASSIGNMENT.
NOT AGAIN.
DIDN'T WE HAVE ANOTHER GUY WHO DIDN'T WORK OUT RECENTLY?
WHY DO PEOPLE ON THIS PLANET QUIT THEIR JOBS SO EASILY?!
TAKE...

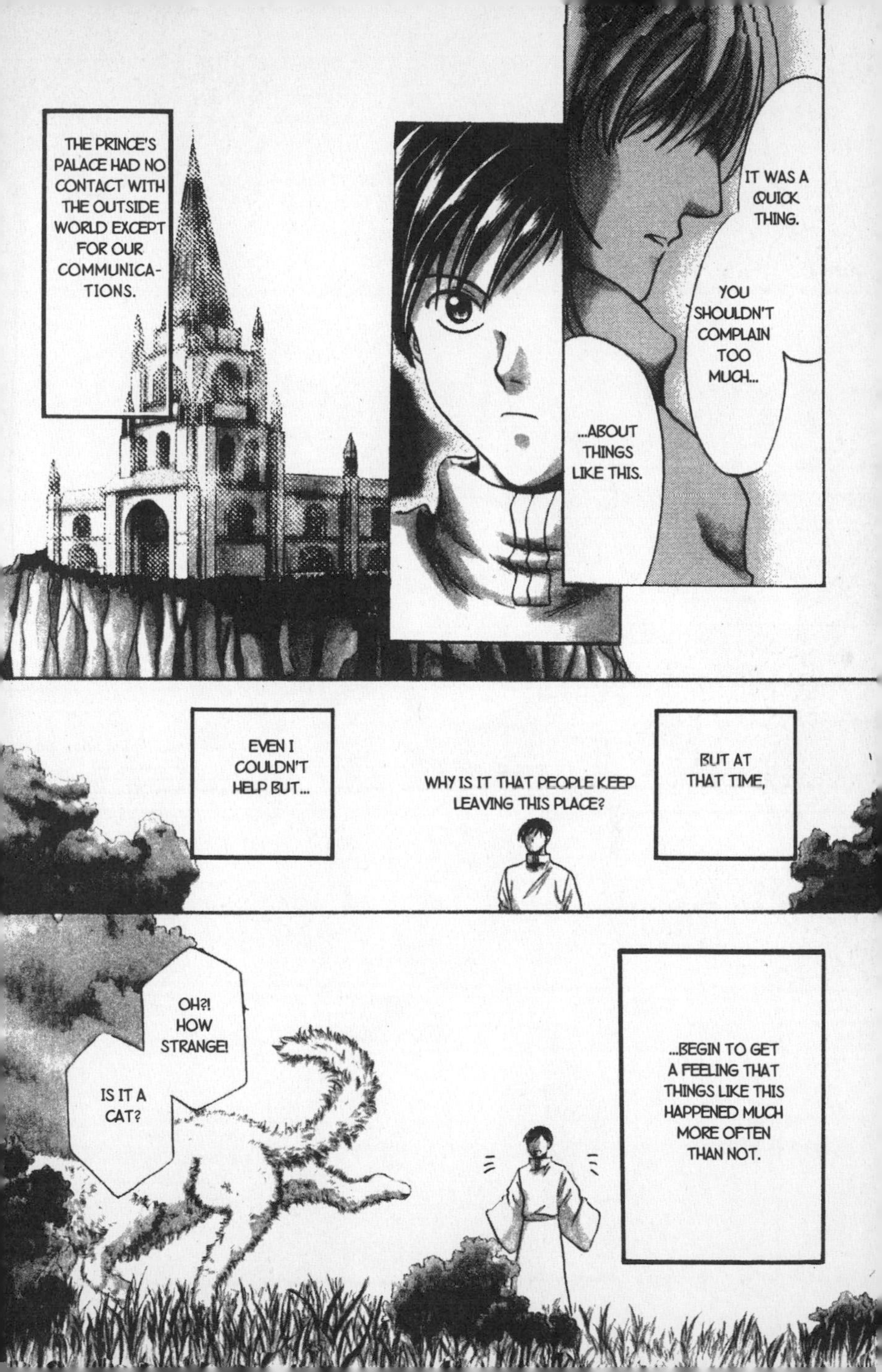
IT WAS A QUICK THING.
YOU SHOULDN'T COMPLAIN TOO MUCH...
...ABOUT THINGS LIKE THIS.
THE PRINCE'S PALACE HAD NO CONTACT WITH THE OUTSIDE WORLD EXCEPT FOR OUR COMMUNICA-TIONS.
BUT AT THAT TIME,
WHY IS IT THAT PEOPLE KEEP LEAVING THIS PLACE?
EVEN I COULDN'T HELP BUT...
...BEGIN TO GET A FEELING THAT THINGS LIKE THIS HAPPENED MUCH MORE OFTEN THAN NOT.
OH?! HOW STRANGE!
IS IT A CAT?

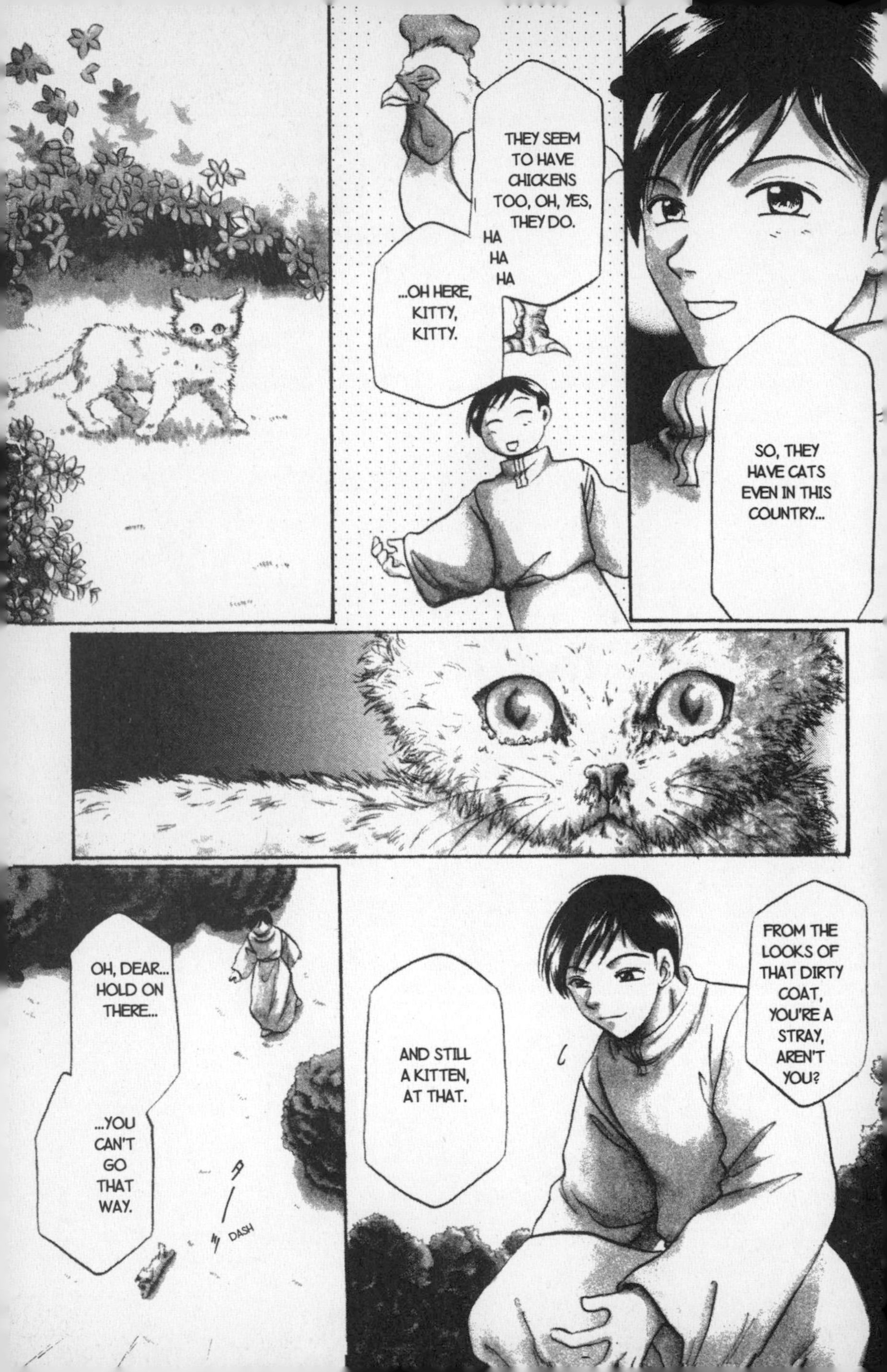
SO, THEY HAVE CATS EVEN IN THIS COUNTRY...
THEY SEEM TO HAVE CHICKENS TOO, OH, YES, THEY DO.
HA HA HA
...OH HERE, KITTY, KITTY.
FROM THE LOOKS OF THAT DIRTY COAT, YOU'RE A STRAY, AREN'T YOU?
AND STILL A KITTEN, AT THAT.
OH, DEAR... HOLD ON THERE...
...YOU CAN'T GO THAT WAY.
DASH

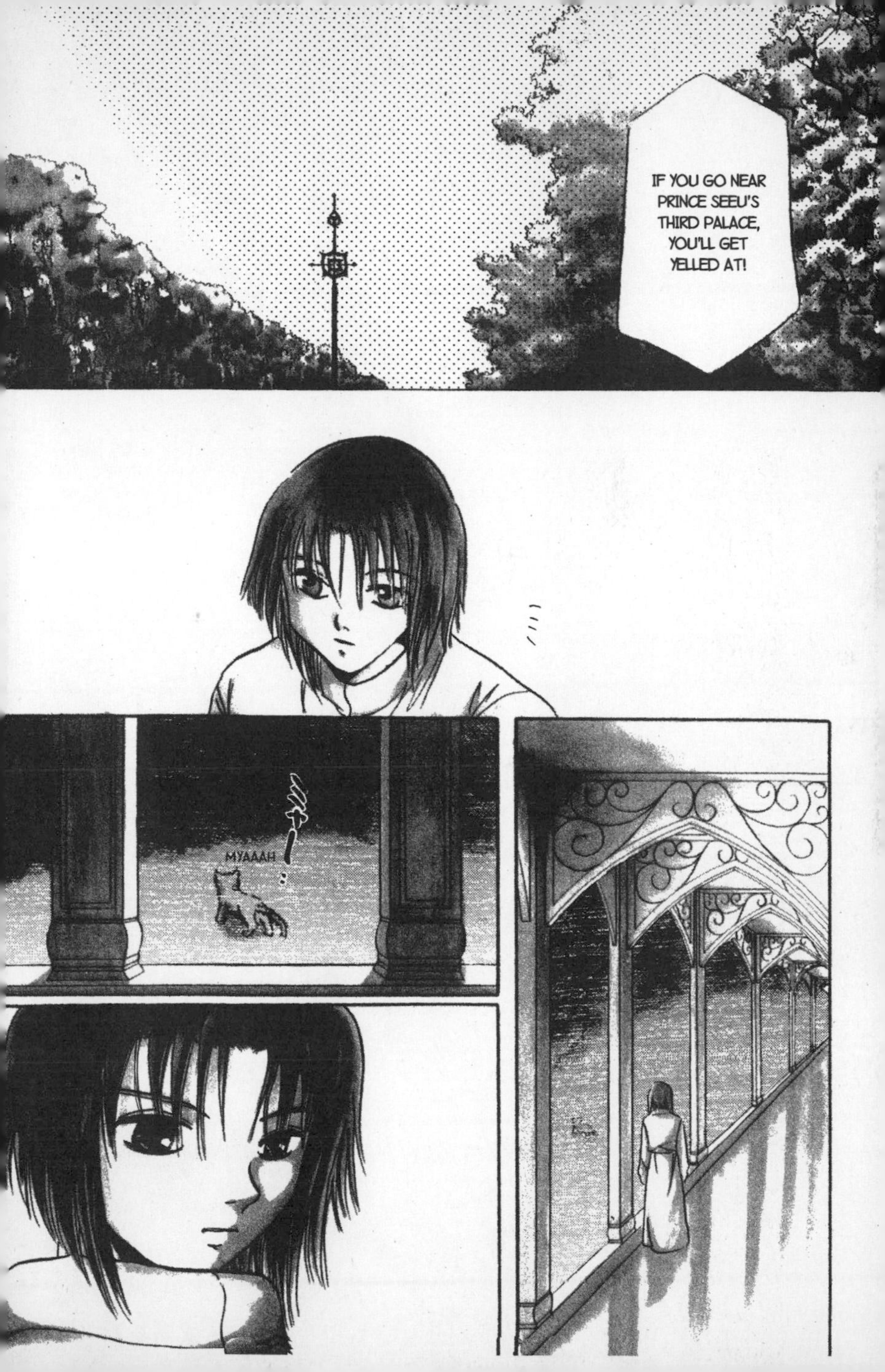
IF YOU GO NEAR PRINCE SEEU'S THIRD PALACE, YOU'LL GET YELLED AT!
MYAAAH

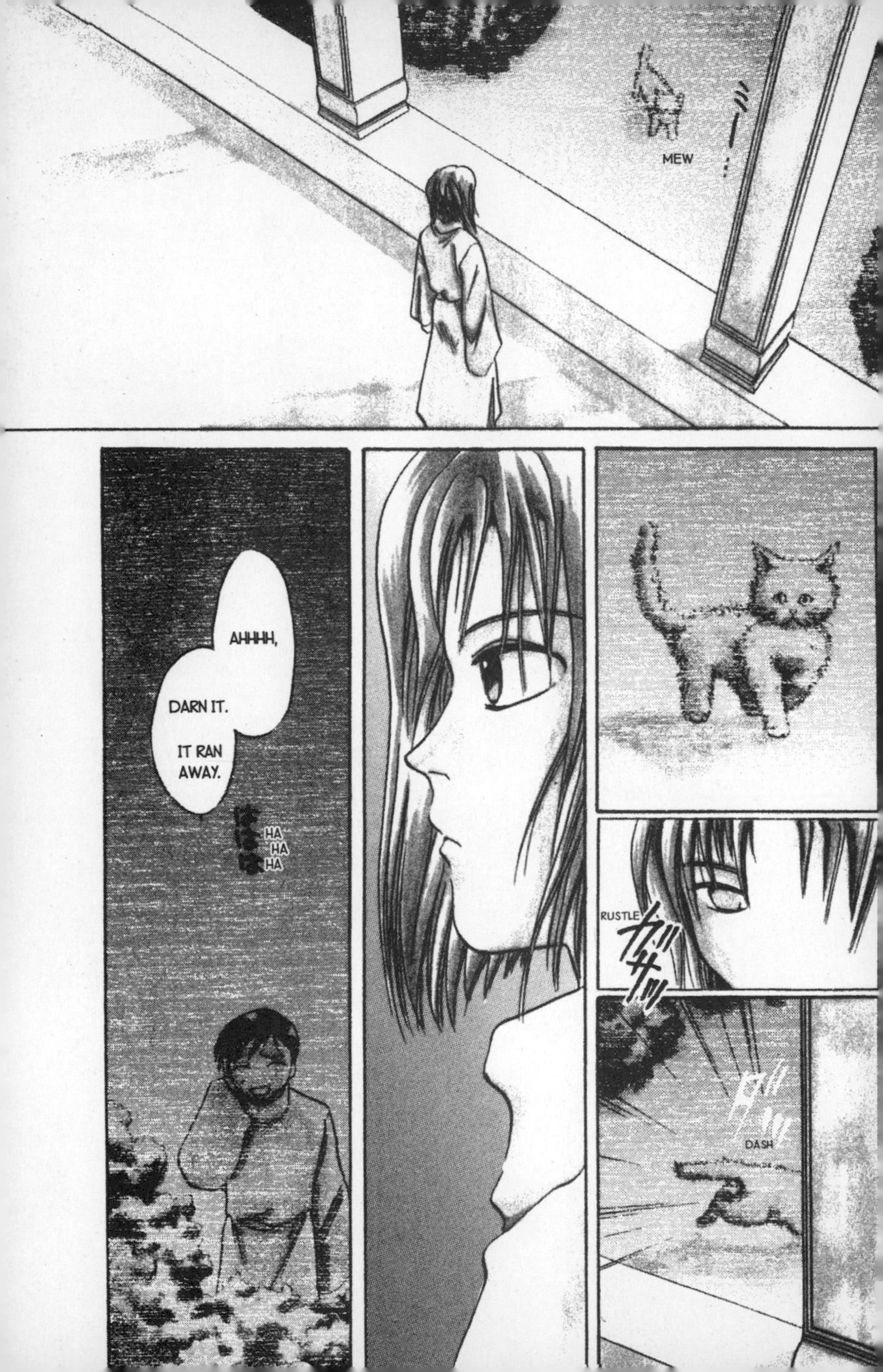
MEW
RUSTLE
DASH
AHHHH,
DARN IT.
IT RAN AWAY.
HA HA HA

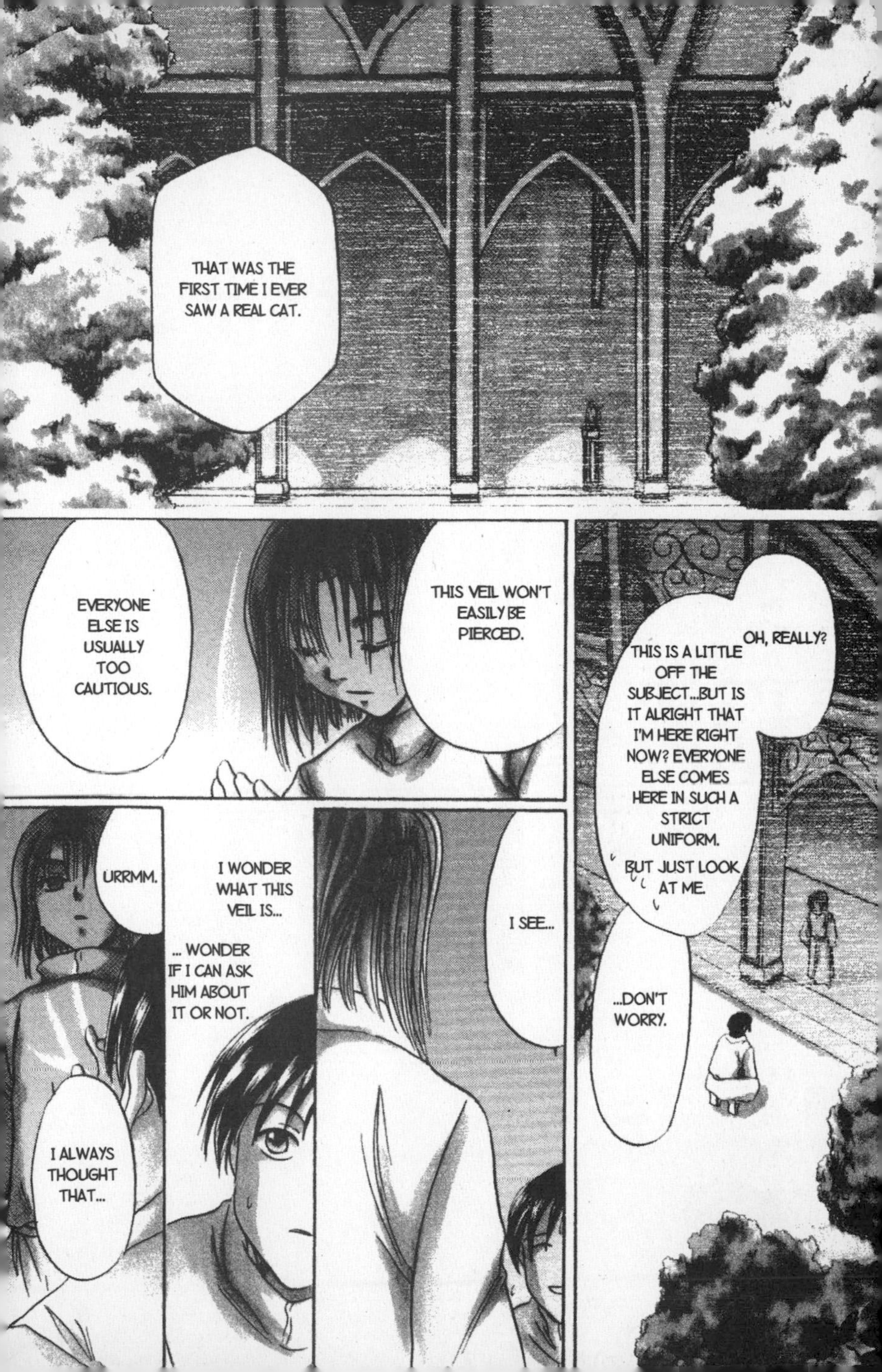
THAT WAS THE FIRST TIME I EVER SAW A REAL CAT.
OH, REALLY?
THIS IS A LITTLE OFF THE SUBJECT...BUT IS IT ALRIGHT THAT I'M HERE RIGHT NOW? EVERYONE ELSE COMES HERE IN SUCH A STRICT UNIFORM.
BUT JUST LOOK AT ME.
...DON'T WORRY.
THIS VEIL WON'T EASILY BE PIERCED.
EVERYONE ELSE IS USUALLY TOO CAUTIOUS.
I SEE...
I WONDER WHAT THIS VEIL IS...
... WONDER IF I CAN ASK HIM ABOUT IT OR NOT.
URRMM.
I ALWAYS THOUGHT THAT...

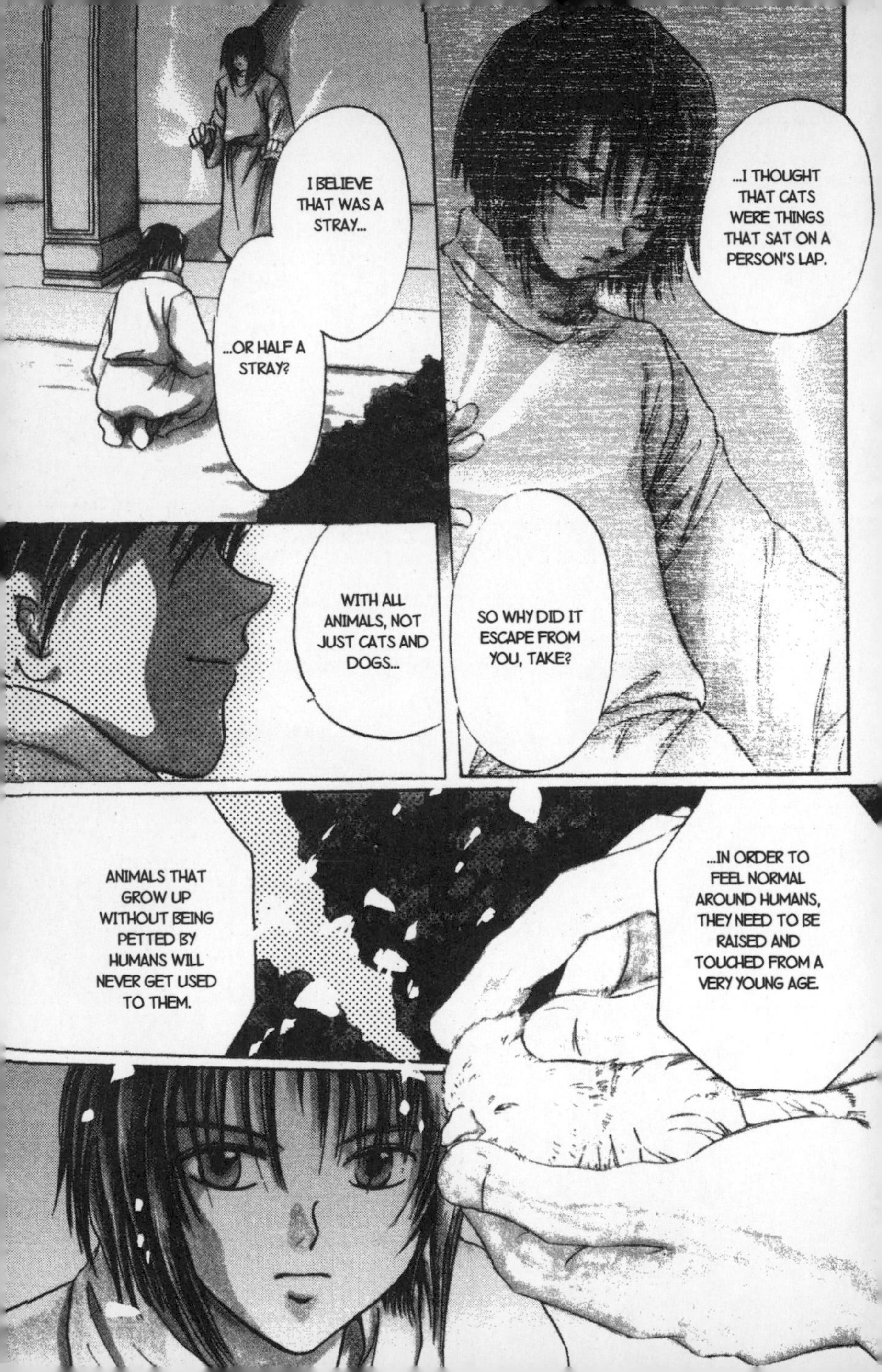
...I THOUGHT THAT CATS WERE THINGS THAT SAT ON A PERSON'S LAP.
SO WHY DID IT ESCAPE FROM YOU, TAKE?
I BELIEVE THAT WAS A STRAY...
...OR HALF A STRAY?
WITH ALL ANIMALS, NOT JUST CATS AND DOGS...
ANIMALS THAT GROW UP WITHOUT BEING PETTED BY HUMANS WILL NEVER GET USED TO THEM.
...IN ORDER TO FEEL NORMAL AROUND HUMANS, THEY NEED TO BE RAISED AND TOUCHED FROM A VERY YOUNG AGE.

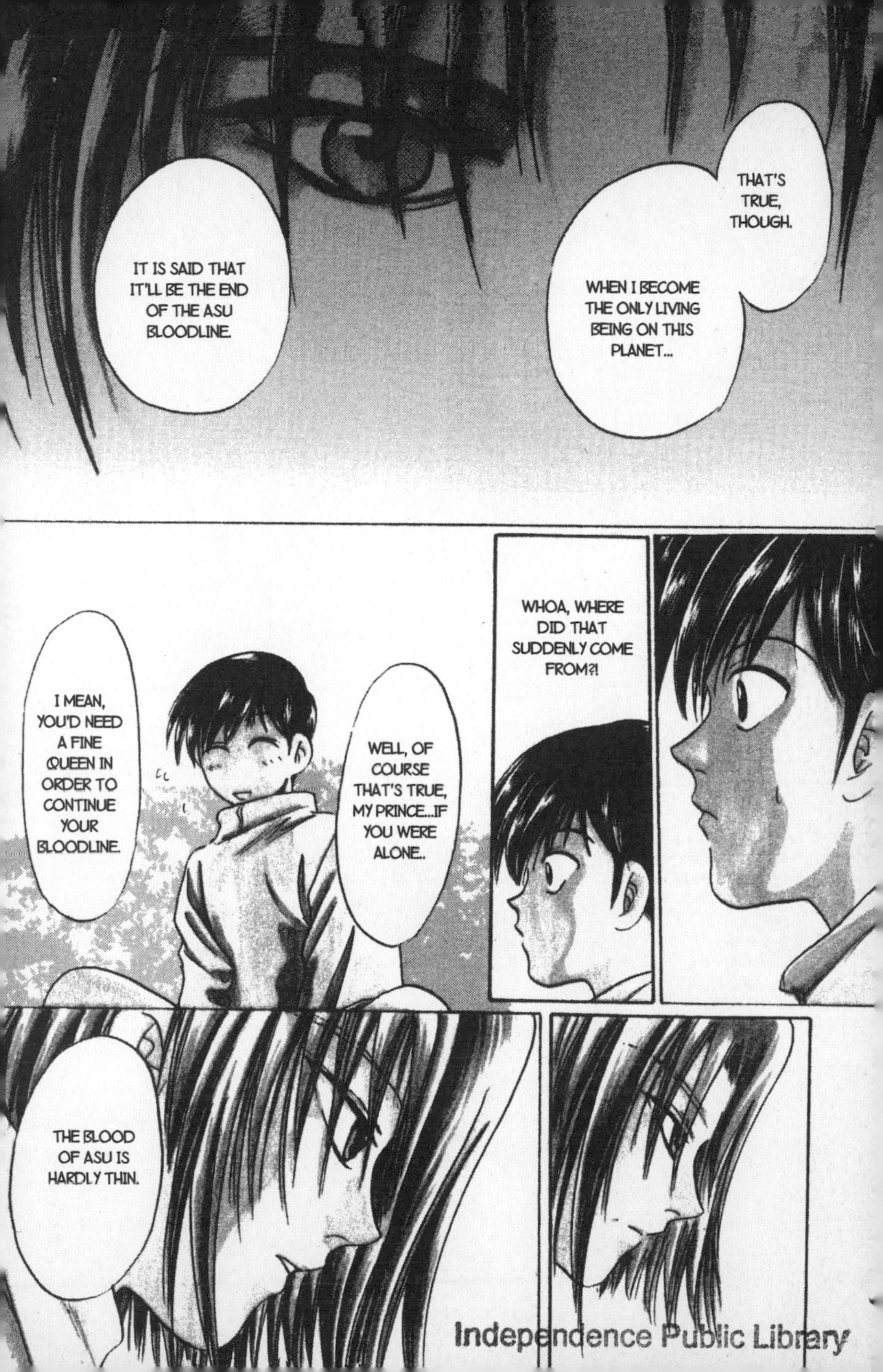
THAT'S TRUE, THOUGH.
WHEN I BECOME THE ONLY LIVING BEING ON THIS PLANET...
IT IS SAID THAT IT'LL BE THE END OF THE ASU BLOODLINE.
WHOA, WHERE DID THAT SUDDENLY COME FROM?!
WELL, OF COURSE THAT'S TRUE, MY PRINCE...IF YOU WERE ALONE..
I MEAN, YOU'D NEED A FINE QUEEN IN ORDER TO CONTINUE YOUR BLOODLINE.
THE BLOOD OF ASU IS HARDLY THIN.

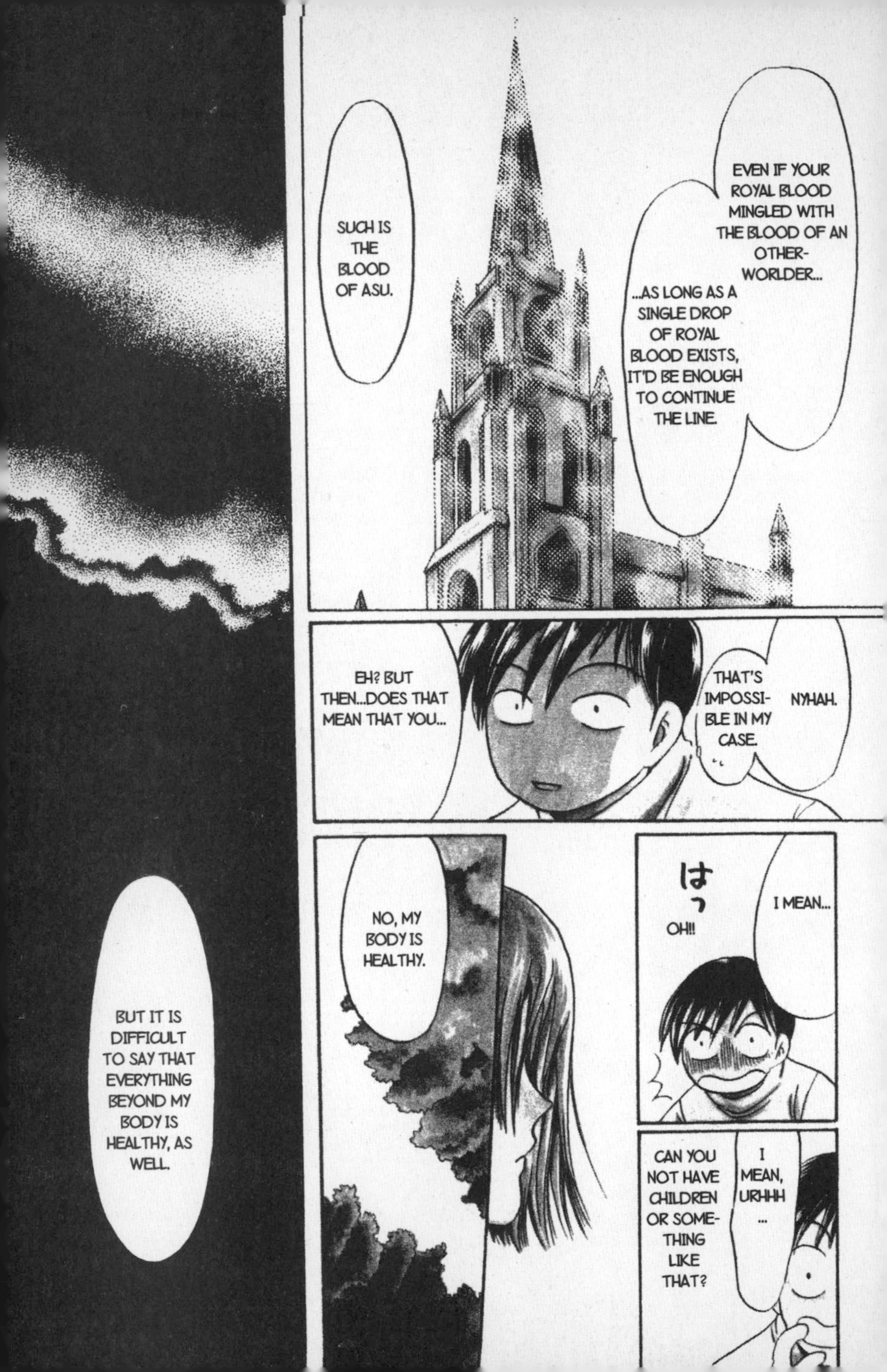
EVEN IF YOUR ROYAL BLOOD MINGLED WITH THE BLOOD OF AN OTHER-WORLDER...
...AS LONG AS A SINGLE DROP OF ROYAL BLOOD EXISTS, IT'D BE ENOUGH TO CONTINUE THE LINE.
SUCH IS THE BLOOD OF ASU.
NYHAH.
THAT'S IMPOSSI-BLE IN MY CASE.
EH? BUT THEN...DOES THAT MEAN THAT YOU...
I MEAN...
はっ
OH!!
I MEAN, URHHH ...
CAN YOU NOT HAVE CHILDREN OR SOME-THING LIKE THAT?
NO, MY BODY IS HEALTHY.
BUT IT IS DIFFICULT TO SAY THAT EVERYTHING BEYOND MY BODY IS HEALTHY, AS WELL.

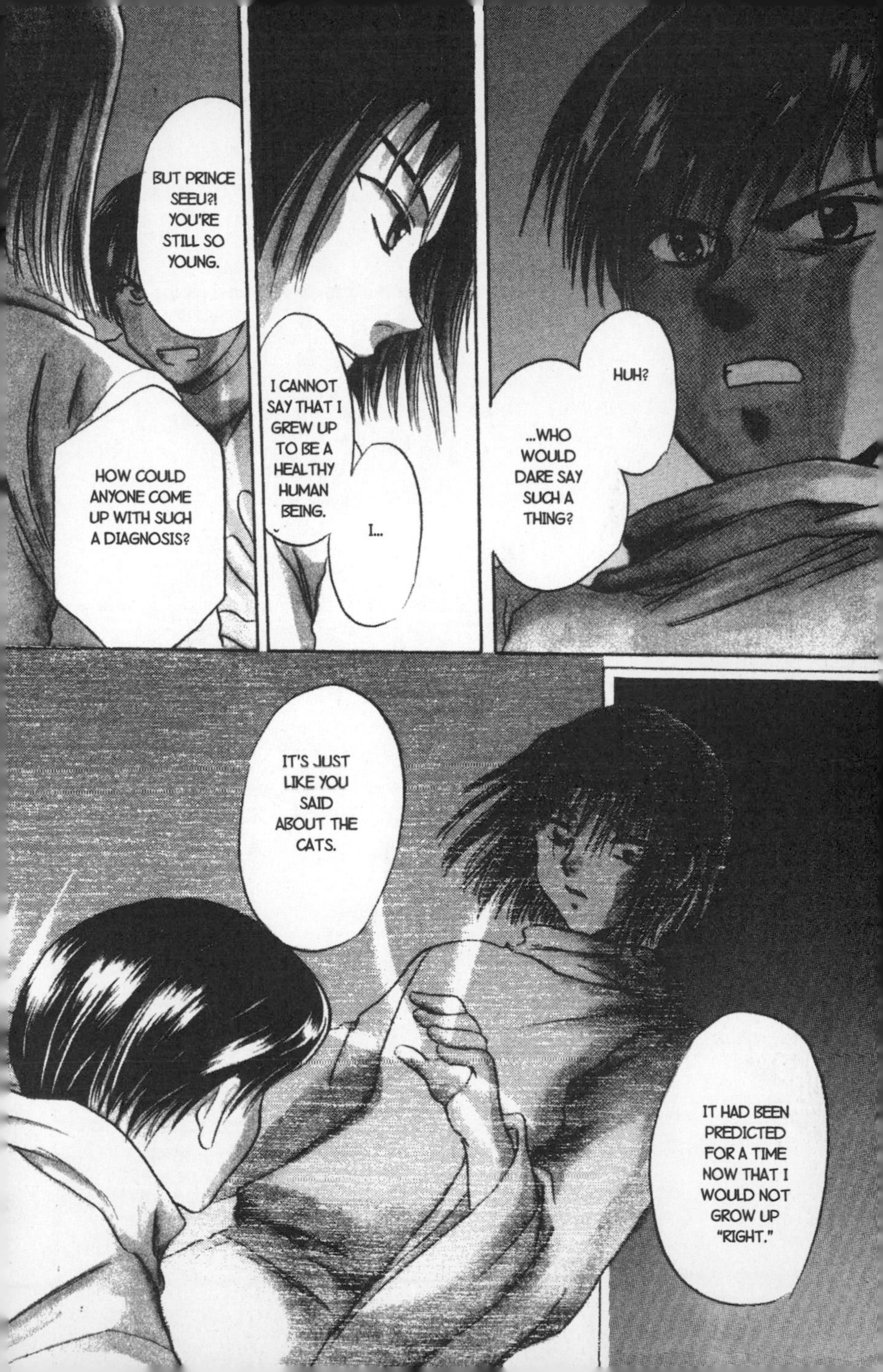
HUH?
...WHO WOULD DARE SAY SUCH A THING?
I...
I CANNOT SAY THAT I GREW UP TO BE A HEALTHY HUMAN BEING.
BUT PRINCE SEEU?! YOU'RE STILL SO YOUNG.
HOW COULD ANYONE COME UP WITH SUCH A DIAGNOSIS?
IT HAD BEEN PREDICTED FOR A TIME NOW THAT I WOULD NOT GROW UP "RIGHT."
IT'S JUST LIKE YOU SAID ABOUT THE CATS.

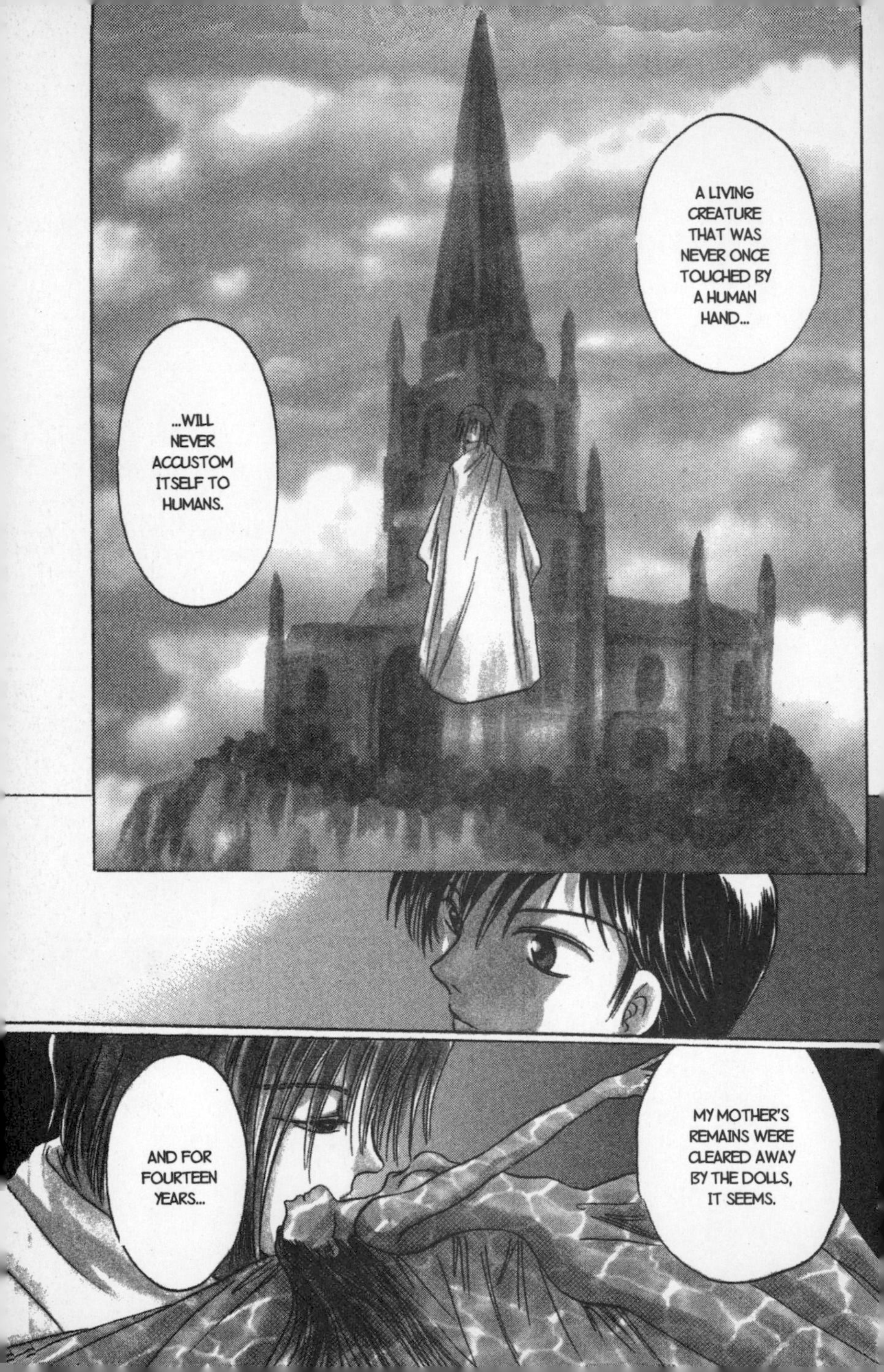
A LIVING CREATURE THAT WAS NEVER ONCE TOUCHED BY A HUMAN HAND...
...WILL NEVER ACCUSTOM ITSELF TO HUMANS.
MY MOTHER'S REMAINS WERE CLEARED AWAY BY THE DOLLS, IT SEEMS.
AND FOR FOURTEEN YEARS...

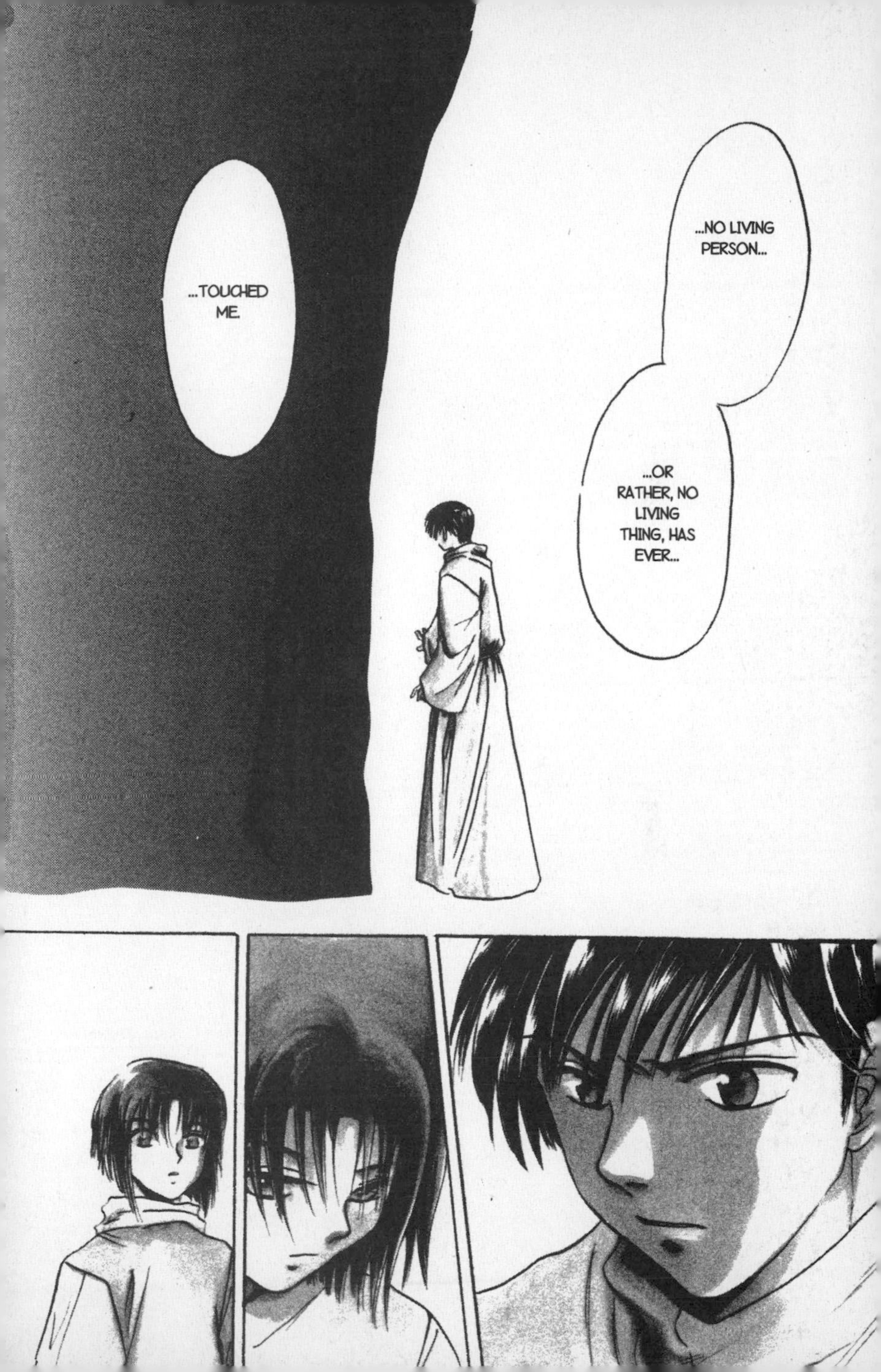
...NO LIVING PERSON...
...OR RATHER, NO LIVING THING, HAS EVER...
...TOUCHED ME.

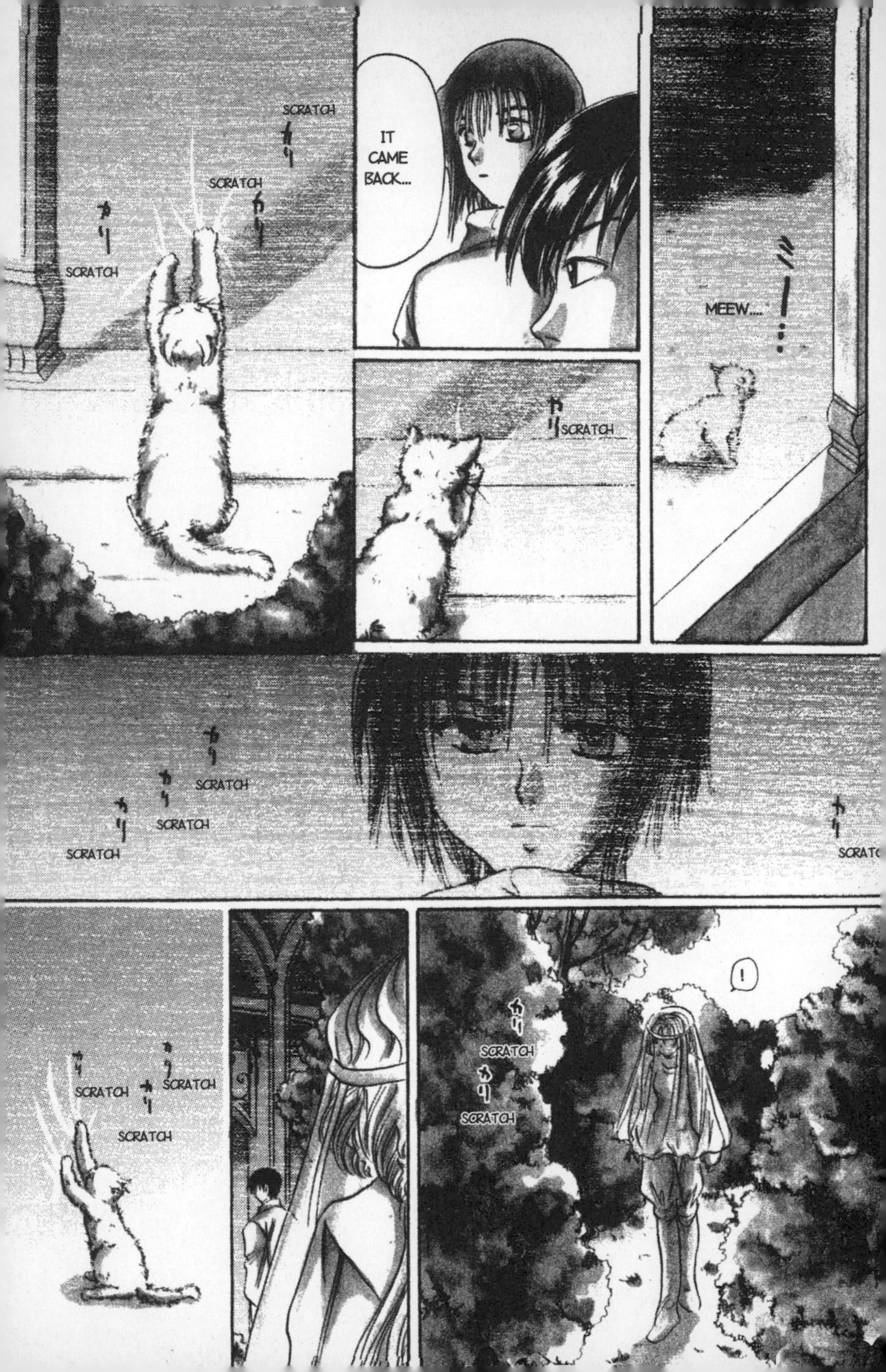
MEEW....
IT CAME BACK...
SCRATCH
SCRATCH
SCRATCH
SCRATCH
SCRATC
SCRATCH
SCRATCH
SCRATCH
!
SCRATCH
SCRATCH
SCRATCH
SCRATCH
SCRATCH

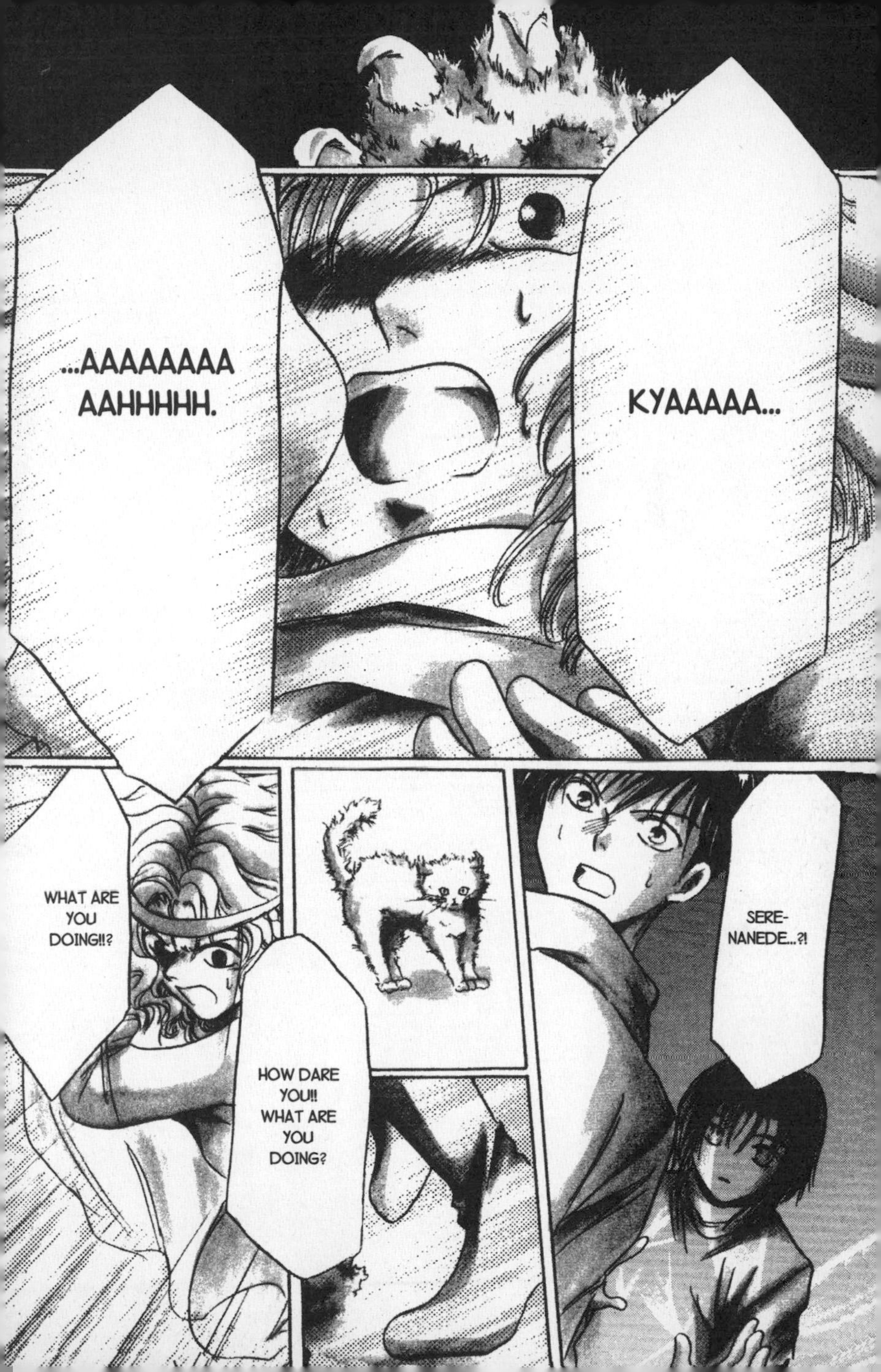
KYAAAAA...
...AAAAAAAA AAHHHHH.
SERE-NANEDE...?!
WHAT ARE YOU DOING!!?
HOW DARE YOU!! WHAT ARE YOU DOING?

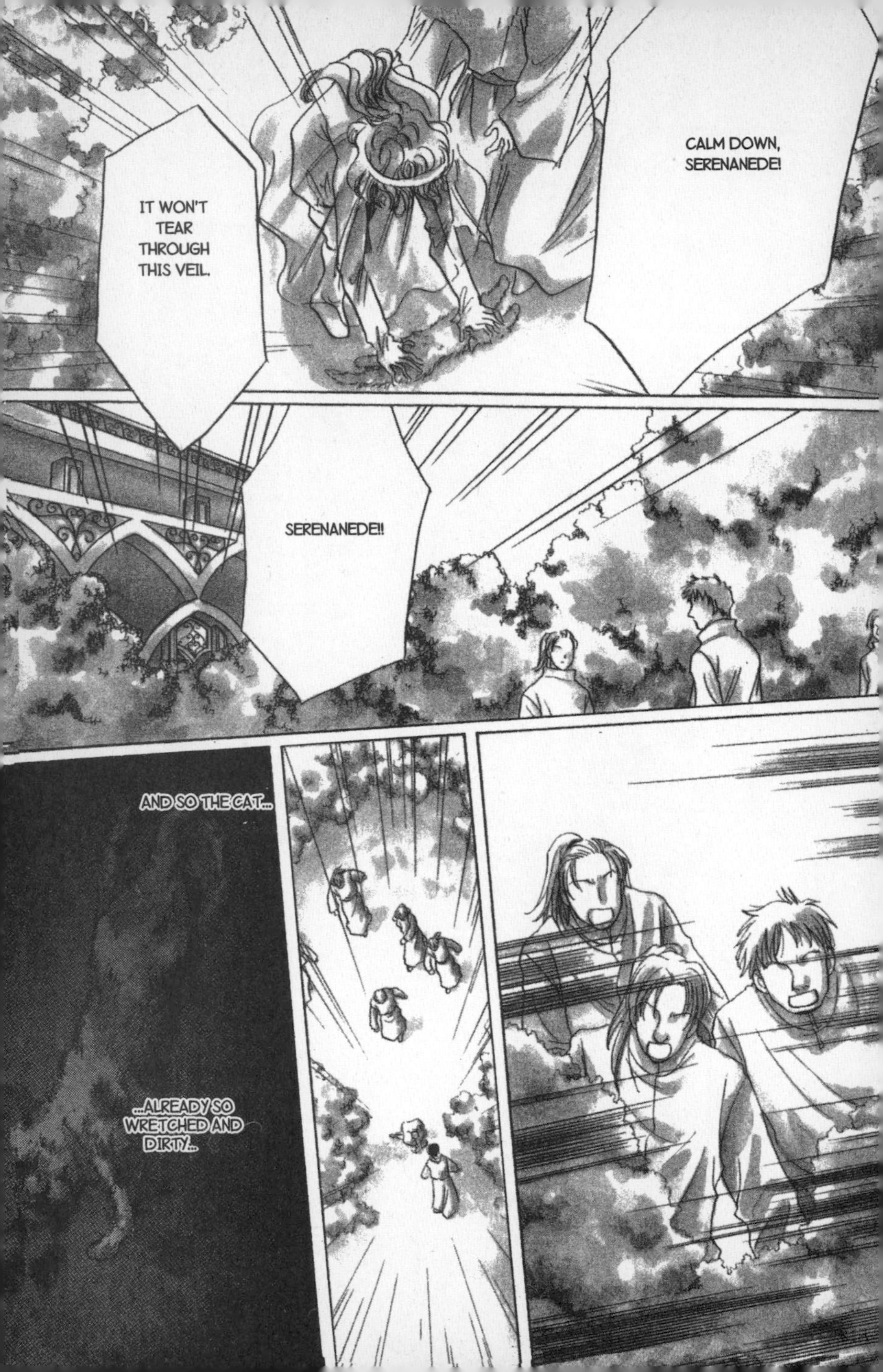
CALM DOWN, SERENANEDE!
IT WON'T TEAR THROUGH THIS VEIL.
SERENANEDE!!
AND SO THE CAT...
...ALREADY SO WRETCHED AND DIRTY...

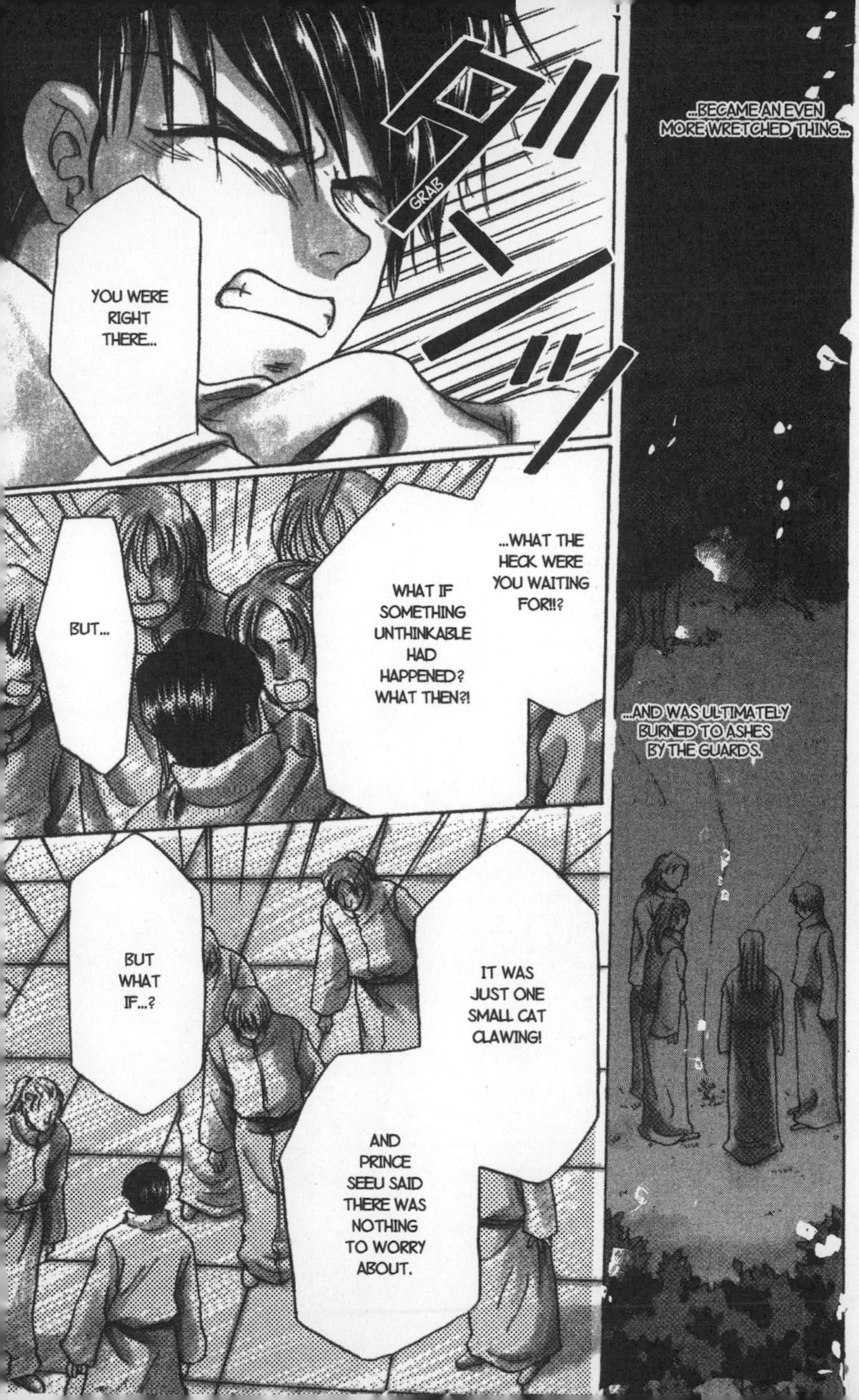
...BECAME AN EVEN MORE WRETCHED THING...
...AND WAS ULTIMATELY BURNED TO ASHES BY THE GUARDS.
GRAB
YOU WERE RIGHT THERE...
...WHAT THE HECK WERE YOU WAITING FOR!!?
WHAT IF SOMETHING UNTHINKABLE HAD HAPPENED? WHAT THEN?!
BUT...
IT WAS JUST ONE SMALL CAT CLAWING!
AND PRINCE SEEU SAID THERE WAS NOTHING TO WORRY ABOUT.
BUT WHAT IF...?

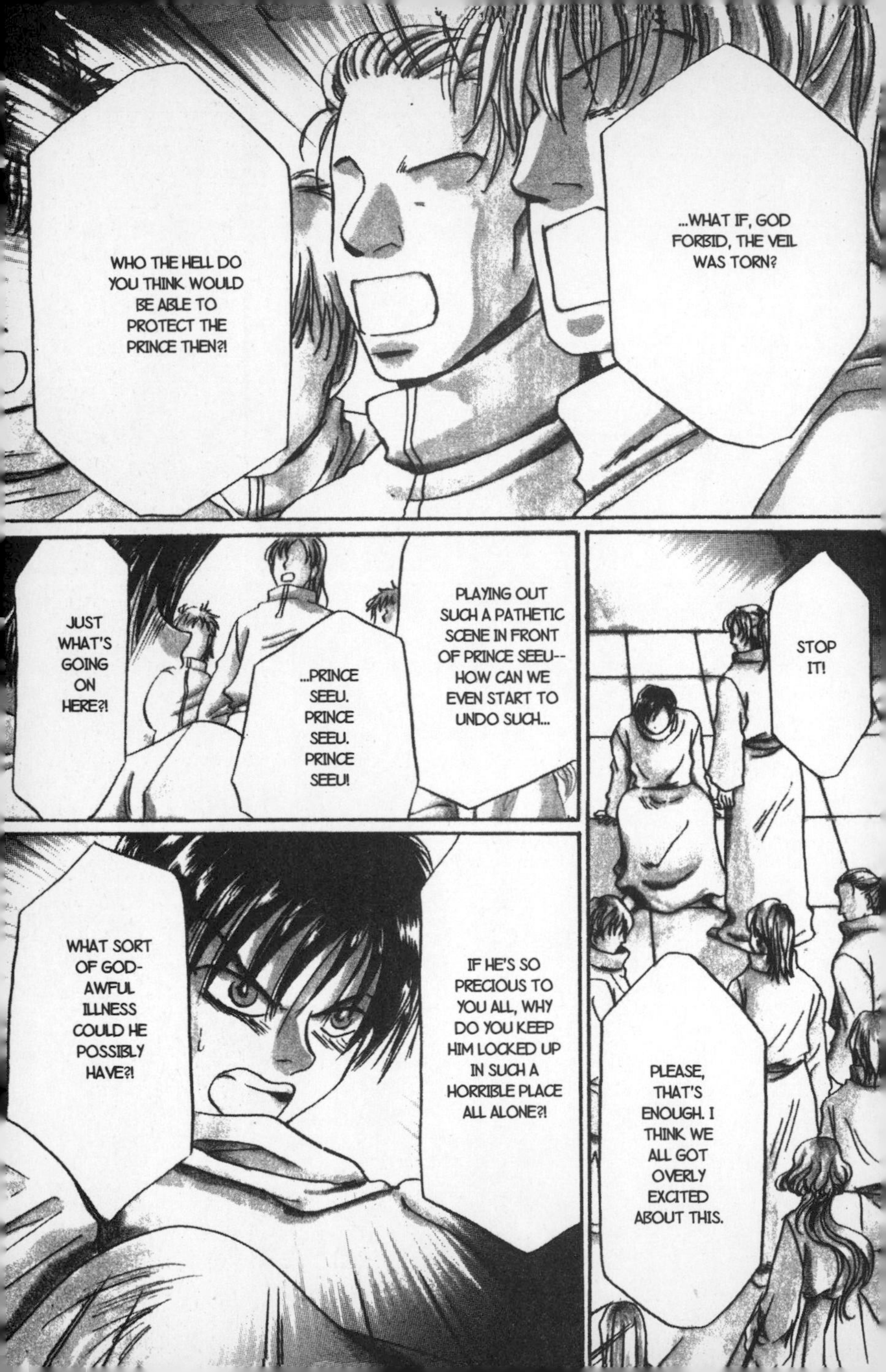
...WHAT IF, GOD FORBID, THE VEIL WAS TORN?
WHO THE HELL DO YOU THINK WOULD BE ABLE TO PROTECT THE PRINCE THEN?!
STOP IT!
PLEASE, THAT'S ENOUGH. I THINK WE ALL GOT OVERLY EXCITED ABOUT THIS.
PLAYING OUT SUCH A PATHETIC SCENE IN FRONT OF PRINCE SEEU-- HOW CAN WE EVEN START TO UNDO SUCH...
...PRINCE SEEU. PRINCE SEEU. PRINCE SEEU!
JUST WHAT'S GOING ON HERE?!
IF HE'S SO PRECIOUS TO YOU ALL, WHY DO YOU KEEP HIM LOCKED UP IN SUCH A HORRIBLE PLACE ALL ALONE?!
WHAT SORT OF GOD-AWFUL ILLNESS COULD HE POSSIBLY HAVE?!

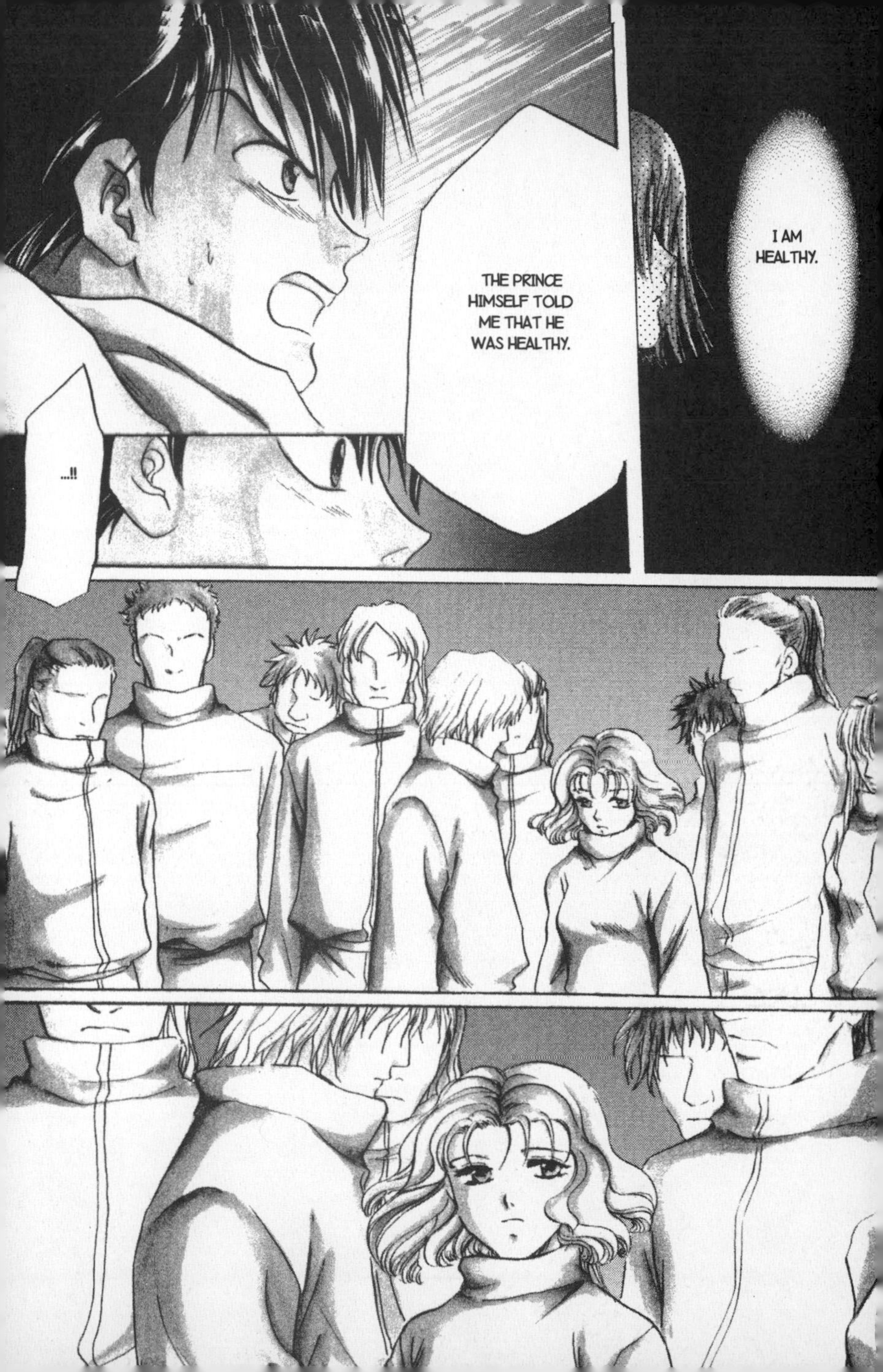
I AM HEALTHY.
THE PRINCE HIMSELF TOLD ME THAT HE WAS HEALTHY.
...!!

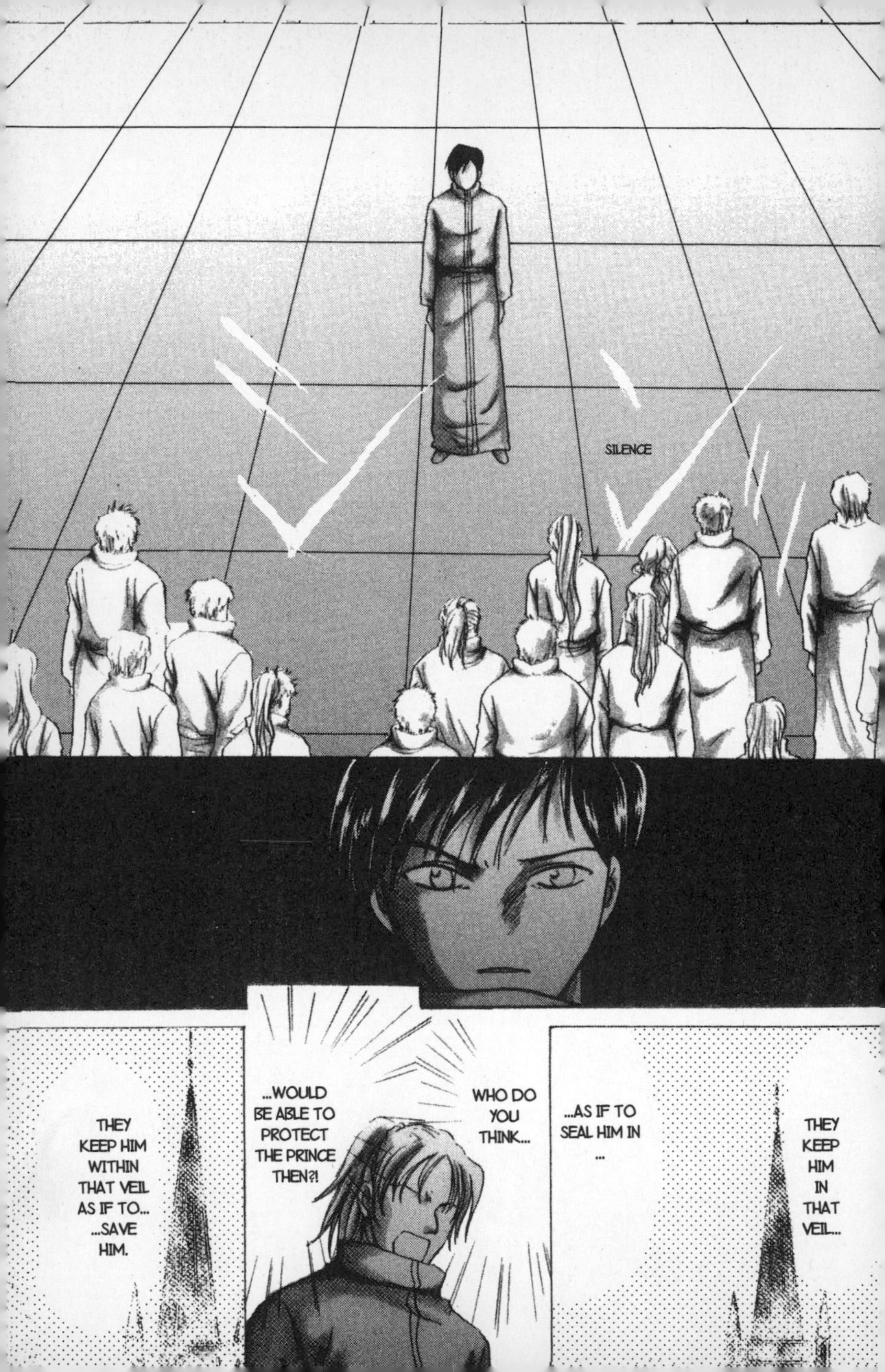
SILENCE
THEY KEEP HIM IN THAT VEIL...
...AS IF TO SEAL HIM IN ...
WHO DO YOU THINK...
...WOULD BE ABLE TO PROTECT THE PRINCE THEN?!
THEY KEEP HIM WITHIN THAT VEIL AS IF TO...
...SAVE HIM.

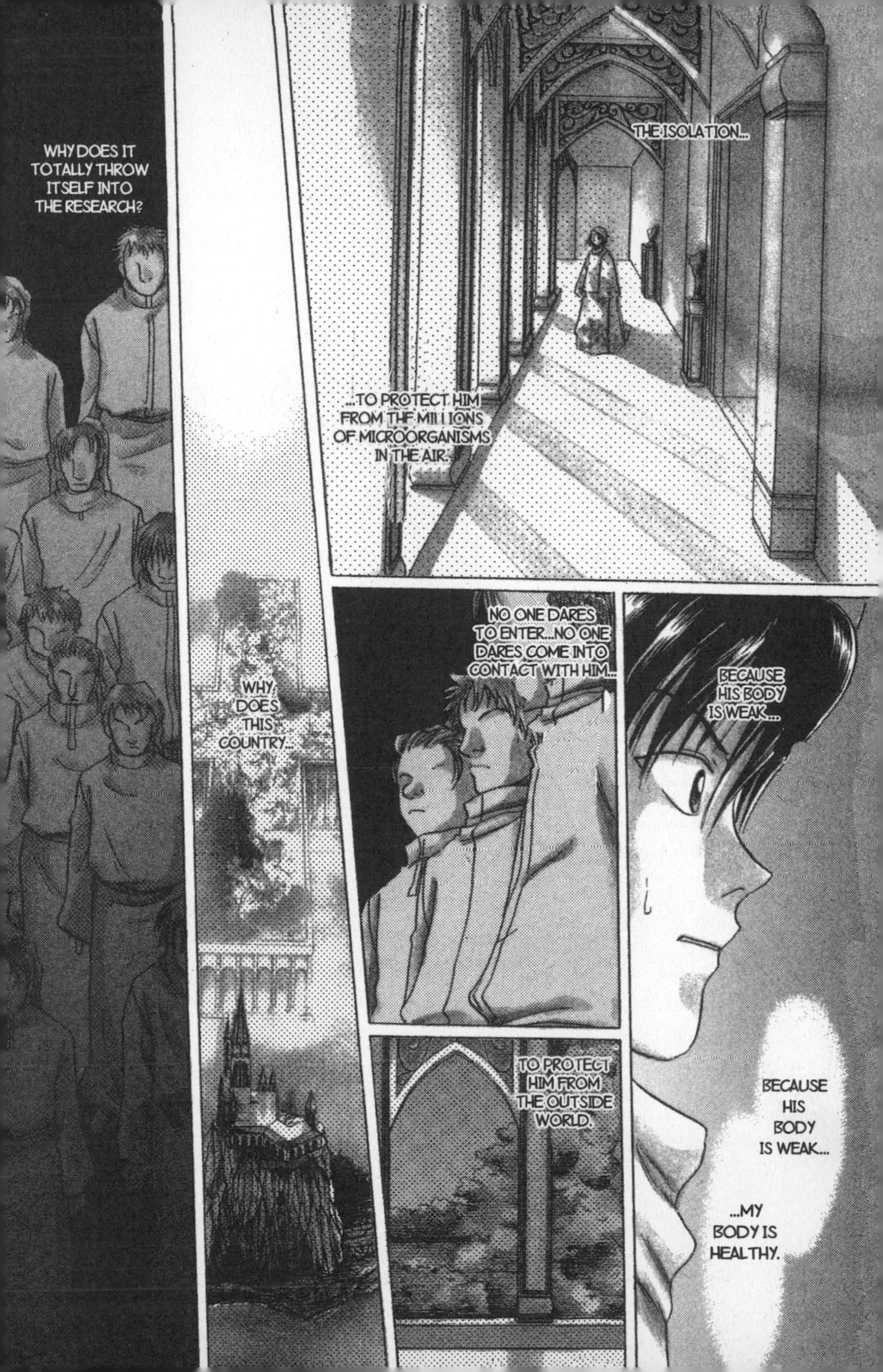
THE ISOLATION...
...TO PROTECT HIM FROM THE MILLIONS OF MICROORGANISMS IN THE AIR.
BECAUSE HIS BODY IS WEAK...
BECAUSE HIS BODY IS WEAK...
...MY BODY IS HEALTHY.
NO ONE DARES TO ENTER...NO ONE DARES COME INTO CONTACT WITH HIM...
TO PROTECT HIM FROM THE OUTSIDE WORLD.
WHY DOES THIS COUNTRY...
WHY DOES IT TOTALLY THROW ITSELF INTO THE RESEARCH?

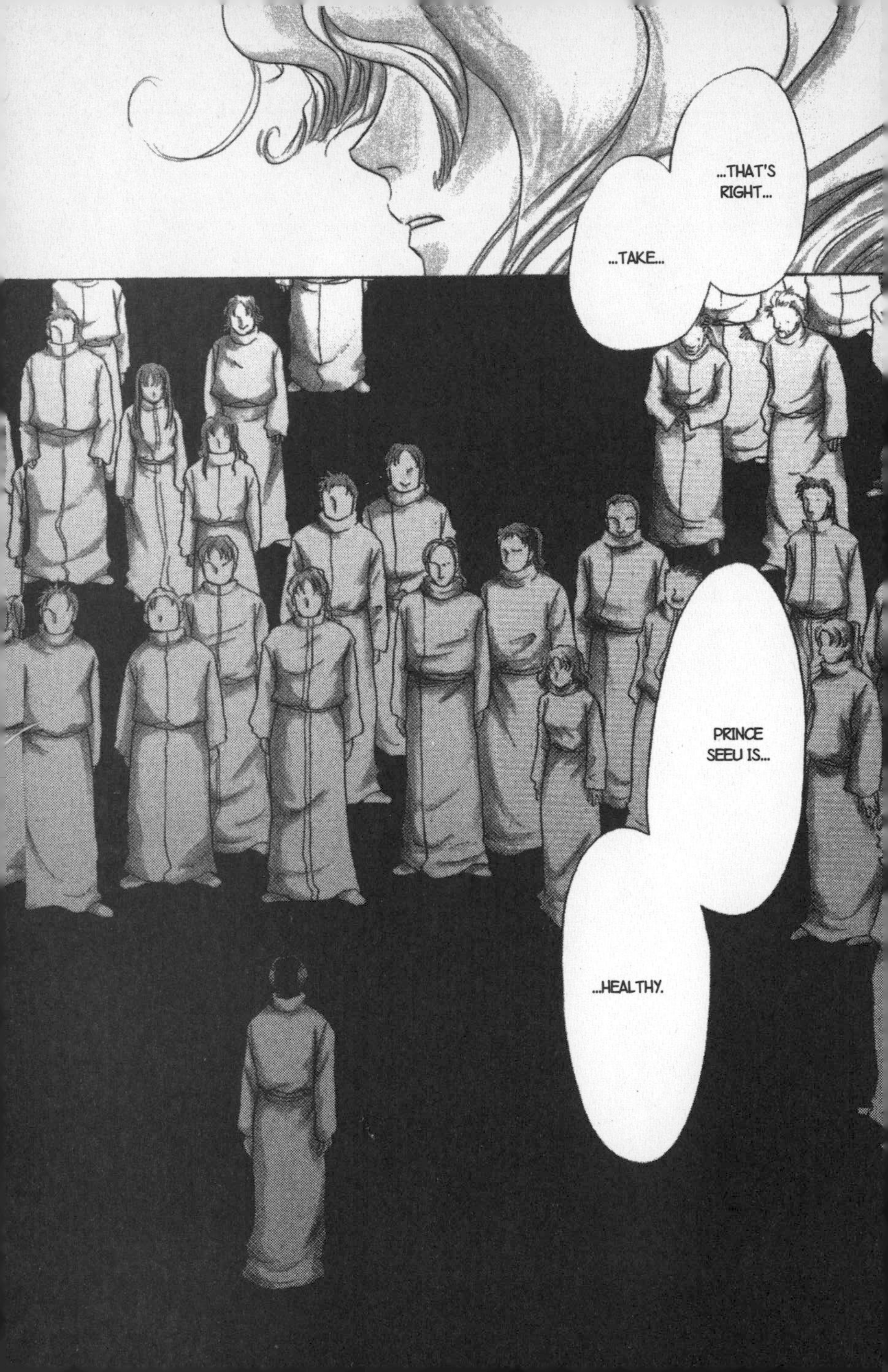
...THAT'S RIGHT...
...TAKE...
PRINCE SEEU IS...
...HEALTHY.

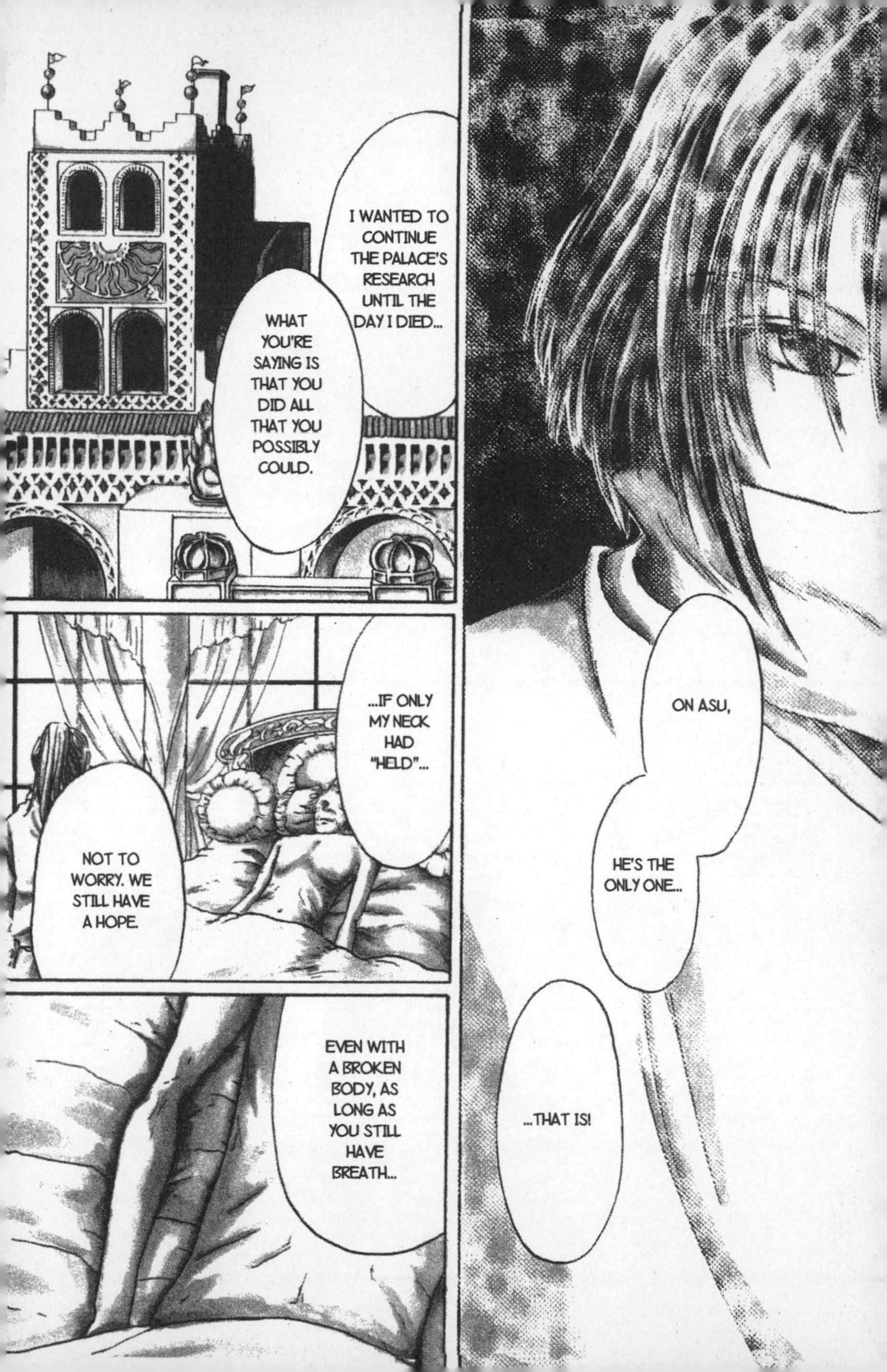
I WANTED TO CONTINUE THE PALACE'S RESEARCH UNTIL THE DAY I DIED...
WHAT YOU'RE SAYING IS THAT YOU DID ALL THAT YOU POSSIBLY COULD.
...IF ONLY MY NECK HAD "HELD"...
NOT TO WORRY. WE STILL HAVE A HOPE.
EVEN WITH A BROKEN BODY, AS LONG AS YOU STILL HAVE BREATH...
ON ASU,
HE'S THE ONLY ONE...
...THAT IS!

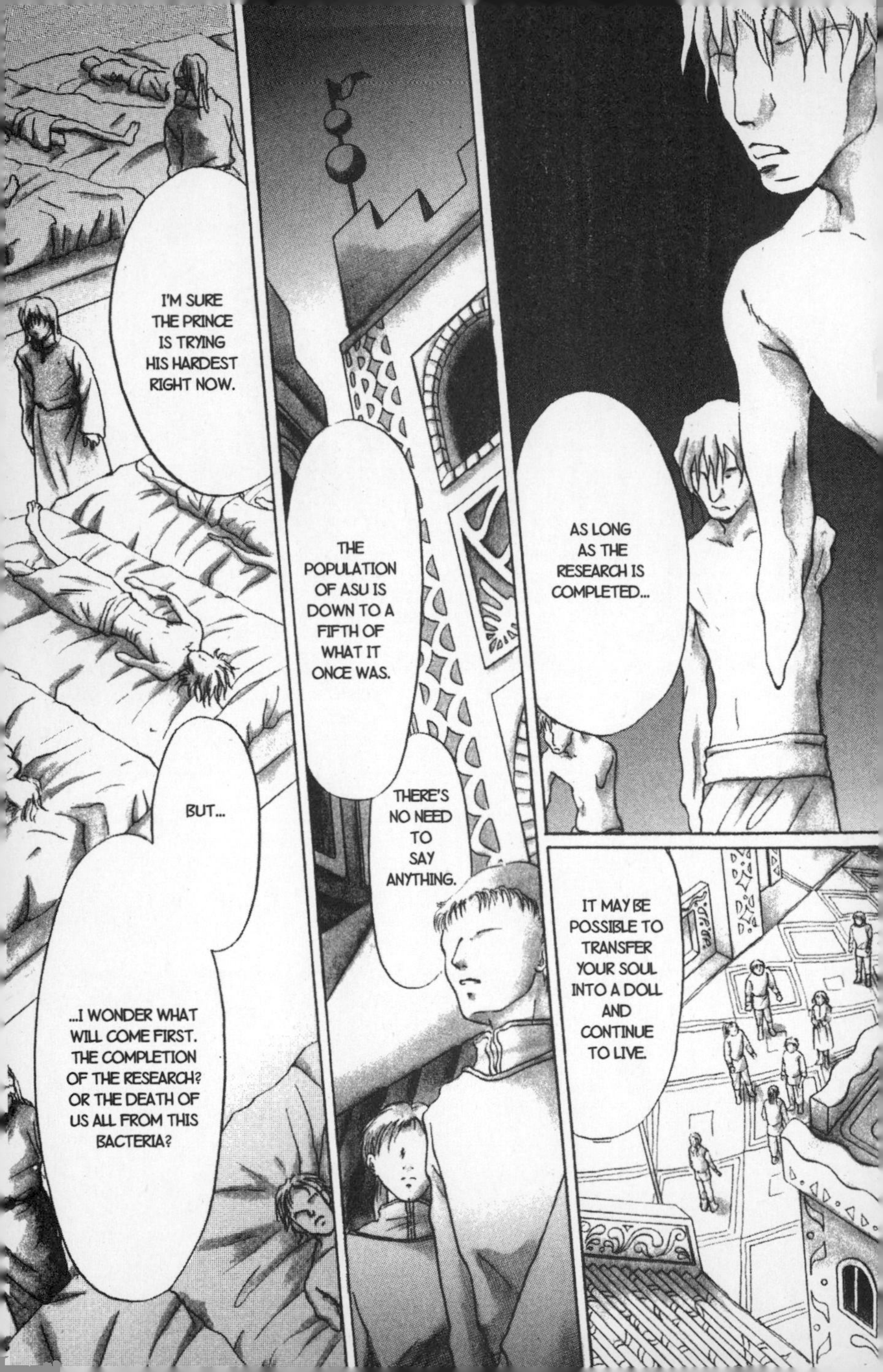
AS LONG AS THE RESEARCH IS COMPLETED...
IT MAY BE POSSIBLE TO TRANSFER YOUR SOUL INTO A DOLL AND CONTINUE TO LIVE.
THE POPULATION OF ASU IS DOWN TO A FIFTH OF WHAT IT ONCE WAS.
THERE'S NO NEED TO SAY ANYTHING.
I'M SURE THE PRINCE IS TRYING HIS HARDEST RIGHT NOW.
BUT...
...I WONDER WHAT WILL COME FIRST. THE COMPLETION OF THE RESEARCH? OR THE DEATH OF US ALL FROM THIS BACTERIA?

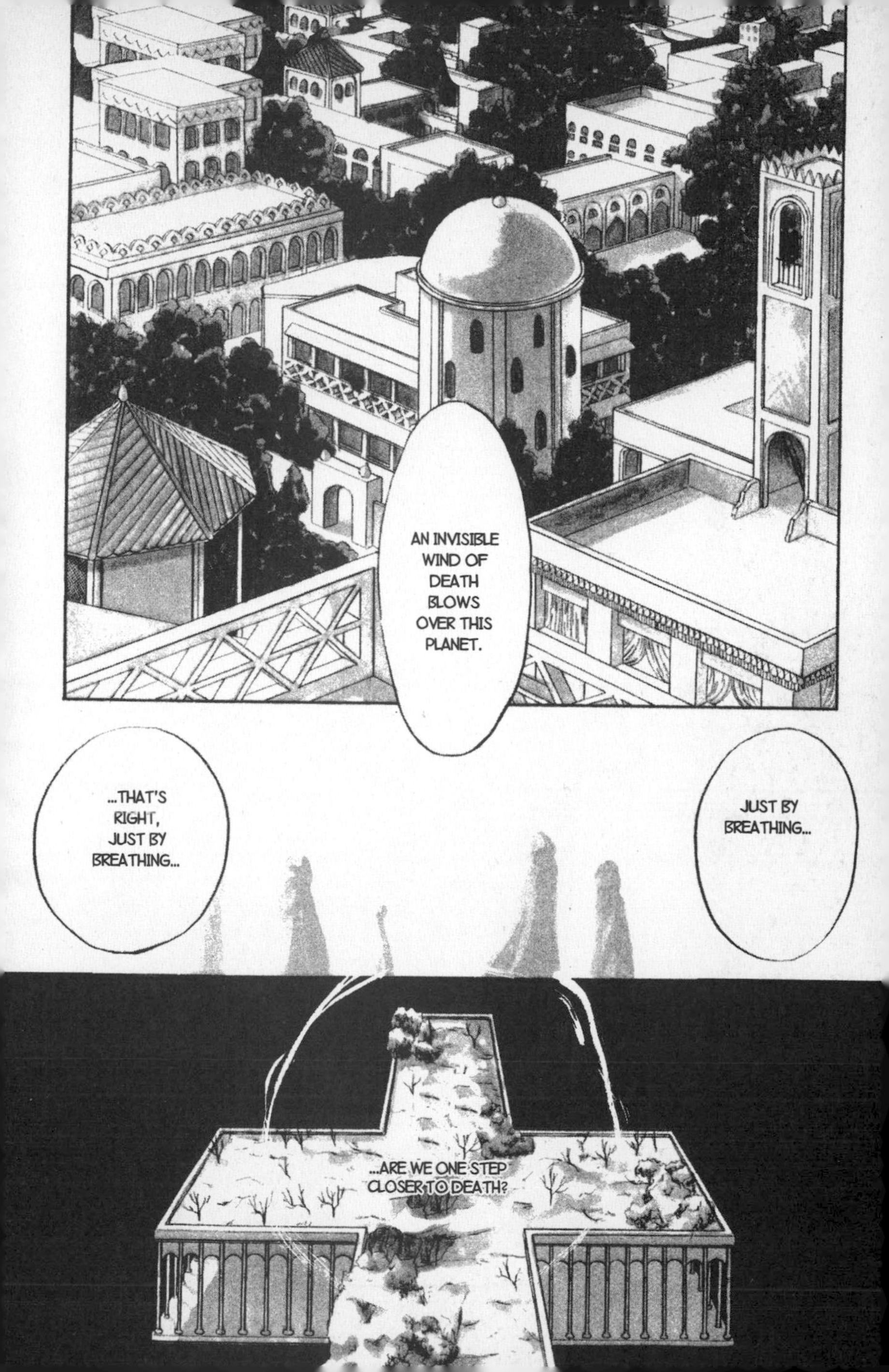
AN INVISIBLE WIND OF DEATH BLOWS OVER THIS PLANET.
JUST BY BREATHING...
...THAT'S RIGHT, JUST BY BREATHING...
...ARE WE ONE STEP CLOSER TO DEATH?

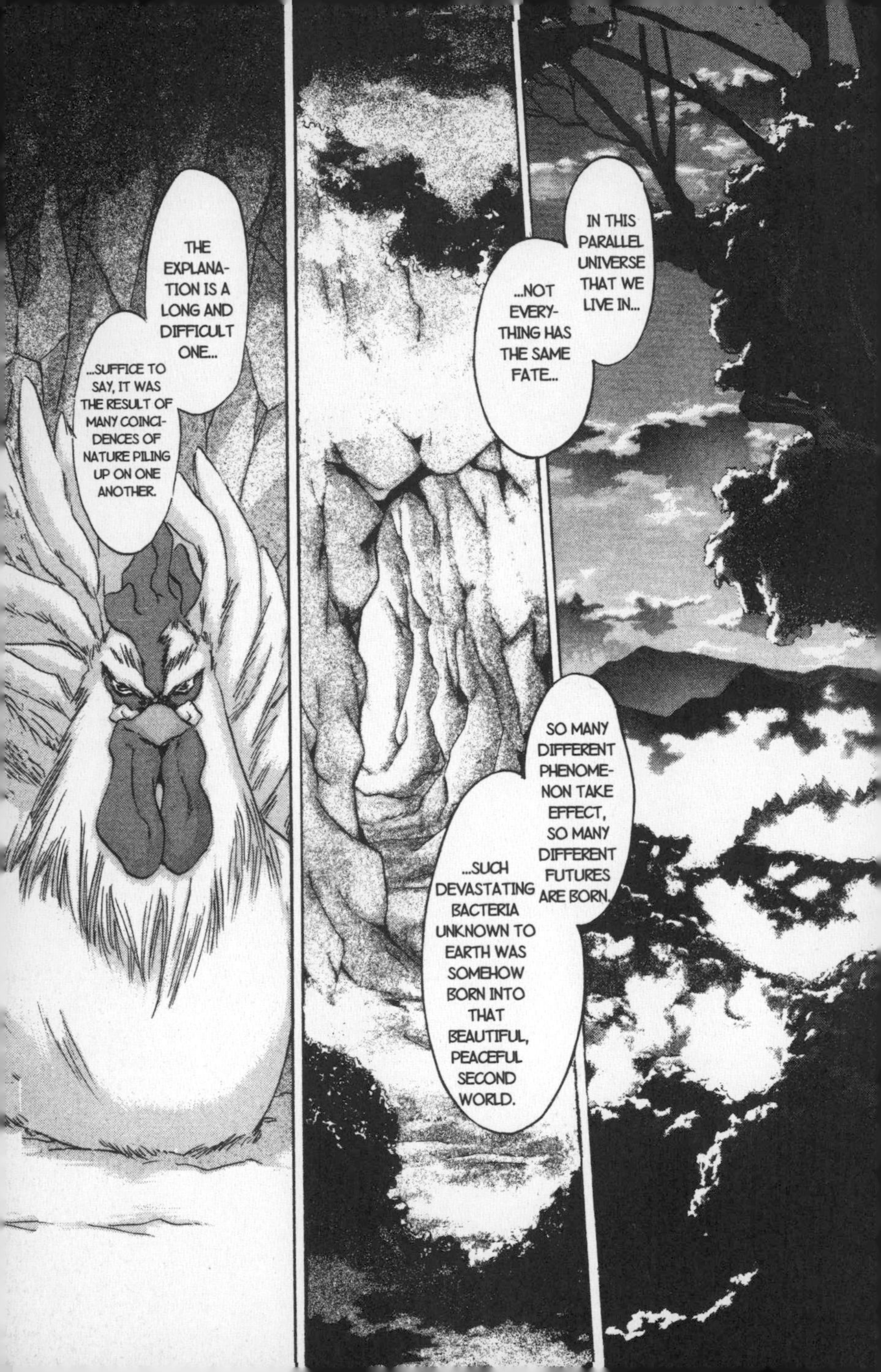
IN THIS PARALLEL UNIVERSE THAT WE LIVE IN...
...NOT EVERYTHING HAS THE SAME FATE...
SO MANY DIFFERENT PHENOMENON TAKE EFFECT, SO MANY DIFFERENT FUTURES ARE BORN.
...SUCH DEVASTATING BACTERIA UNKNOWN TO EARTH WAS SOMEHOW BORN INTO THAT BEAUTIFUL, PEACEFUL SECOND WORLD.
THE EXPLANATION IS A LONG AND DIFFICULT ONE...
...SUFFICE TO SAY, IT WAS THE RESULT OF MANY COINCIDENCES OF NATURE PILING UP ON ONE ANOTHER.

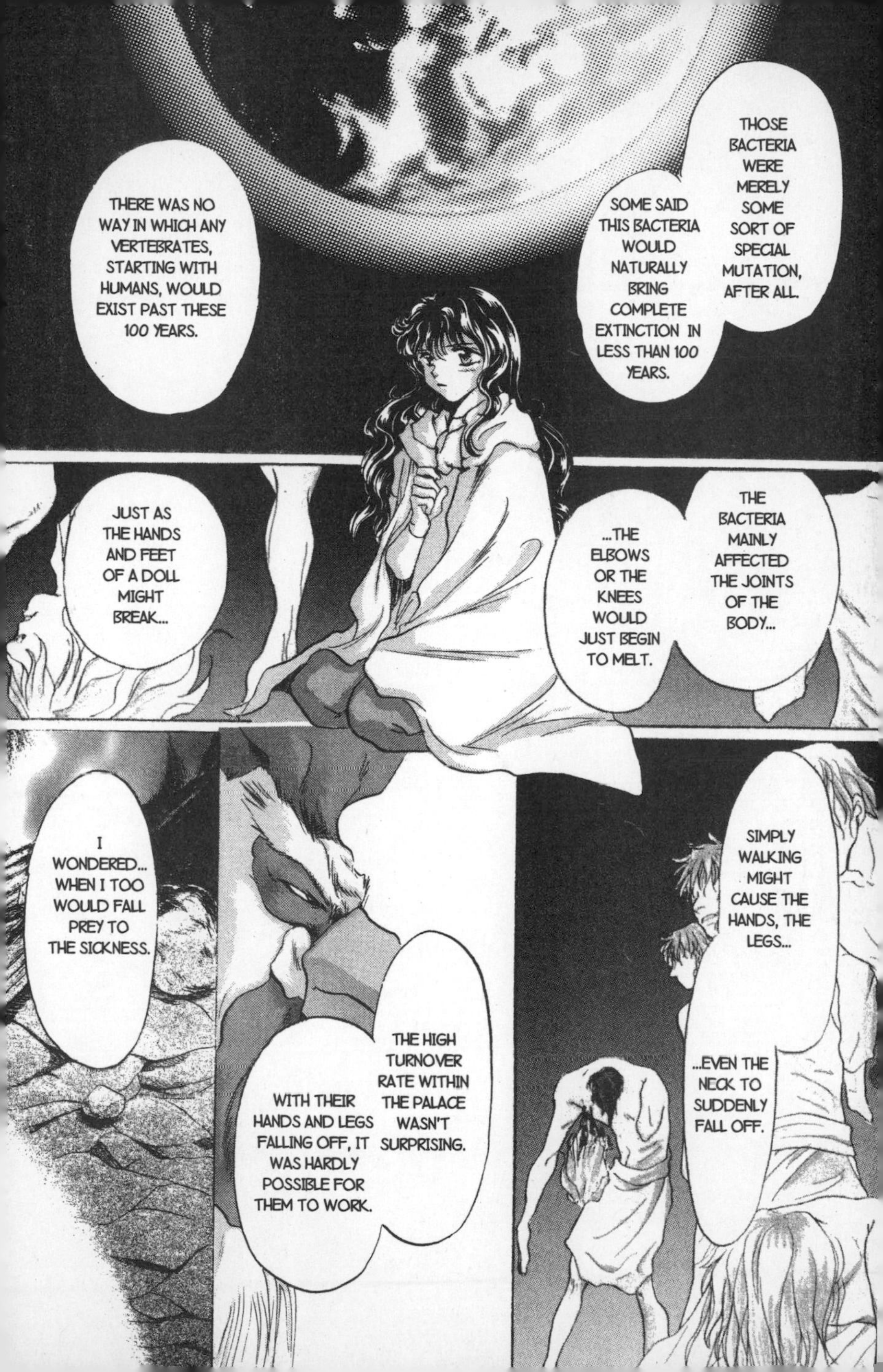
THOSE BACTERIA WERE MERELY SOME SORT OF SPECIAL MUTATION, AFTER ALL.
SOME SAID THIS BACTERIA WOULD NATURALLY BRING COMPLETE EXTINCTION IN LESS THAN 100 YEARS.
THERE WAS NO WAY IN WHICH ANY VERTEBRATES, STARTING WITH HUMANS, WOULD EXIST PAST THESE 100 YEARS.
THE BACTERIA MAINLY AFFECTED THE JOINTS OF THE BODY...
...THE ELBOWS OR THE KNEES WOULD JUST BEGIN TO MELT.
JUST AS THE HANDS AND FEET OF A DOLL MIGHT BREAK...
SIMPLY WALKING MIGHT CAUSE THE HANDS, THE LEGS...
...EVEN THE NECK TO SUDDENLY FALL OFF.
THE HIGH TURNOVER RATE WITHIN THE PALACE WASN'T SURPRISING.
WITH THEIR HANDS AND LEGS FALLING OFF, IT WAS HARDLY POSSIBLE FOR THEM TO WORK.
I WONDERED... WHEN I TOO WOULD FALL PREY TO THE SICKNESS.

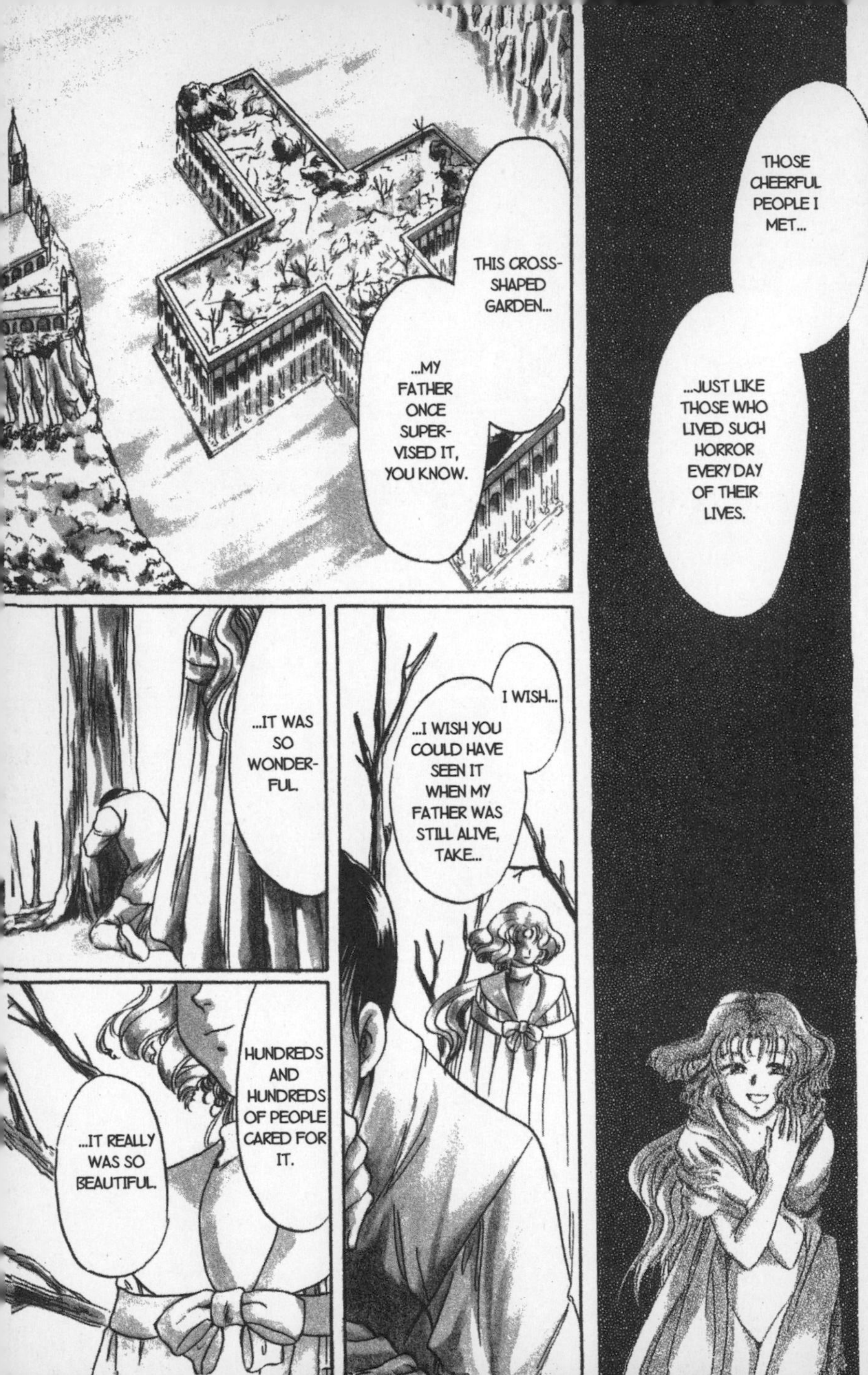
THOSE CHEERFUL PEOPLE I MET...
...JUST LIKE THOSE WHO LIVED SUCH HORROR EVERY DAY OF THEIR LIVES.
THIS CROSS-SHAPED GARDEN...
...MY FATHER ONCE SUPER-VISED IT, YOU KNOW.
I WISH...
...I WISH YOU COULD HAVE SEEN IT WHEN MY FATHER WAS STILL ALIVE, TAKE...
...IT WAS SO WONDER-FUL.
HUNDREDS AND HUNDREDS OF PEOPLE CARED FOR IT.
...IT REALLY WAS SO BEAUTIFUL.

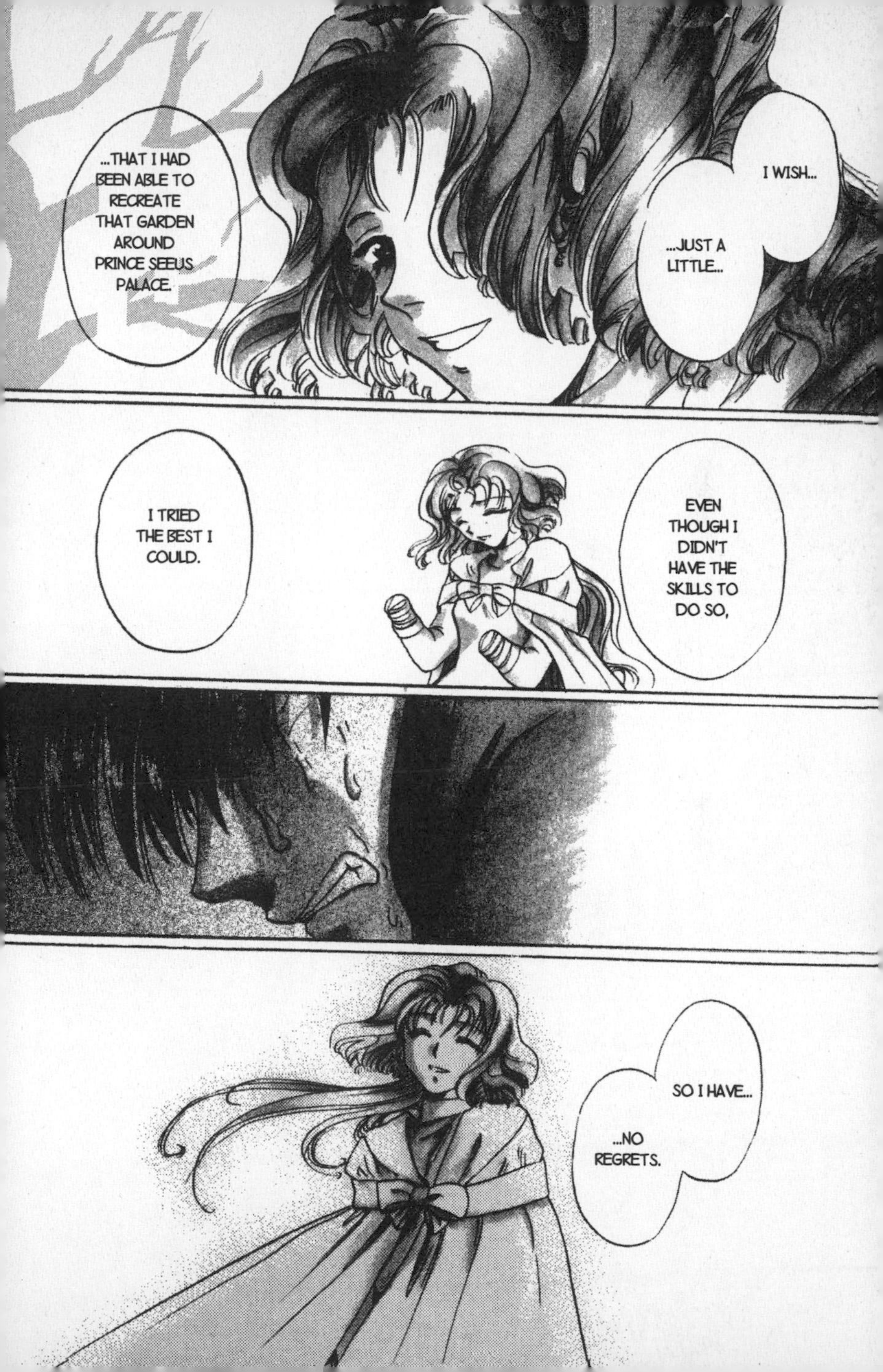
I WISH...
...JUST A LITTLE...
...THAT I HAD BEEN ABLE TO RECREATE THAT GARDEN AROUND PRINCE SEEUS PALACE.
EVEN THOUGH I DIDN'T HAVE THE SKILLS TO DO SO,
I TRIED THE BEST I COULD.
SO I HAVE...
...NO REGRETS.

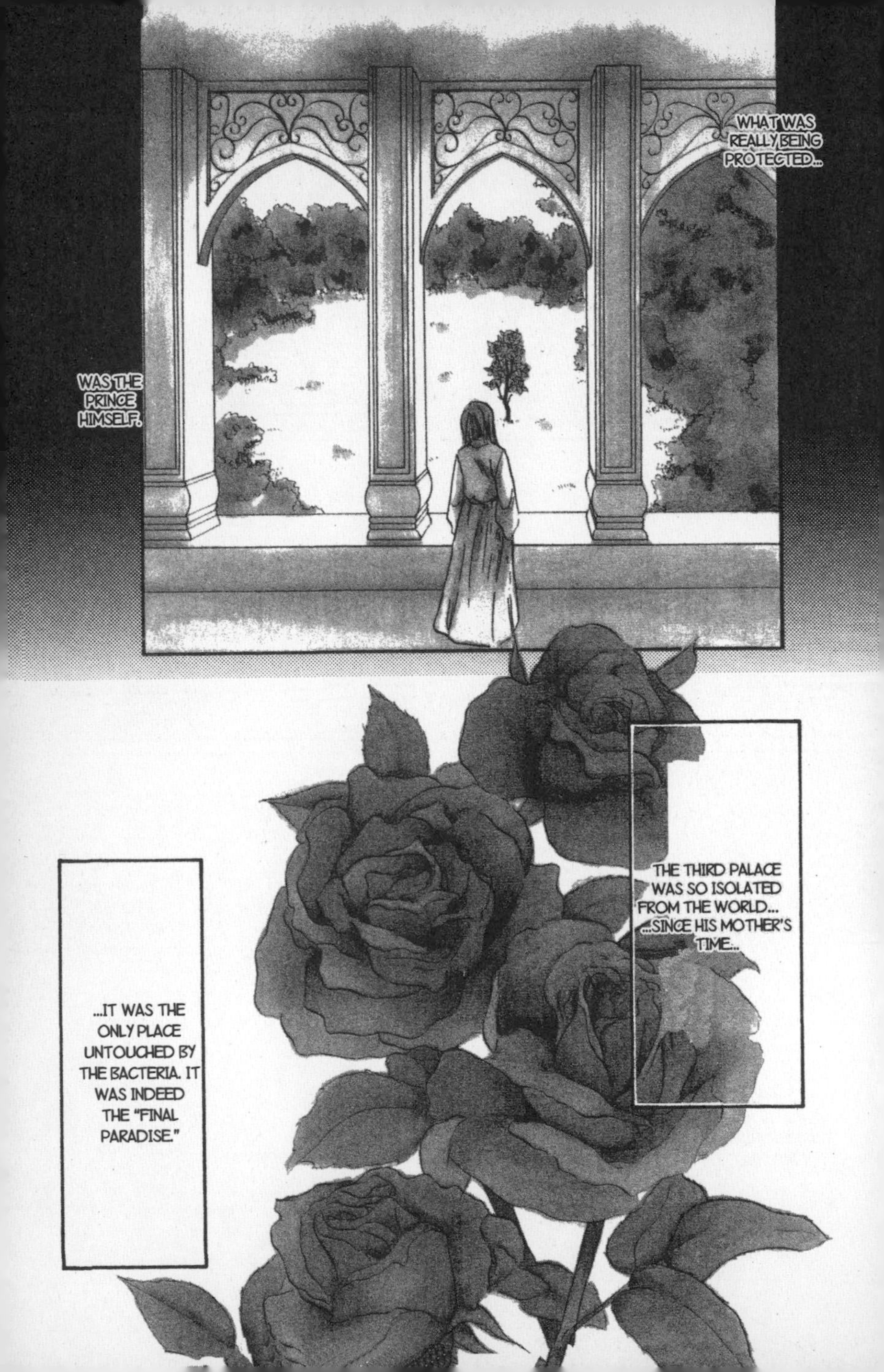
WHAT WAS REALLY BEING PROTECTED...
WAS THE PRINCE HIMSELF.
THE THIRD PALACE WAS SO ISOLATED FROM THE WORLD... ...SINCE HIS MOTHER'S TIME...
...IT WAS THE ONLY PLACE UNTOUCHED BY THE BACTERIA. IT WAS INDEED THE "FINAL PARADISE."

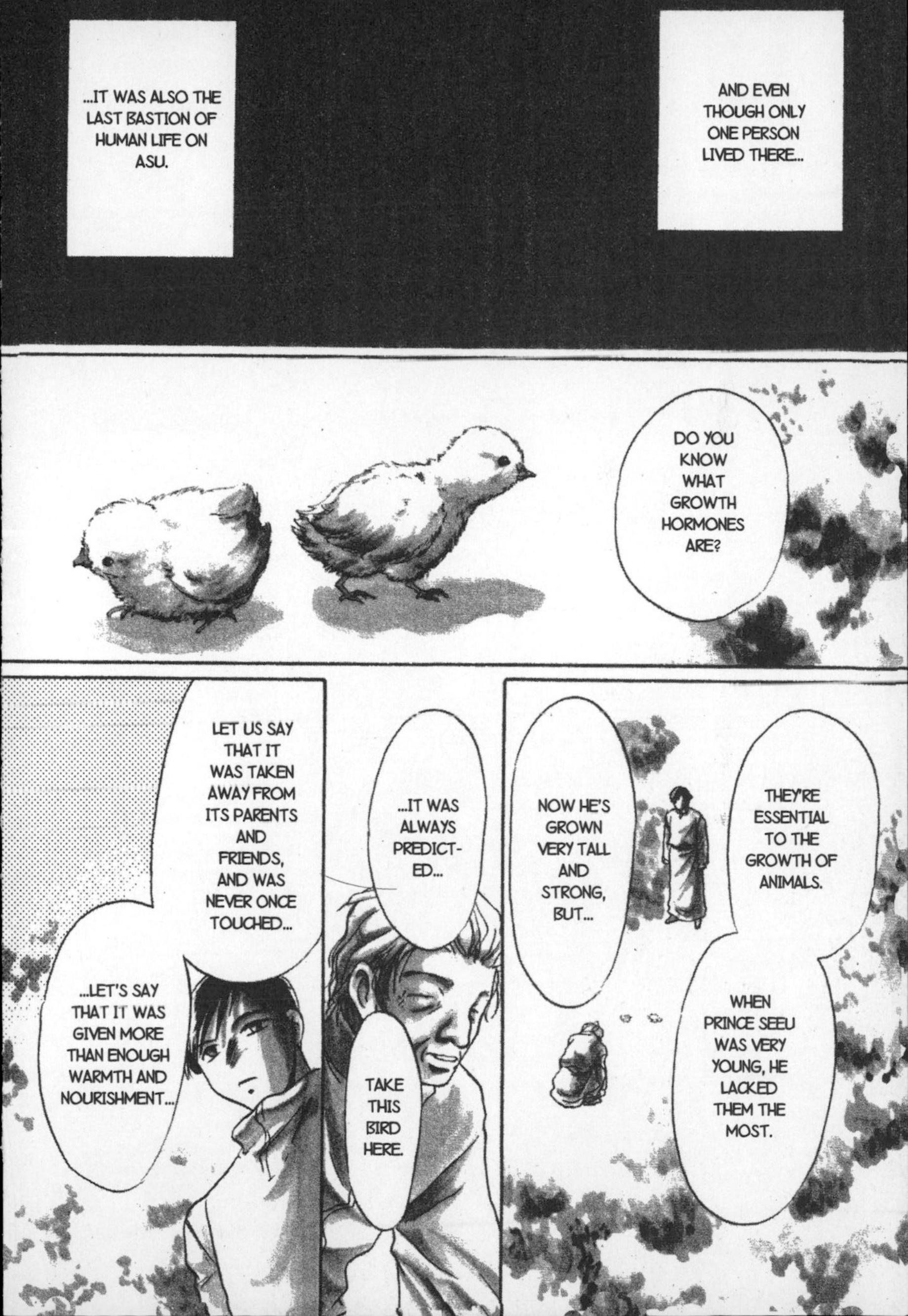
AND EVEN THOUGH ONLY ONE PERSON LIVED THERE...
...IT WAS ALSO THE LAST BASTION OF HUMAN LIFE ON ASU.
DO YOU KNOW WHAT GROWTH HORMONES ARE?
THEY'RE ESSENTIAL TO THE GROWTH OF ANIMALS.
WHEN PRINCE SEEU WAS VERY YOUNG, HE LACKED THEM THE MOST.
NOW HE'S GROWN VERY TALL AND STRONG, BUT...
...IT WAS ALWAYS PREDICT-ED...
TAKE THIS BIRD HERE.
LET US SAY THAT IT WAS TAKEN AWAY FROM ITS PARENTS AND FRIENDS, AND WAS NEVER ONCE TOUCHED...
...LET'S SAY THAT IT WAS GIVEN MORE THAN ENOUGH WARMTH AND NOURISHMENT...

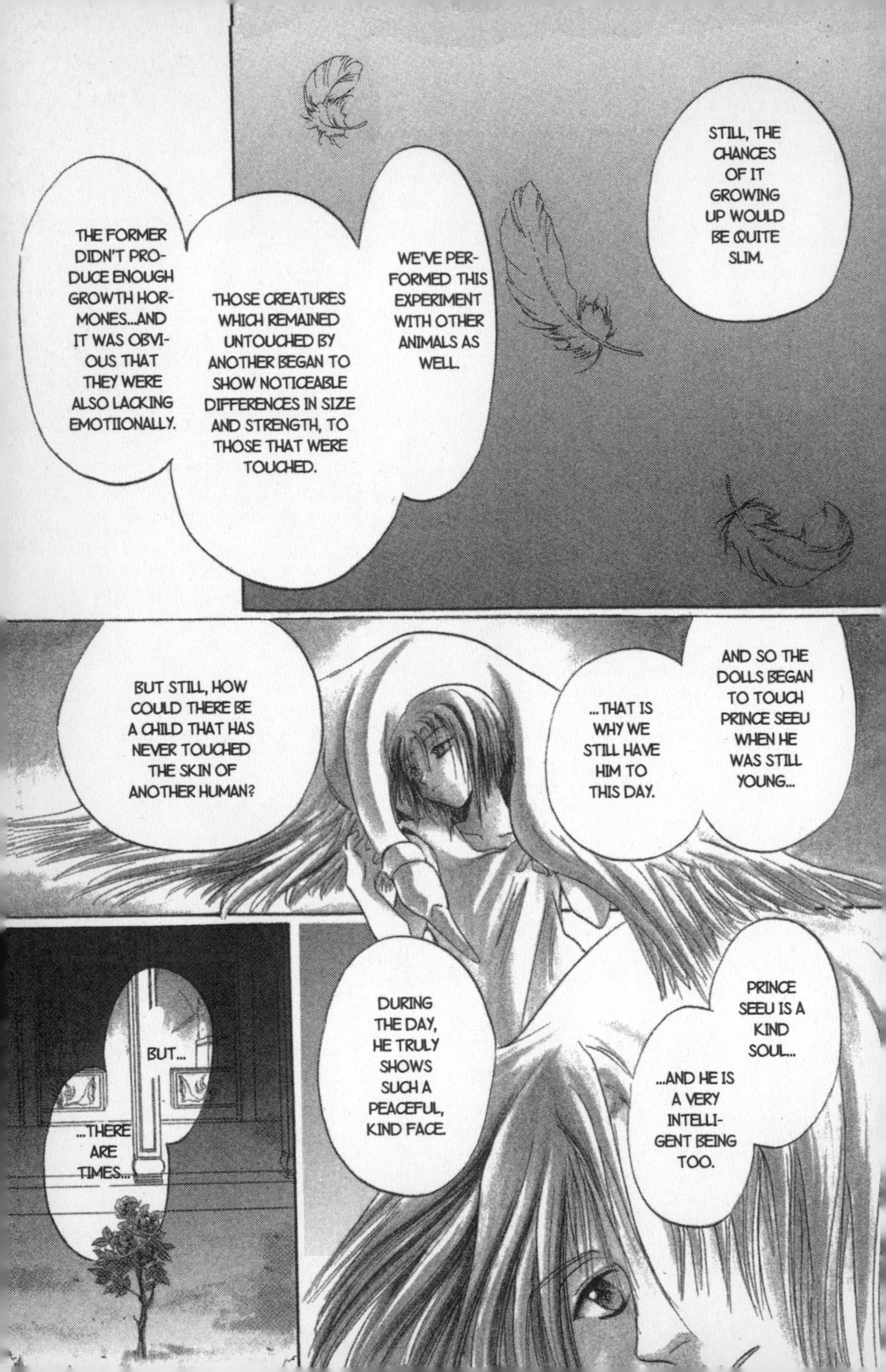
STILL, THE CHANCES OF IT GROWING UP WOULD BE QUITE SLIM.
WE'VE PER- FORMED THIS EXPERIMENT WITH OTHER ANIMALS AS WELL.
THOSE CREATURES WHICH REMAINED UNTOUCHED BY ANOTHER BEGAN TO SHOW NOTICEABLE DIFFERENCES IN SIZE AND STRENGTH, TO THOSE THAT WERE TOUCHED.
THE FORMER DIDN'T PRO- DUCE ENOUGH GROWTH HOR- MONES...AND IT WAS OBVI- OUS THAT THEY WERE ALSO LACKING EMOTIIONALLY.
AND SO THE DOLLS BEGAN TO TOUCH PRINCE SEEU WHEN HE WAS STILL YOUNG...
...THAT IS WHY WE STILL HAVE HIM TO THIS DAY.
BUT STILL, HOW COULD THERE BE A CHILD THAT HAS NEVER TOUCHED THE SKIN OF ANOTHER HUMAN?
PRINCE SEEU IS A KIND SOUL...
...AND HE IS A VERY INTELLI- GENT BEING TOO.
DURING THE DAY, HE TRULY SHOWS SUCH A PEACEFUL, KIND FACE.
BUT...
...THERE ARE TIMES...

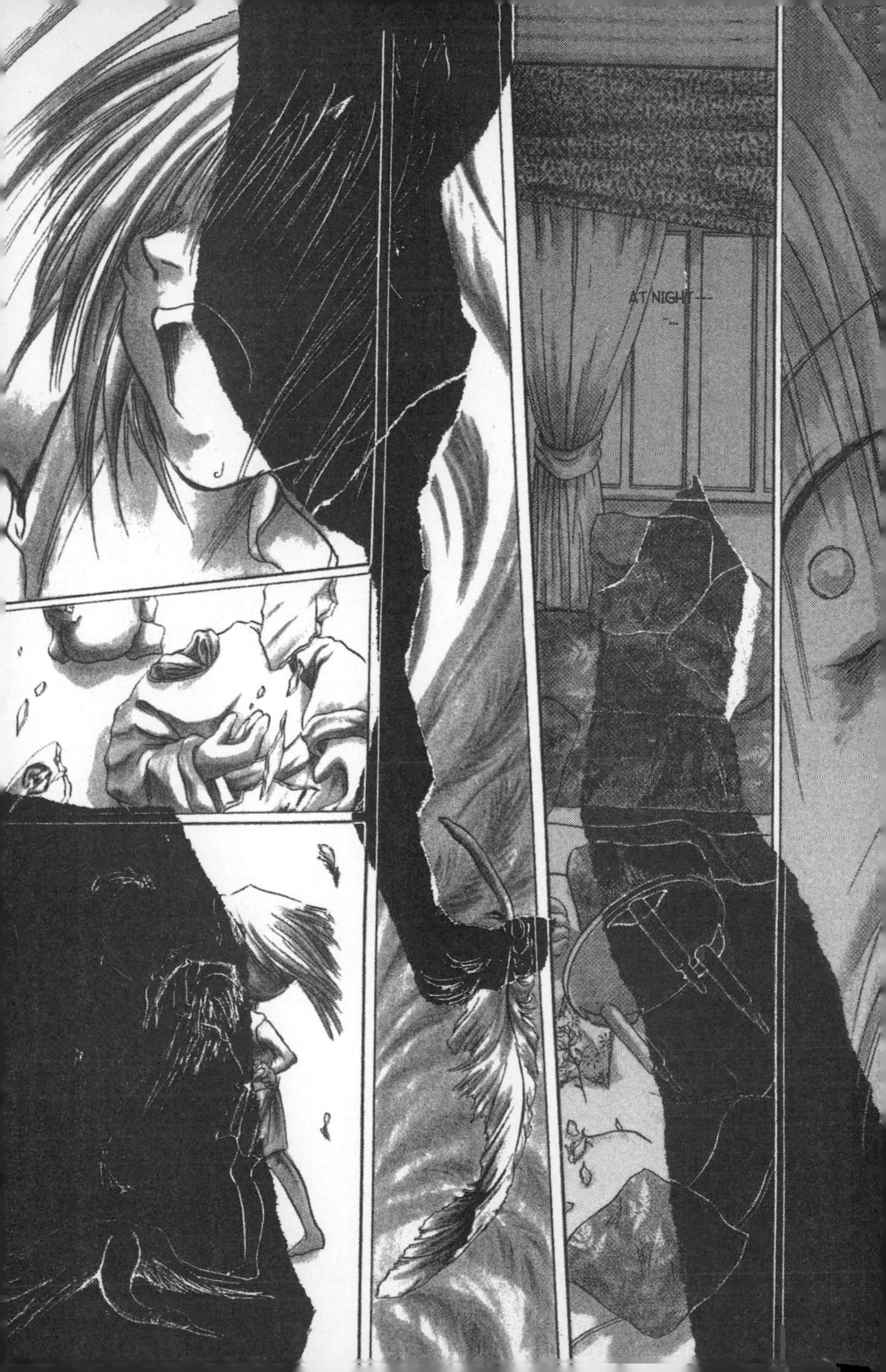
AT NIGHT —

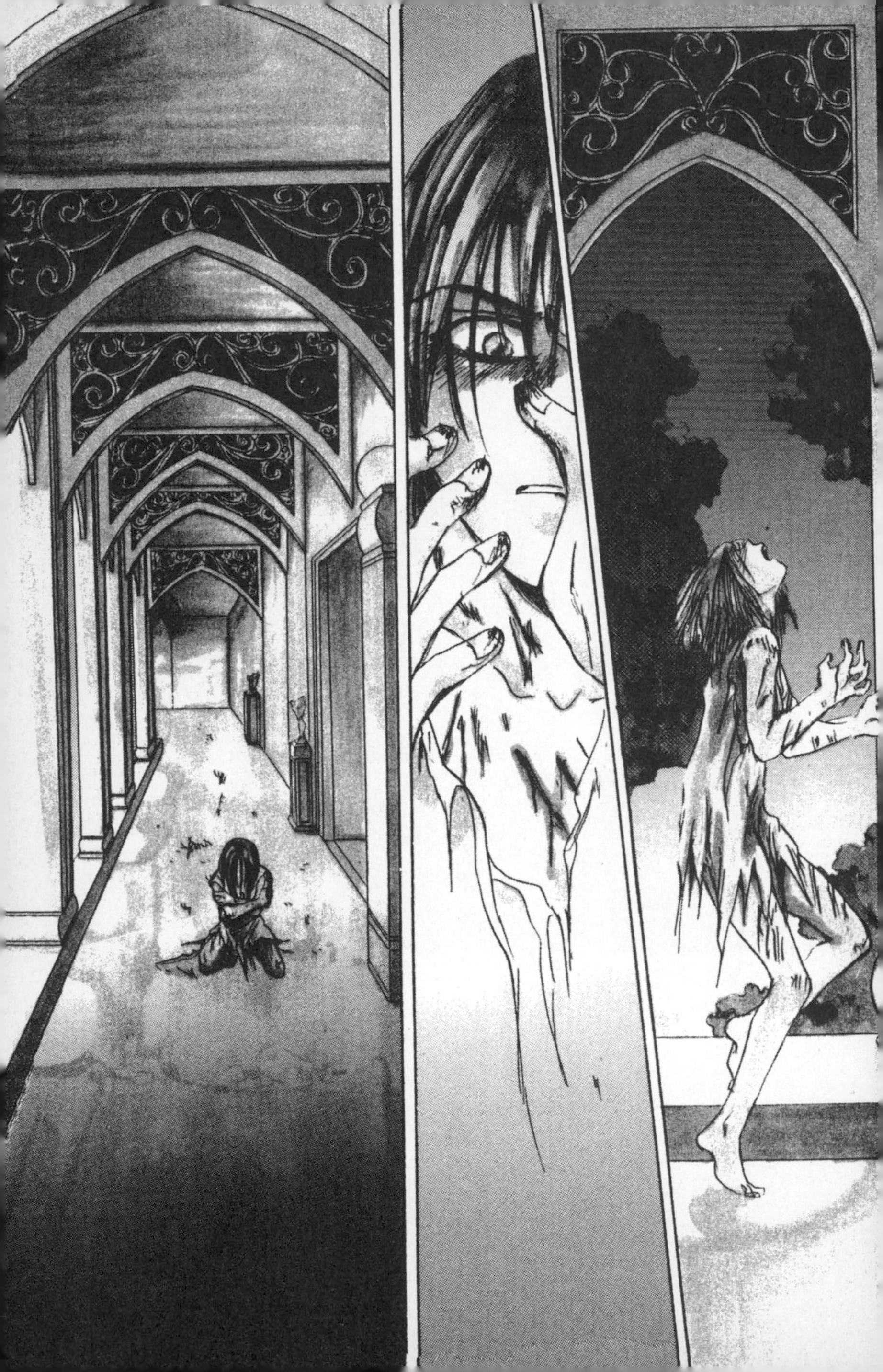

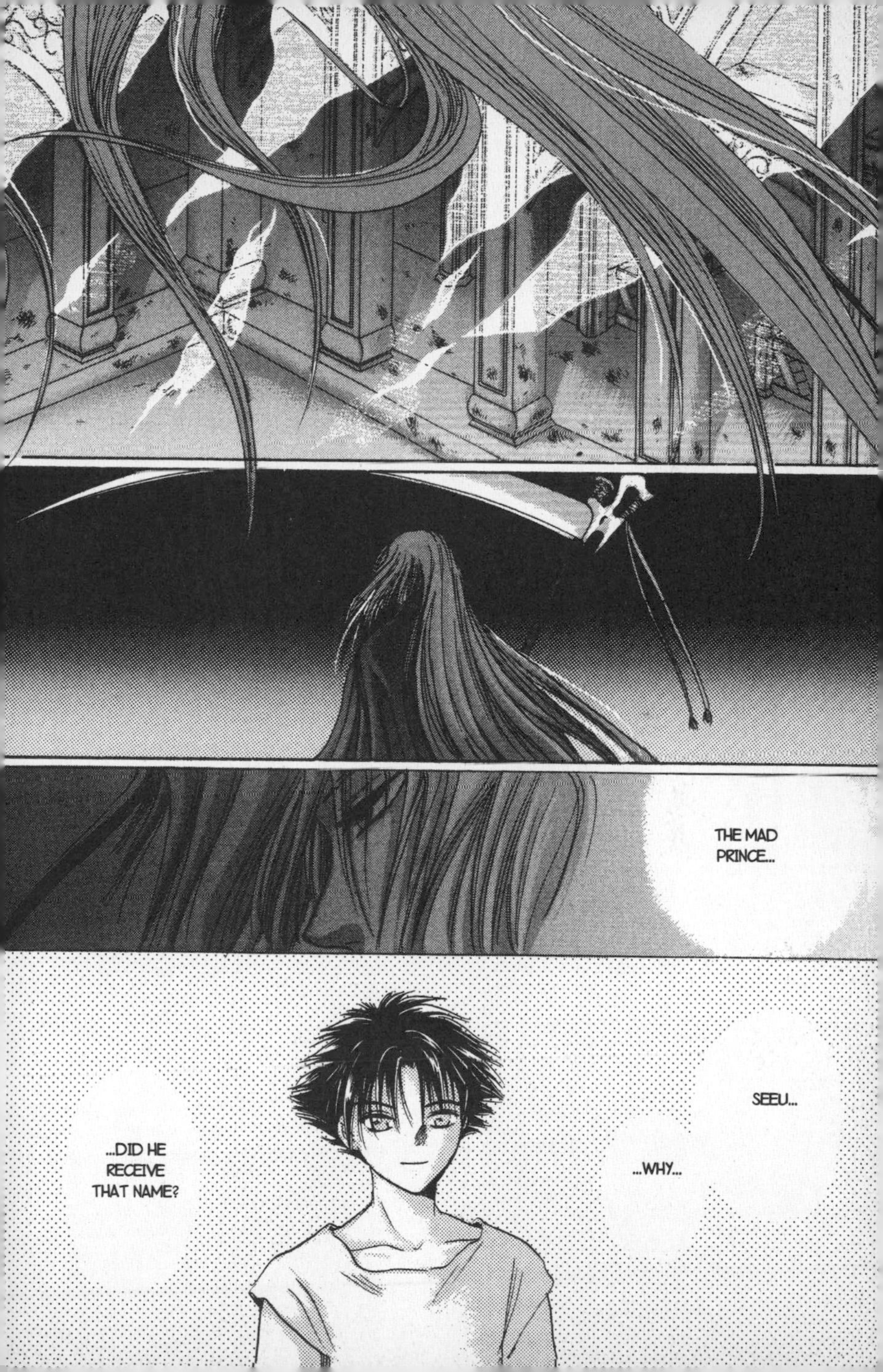
THE MAD PRINCE...
SEEU...
...WHY...
...DID HE RECEIVE THAT NAME?

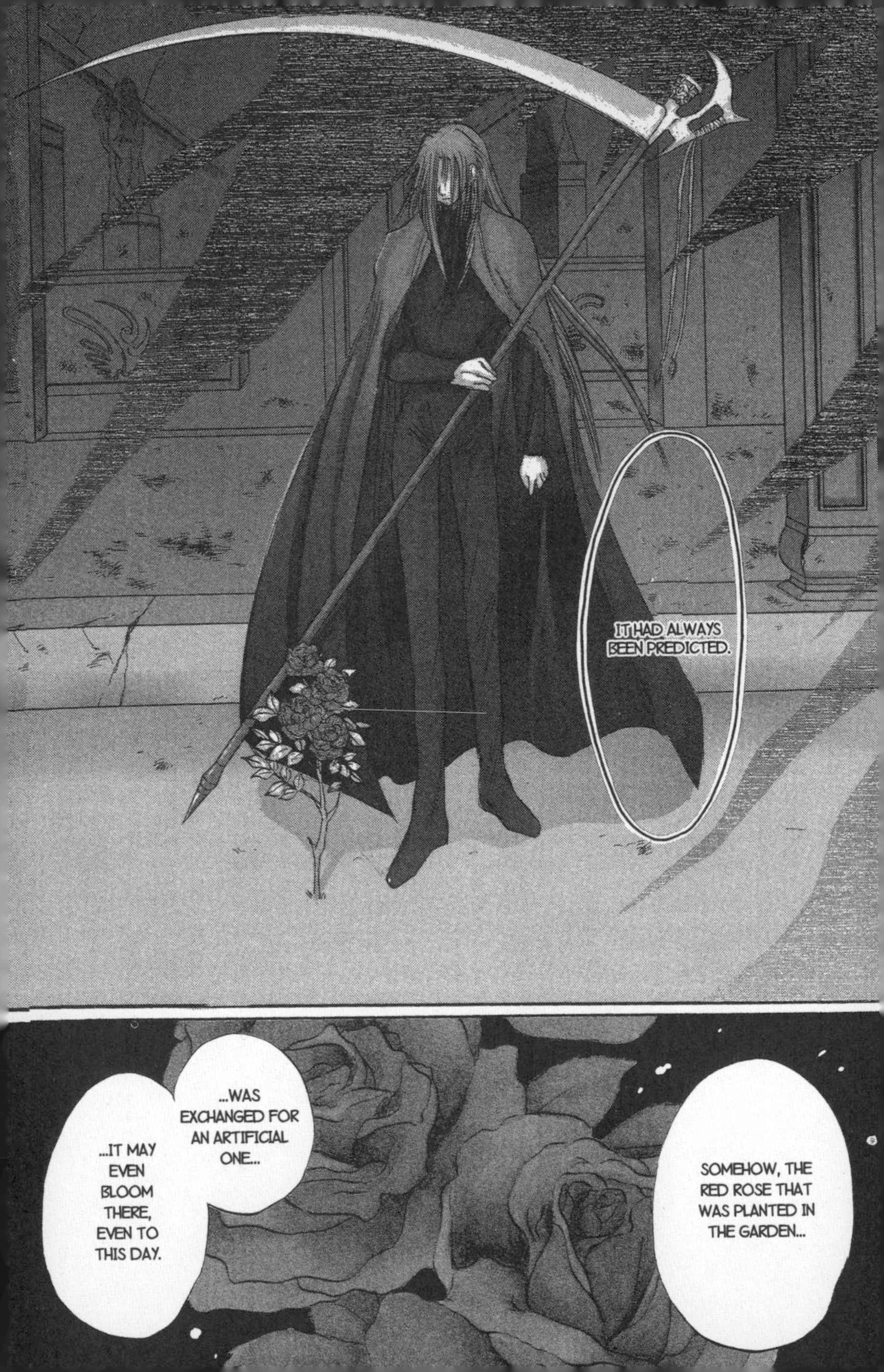
IT HAD ALWAYS BEEN PREDICTED.
SOMEHOW, THE RED ROSE THAT WAS PLANTED IN THE GARDEN...
...WAS EXCHANGED FOR AN ARTIFICIAL ONE...
...IT MAY EVEN BLOOM THERE, EVEN TO THIS DAY.

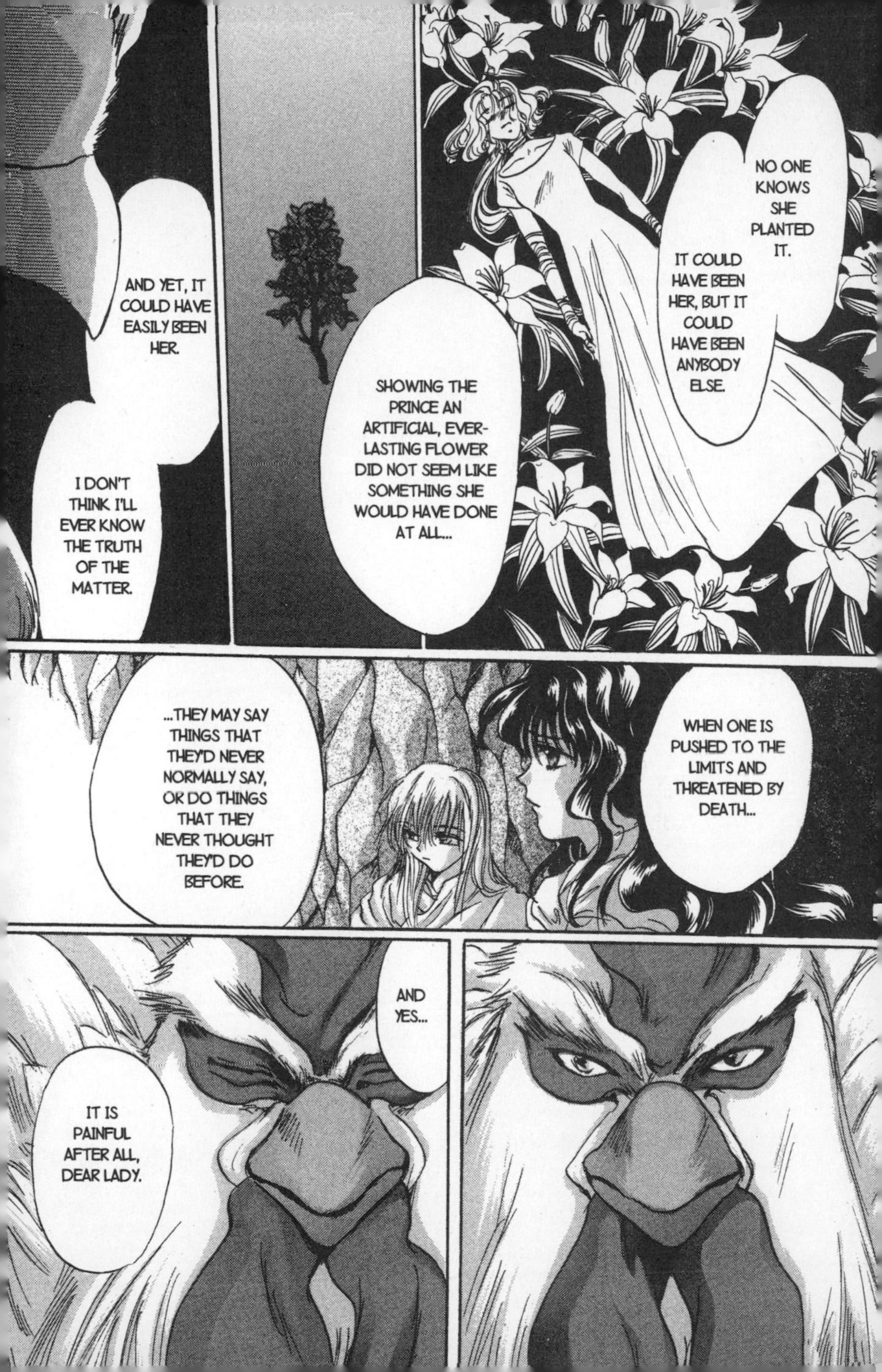
NO ONE KNOWS SHE PLANTED IT.
IT COULD HAVE BEEN HER, BUT IT COULD HAVE BEEN ANYBODY ELSE.
SHOWING THE PRINCE AN ARTIFICIAL, EVER-LASTING FLOWER DID NOT SEEM LIKE SOMETHING SHE WOULD HAVE DONE AT ALL...
AND YET, IT COULD HAVE EASILY BEEN HER.
I DON'T THINK I'LL EVER KNOW THE TRUTH OF THE MATTER.
WHEN ONE IS PUSHED TO THE LIMITS AND THREATENED BY DEATH...
...THEY MAY SAY THINGS THAT THEY'D NEVER NORMALLY SAY, OR DO THINGS THAT THEY NEVER THOUGHT THEY'D DO BEFORE.
AND YES...
IT IS PAINFUL AFTER ALL, DEAR LADY.

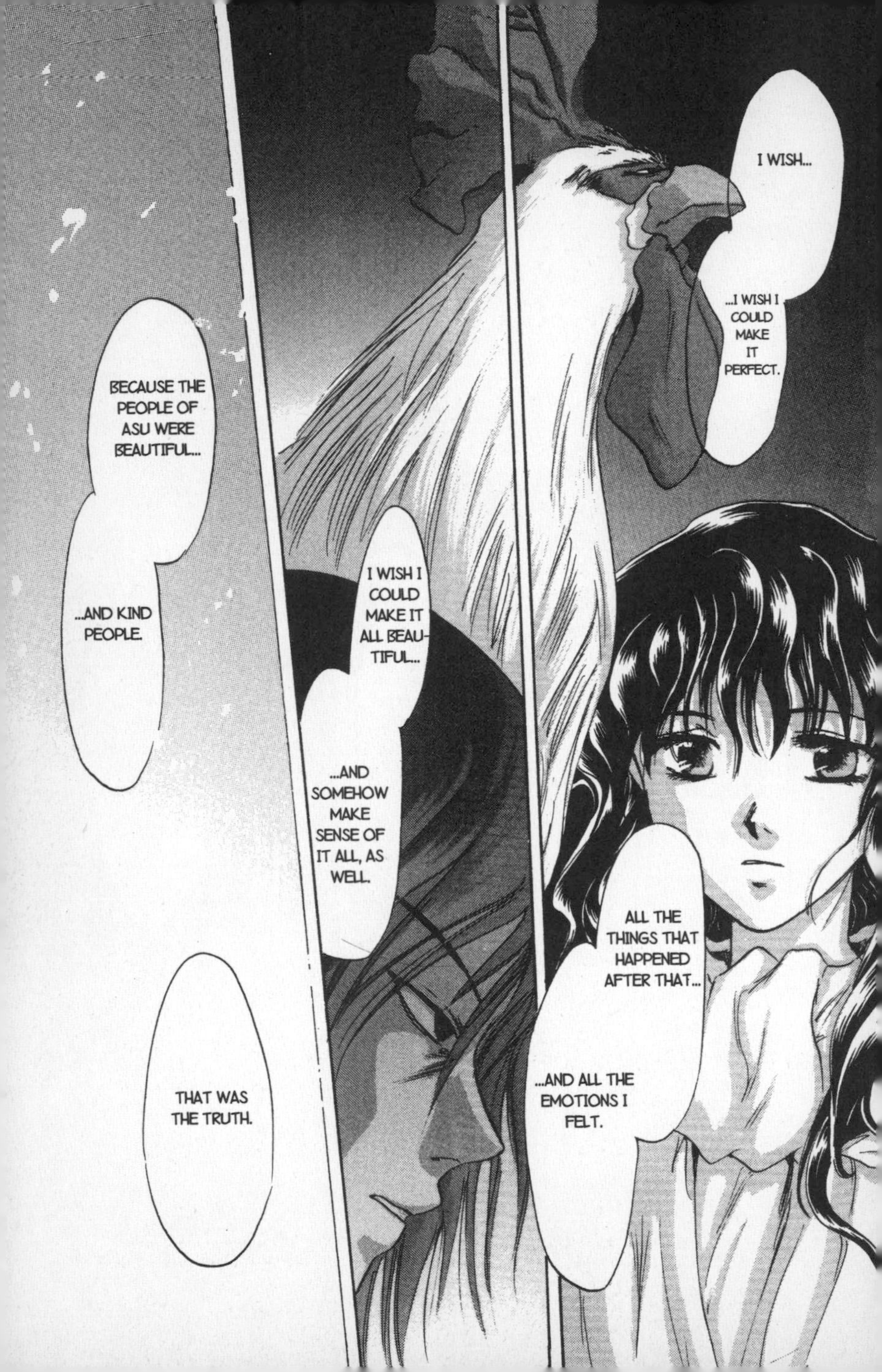
I WISH...
...I WISH I COULD MAKE IT PERFECT.
ALL THE THINGS THAT HAPPENED AFTER THAT...
...AND ALL THE EMOTIONS I FELT.
I WISH I COULD MAKE IT ALL BEAU-TIFUL...
...AND SOMEHOW MAKE SENSE OF IT ALL, AS WELL.
BECAUSE THE PEOPLE OF ASU WERE BEAUTIFUL...
...AND KIND PEOPLE.
THAT WAS THE TRUTH.

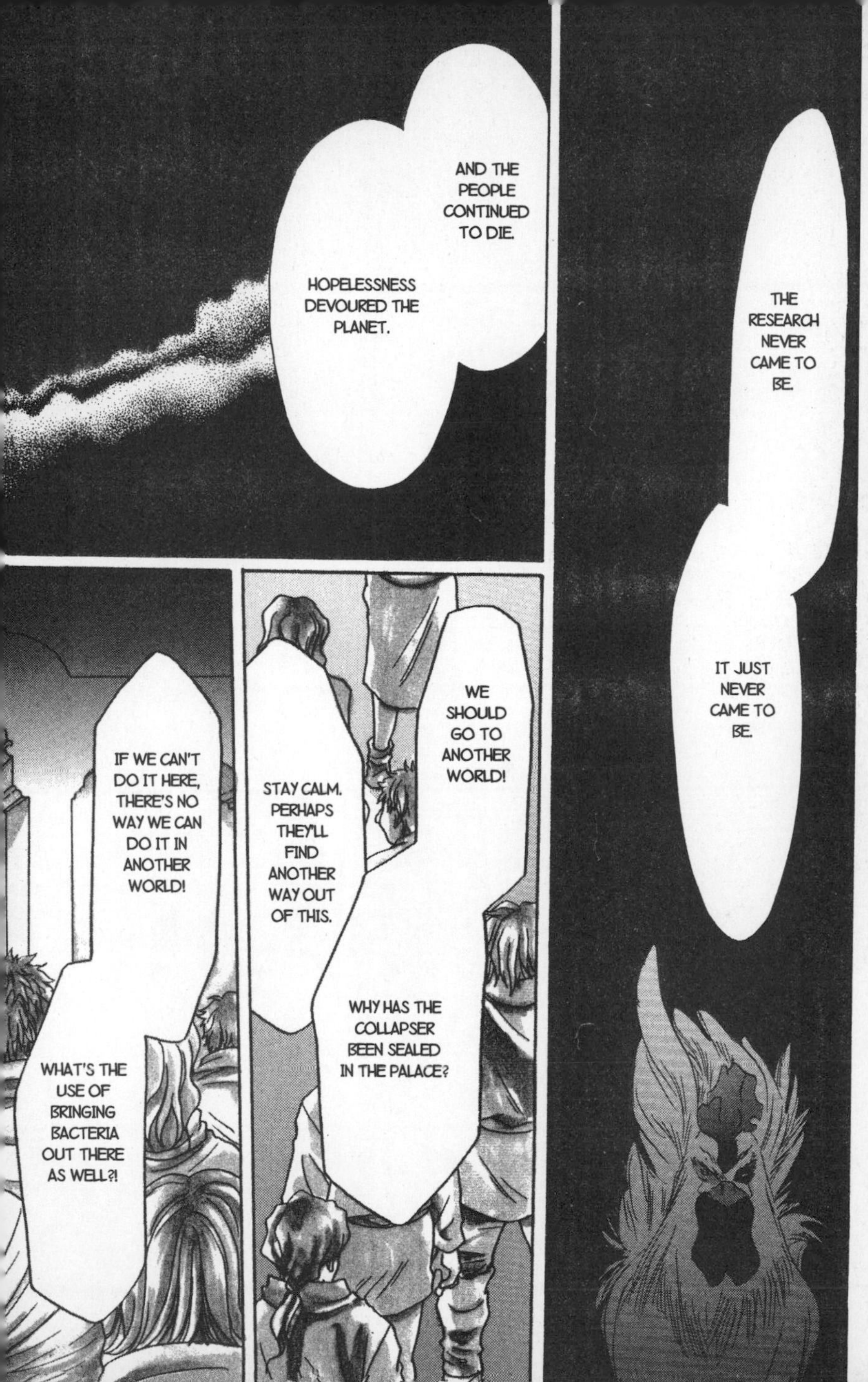
THE RESEARCH NEVER CAME TO BE.
IT JUST NEVER CAME TO BE.
AND THE PEOPLE CONTINUED TO DIE.
HOPELESSNESS DEVOURED THE PLANET.
WE SHOULD GO TO ANOTHER WORLD!
STAY CALM. PERHAPS THEY'LL FIND ANOTHER WAY OUT OF THIS.
WHY HAS THE COLLAPSER BEEN SEALED IN THE PALACE?
IF WE CAN'T DO IT HERE, THERE'S NO WAY WE CAN DO IT IN ANOTHER WORLD!
WHAT'S THE USE OF BRINGING BACTERIA OUT THERE AS WELL?!

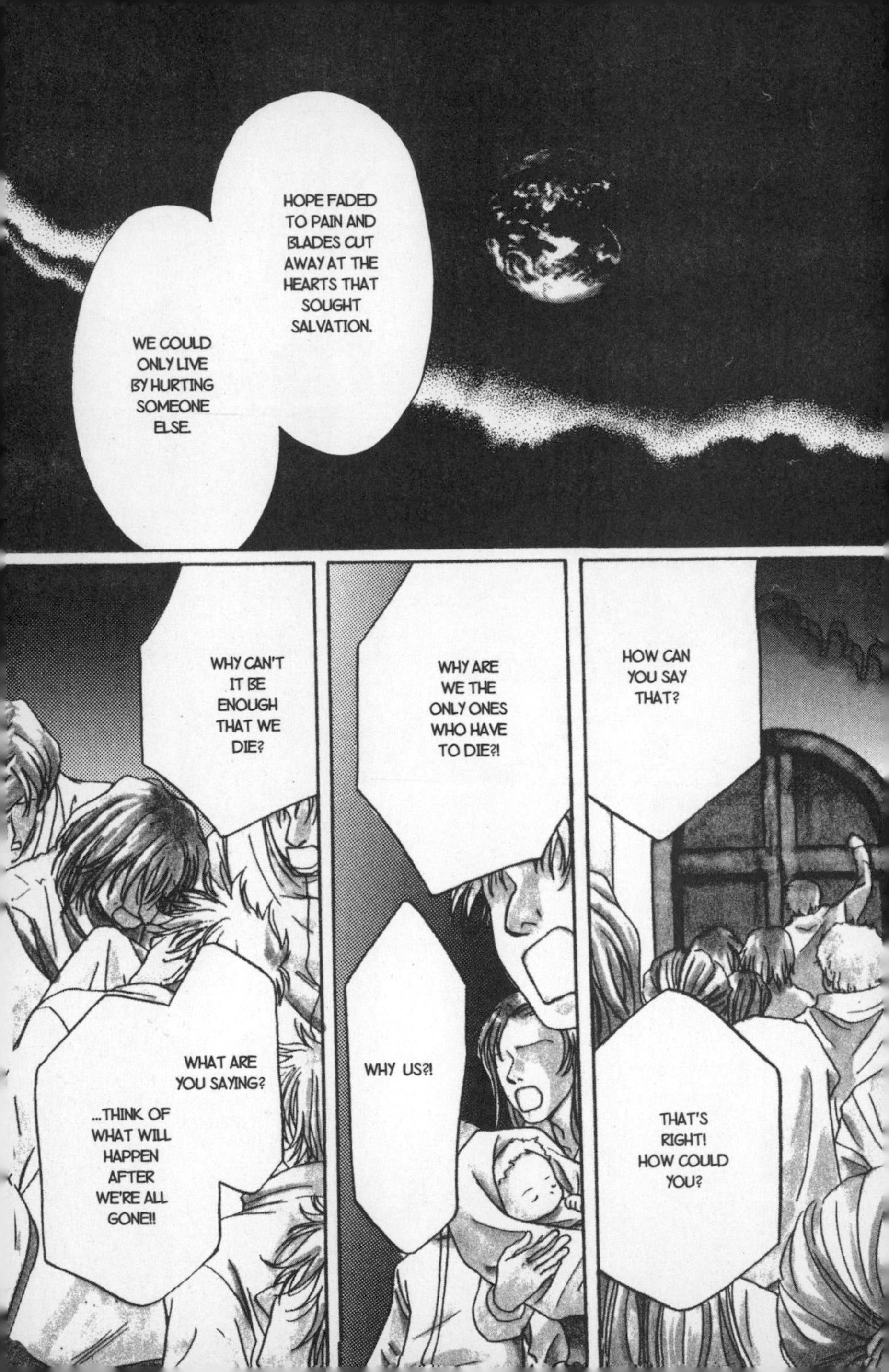
HOPE FADED TO PAIN AND BLADES CUT AWAY AT THE HEARTS THAT SOUGHT SALVATION.
WE COULD ONLY LIVE BY HURTING SOMEONE ELSE.
HOW CAN YOU SAY THAT?
THAT'S RIGHT! HOW COULD YOU?
WHY ARE WE THE ONLY ONES WHO HAVE TO DIE?!
WHY US?!
WHY CAN'T IT BE ENOUGH THAT WE DIE?
WHAT ARE YOU SAYING?
...THINK OF WHAT WILL HAPPEN AFTER WE'RE ALL GONE!!

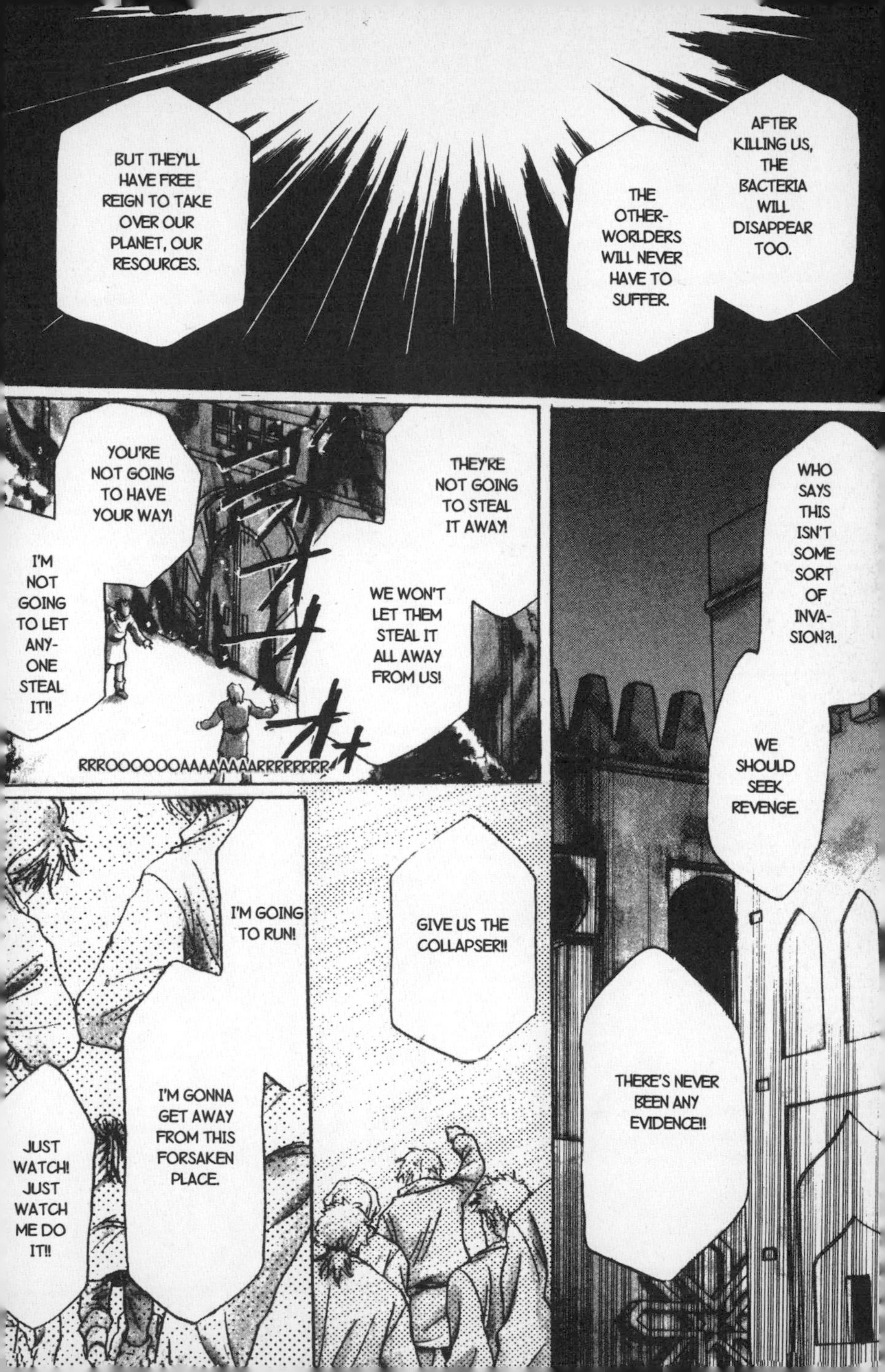
AFTER KILLING US, THE BACTERIA WILL DISAPPEAR TOO.
THE OTHER-WORLDERS WILL NEVER HAVE TO SUFFER.
BUT THEY'LL HAVE FREE REIGN TO TAKE OVER OUR PLANET, OUR RESOURCES.
WHO SAYS THIS ISN'T SOME SORT OF INVASION?!.
WE SHOULD SEEK REVENGE.
THERE'S NEVER BEEN ANY EVIDENCE!!
THEY'RE NOT GOING TO STEAL IT AWAY!
WE WON'T LET THEM STEAL IT ALL AWAY FROM US!
YOU'RE NOT GOING TO HAVE YOUR WAY!
I'M NOT GOING TO LET ANY-ONE STEAL IT!!
RRROOOOOOAAAAAAARRRRRRR
GIVE US THE COLLAPSER!!
I'M GOING TO RUN!
I'M GONNA GET AWAY FROM THIS FORSAKEN PLACE.
JUST WATCH! JUST WATCH ME DO IT!!

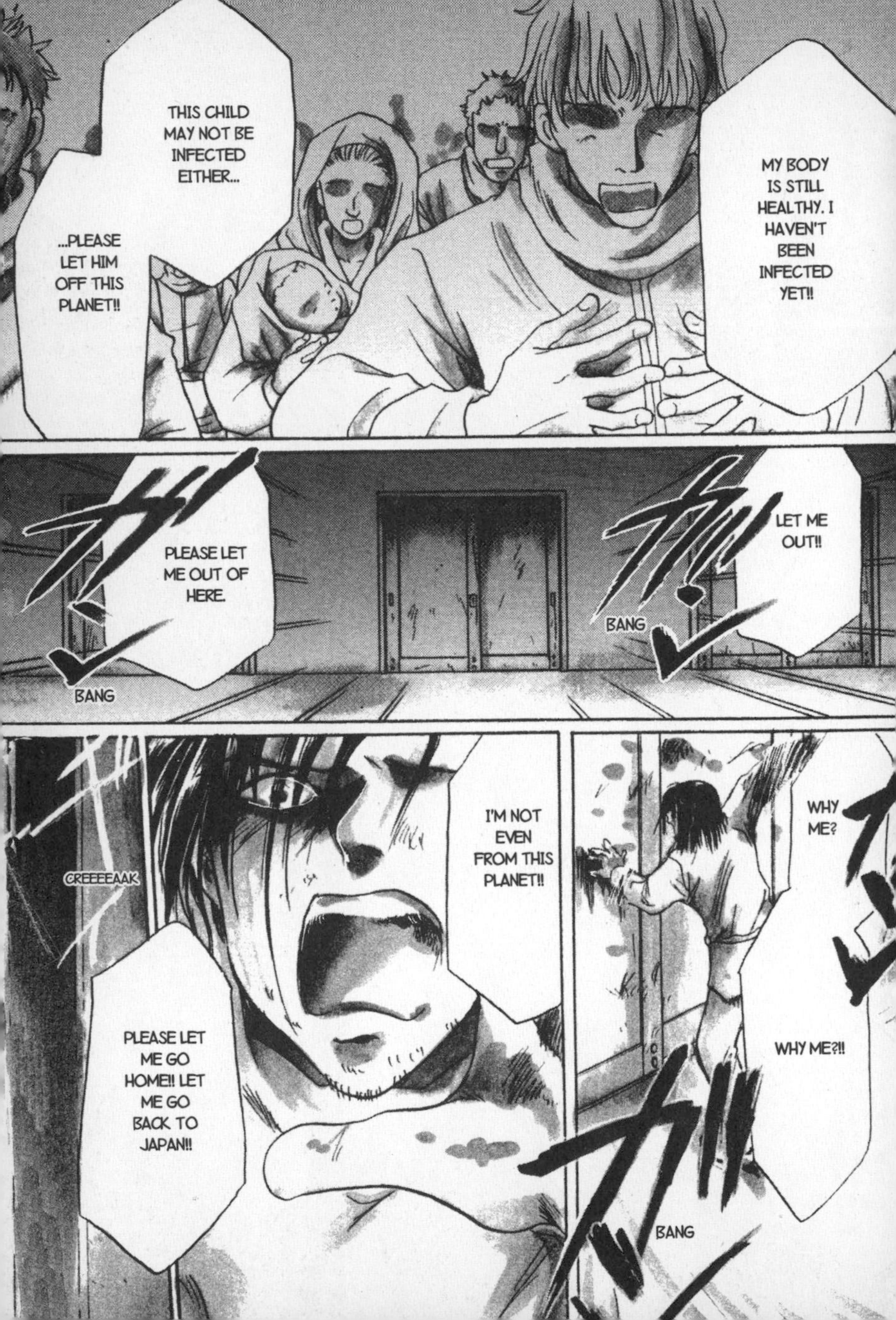
MY BODY IS STILL HEALTHY. I HAVEN'T BEEN INFECTED YET!!
THIS CHILD MAY NOT BE INFECTED EITHER...
...PLEASE LET HIM OFF THIS PLANET!!
LET ME OUT!!
BANG
PLEASE LET ME OUT OF HERE.
BANG
WHY ME?
WHY ME?!!
BANG
I'M NOT EVEN FROM THIS PLANET!!
CREEEEAAK
PLEASE LET ME GO HOME!! LET ME GO BACK TO JAPAN!!

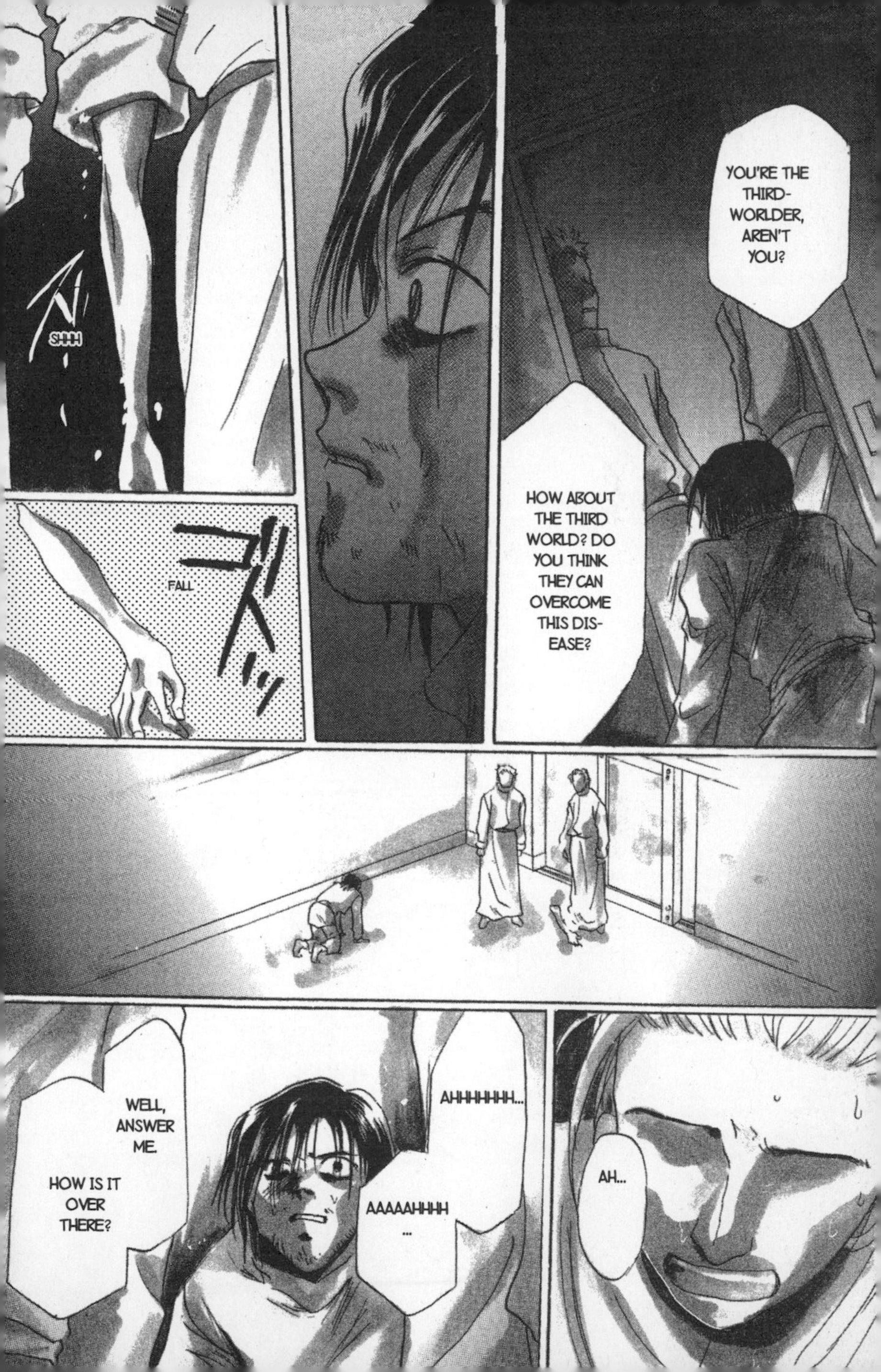
YOU'RE THE THIRD-WORLDER, AREN'T YOU?
HOW ABOUT THE THIRD WORLD? DO YOU THINK THEY CAN OVERCOME THIS DIS-EASE?
SHHH
FALL
AH...
AHHHHHHH...
WELL, ANSWER ME.
AAAAAHHHH ...
HOW IS IT OVER THERE?

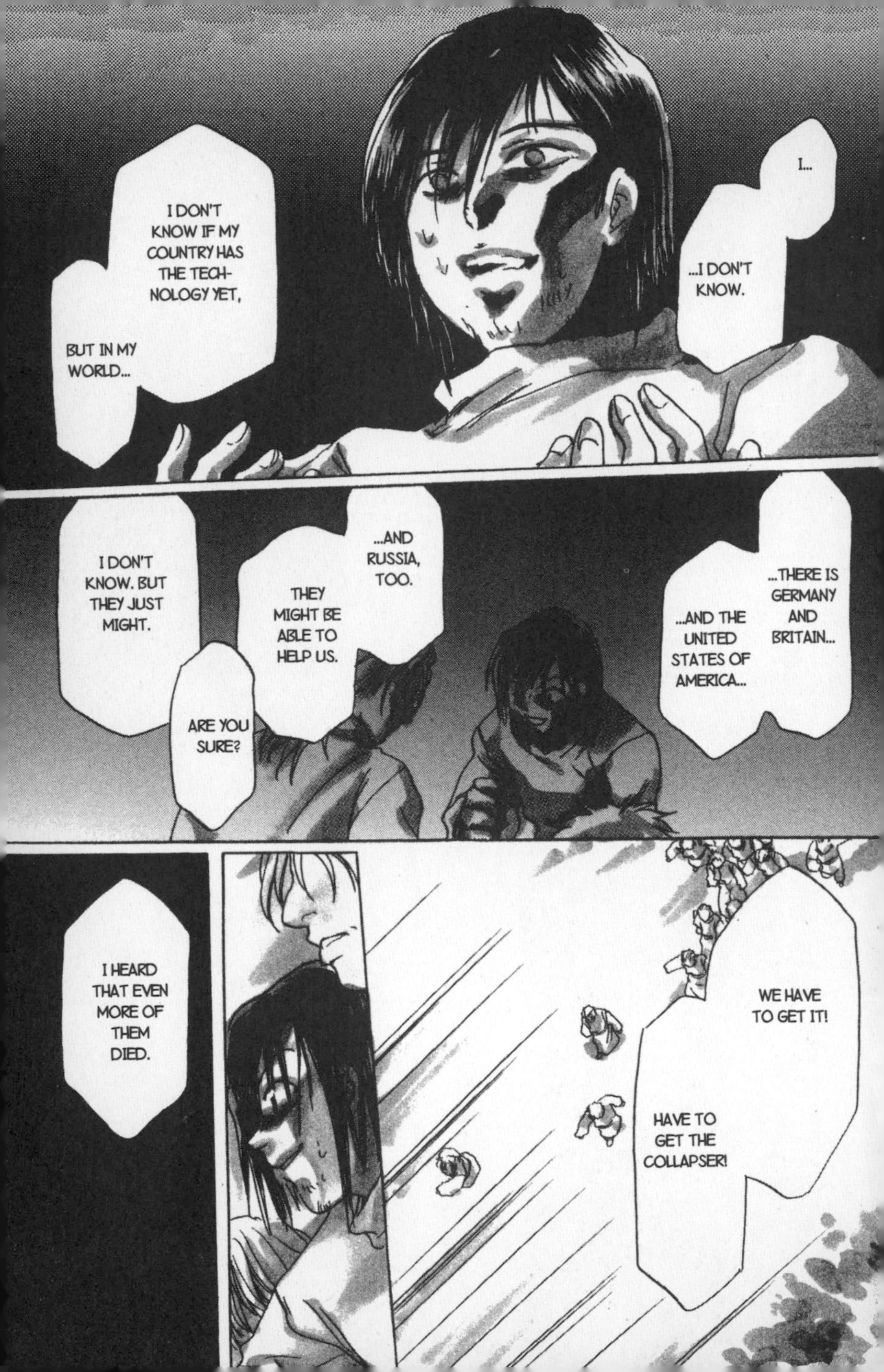
I...
...I DON'T KNOW.
I DON'T KNOW IF MY COUNTRY HAS THE TECH-NOLOGY YET,
BUT IN MY WORLD...
...THERE IS GERMANY AND BRITAIN...
...AND THE UNITED STATES OF AMERICA...
...AND RUSSIA, TOO.
THEY MIGHT BE ABLE TO HELP US.
ARE YOU SURE?
I DON'T KNOW. BUT THEY JUST MIGHT.
WE HAVE TO GET IT!
HAVE TO GET THE COLLAPSER!
I HEARD THAT EVEN MORE OF THEM DIED.

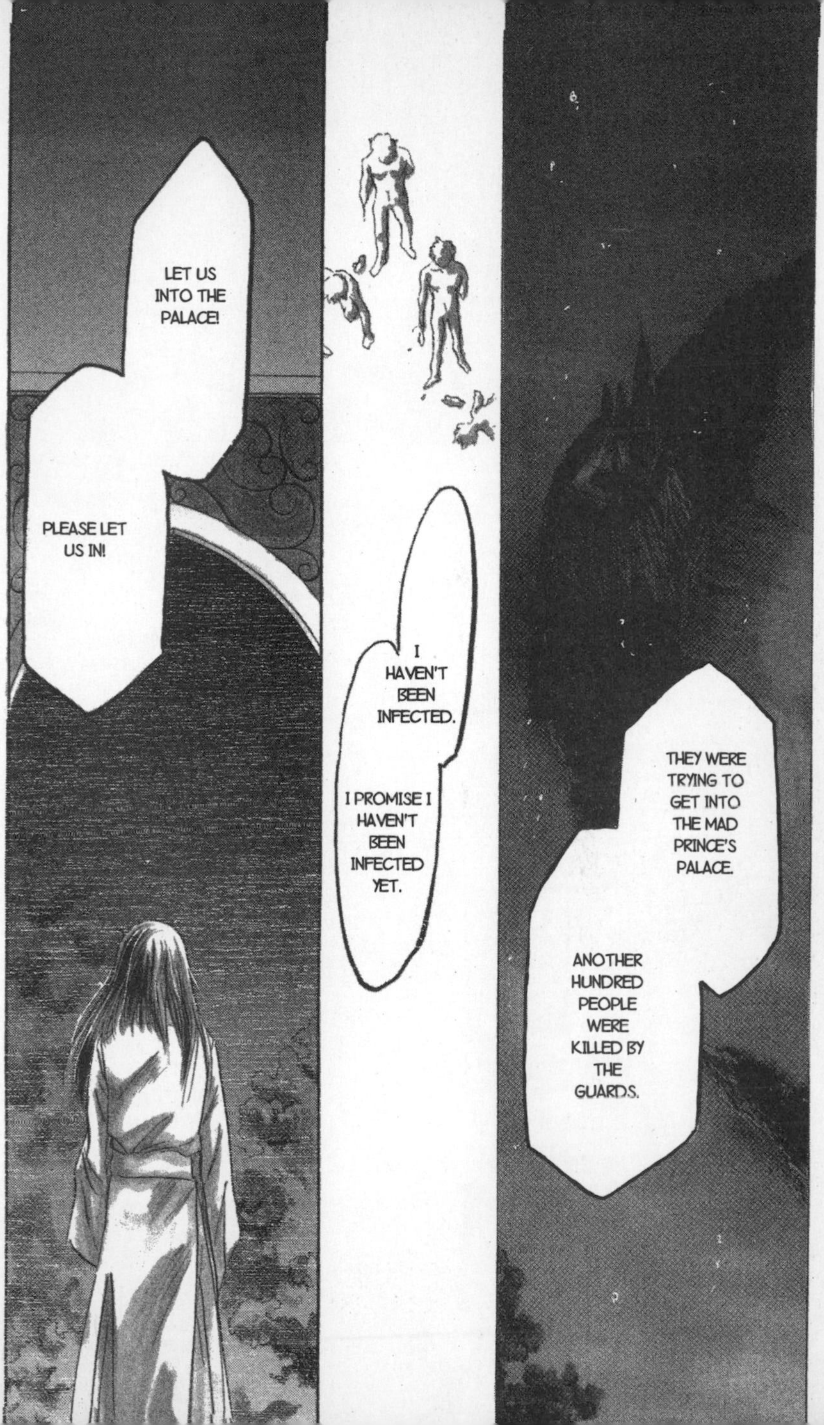
THEY WERE TRYING TO GET INTO THE MAD PRINCE'S PALACE.
ANOTHER HUNDRED PEOPLE WERE KILLED BY THE GUARDS.
I HAVEN'T BEEN INFECTED.
I PROMISE I HAVEN'T BEEN INFECTED YET.
LET US INTO THE PALACE!
PLEASE LET US IN!

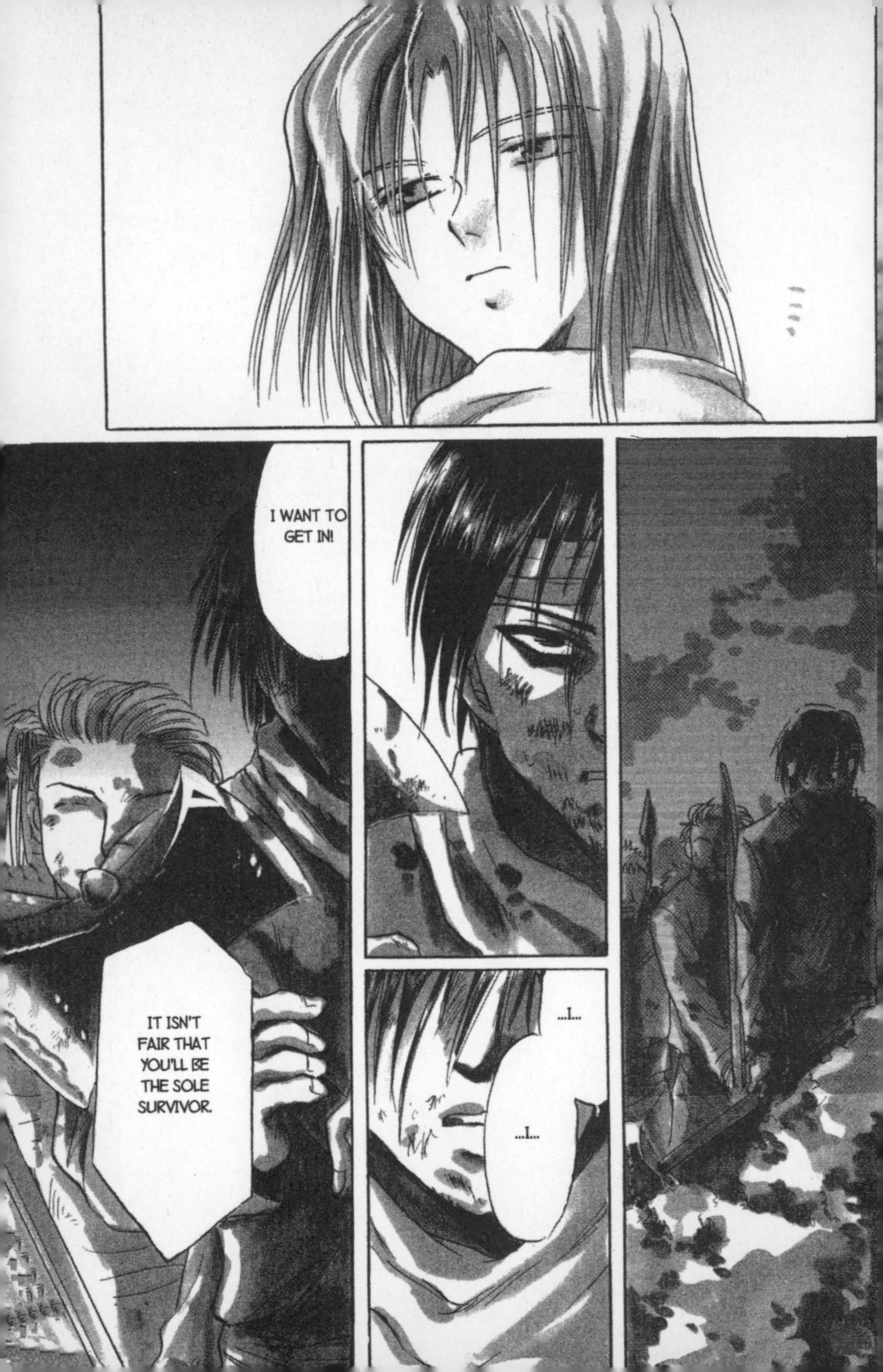
...I...
...I...
I WANT TO GET IN!
IT ISN'T FAIR THAT YOU'LL BE THE SOLE SURVIVOR.

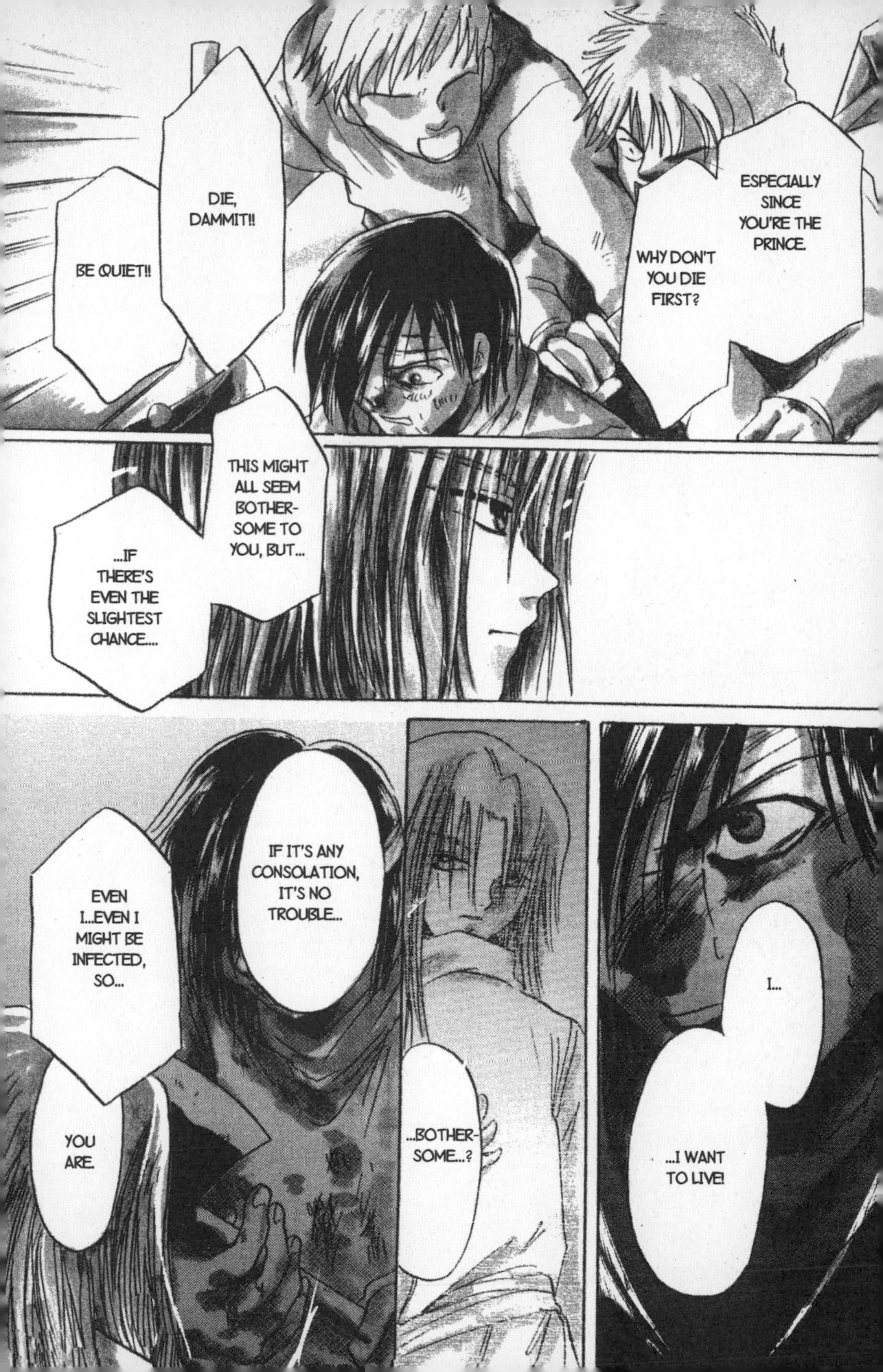
WHY DON'T YOU DIE FIRST?
ESPECIALLY SINCE YOU'RE THE PRINCE.
DIE, DAMMIT!!
BE QUIET!!
THIS MIGHT ALL SEEM BOTHER-SOME TO YOU, BUT...
...IF THERE'S EVEN THE SLIGHTEST CHANCE...
I...
...I WANT TO LIVE!
...BOTHER-SOME...?
IF IT'S ANY CONSOLATION, IT'S NO TROUBLE...
EVEN I...EVEN I MIGHT BE INFECTED, SO...
YOU ARE.

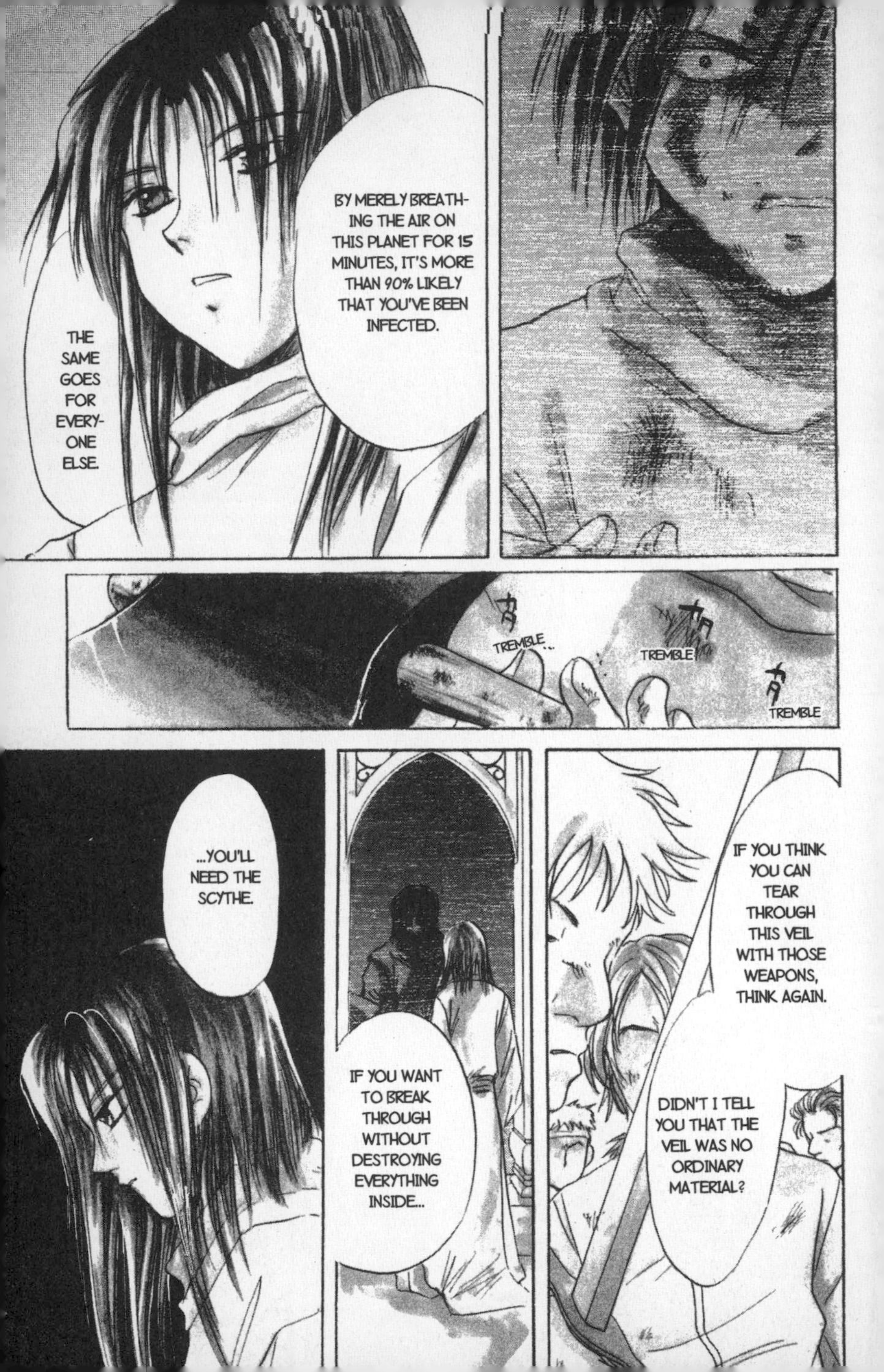
BY MERELY BREATHING THE AIR ON THIS PLANET FOR 15 MINUTES, IT'S MORE THAN 90% LIKELY THAT YOU'VE BEEN INFECTED.
THE SAME GOES FOR EVERYONE ELSE.
TREMBLE
TREMBLE
TREMBLE...
IF YOU THINK YOU CAN TEAR THROUGH THIS VEIL WITH THOSE WEAPONS, THINK AGAIN.
DIDN'T I TELL YOU THAT THE VEIL WAS NO ORDINARY MATERIAL?
IF YOU WANT TO BREAK THROUGH WITHOUT DESTROYING EVERYTHING INSIDE...
...YOU'LL NEED THE SCYTHE.

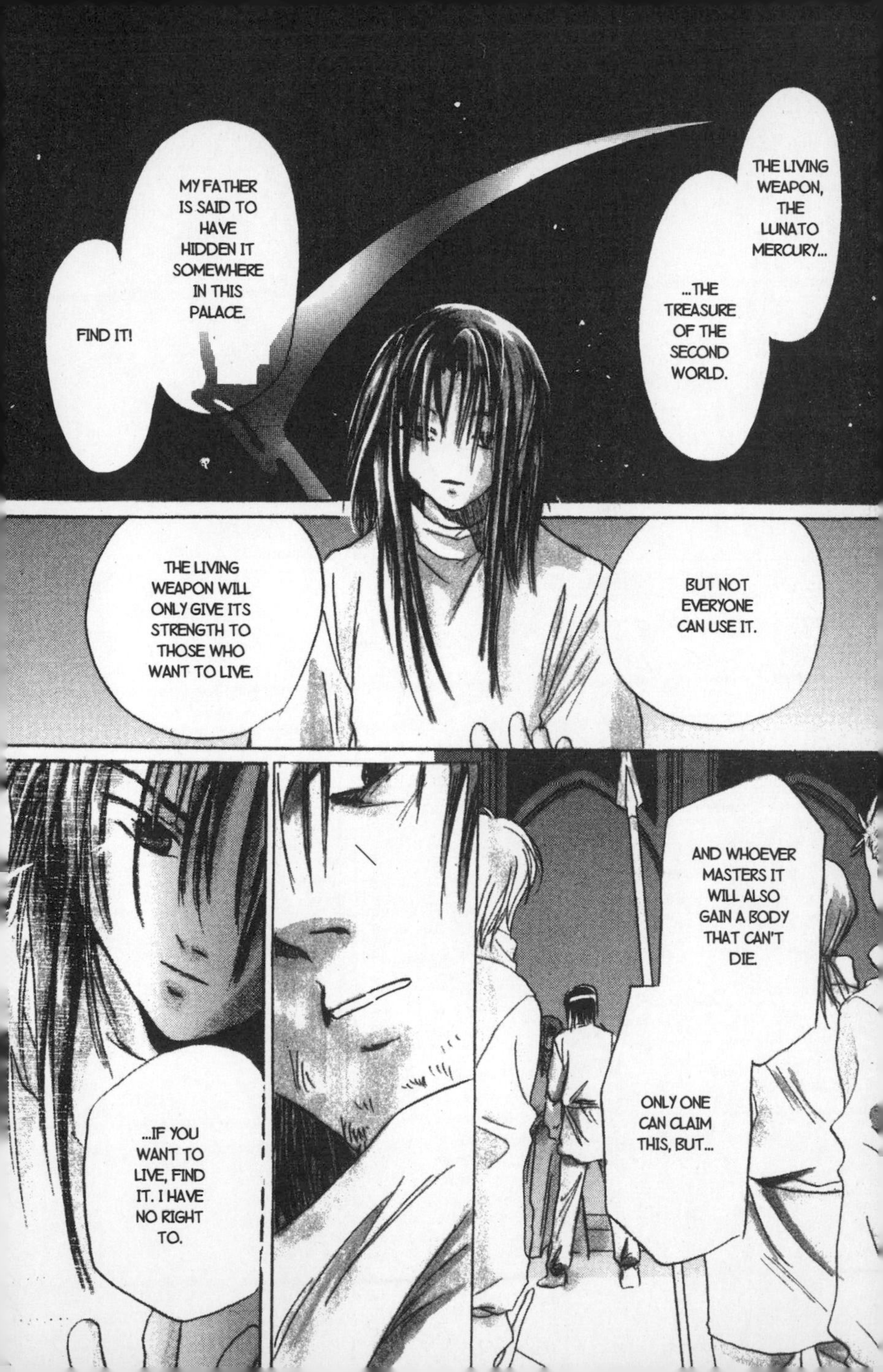
THE LIVING WEAPON, THE LUNATO MERCURY...
...THE TREASURE OF THE SECOND WORLD.
MY FATHER IS SAID TO HAVE HIDDEN IT SOMEWHERE IN THIS PALACE.
FIND IT!
BUT NOT EVERYONE CAN USE IT.
THE LIVING WEAPON WILL ONLY GIVE ITS STRENGTH TO THOSE WHO WANT TO LIVE.
AND WHOEVER MASTERS IT WILL ALSO GAIN A BODY THAT CAN'T DIE.
ONLY ONE CAN CLAIM THIS, BUT...
...IF YOU WANT TO LIVE, FIND IT. I HAVE NO RIGHT TO.

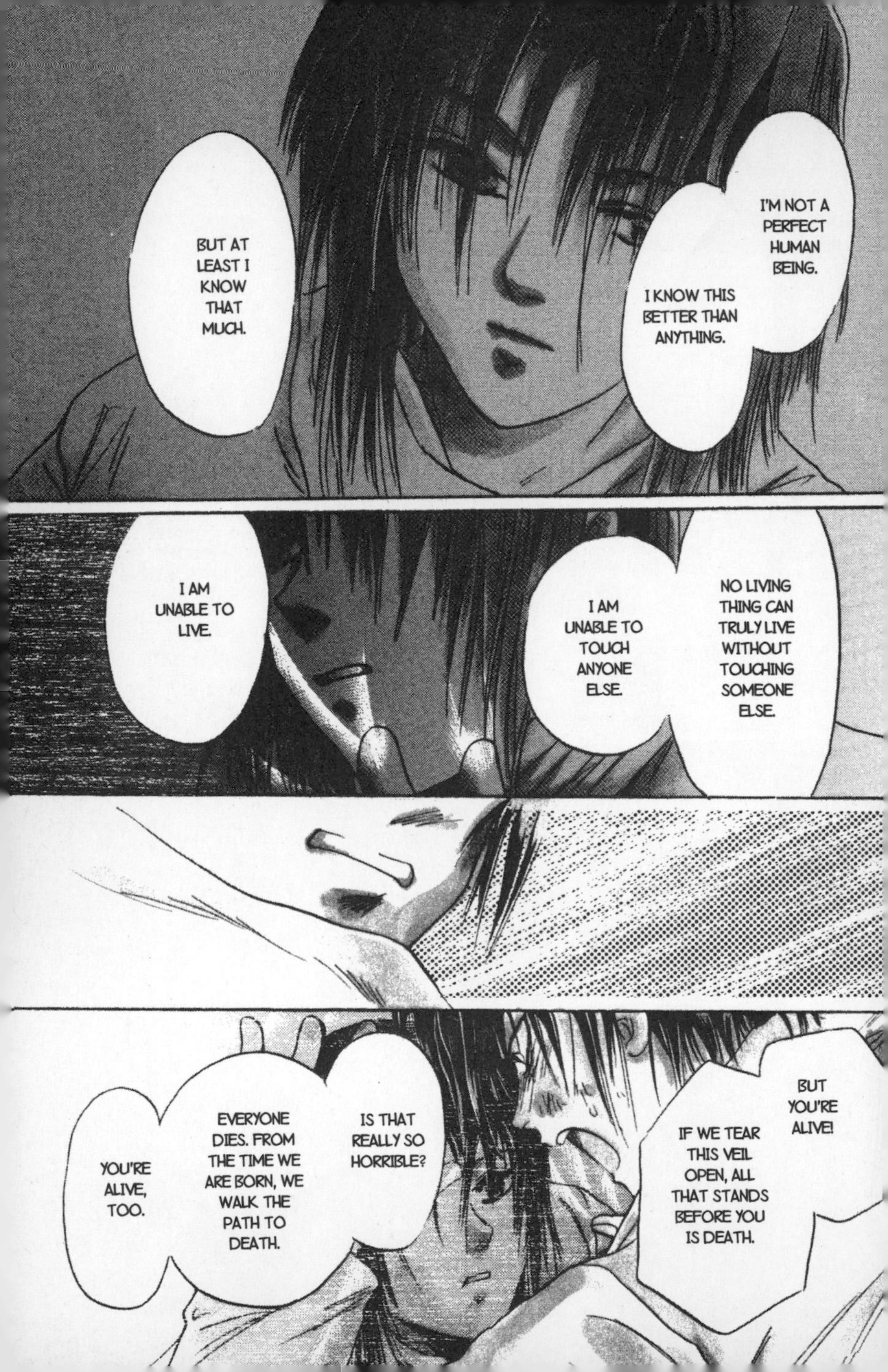
I'M NOT A PERFECT HUMAN BEING.
I KNOW THIS BETTER THAN ANYTHING.
BUT AT LEAST I KNOW THAT MUCH.
NO LIVING THING CAN TRULY LIVE WITHOUT TOUCHING SOMEONE ELSE.
I AM UNABLE TO TOUCH ANYONE ELSE.
I AM UNABLE TO LIVE.
BUT YOU'RE ALIVE!
IF WE TEAR THIS VEIL OPEN, ALL THAT STANDS BEFORE YOU IS DEATH.
IS THAT REALLY SO HORRIBLE?
EVERYONE DIES. FROM THE TIME WE ARE BORN, WE WALK THE PATH TO DEATH.
YOU'RE ALIVE, TOO.

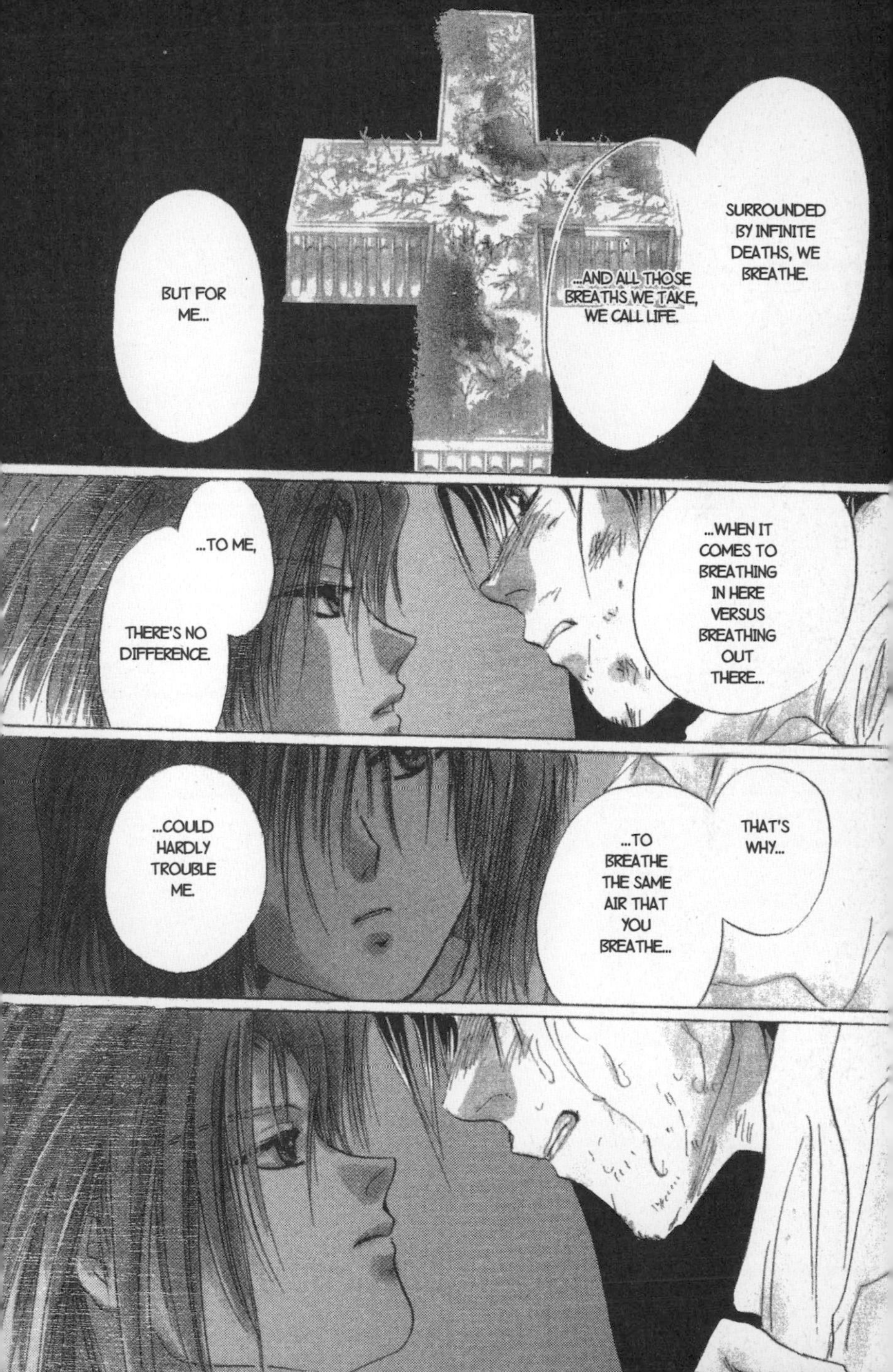
SURROUNDED BY INFINITE DEATHS, WE BREATHE.
...AND ALL THOSE BREATHS WE TAKE, WE CALL LIFE.
BUT FOR ME...
...WHEN IT COMES TO BREATHING IN HERE VERSUS BREATHING OUT THERE...
...TO ME,
THERE'S NO DIFFERENCE.
THAT'S WHY...
...TO BREATHE THE SAME AIR THAT YOU BREATHE...
...COULD HARDLY TROUBLE ME.

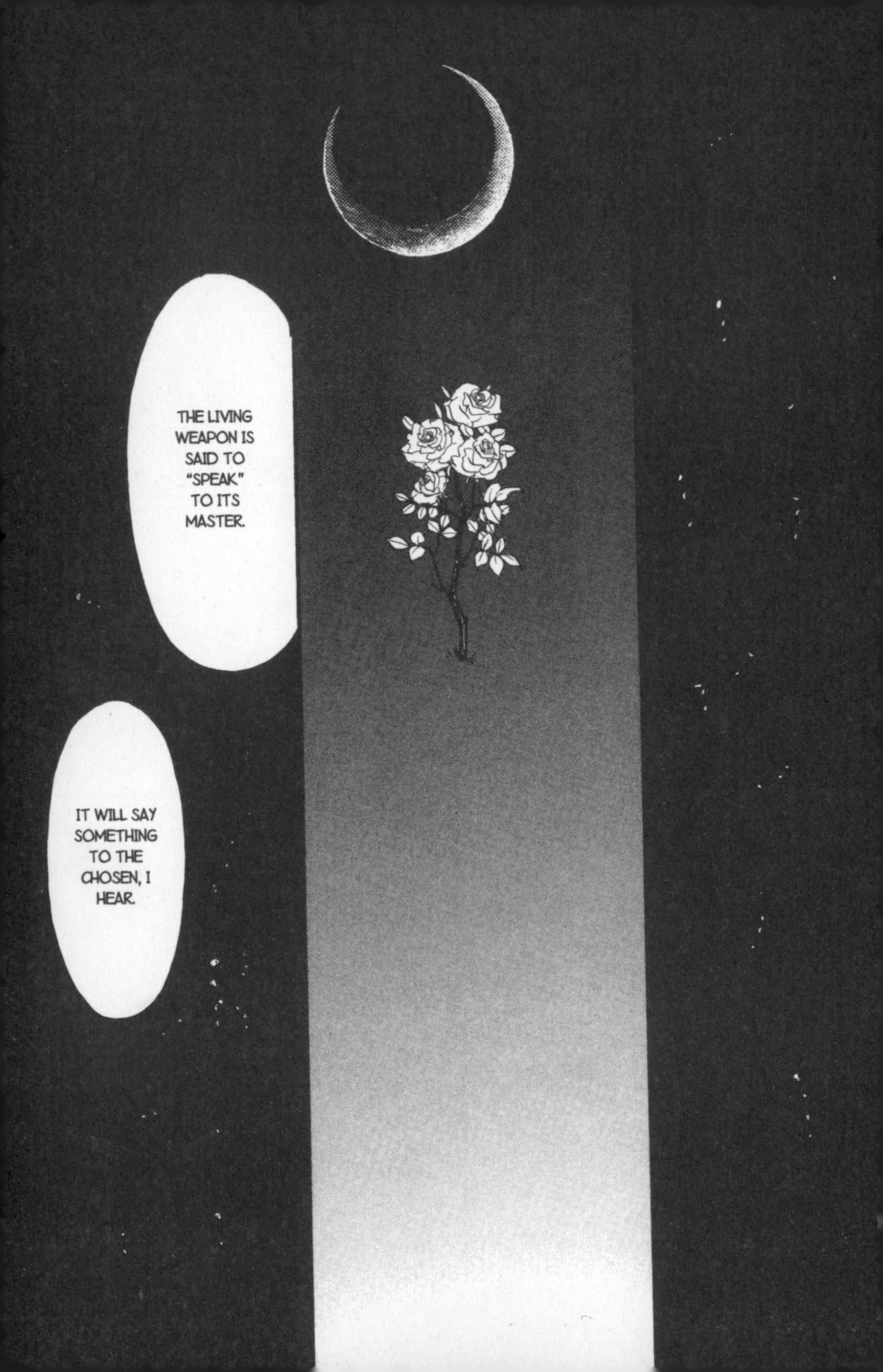
THE LIVING WEAPON IS SAID TO "SPEAK" TO ITS MASTER.
IT WILL SAY SOMETHING TO THE CHOSEN, I HEAR.

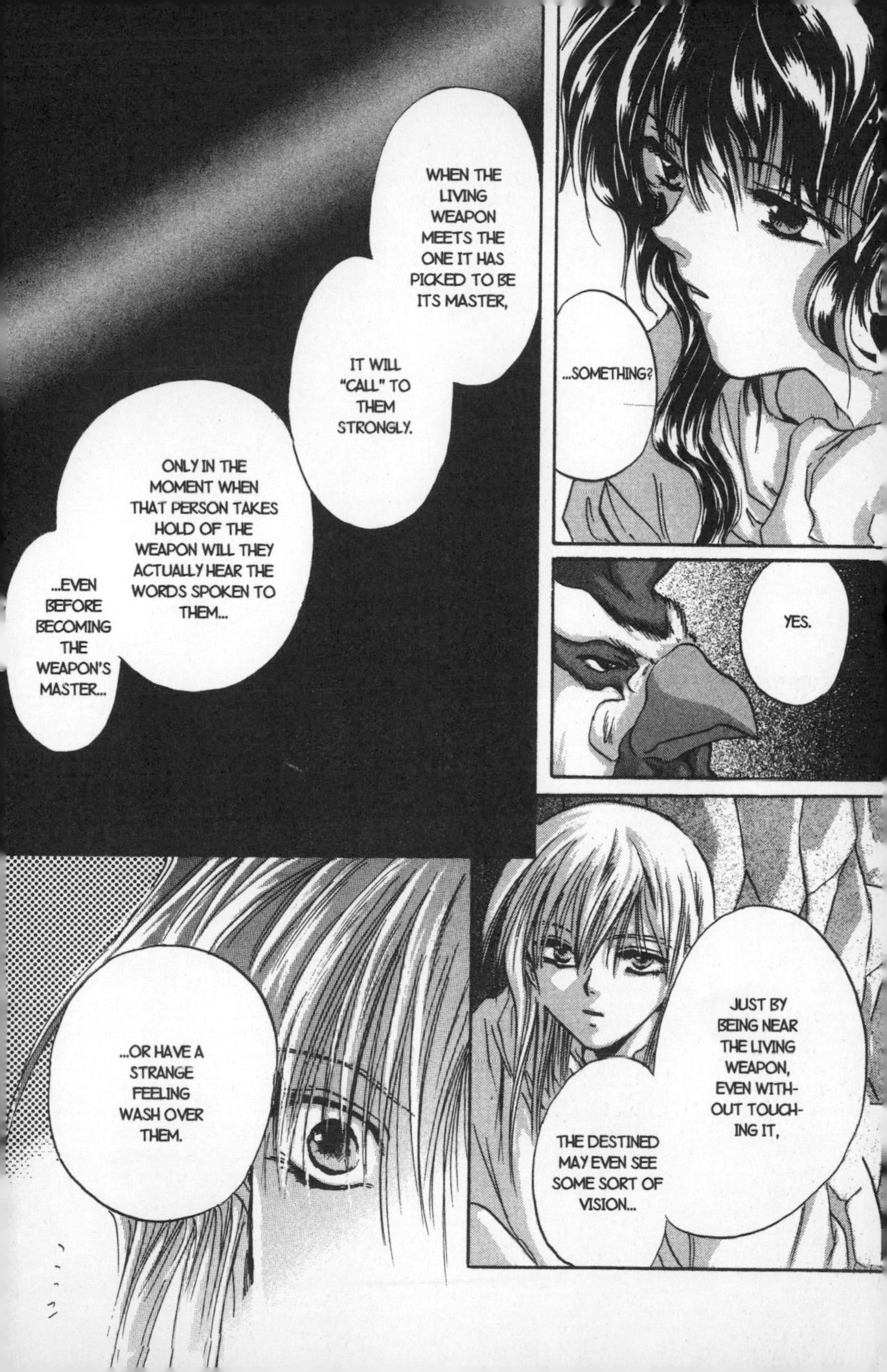
...SOMETHING?
YES.
WHEN THE LIVING WEAPON MEETS THE ONE IT HAS PICKED TO BE ITS MASTER,
IT WILL "CALL" TO THEM STRONGLY.
ONLY IN THE MOMENT WHEN THAT PERSON TAKES HOLD OF THE WEAPON WILL THEY ACTUALLY HEAR THE WORDS SPOKEN TO THEM...
...EVEN BEFORE BECOMING THE WEAPON'S MASTER...
JUST BY BEING NEAR THE LIVING WEAPON, EVEN WITH-OUT TOUCH-ING IT,
THE DESTINED MAY EVEN SEE SOME SORT OF VISION...
...OR HAVE A STRANGE FEELING WASH OVER THEM.

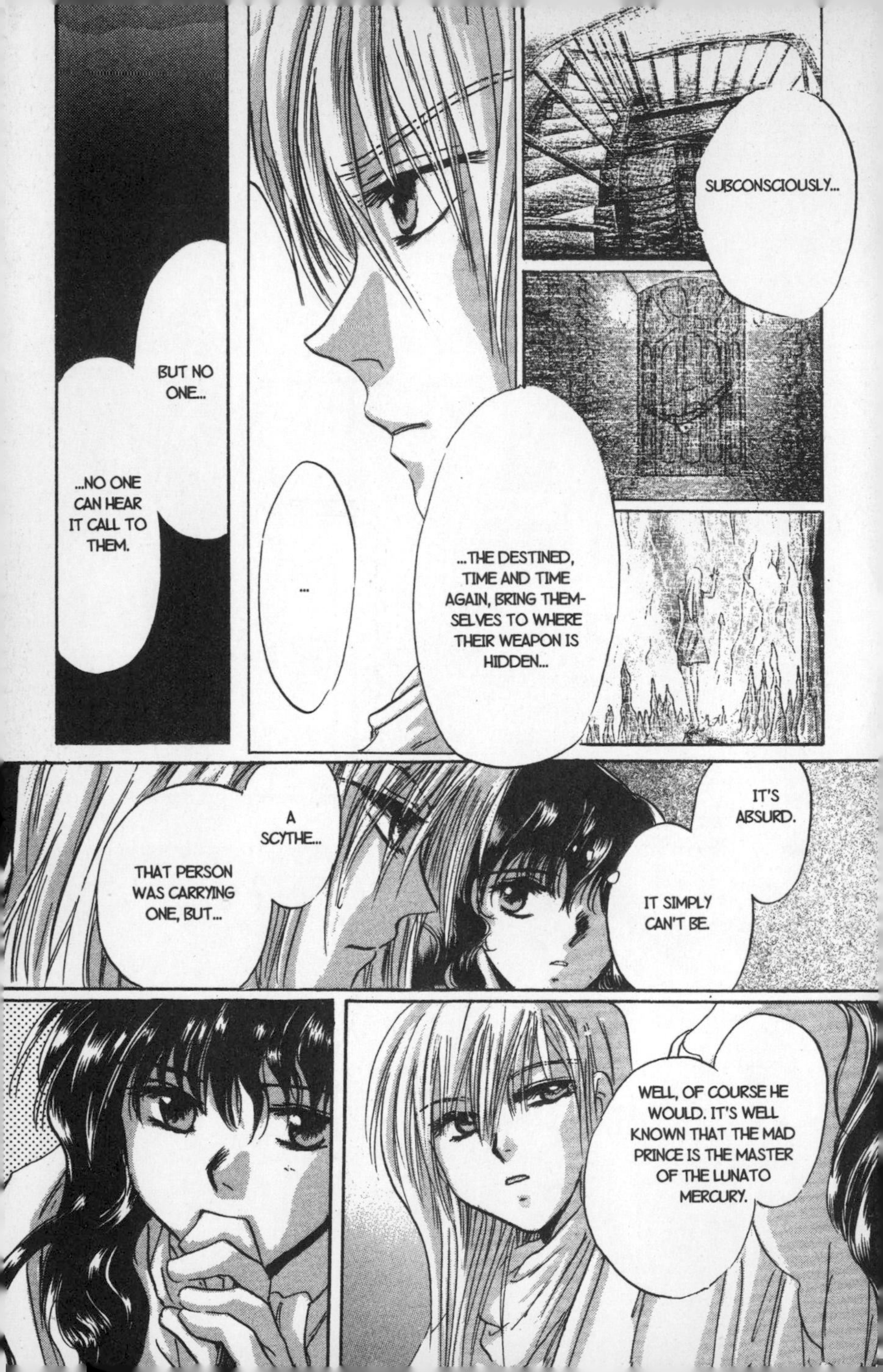
SUBCONSCIOUSLY...
...THE DESTINED, TIME AND TIME AGAIN, BRING THEM-SELVES TO WHERE THEIR WEAPON IS HIDDEN...
...
BUT NO ONE...
...NO ONE CAN HEAR IT CALL TO THEM.
IT'S ABSURD.
IT SIMPLY CAN'T BE.
A SCYTHE...
THAT PERSON WAS CARRYING ONE, BUT...
WELL, OF COURSE HE WOULD. IT'S WELL KNOWN THAT THE MAD PRINCE IS THE MASTER OF THE LUNATO MERCURY.

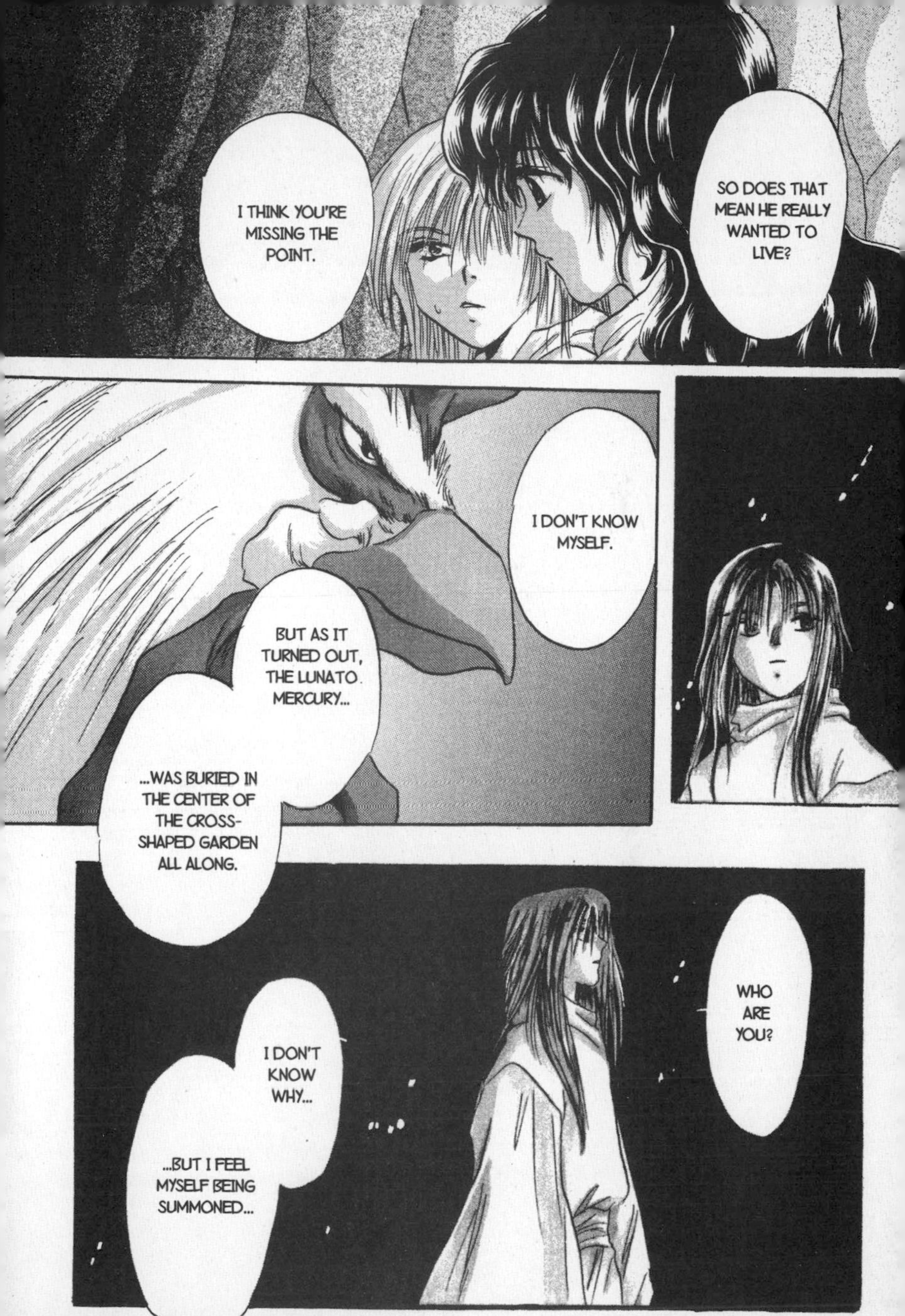
SO DOES THAT MEAN HE REALLY WANTED TO LIVE?
I THINK YOU'RE MISSING THE POINT.
I DON'T KNOW MYSELF.
BUT AS IT TURNED OUT, THE LUNATO MERCURY...
...WAS BURIED IN THE CENTER OF THE CROSS-SHAPED GARDEN ALL ALONG.
WHO ARE YOU?
I DON'T KNOW WHY...
...BUT I FEEL MYSELF BEING SUMMONED...

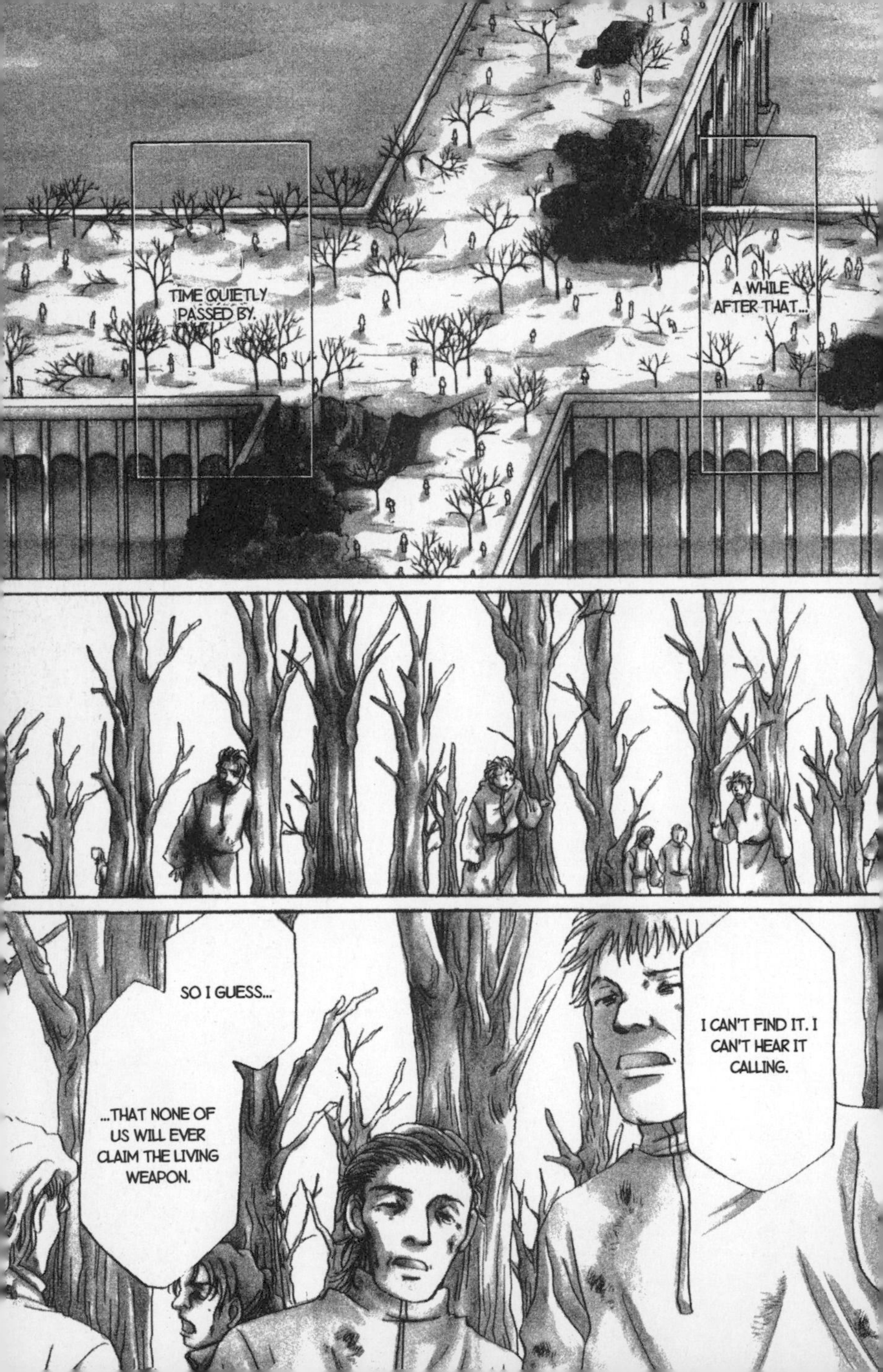
A WHILE AFTER THAT...
TIME QUIETLY PASSED BY.
I CAN'T FIND IT. I CAN'T HEAR IT CALLING.
SO I GUESS...
...THAT NONE OF US WILL EVER CLAIM THE LIVING WEAPON.

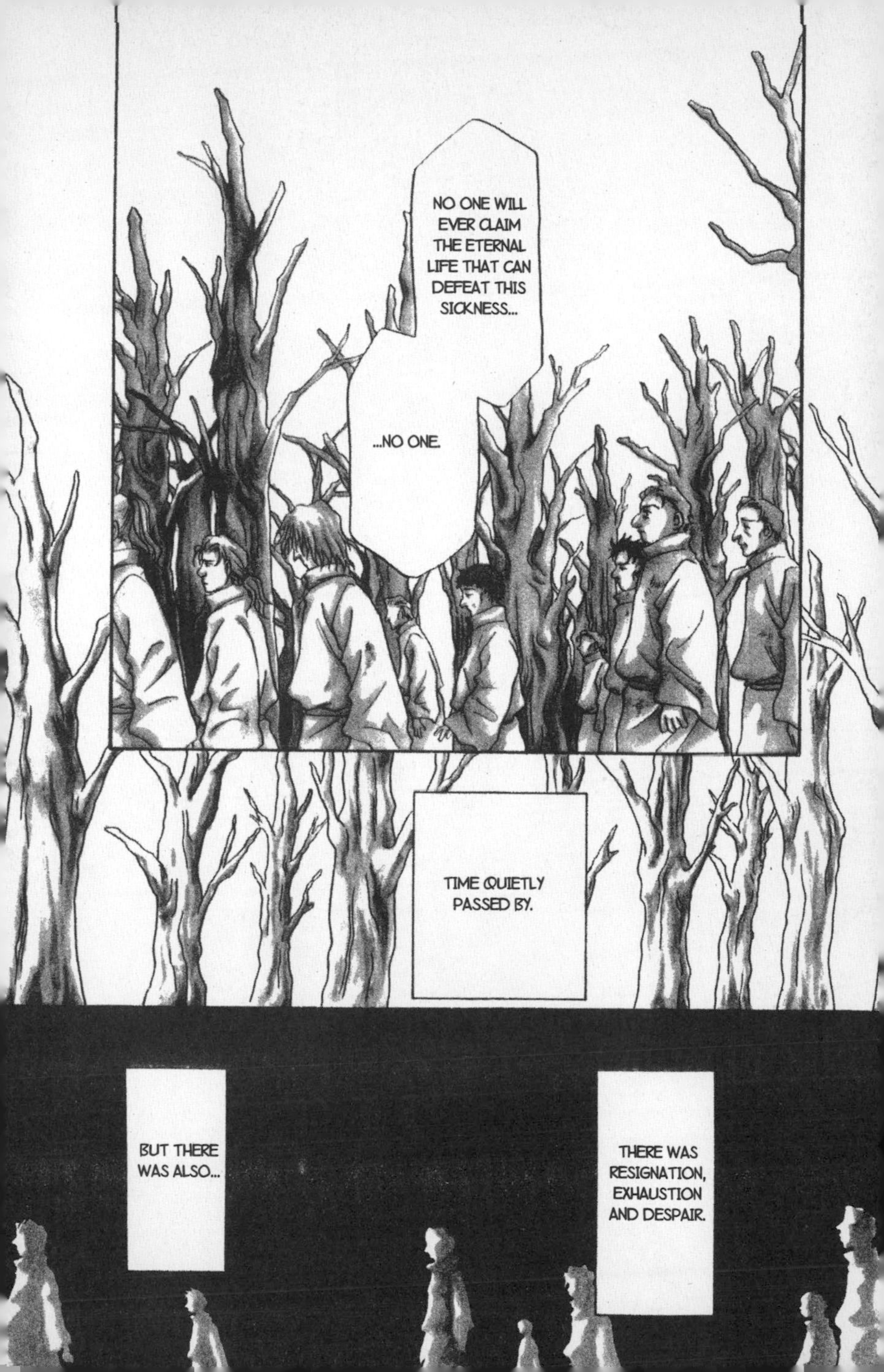
NO ONE WILL EVER CLAIM THE ETERNAL LIFE THAT CAN DEFEAT THIS SICKNESS...
...NO ONE.
TIME QUIETLY PASSED BY.
THERE WAS RESIGNATION, EXHAUSTION AND DESPAIR.
BUT THERE WAS ALSO...

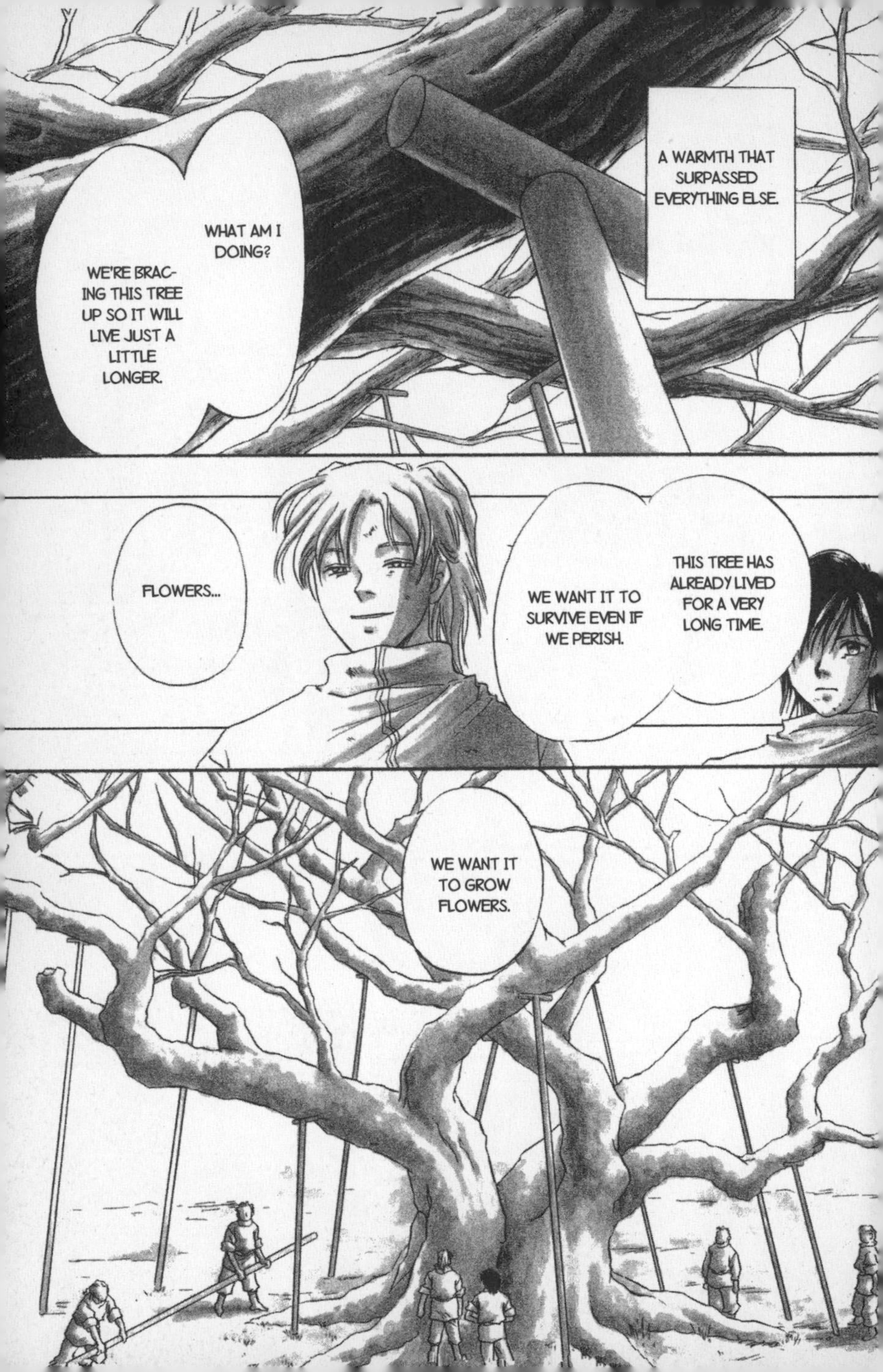
A WARMTH THAT SURPASSED EVERYTHING ELSE.
WHAT AM I DOING?
WE'RE BRAC-ING THIS TREE UP SO IT WILL LIVE JUST A LITTLE LONGER.
THIS TREE HAS ALREADY LIVED FOR A VERY LONG TIME.
WE WANT IT TO SURVIVE EVEN IF WE PERISH.
FLOWERS...
WE WANT IT TO GROW FLOWERS.

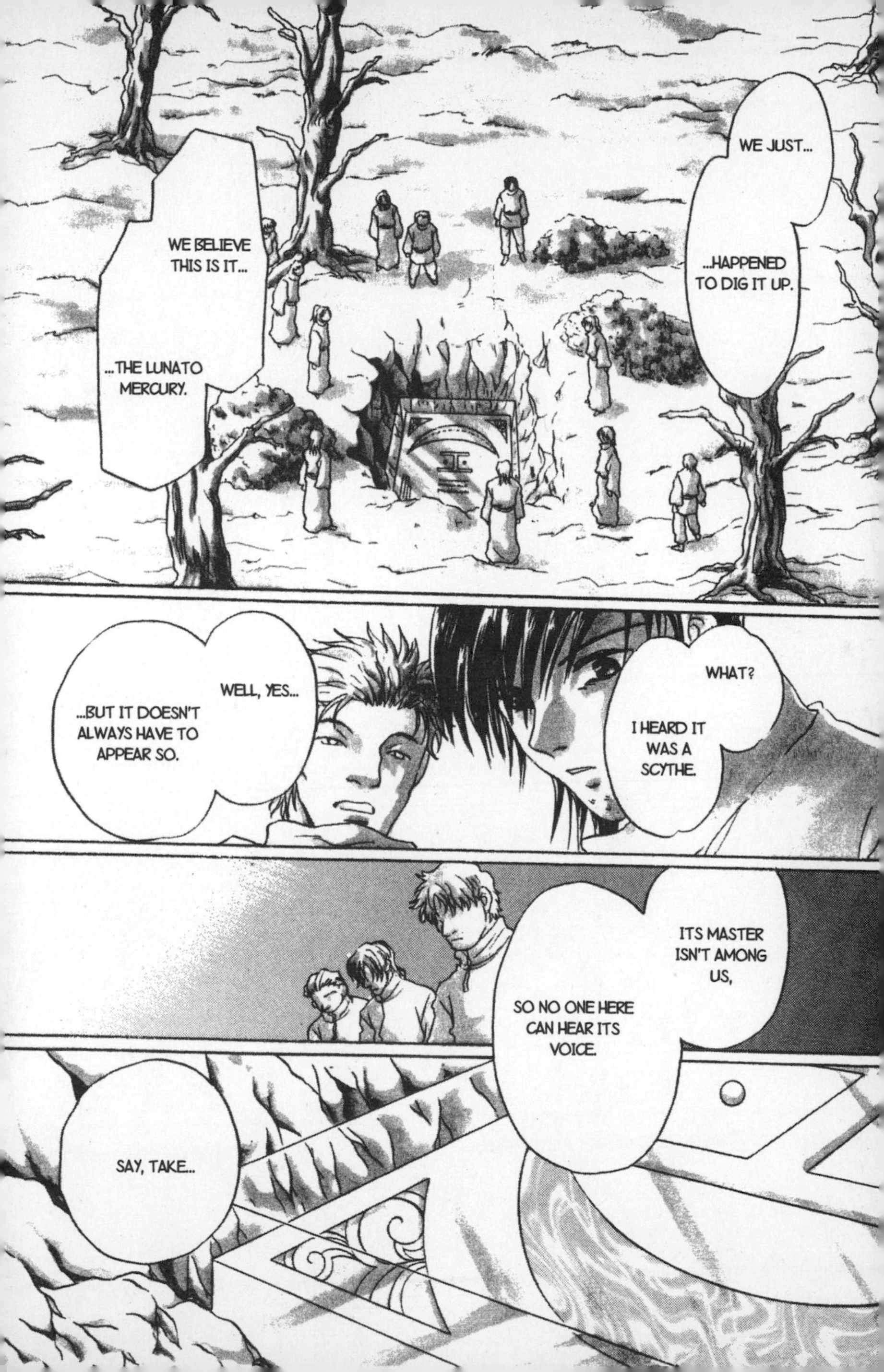
WE JUST...
...HAPPENED TO DIG IT UP.
WE BELIEVE THIS IS IT...
...THE LUNATO MERCURY.
WHAT?
I HEARD IT WAS A SCYTHE.
WELL, YES...
...BUT IT DOESN'T ALWAYS HAVE TO APPEAR SO.
ITS MASTER ISN'T AMONG US,
SO NO ONE HERE CAN HEAR ITS VOICE.
SAY, TAKE...

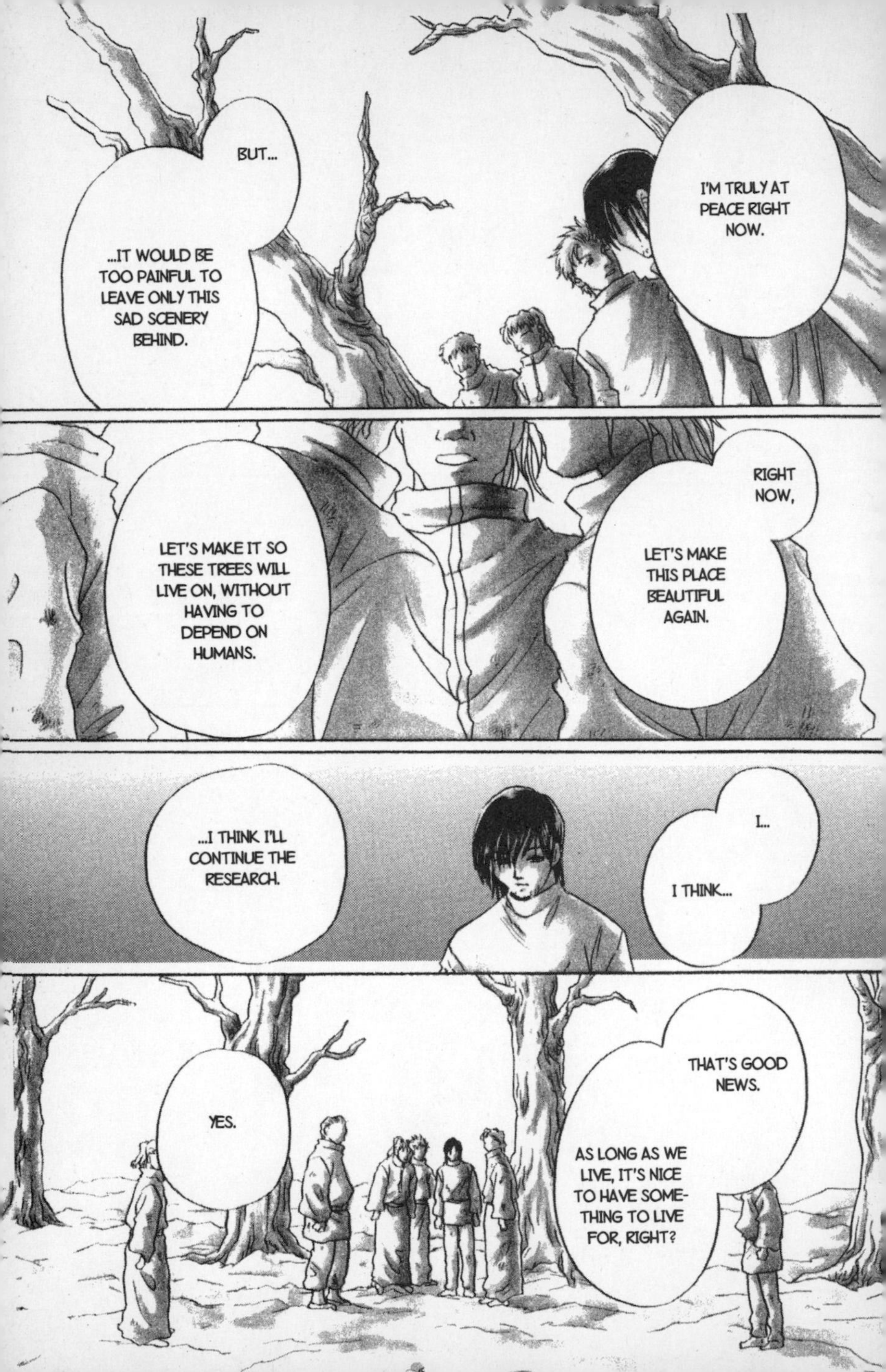
I'M TRULY AT PEACE RIGHT NOW.
BUT...
...IT WOULD BE TOO PAINFUL TO LEAVE ONLY THIS SAD SCENERY BEHIND.
RIGHT NOW,
LET'S MAKE THIS PLACE BEAUTIFUL AGAIN.
LET'S MAKE IT SO THESE TREES WILL LIVE ON, WITHOUT HAVING TO DEPEND ON HUMANS.
I...
I THINK...
...I THINK I'LL CONTINUE THE RESEARCH.
THAT'S GOOD NEWS.
AS LONG AS WE LIVE, IT'S NICE TO HAVE SOME-THING TO LIVE FOR, RIGHT?
YES.

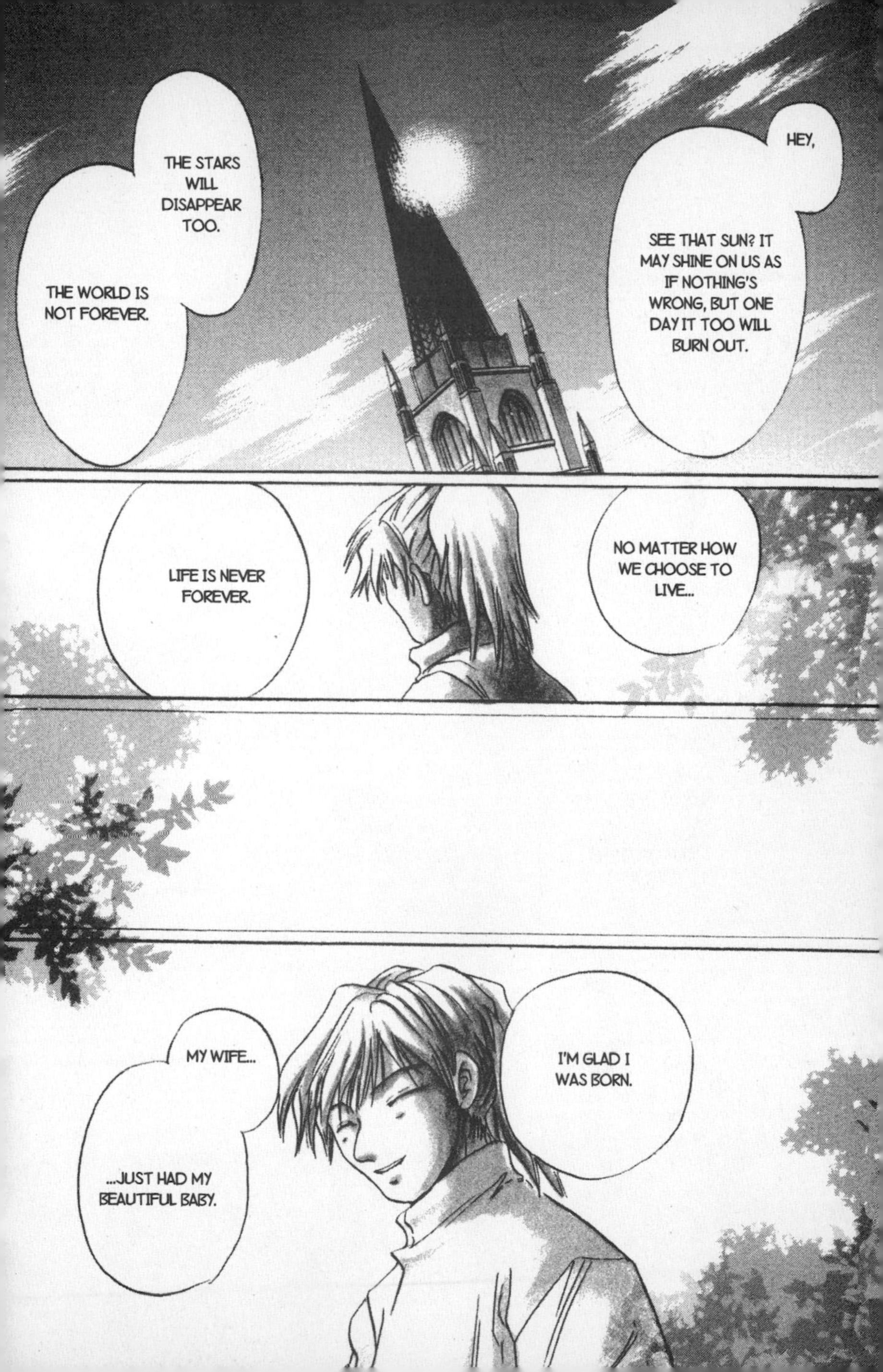
HEY,
SEE THAT SUN? IT MAY SHINE ON US AS IF NOTHING'S WRONG, BUT ONE DAY IT TOO WILL BURN OUT.
THE STARS WILL DISAPPEAR TOO.
THE WORLD IS NOT FOREVER.
NO MATTER HOW WE CHOOSE TO LIVE...
LIFE IS NEVER FOREVER.
I'M GLAD I WAS BORN.
MY WIFE...
...JUST HAD MY BEAUTIFUL BABY.

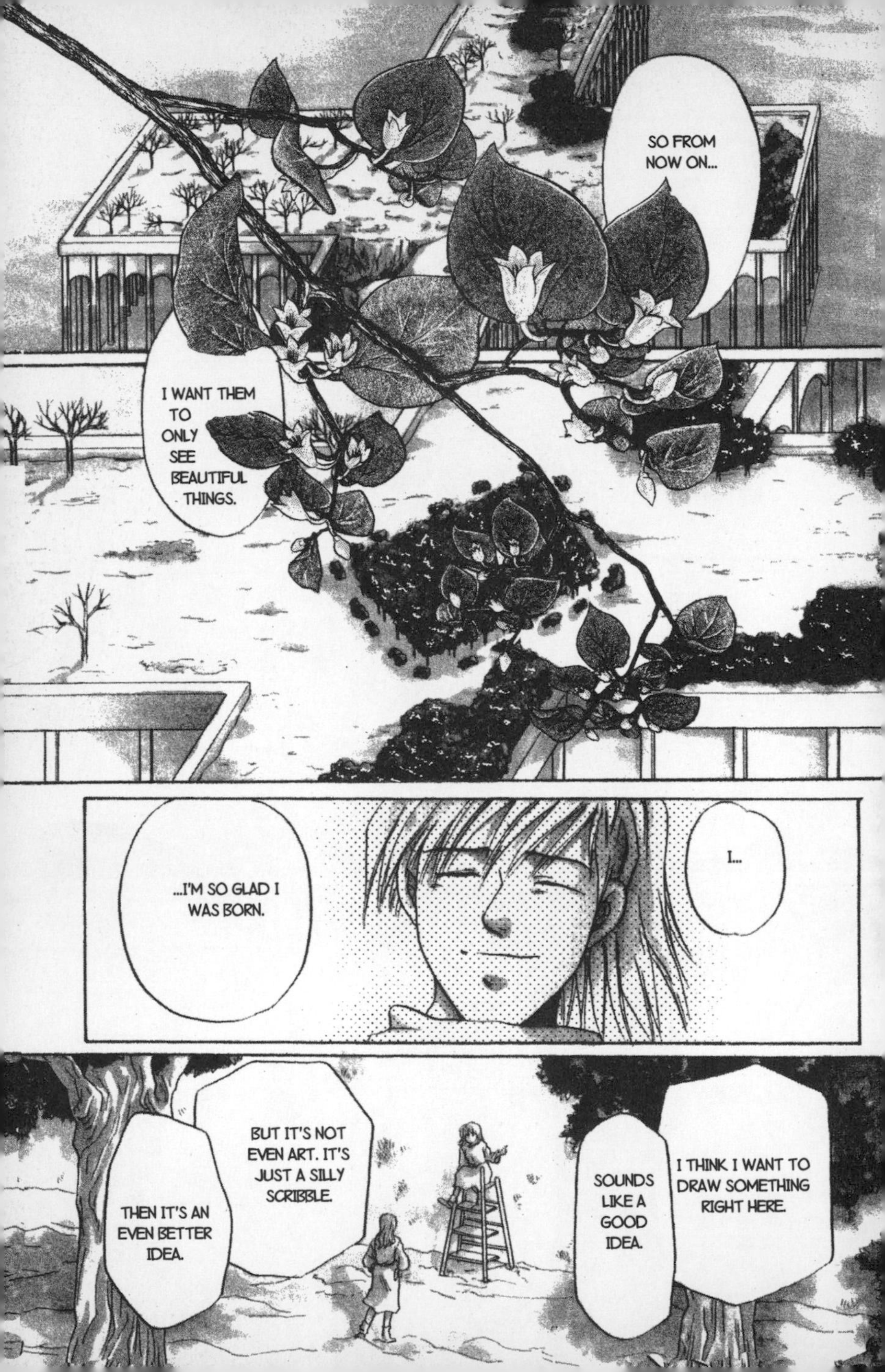
SO FROM NOW ON...
I WANT THEM TO ONLY SEE BEAUTIFUL THINGS.
I...
...I'M SO GLAD I WAS BORN.
I THINK I WANT TO DRAW SOMETHING RIGHT HERE.
SOUNDS LIKE A GOOD IDEA.
BUT IT'S NOT EVEN ART. IT'S JUST A SILLY SCRIBBLE.
THEN IT'S AN EVEN BETTER IDEA.

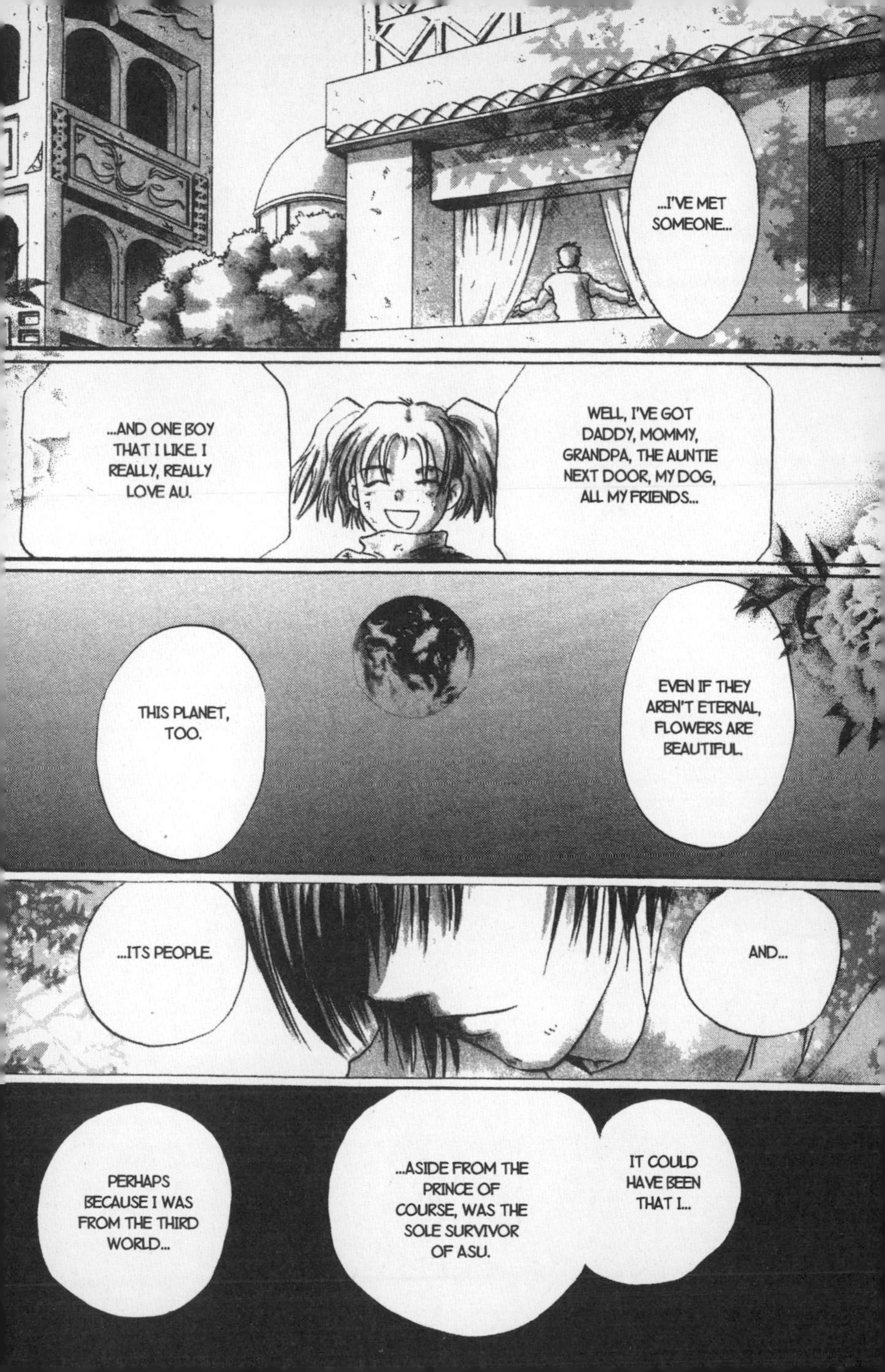
...I'VE MET SOMEONE...
WELL, I'VE GOT DADDY, MOMMY, GRANDPA, THE AUNTIE NEXT DOOR, MY DOG, ALL MY FRIENDS...
...AND ONE BOY THAT I LIKE. I REALLY, REALLY LOVE AU.
EVEN IF THEY AREN'T ETERNAL, FLOWERS ARE BEAUTIFUL.
THIS PLANET, TOO.
AND...
...ITS PEOPLE.
IT COULD HAVE BEEN THAT I...
...ASIDE FROM THE PRINCE OF COURSE, WAS THE SOLE SURVIVOR OF ASU.
PERHAPS BECAUSE I WAS FROM THE THIRD WORLD...

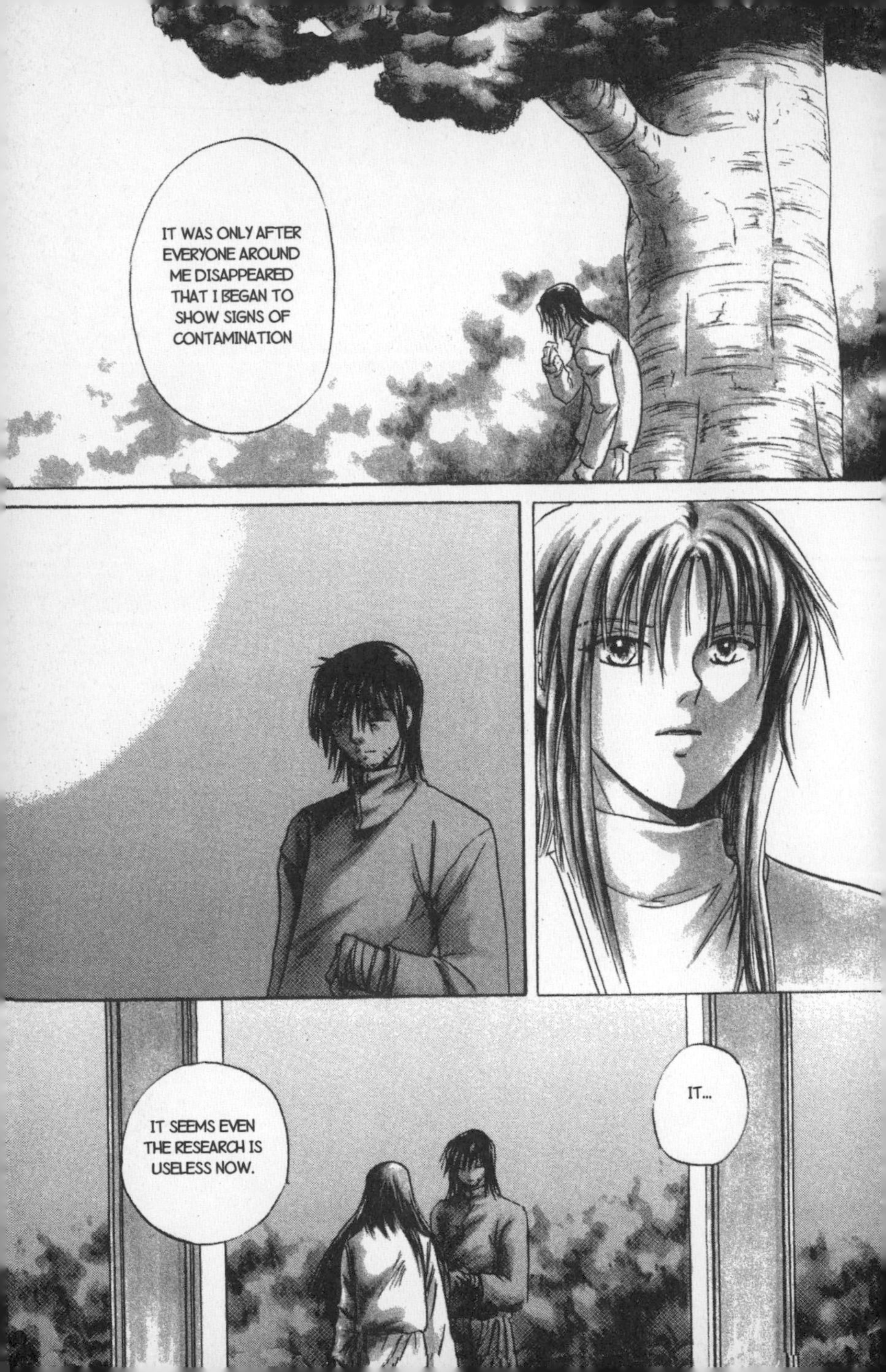
IT WAS ONLY AFTER EVERYONE AROUND ME DISAPPEARED THAT I BEGAN TO SHOW SIGNS OF CONTAMINATION
IT...
IT SEEMS EVEN THE RESEARCH IS USELESS NOW.

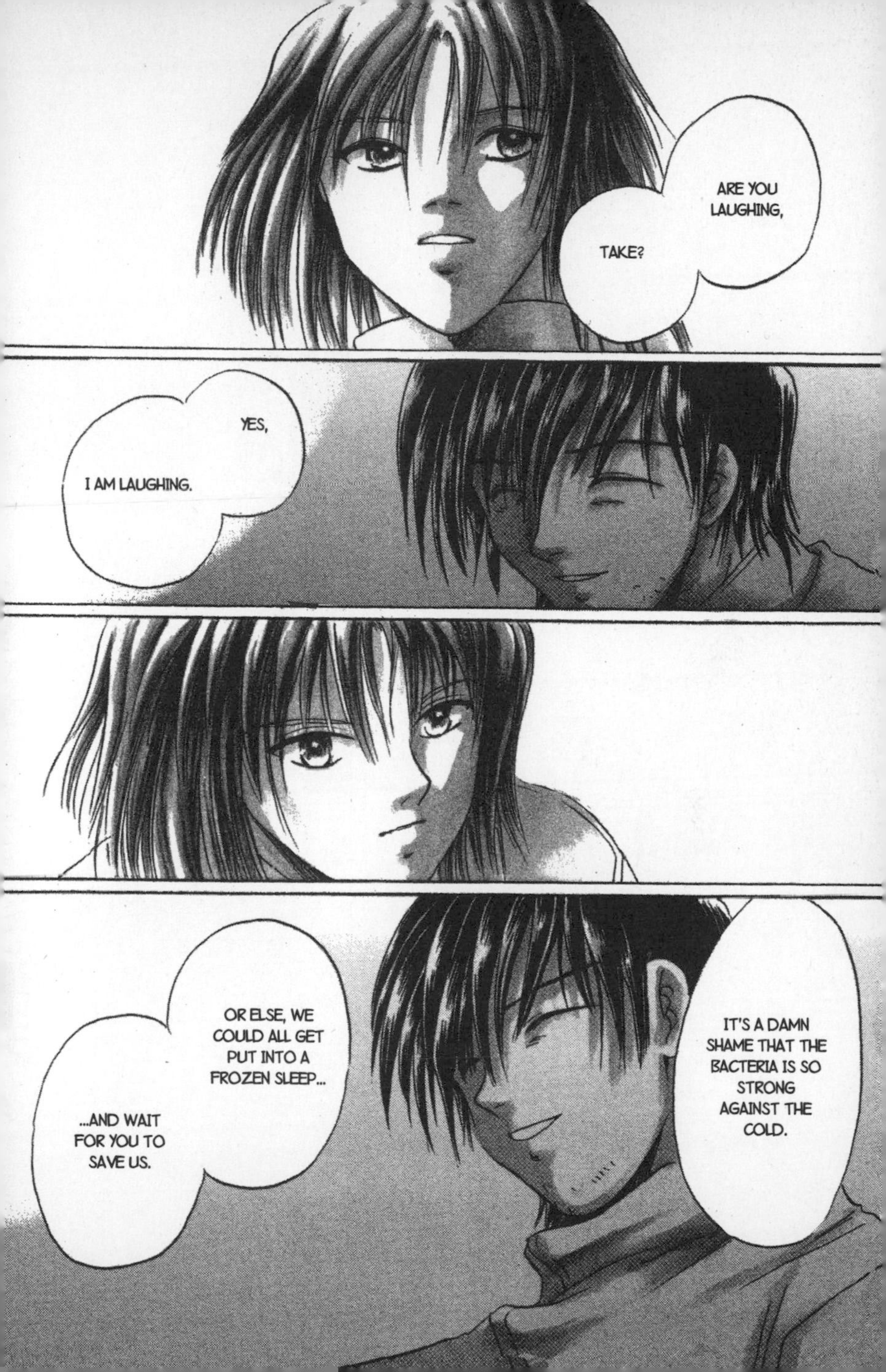
ARE YOU LAUGHING,
TAKE?
YES,
I AM LAUGHING.
IT'S A DAMN SHAME THAT THE BACTERIA IS SO STRONG AGAINST THE COLD.
OR ELSE, WE COULD ALL GET PUT INTO A FROZEN SLEEP...
...AND WAIT FOR YOU TO SAVE US.

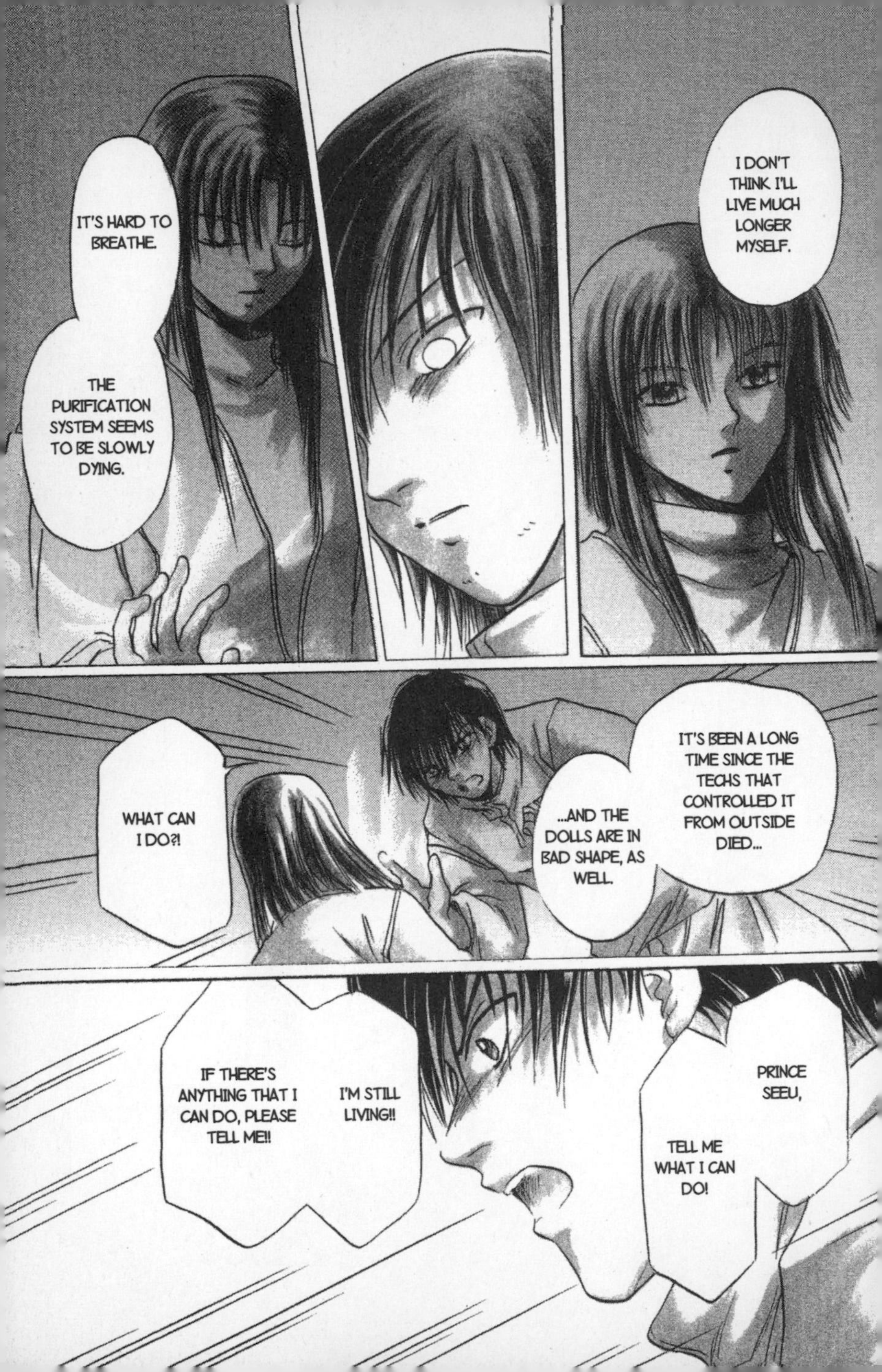
I DON'T THINK I'LL LIVE MUCH LONGER MYSELF.
IT'S HARD TO BREATHE.
THE PURIFICATION SYSTEM SEEMS TO BE SLOWLY DYING.
IT'S BEEN A LONG TIME SINCE THE TECHS THAT CONTROLLED IT FROM OUTSIDE DIED...
...AND THE DOLLS ARE IN BAD SHAPE, AS WELL.
WHAT CAN I DO?!
PRINCE SEEU,
TELL ME WHAT I CAN DO!
I'M STILL LIVING!!
IF THERE'S ANYTHING THAT I CAN DO, PLEASE TELL ME!!

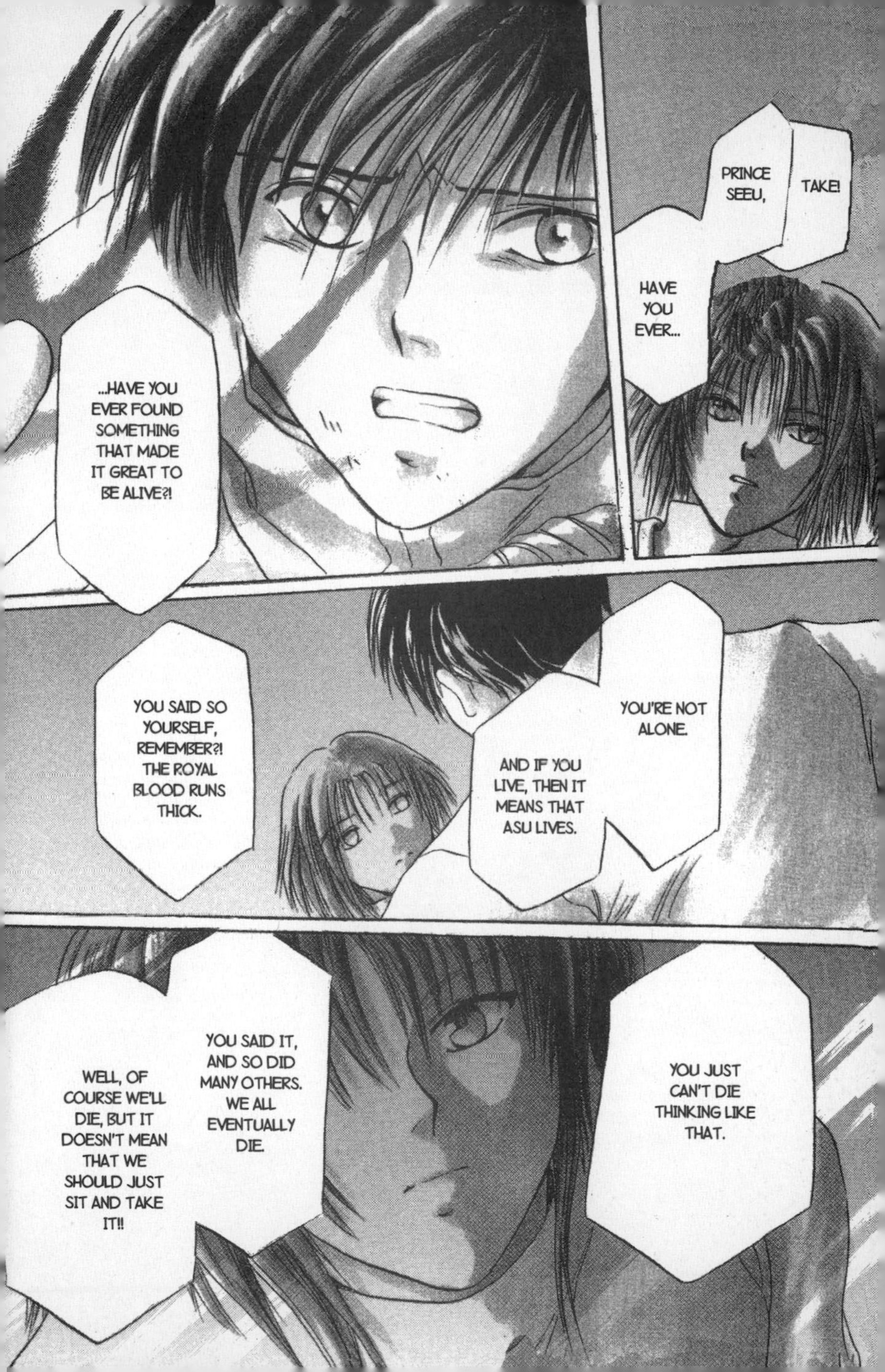
TAKE!
PRINCE SEEU,
HAVE YOU EVER...
...HAVE YOU EVER FOUND SOMETHING THAT MADE IT GREAT TO BE ALIVE?!
YOU'RE NOT ALONE.
AND IF YOU LIVE, THEN IT MEANS THAT ASU LIVES.
YOU SAID SO YOURSELF, REMEMBER?! THE ROYAL BLOOD RUNS THICK.
YOU JUST CAN'T DIE THINKING LIKE THAT.
YOU SAID IT, AND SO DID MANY OTHERS. WE ALL EVENTUALLY DIE.
WELL, OF COURSE WE'LL DIE, BUT IT DOESN'T MEAN THAT WE SHOULD JUST SIT AND TAKE IT!!

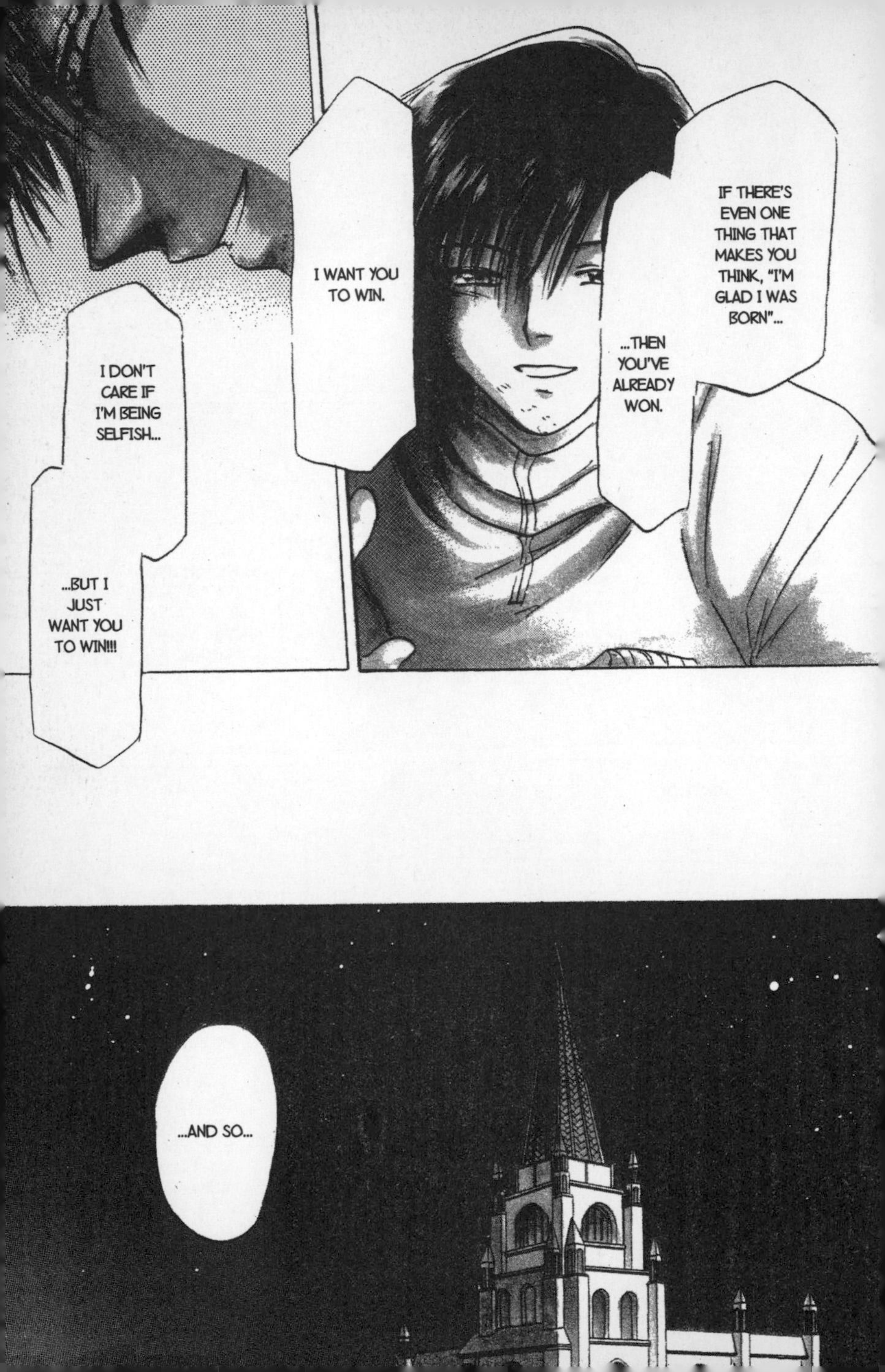
IF THERE'S EVEN ONE THING THAT MAKES YOU THINK, "I'M GLAD I WAS BORN"...
...THEN YOU'VE ALREADY WON.
I WANT YOU TO WIN.
I DON'T CARE IF I'M BEING SELFISH...
...BUT I JUST WANT YOU TO WIN!!!
...AND SO...

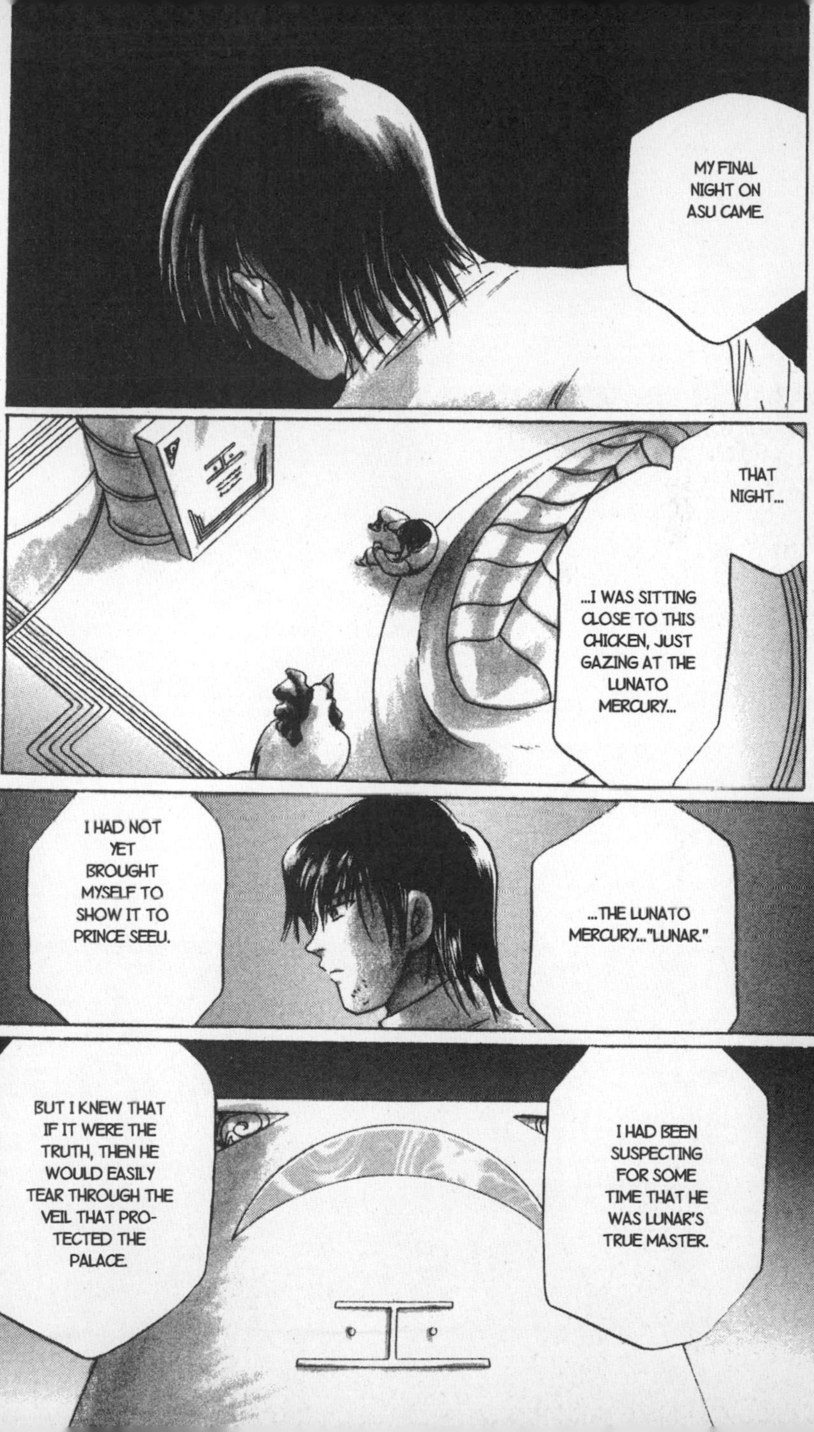
MY FINAL NIGHT ON ASU CAME.
THAT NIGHT...
...I WAS SITTING CLOSE TO THIS CHICKEN, JUST GAZING AT THE LUNATO MERCURY...
...THE LUNATO MERCURY..."LUNAR."
I HAD NOT YET BROUGHT MYSELF TO SHOW IT TO PRINCE SEEU.
I HAD BEEN SUSPECTING FOR SOME TIME THAT HE WAS LUNAR'S TRUE MASTER.
BUT I KNEW THAT IF IT WERE THE TRUTH, THEN HE WOULD EASILY TEAR THROUGH THE VEIL THAT PRO-TECTED THE PALACE.

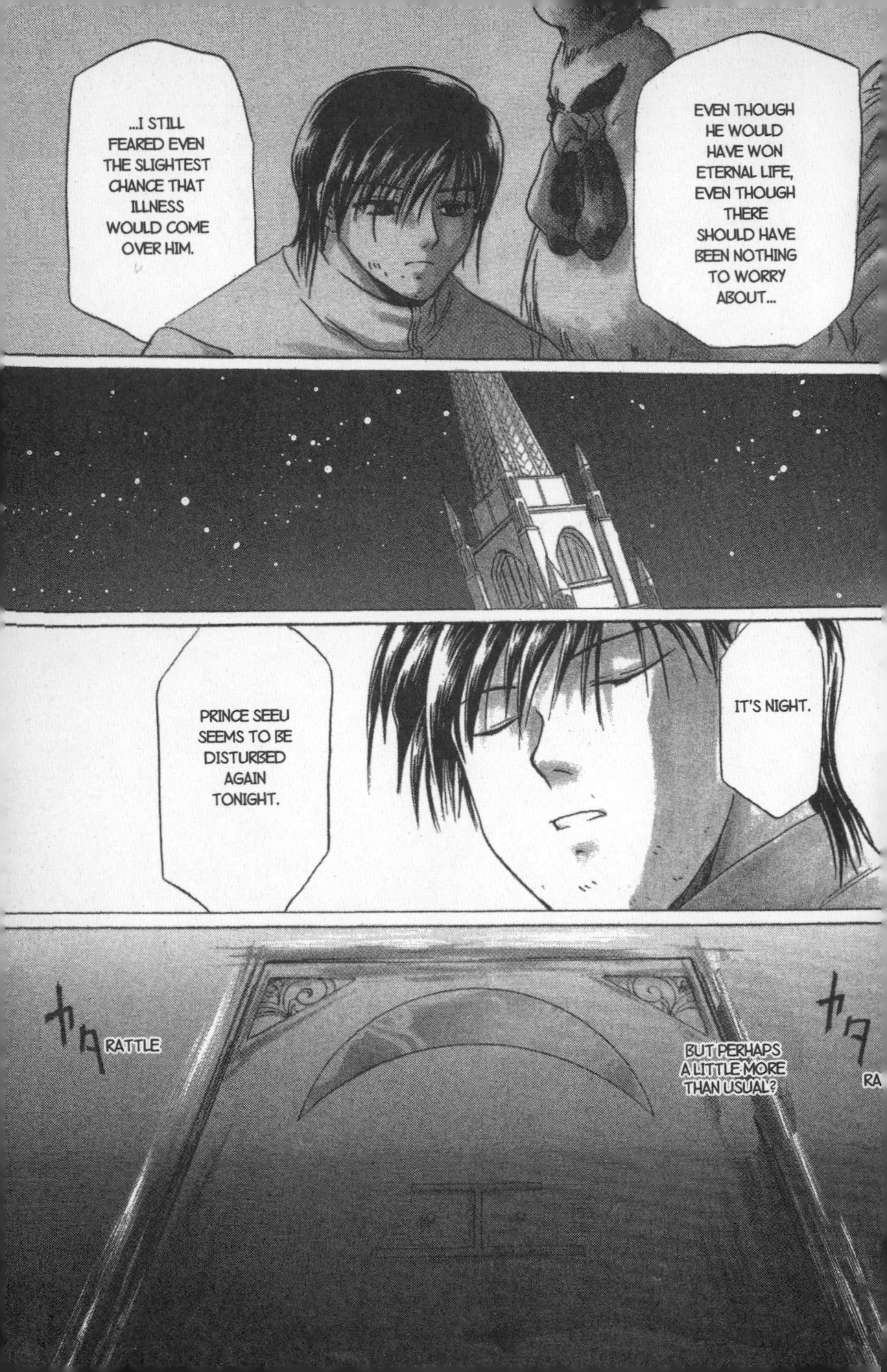
EVEN THOUGH HE WOULD HAVE WON ETERNAL LIFE, EVEN THOUGH THERE SHOULD HAVE BEEN NOTHING TO WORRY ABOUT...
...I STILL FEARED EVEN THE SLIGHTEST CHANCE THAT ILLNESS WOULD COME OVER HIM.
IT'S NIGHT.
PRINCE SEEU SEEMS TO BE DISTURBED AGAIN TONIGHT.
カタ
RA
BUT PERHAPS A LITTLE MORE THAN USUAL?
カタ
RATTLE

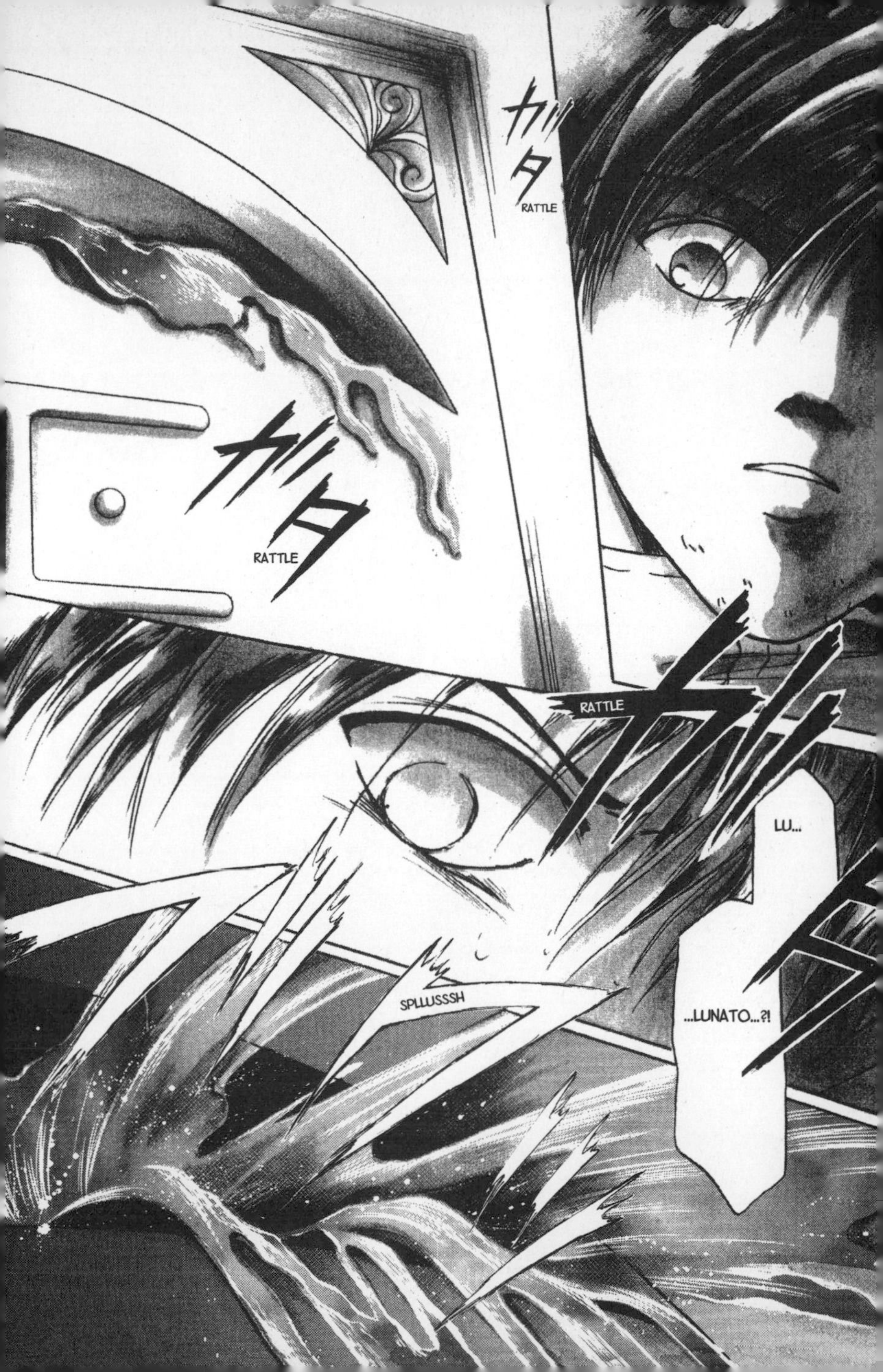
カタ
RATTLE
カタ
RATTLE
カタ
RATTLE
LU...
...LUNATO...?!
SPLLUSSSH

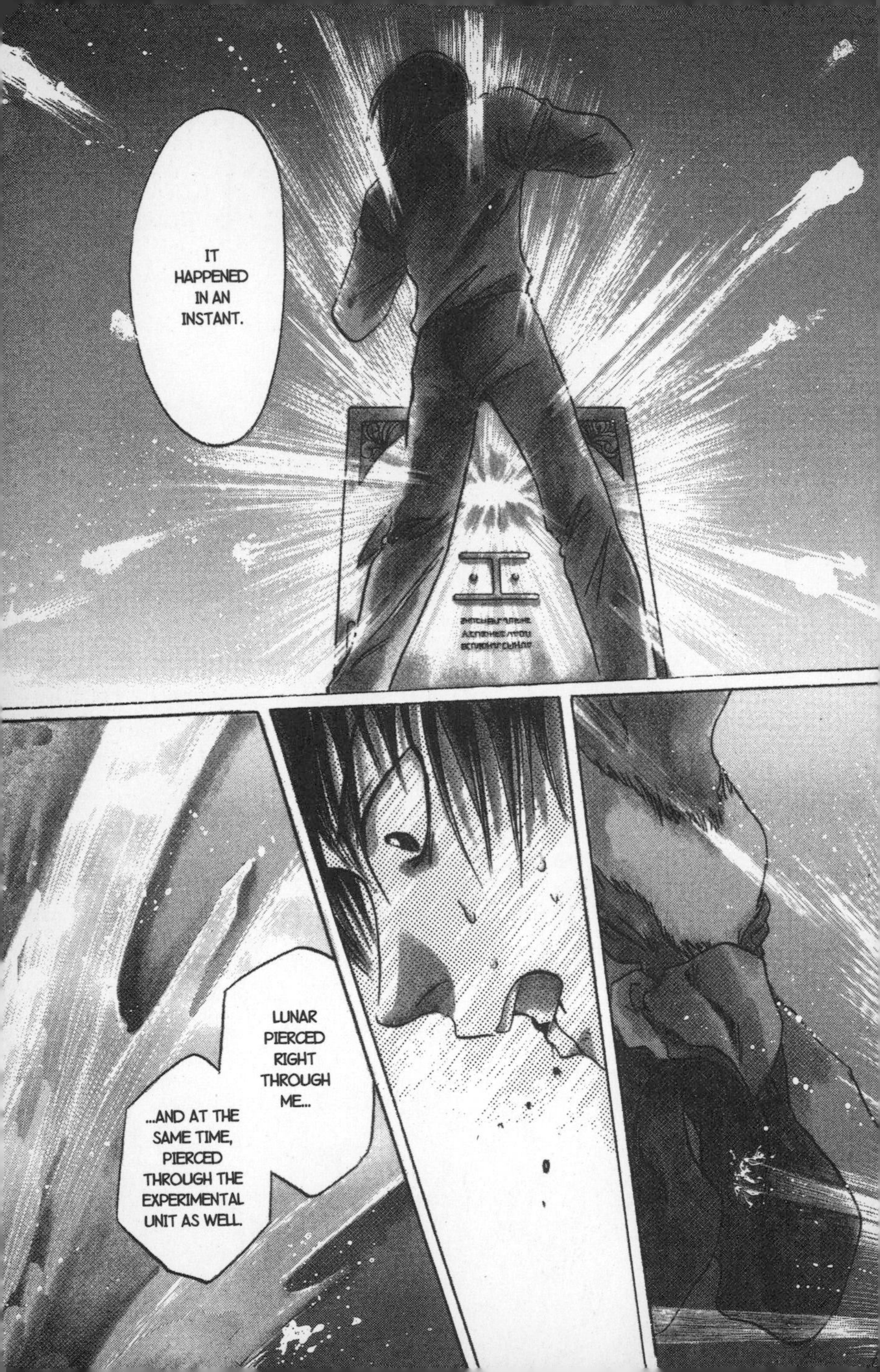
IT HAPPENED IN AN INSTANT.
LUNAR PIERCED RIGHT THROUGH ME...
...AND AT THE SAME TIME, PIERCED THROUGH THE EXPERIMENTAL UNIT AS WELL.

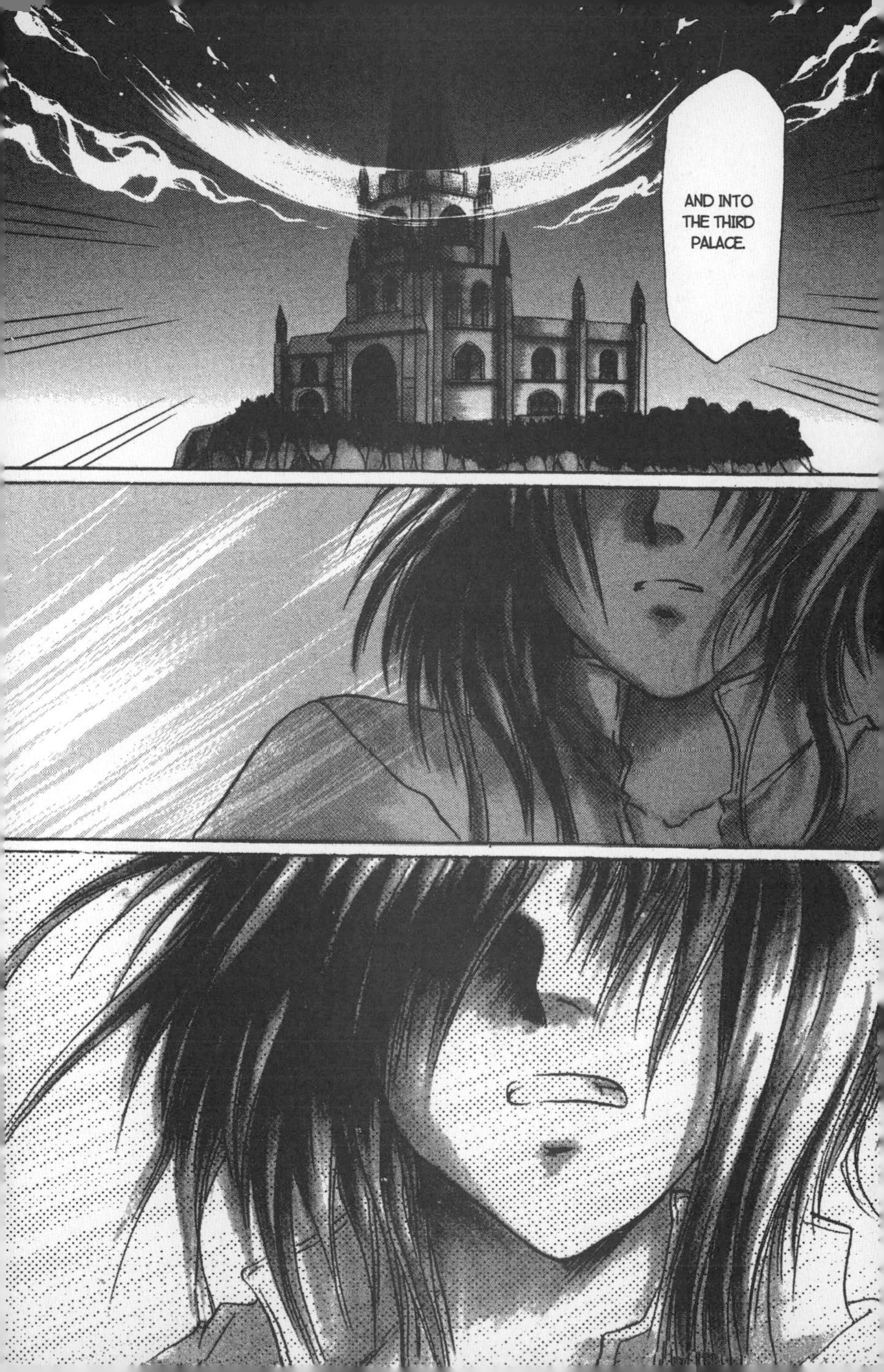
AND INTO THE THIRD PALACE.

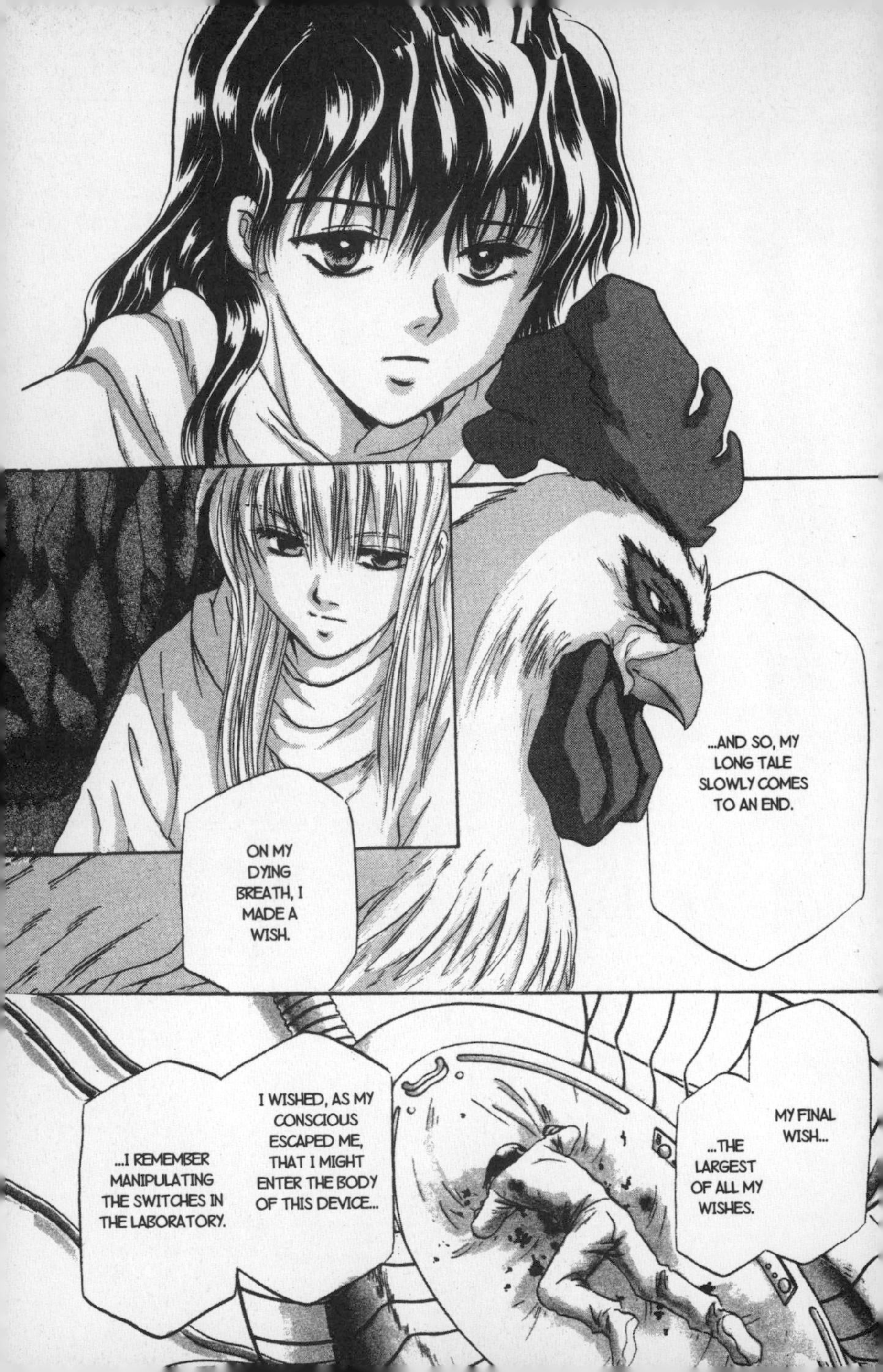
...AND SO, MY LONG TALE SLOWLY COMES TO AN END.
ON MY DYING BREATH, I MADE A WISH.
MY FINAL WISH...
...THE LARGEST OF ALL MY WISHES.
I WISHED, AS MY CONSCIOUS ESCAPED ME, THAT I MIGHT ENTER THE BODY OF THIS DEVICE...
...I REMEMBER MANIPULATING THE SWITCHES IN THE LABORATORY.

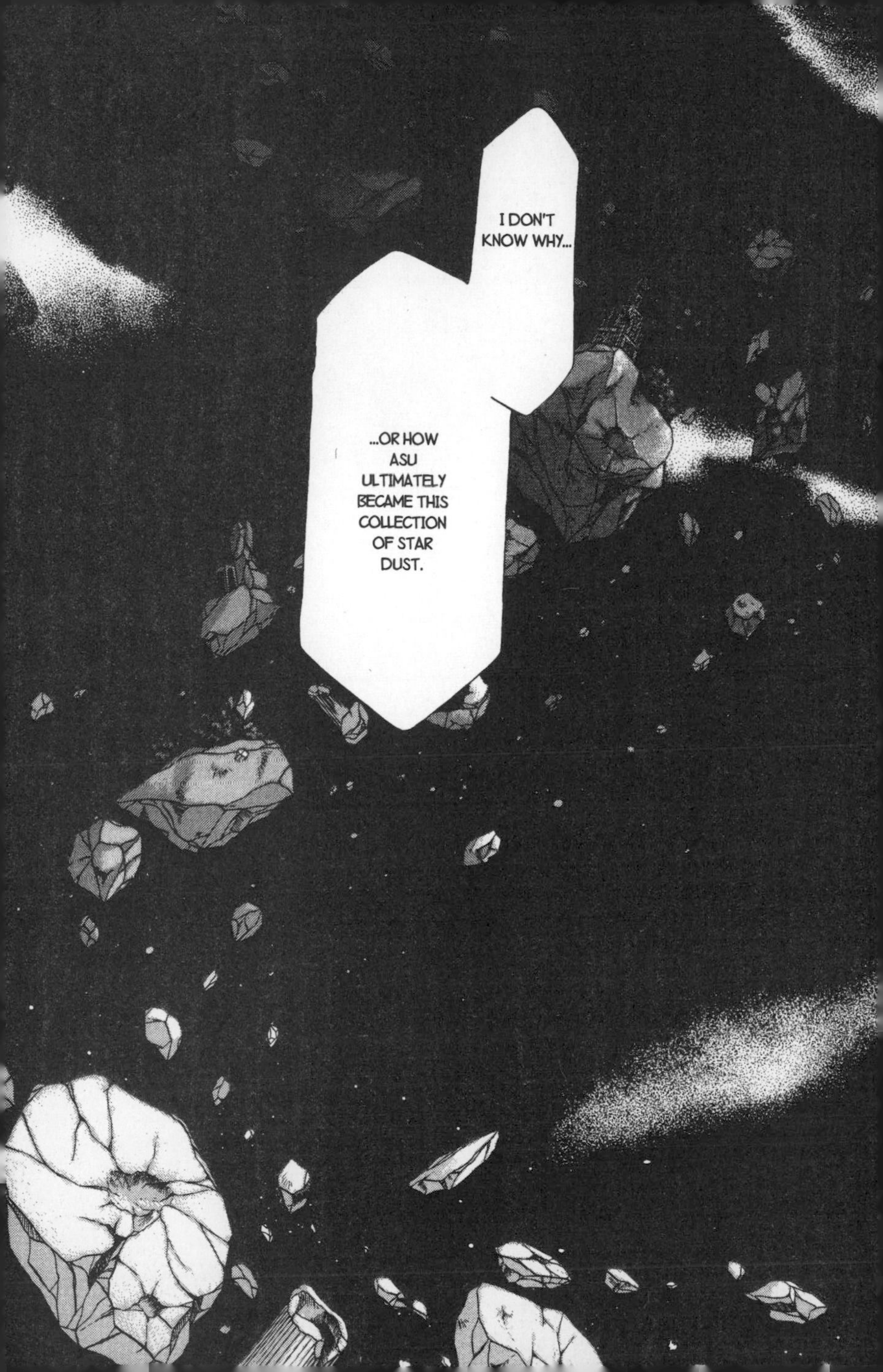
I DON'T KNOW WHY...
...OR HOW ASU ULTIMATELY BECAME THIS COLLECTION OF STAR DUST.

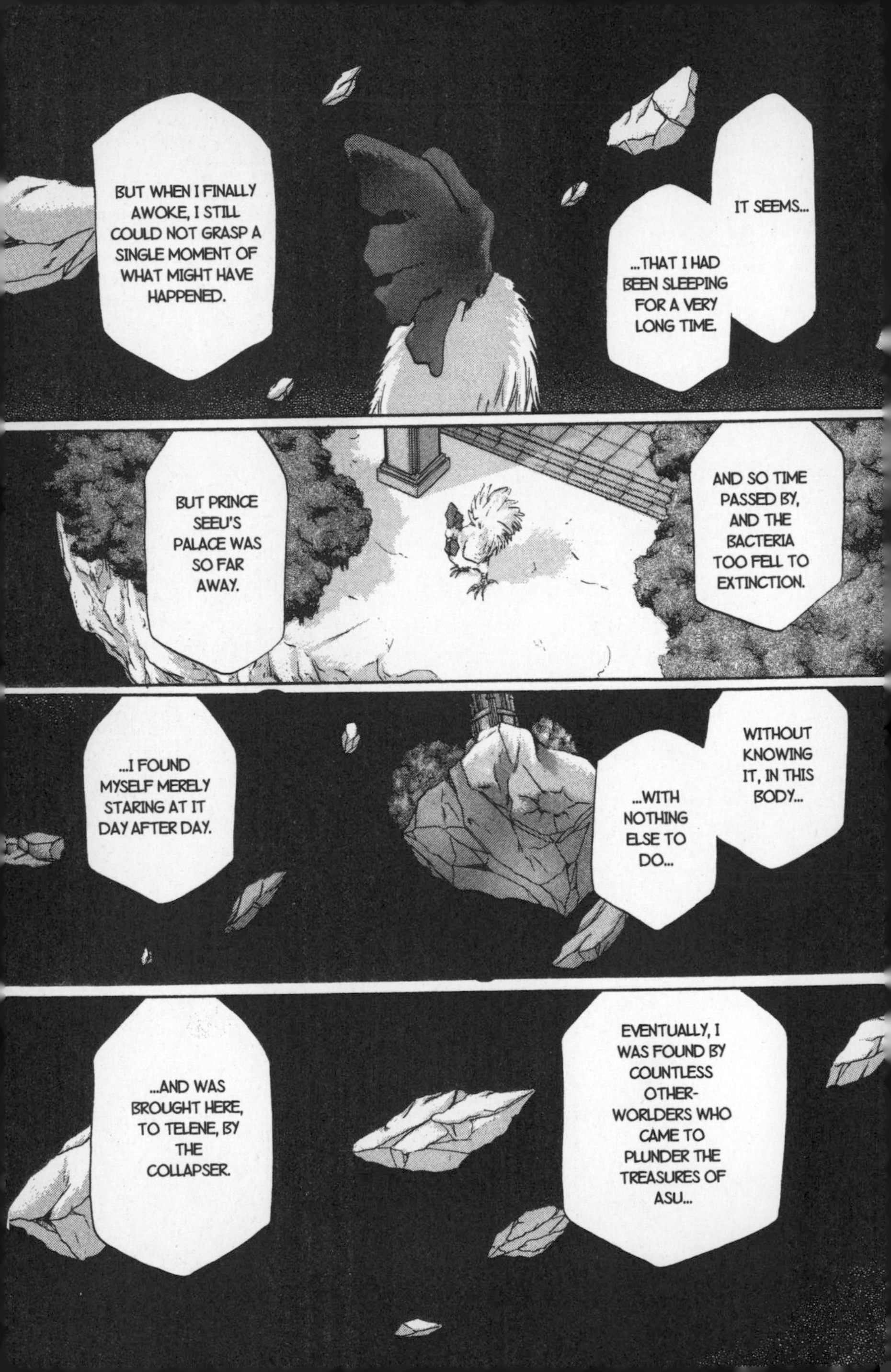
IT SEEMS...
...THAT I HAD BEEN SLEEPING FOR A VERY LONG TIME.
BUT WHEN I FINALLY AWOKE, I STILL COULD NOT GRASP A SINGLE MOMENT OF WHAT MIGHT HAVE HAPPENED.
AND SO TIME PASSED BY, AND THE BACTERIA TOO FELL TO EXTINCTION.
BUT PRINCE SEEU'S PALACE WAS SO FAR AWAY.
WITHOUT KNOWING IT, IN THIS BODY...
...WITH NOTHING ELSE TO DO...
...I FOUND MYSELF MERELY STARING AT IT DAY AFTER DAY.
EVENTUALLY, I WAS FOUND BY COUNTLESS OTHER-WORLDERS WHO CAME TO PLUNDER THE TREASURES OF ASU...
...AND WAS BROUGHT HERE, TO TELENE, BY THE COLLAPSER.

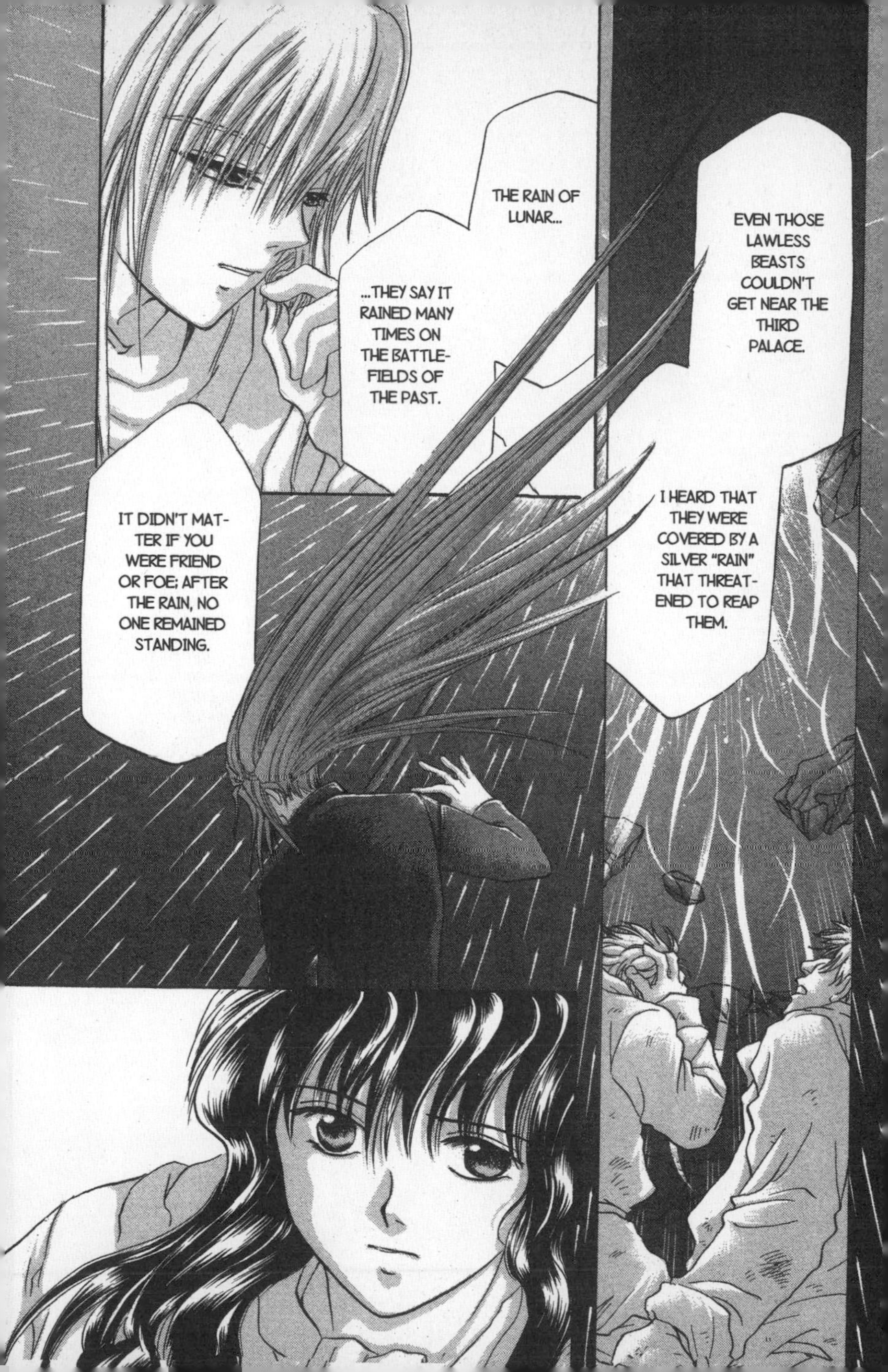
EVEN THOSE LAWLESS BEASTS COULDN'T GET NEAR THE THIRD PALACE.
I HEARD THAT THEY WERE COVERED BY A SILVER "RAIN" THAT THREAT-ENED TO REAP THEM.
THE RAIN OF LUNAR...
...THEY SAY IT RAINED MANY TIMES ON THE BATTLE-FIELDS OF THE PAST.
IT DIDN'T MAT-TER IF YOU WERE FRIEND OR FOE; AFTER THE RAIN, NO ONE REMAINED STANDING.

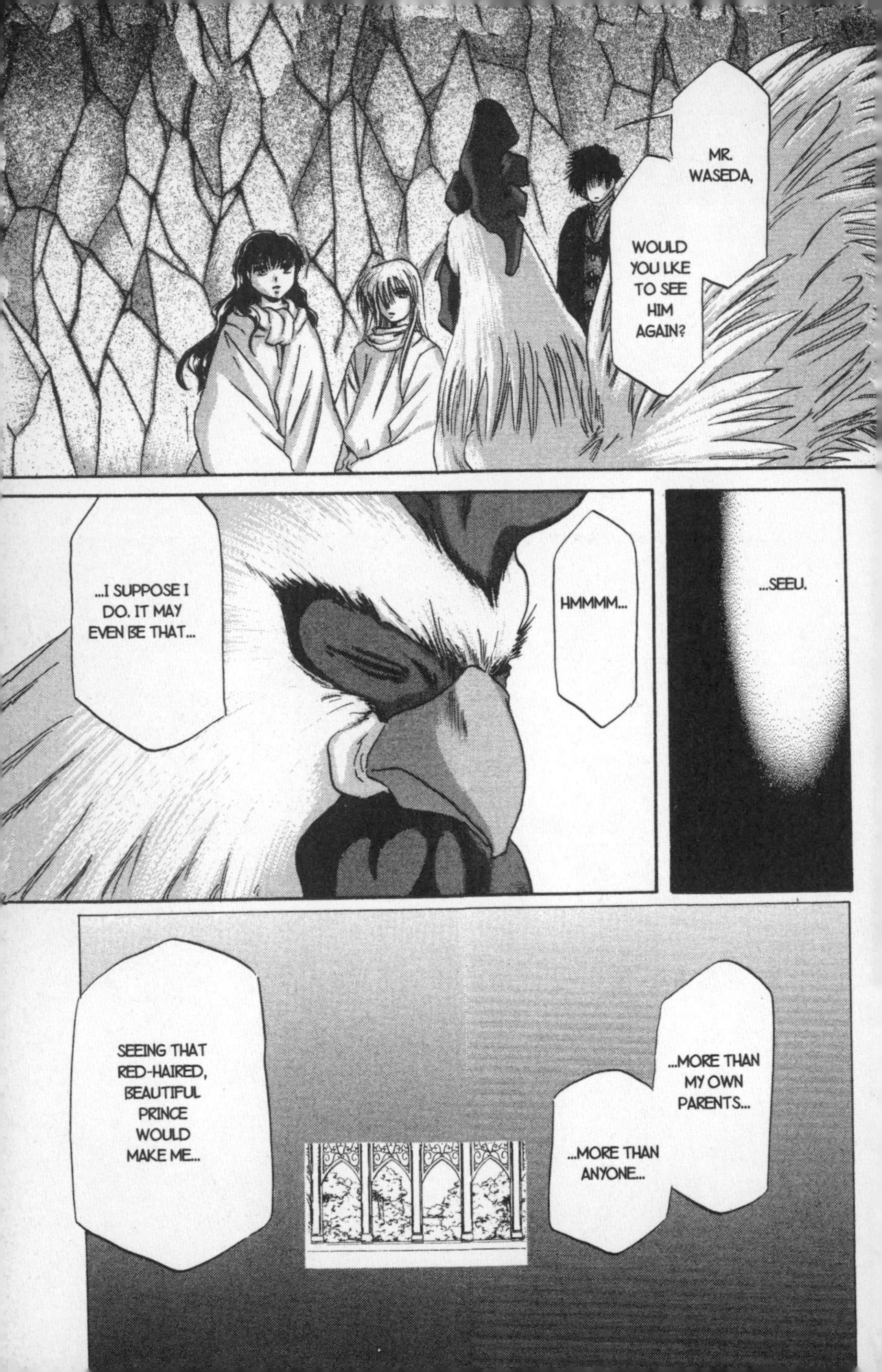
MR. WASEDA,
WOULD YOU LKE TO SEE HIM AGAIN?
...SEEU.
HMMMM...
...I SUPPOSE I DO. IT MAY EVEN BE THAT...
...MORE THAN MY OWN PARENTS...
...MORE THAN ANYONE...
SEEING THAT RED-HAIRED, BEAUTIFUL PRINCE WOULD MAKE ME...

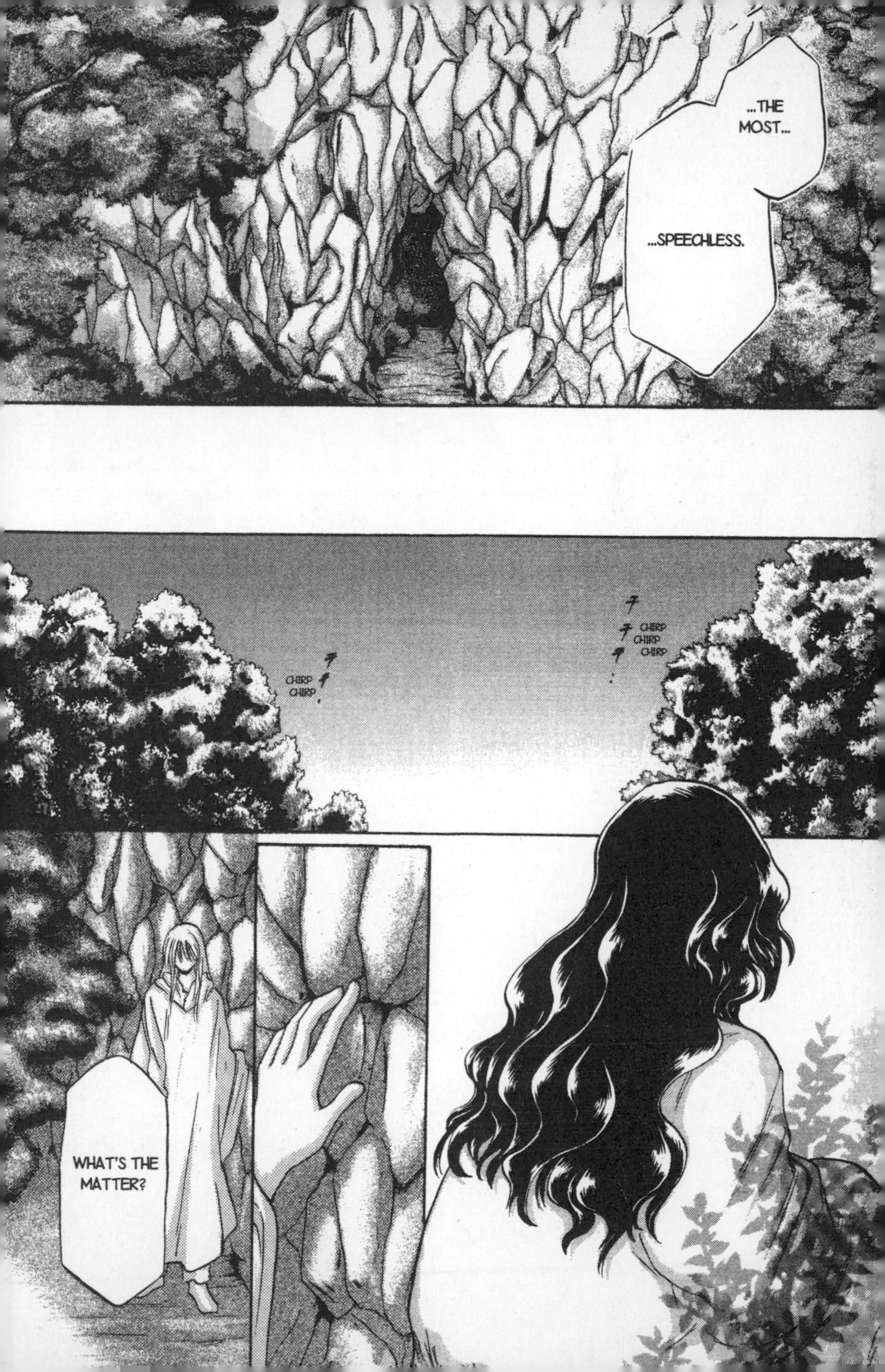
...THE MOST...
...SPEECHLESS.
CHIRP CHIRP CHIRP
CHIRP CHIRP
WHAT'S THE MATTER?

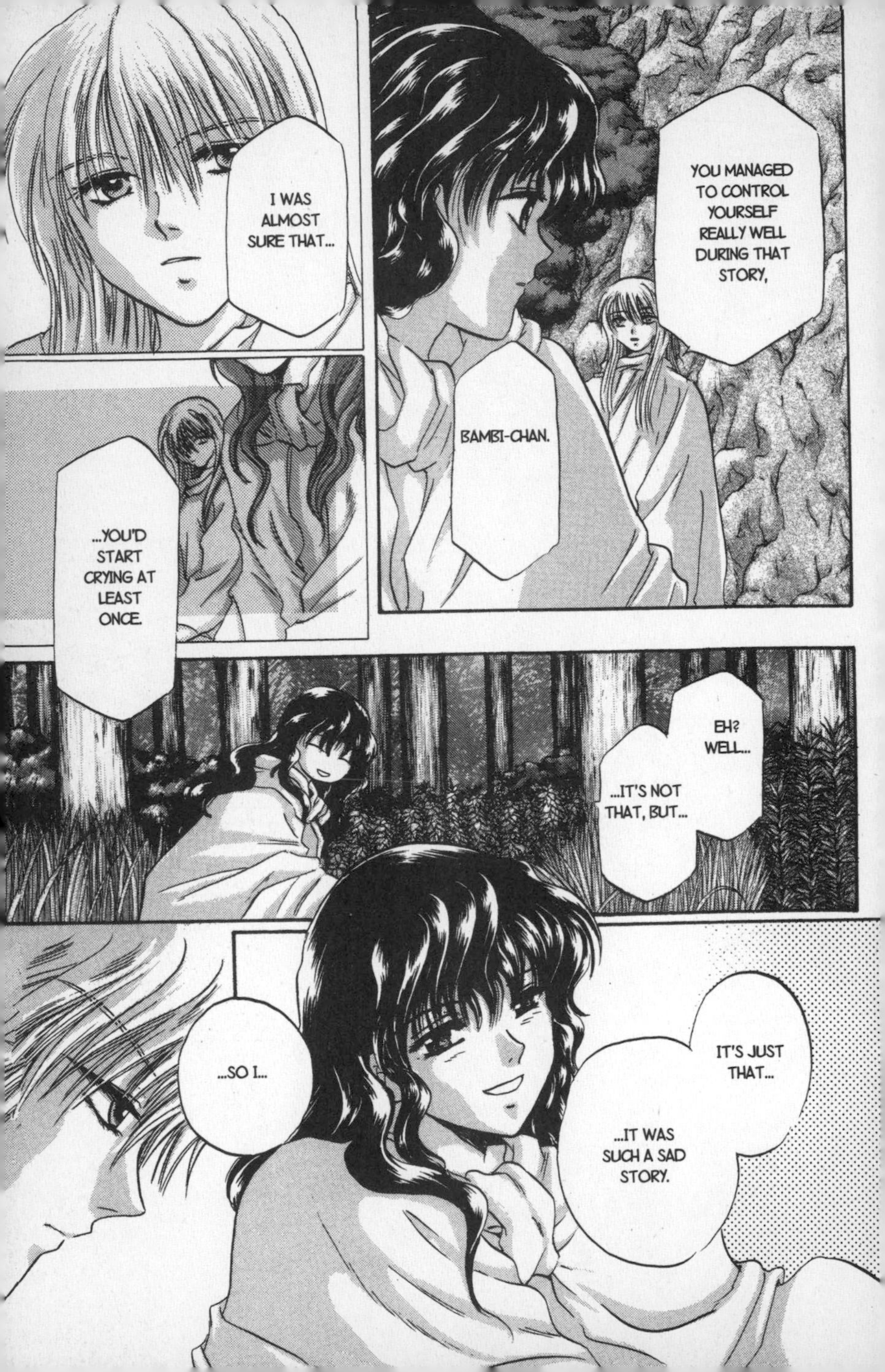
YOU MANAGED TO CONTROL YOURSELF REALLY WELL DURING THAT STORY,
BAMBI-CHAN.
I WAS ALMOST SURE THAT...
...YOU'D START CRYING AT LEAST ONCE.
EH? WELL...
...IT'S NOT THAT, BUT...
IT'S JUST THAT...
...IT WAS SUCH A SAD STORY.
...SO I...

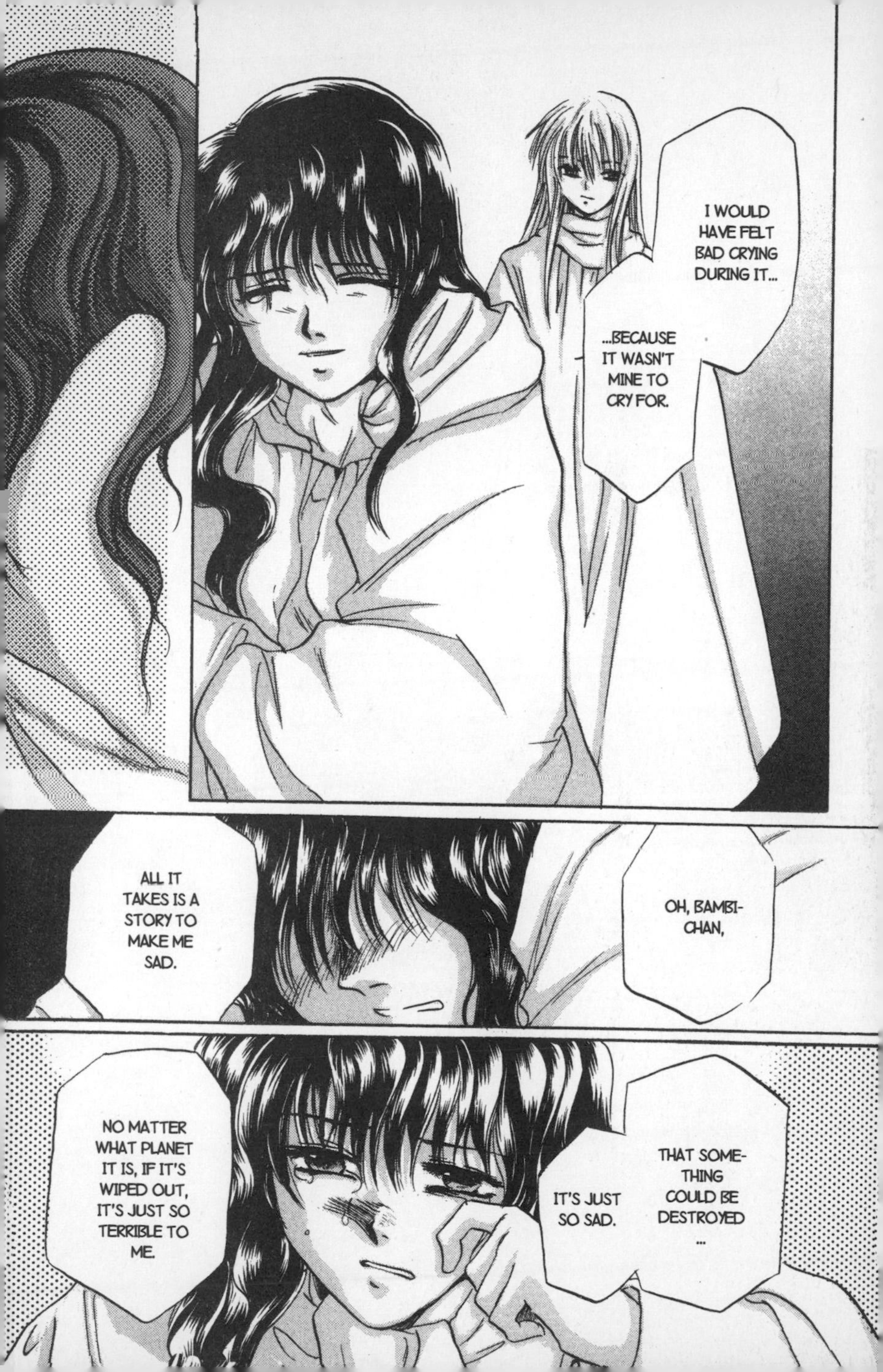
I WOULD HAVE FELT BAD CRYING DURING IT...
...BECAUSE IT WASN'T MINE TO CRY FOR.
OH, BAMBI-CHAN,
ALL IT TAKES IS A STORY TO MAKE ME SAD.
THAT SOMETHING COULD BE DESTROYED ...
IT'S JUST SO SAD.
NO MATTER WHAT PLANET IT IS, IF IT'S WIPED OUT, IT'S JUST SO TERRIBLE TO ME.

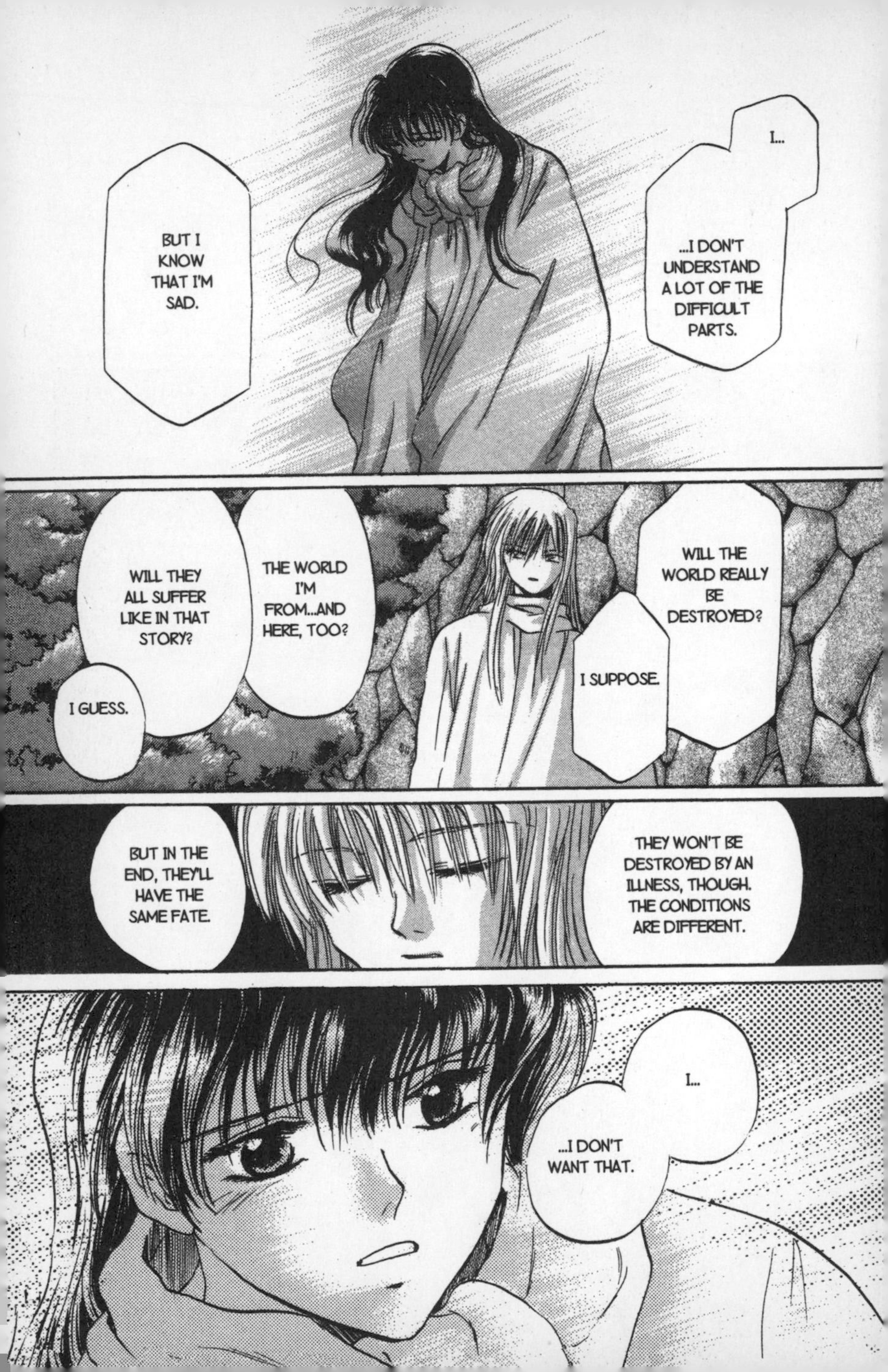
I...
...I DON'T UNDERSTAND A LOT OF THE DIFFICULT PARTS.
BUT I KNOW THAT I'M SAD.
WILL THE WORLD REALLY BE DESTROYED?
I SUPPOSE.
THE WORLD I'M FROM...AND HERE, TOO?
WILL THEY ALL SUFFER LIKE IN THAT STORY?
I GUESS.
THEY WON'T BE DESTROYED BY AN ILLNESS, THOUGH. THE CONDITIONS ARE DIFFERENT.
BUT IN THE END, THEY'LL HAVE THE SAME FATE.
I...
...I DON'T WANT THAT.

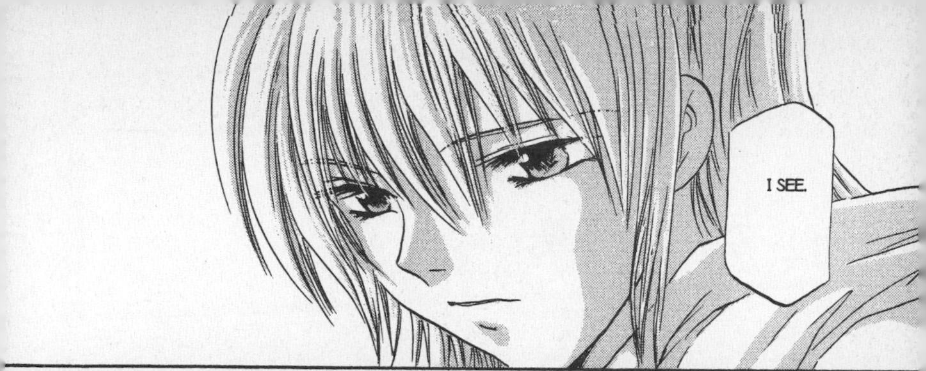
I SEE.

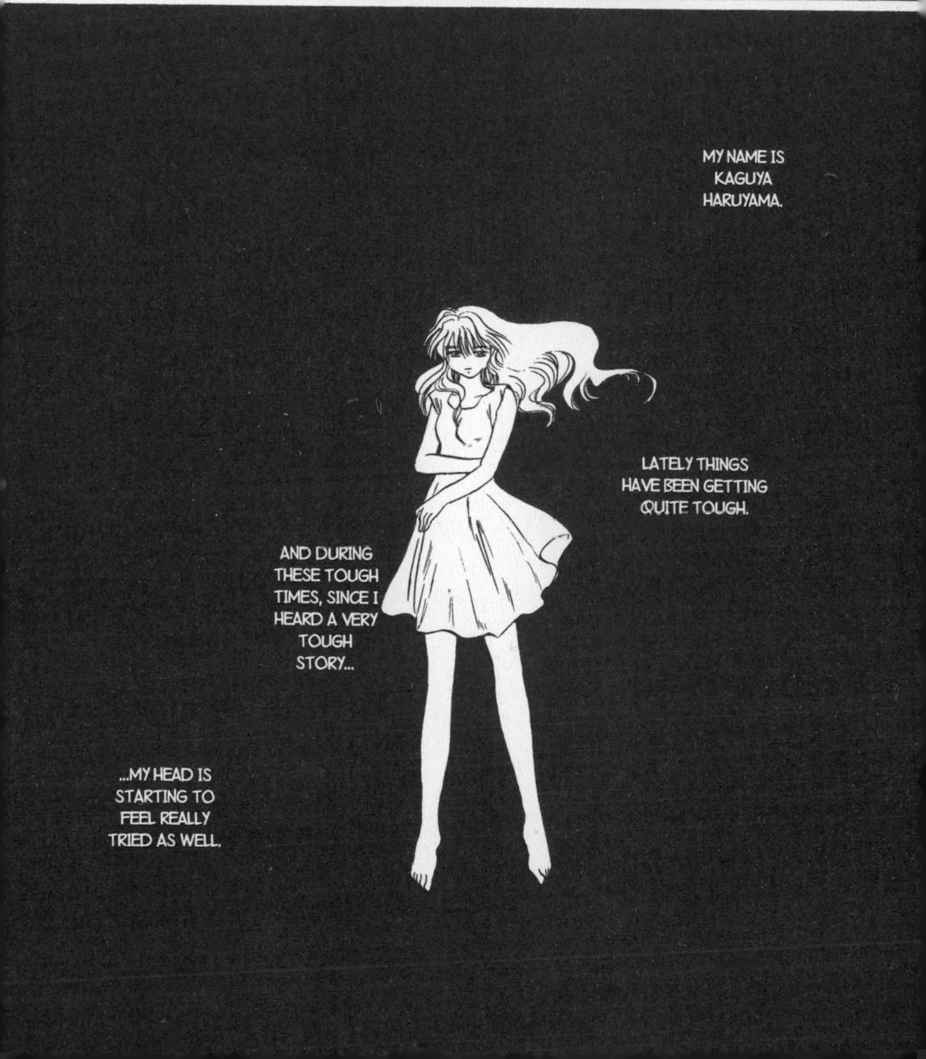
MY NAME IS KAGUYA HARUYAMA.
LATELY THINGS HAVE BEEN GETTING QUITE TOUGH.
AND DURING THESE TOUGH TIMES, SINCE I HEARD A VERY TOUGH STORY...
...MY HEAD IS STARTING TO FEEL REALLY TRIED AS WELL.

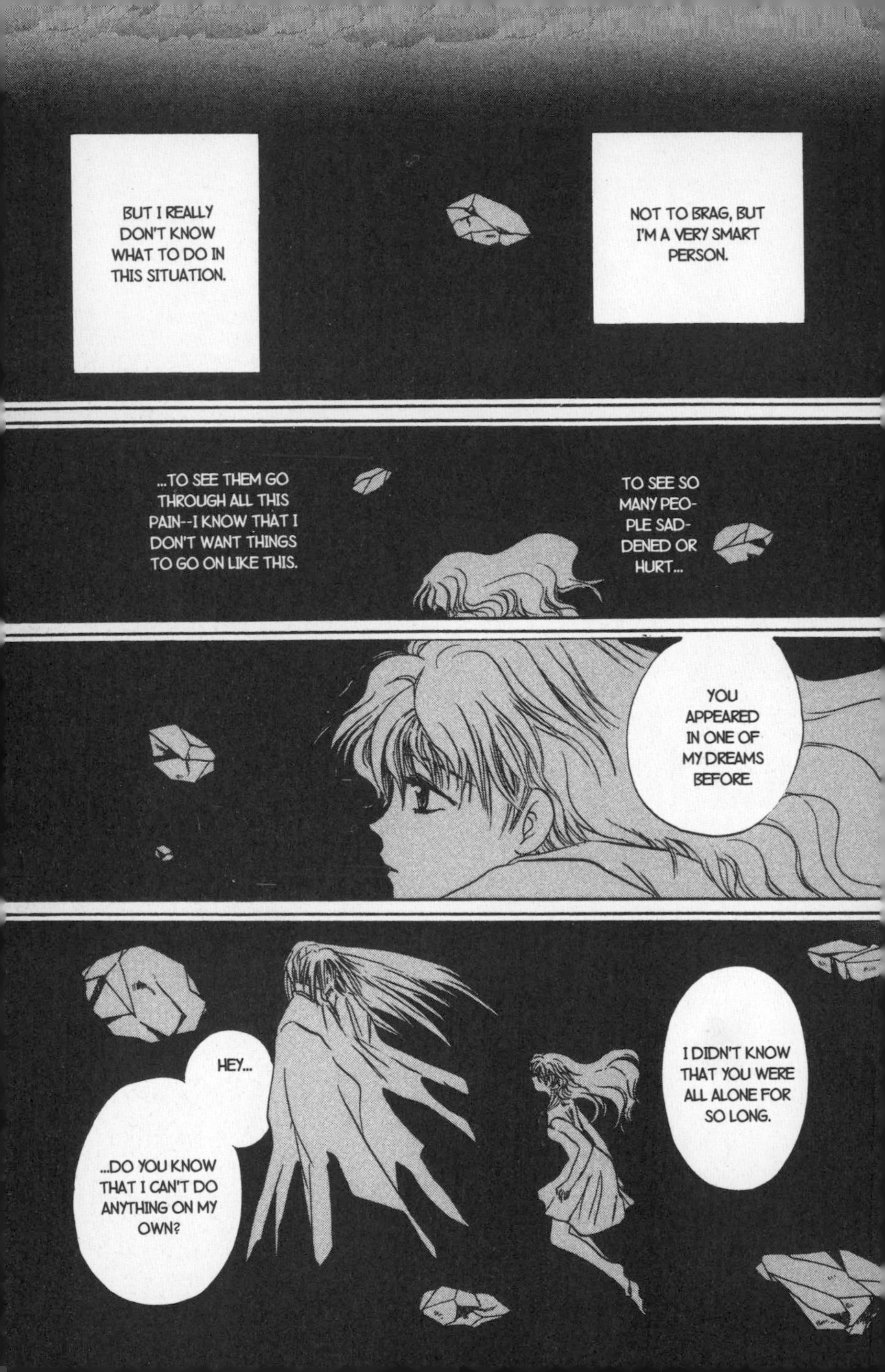
NOT TO BRAG, BUT I'M A VERY SMART PERSON.
BUT I REALLY DON'T KNOW WHAT TO DO IN THIS SITUATION.
TO SEE SO MANY PEO-PLE SAD-DENED OR HURT...
...TO SEE THEM GO THROUGH ALL THIS PAIN--I KNOW THAT I DON'T WANT THINGS TO GO ON LIKE THIS.
YOU APPEARED IN ONE OF MY DREAMS BEFORE.
I DIDN'T KNOW THAT YOU WERE ALL ALONE FOR SO LONG.
HEY...
...DO YOU KNOW THAT I CAN'T DO ANYTHING ON MY OWN?

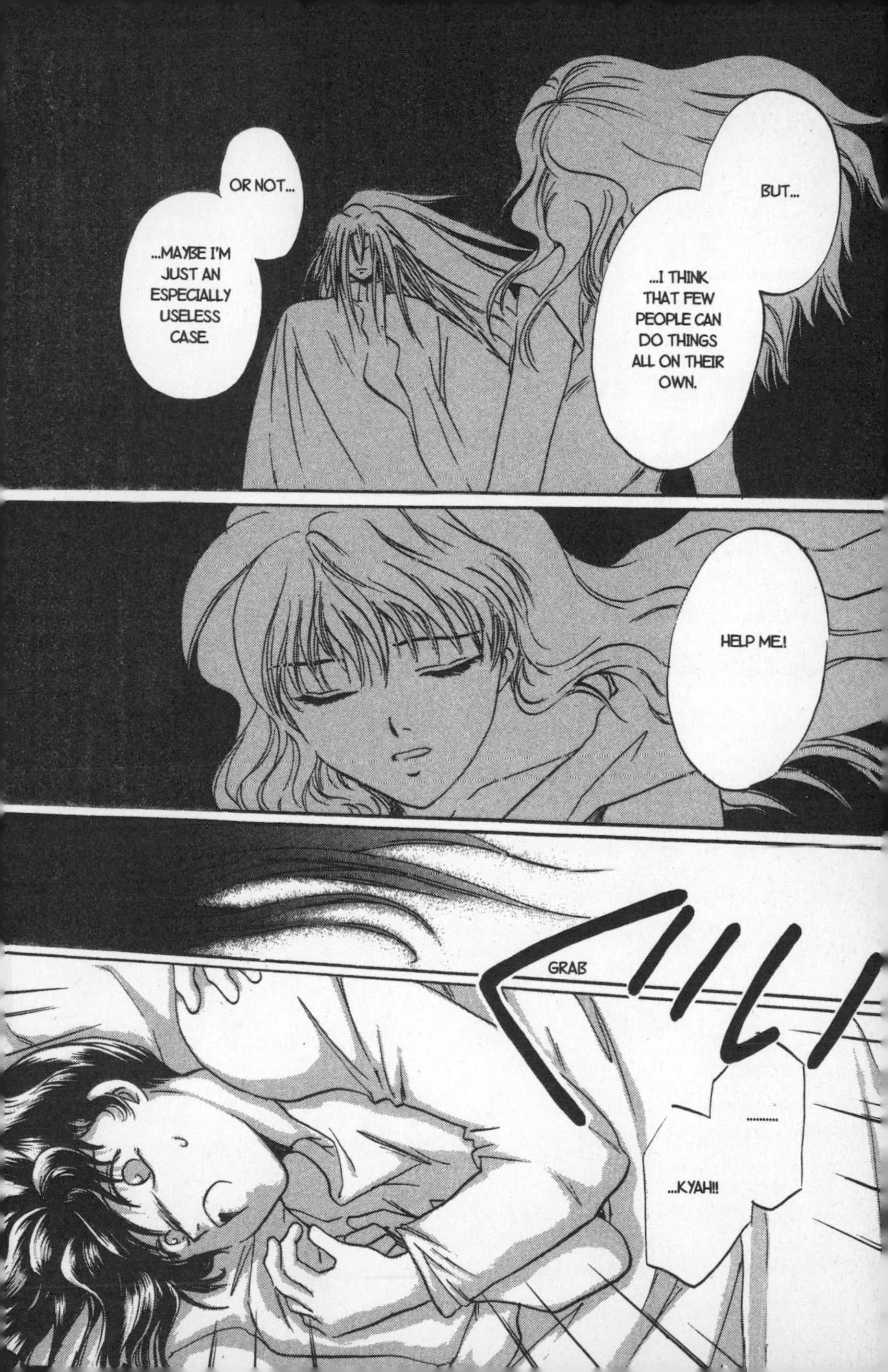
BUT...
...I THINK THAT FEW PEOPLE CAN DO THINGS ALL ON THEIR OWN.
OR NOT...
...MAYBE I'M JUST AN ESPECIALLY USELESS CASE.
HELP ME!
GRAB
....
...KYAH!!

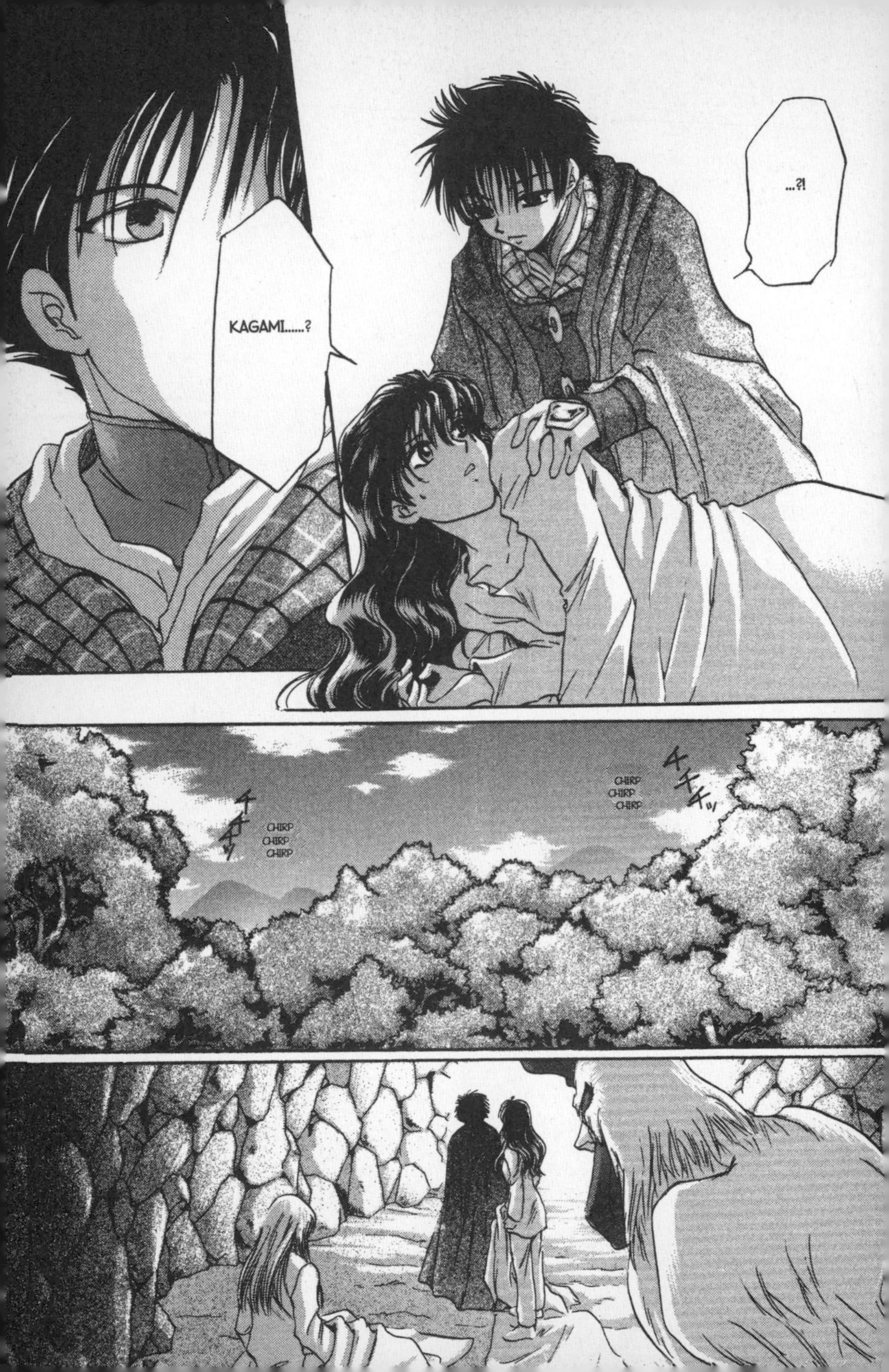
...?!
KAGAMI......?
CHIRP CHIRP CHIRP
CHIRP CHIRP CHIRP

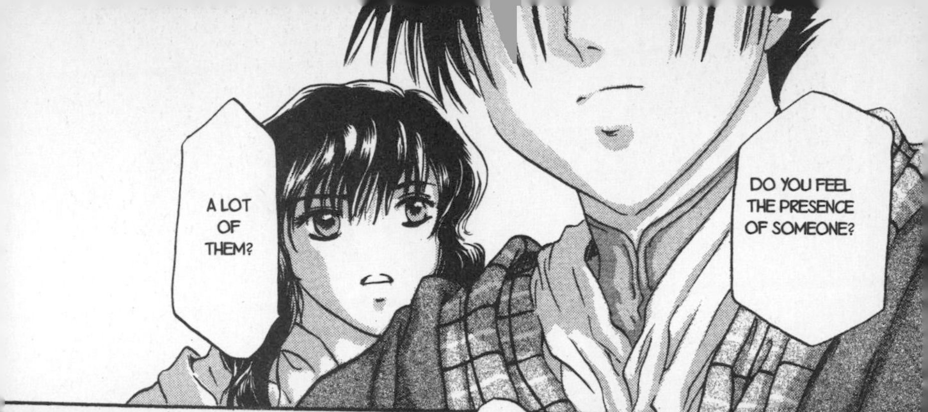
DO YOU FEEL THE PRESENCE OF SOMEONE?
A LOT OF THEM?

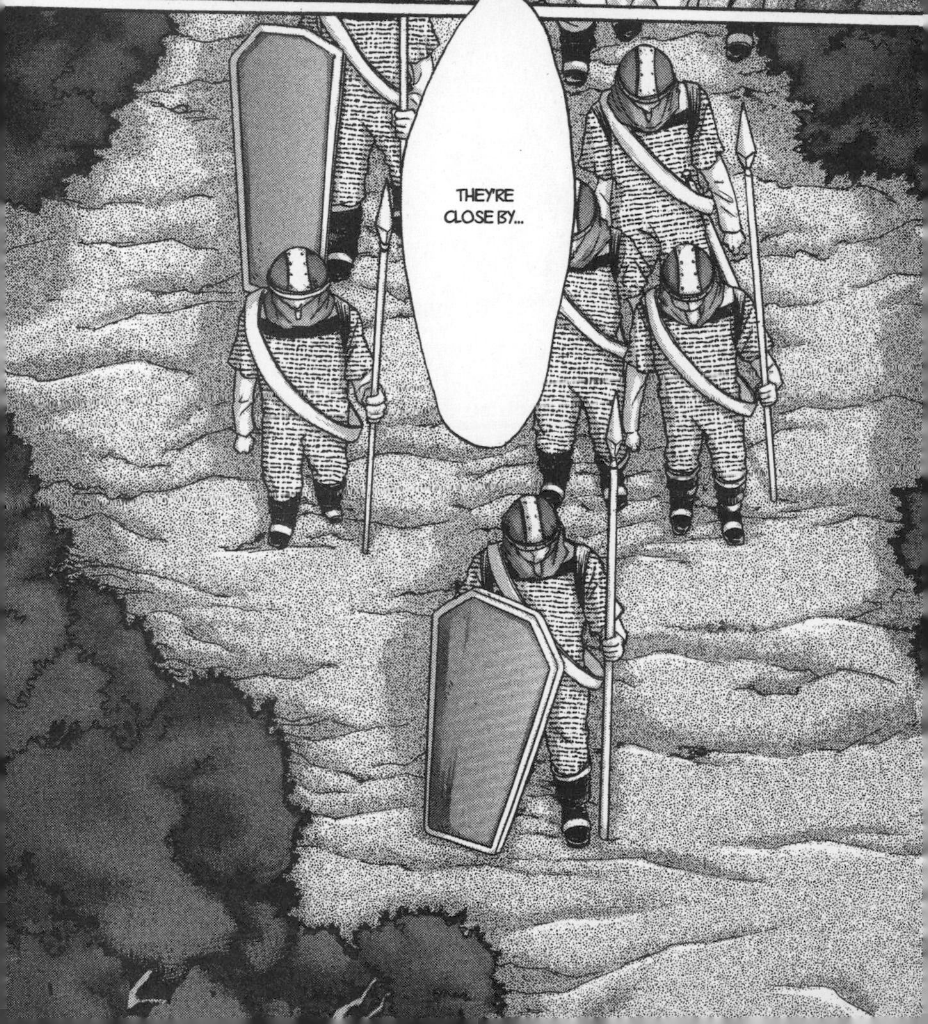
THEY'RE CLOSE BY...

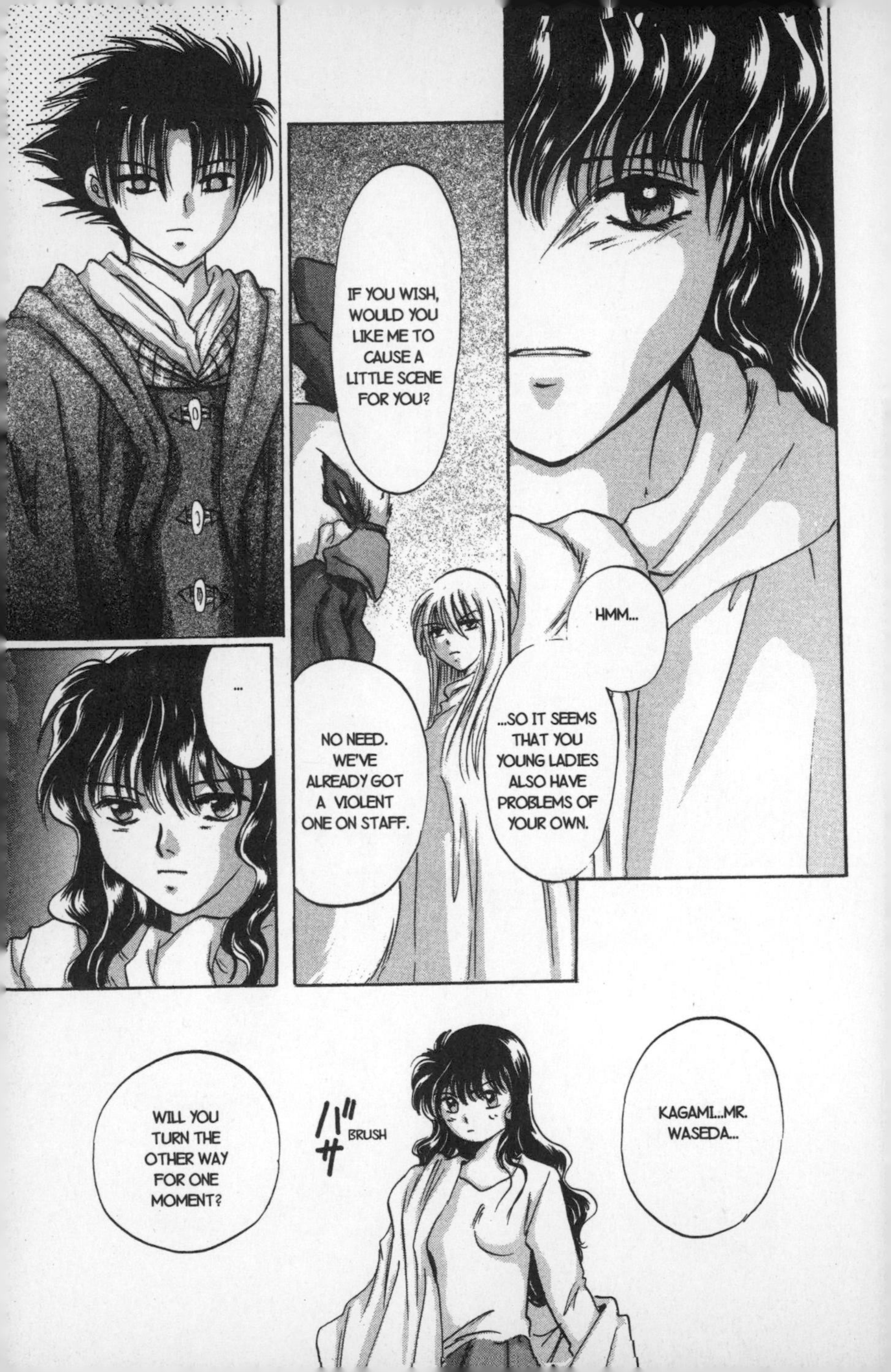
HMM...
...SO IT SEEMS THAT YOU YOUNG LADIES ALSO HAVE PROBLEMS OF YOUR OWN.
IF YOU WISH, WOULD YOU LIKE ME TO CAUSE A LITTLE SCENE FOR YOU?
NO NEED. WE'VE ALREADY GOT A VIOLENT ONE ON STAFF.
...
KAGAMI...MR. WASEDA...
BRUSH
WILL YOU TURN THE OTHER WAY FOR ONE MOMENT?

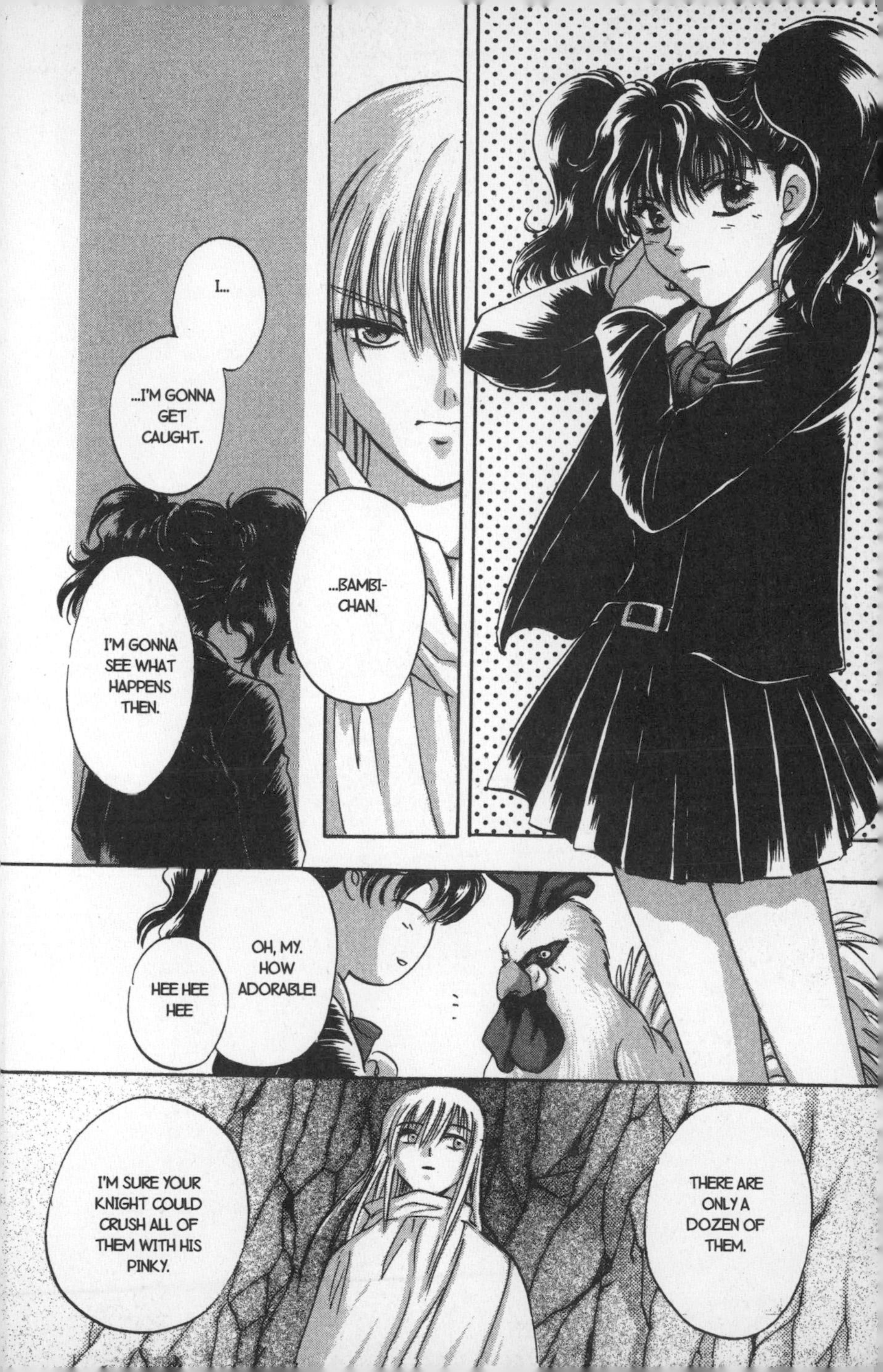

...BAMBI-CHAN.
I...
...I'M GONNA GET CAUGHT.
I'M GONNA SEE WHAT HAPPENS THEN.
OH, MY. HOW ADORABLE!
HEE HEE HEE
THERE ARE ONLY A DOZEN OF THEM.
I'M SURE YOUR KNIGHT COULD CRUSH ALL OF THEM WITH HIS PINKY.

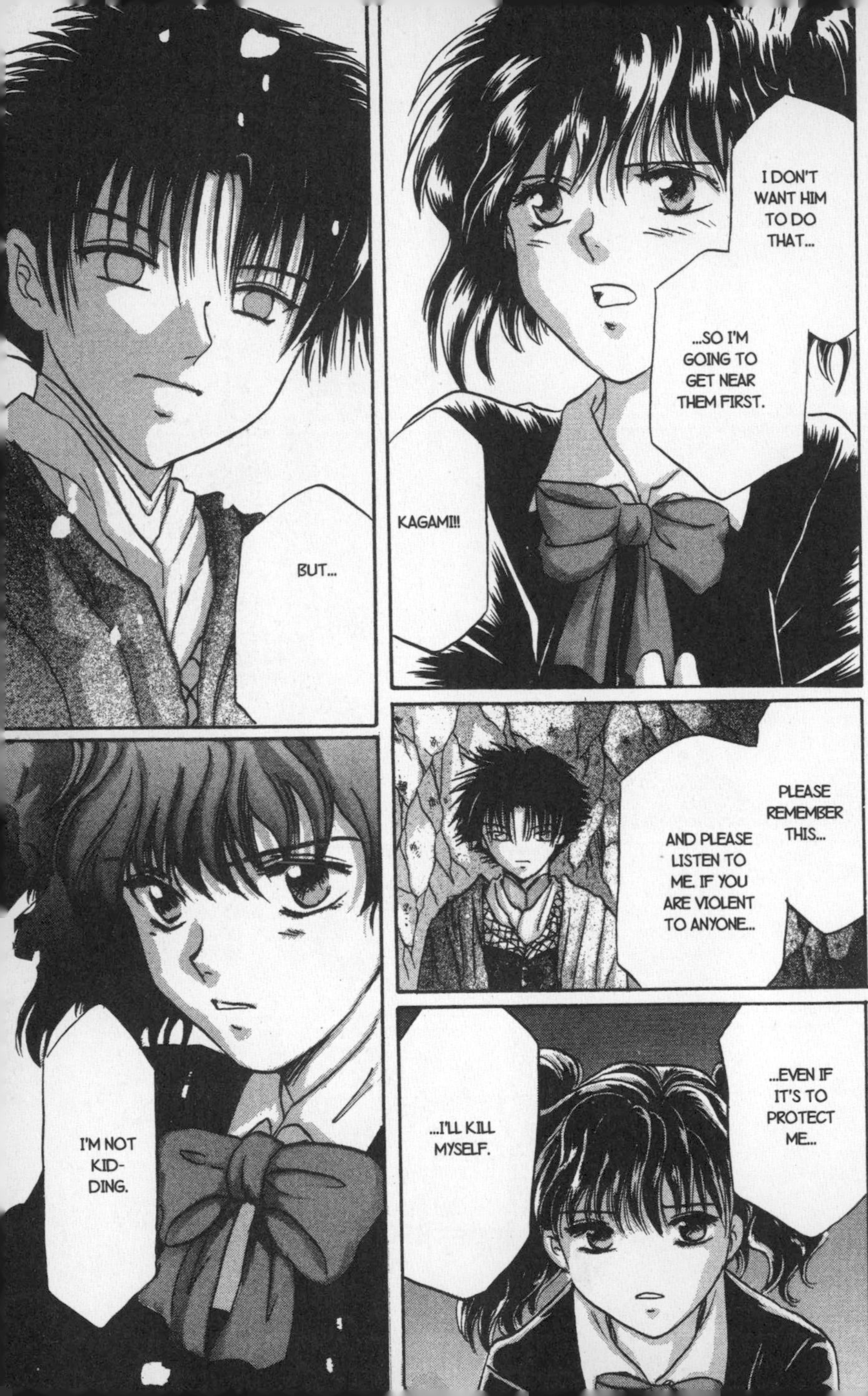
I DON'T WANT HIM TO DO THAT...
...SO I'M GOING TO GET NEAR THEM FIRST.
KAGAMI!!
BUT...
PLEASE REMEMBER THIS...
AND PLEASE LISTEN TO ME. IF YOU ARE VIOLENT TO ANYONE...
...EVEN IF IT'S TO PROTECT ME...
...I'LL KILL MYSELF.
I'M NOT KID-DING.

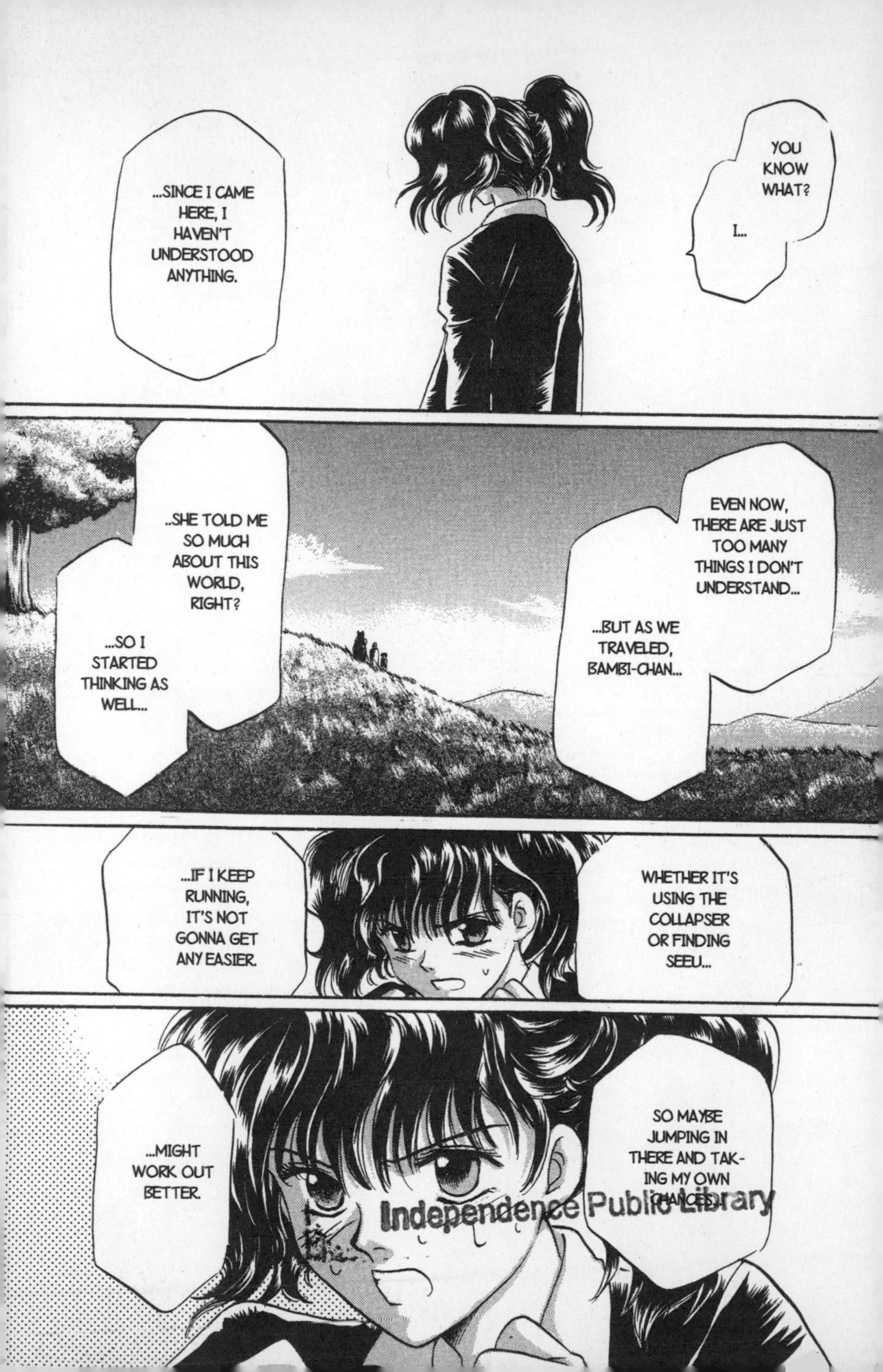
YOU KNOW WHAT?
I...
...SINCE I CAME HERE, I HAVEN'T UNDERSTOOD ANYTHING.
EVEN NOW, THERE ARE JUST TOO MANY THINGS I DON'T UNDERSTAND...
...BUT AS WE TRAVELED, BAMBI-CHAN...
..SHE TOLD ME SO MUCH ABOUT THIS WORLD, RIGHT?
...SO I STARTED THINKING AS WELL...
WHETHER IT'S USING THE COLLAPSER OR FINDING SEEU...
...IF I KEEP RUNNING, IT'S NOT GONNA GET ANY EASIER.
SO MAYBE JUMPING IN THERE AND TAK-ING MY OWN CHANCES...
...MIGHT WORK OUT BETTER.

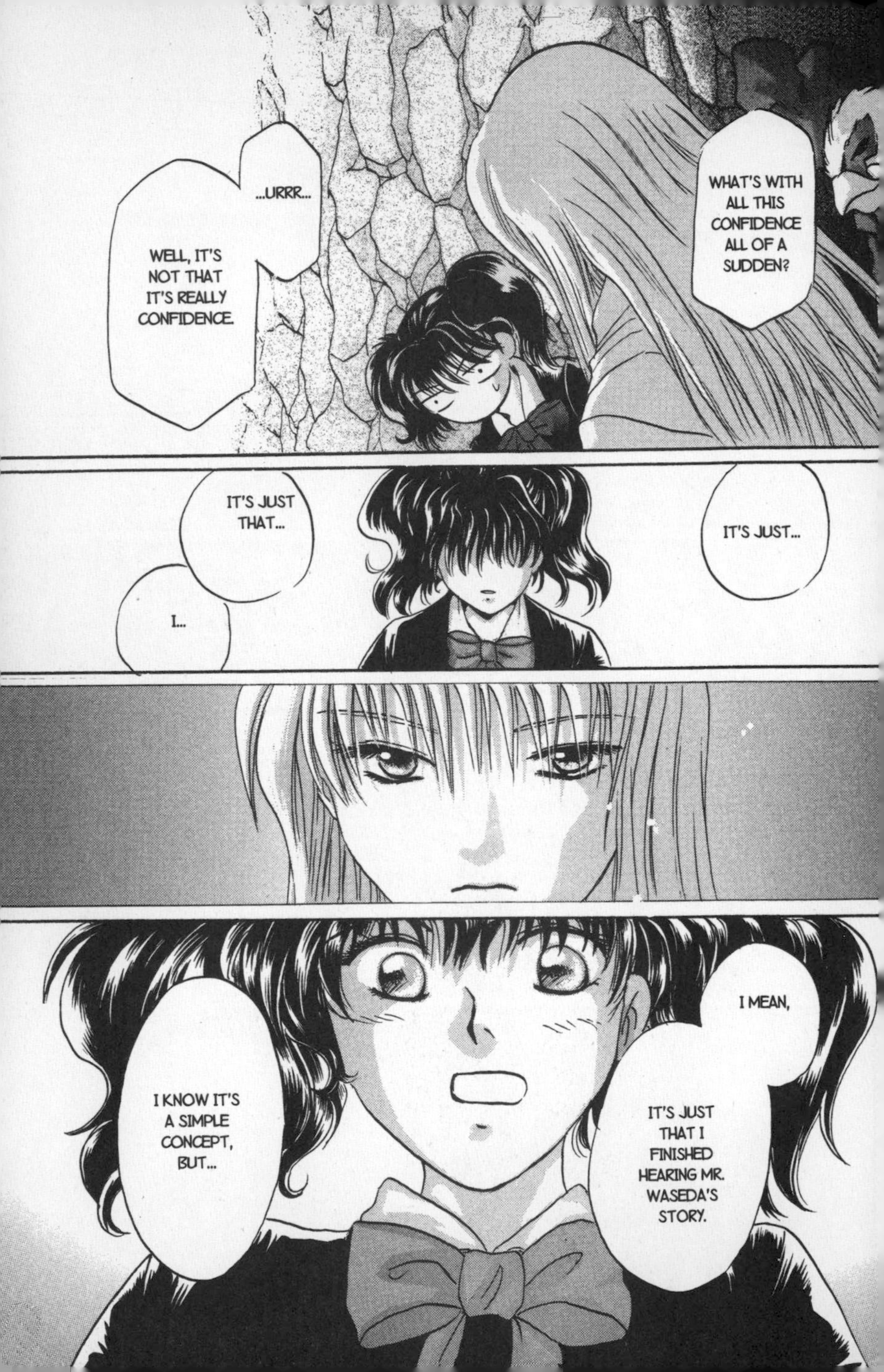
WHAT'S WITH ALL THIS CONFIDENCE ALL OF A SUDDEN?
...URRR...
WELL, IT'S NOT THAT IT'S REALLY CONFIDENCE.
IT'S JUST...
IT'S JUST THAT...
I...
I MEAN,
IT'S JUST THAT I FINISHED HEARING MR. WASEDA'S STORY.
I KNOW IT'S A SIMPLE CONCEPT, BUT...

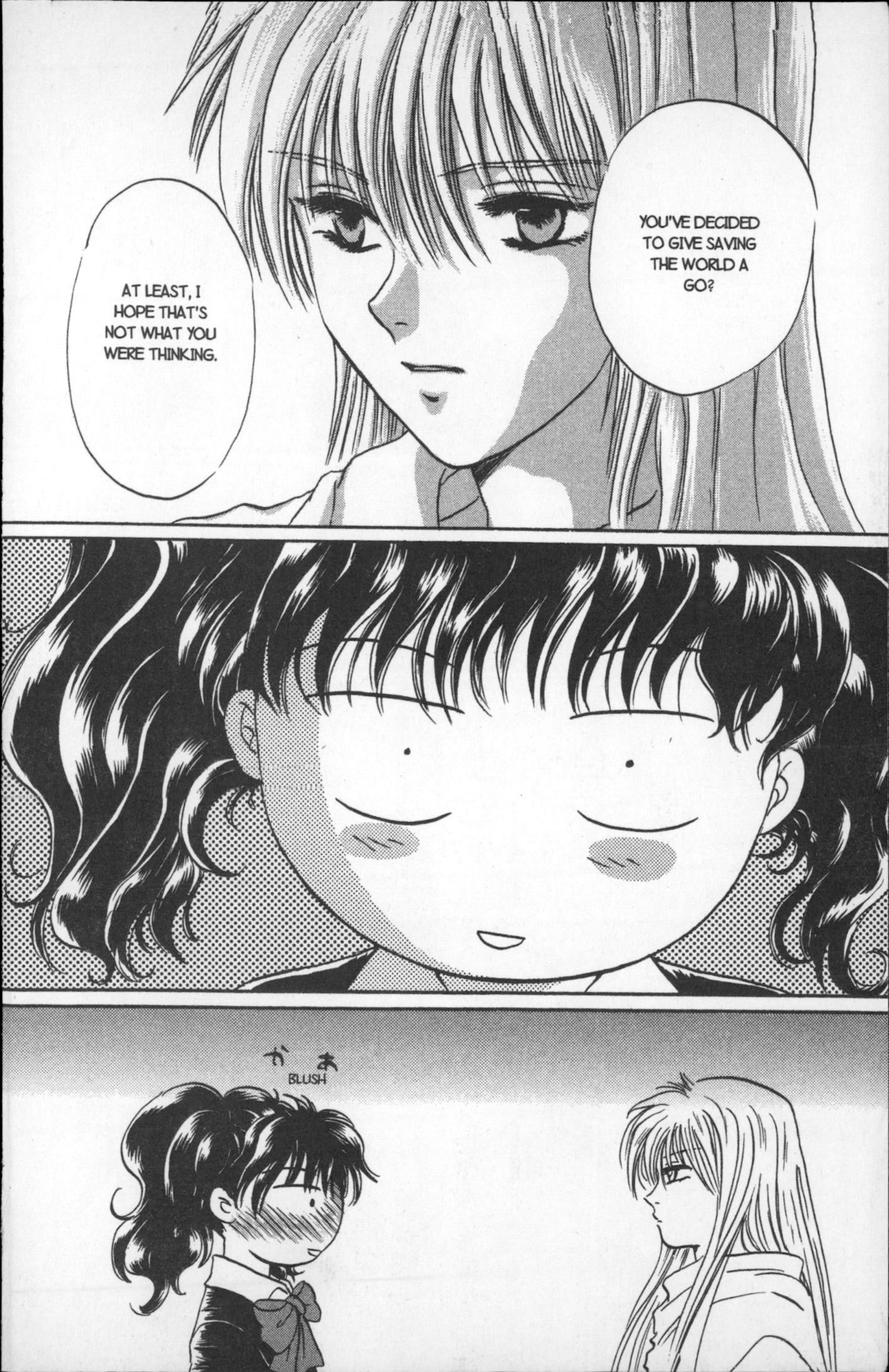
YOU'VE DECIDED TO GIVE SAVING THE WORLD A GO?
AT LEAST, I HOPE THAT'S NOT WHAT YOU WERE THINKING.
かあ
BLUSH

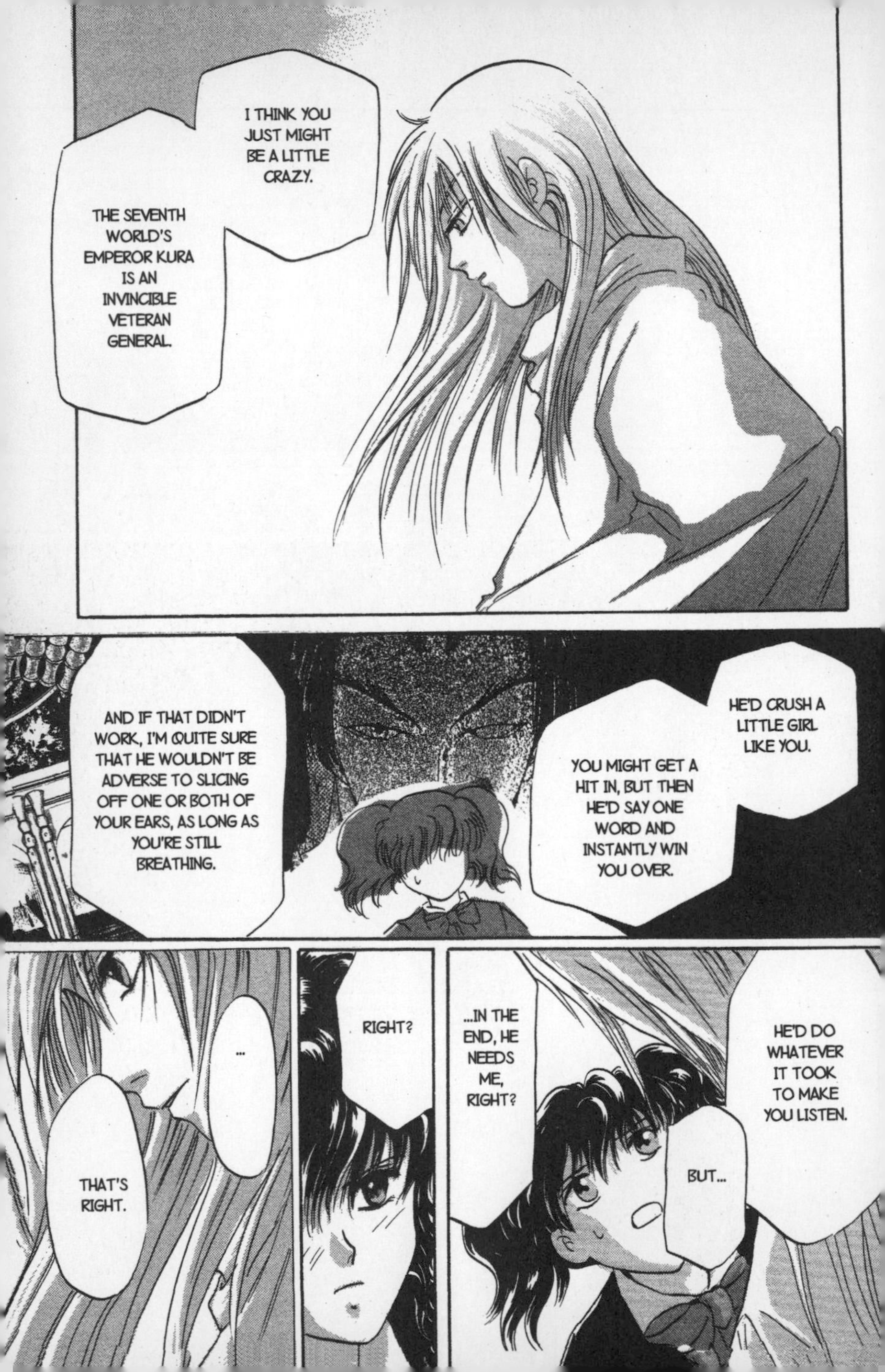
I THINK YOU JUST MIGHT BE A LITTLE CRAZY.
THE SEVENTH WORLD'S EMPEROR KURA IS AN INVINCIBLE VETERAN GENERAL.
HE'D CRUSH A LITTLE GIRL LIKE YOU.
YOU MIGHT GET A HIT IN, BUT THEN HE'D SAY ONE WORD AND INSTANTLY WIN YOU OVER.
AND IF THAT DIDN'T WORK, I'M QUITE SURE THAT HE WOULDN'T BE ADVERSE TO SLICING OFF ONE OR BOTH OF YOUR EARS, AS LONG AS YOU'RE STILL BREATHING.
HE'D DO WHATEVER IT TOOK TO MAKE YOU LISTEN.
BUT...
...IN THE END, HE NEEDS ME, RIGHT?
RIGHT?
...
THAT'S RIGHT.

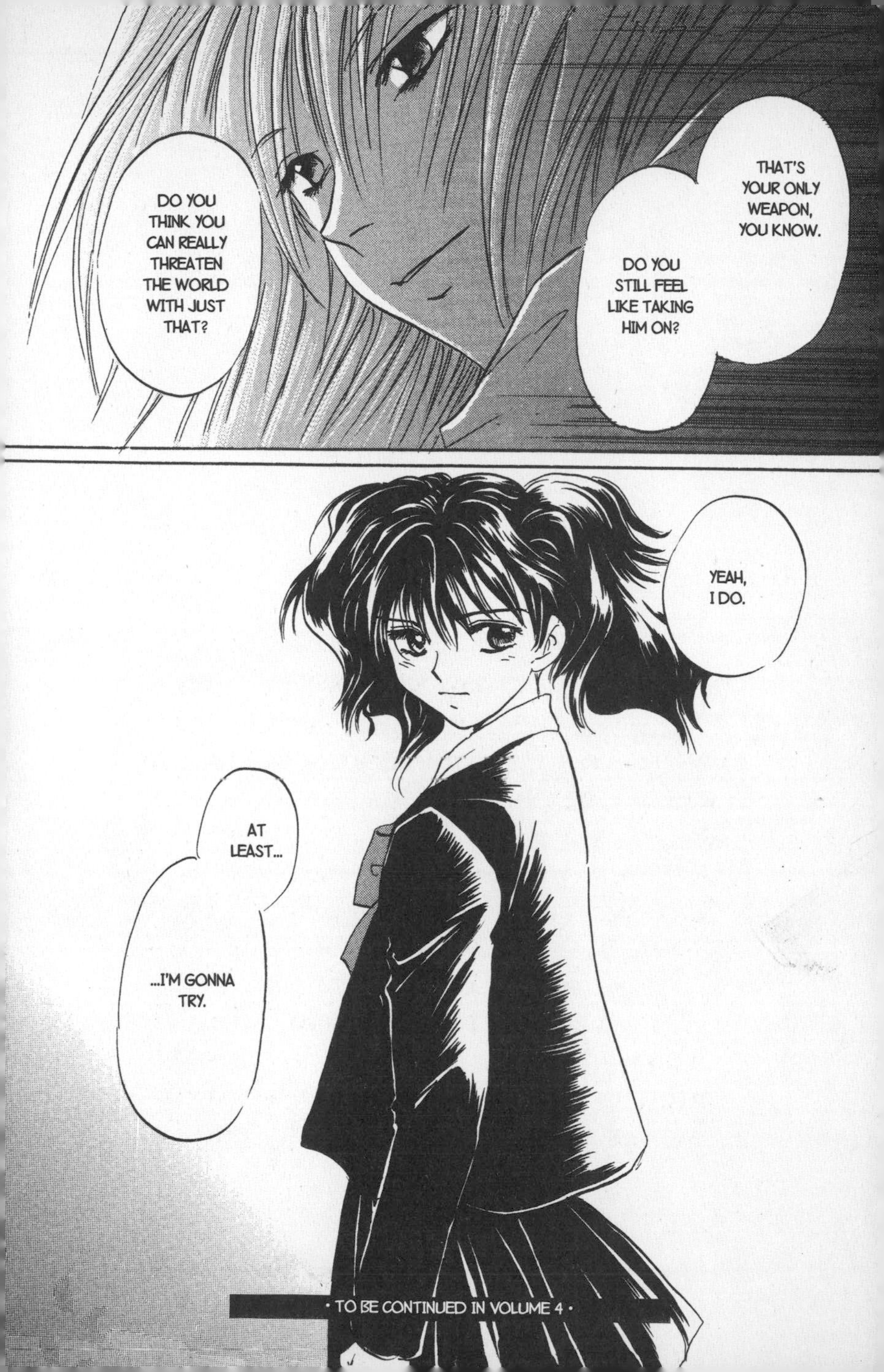
THAT'S YOUR ONLY WEAPON, YOU KNOW.
DO YOU STILL FEEL LIKE TAKING HIM ON?
DO YOU THINK YOU CAN REALLY THREATEN THE WORLD WITH JUST THAT?
YEAH, I DO.
AT LEAST...
...I'M GONNA TRY.
• TO BE CONTINUED IN VOLUME 4 •

Planet Ladder 4
Coming in December

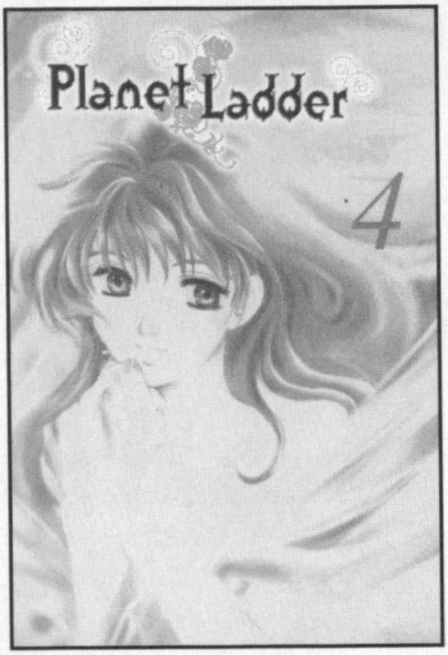
Planet Ladder
4

Orphaned in a war she can't remember, Kaguya is happy with her adopted family on this mysterious planet she now calls home. But chaos returns when a mysterious boy tells her of her past as a princess from another world. With her trusty guardian, Gold, by her side, Kaguya sets out on a journey from world to world to claim her birthright. Courted by some, hunted by others, Kaguya's destiny is feared by all, for it is her fate to decide which worlds will rule, and which shall die.

ST

This is the back of the book.
ou wouldn't want to spoil a great ending!

This book is printed "manga-style," in the authentic Japanese right-to-left ormat. Since none of the artwork has been flipped or altered, readers get to experience the story just as the creator intended. You've been asking for it, so TOKYOPOP® delivered: authentic, hot-off-the-press, and far more fun!

DIRECTIONS

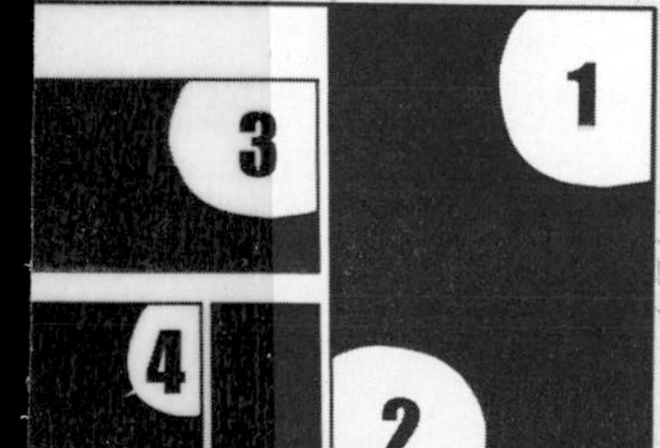
1
2
3
4
5
6
7
8
9
0

If this is your first time reading manga-style, here's a quick guide to help you understand how it works.

It's easy... just start in the top right panel and follow the numbers. Have fun, and look for more 100% authentic manga from TOKYOPOP®!

100% AUTHENTIC MANGA

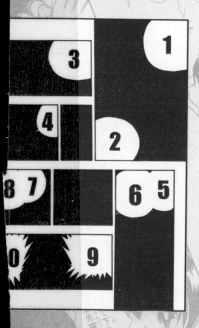